MY
AMERICAN
TERRORISTS

HOME GROWN FAMILY TERRORISTS...DOES SHE ESCAPE?

AMERICA

MY AMERICAN TERRORISTS

HOME GROWN FAMILY TERRORISTS...DOES SHE ESCAPE?

AMERICA

ARPress
ILLUMINATING IDEAS
EMPOWERING VOICES

ARPress
45 Dan Road Suite 15
Canton MA 02021
  Hotline: 1(888) 821-0229
  Fax: 1(508) 545-7580

Ordering Information:
Quantity sales. Special discounts are available on quantity purchases by corporations, associations, and others. For details, contact the publisher at the address above.

Printed in the United States of America.

ISBN-13:   Softcover   979-8-89676-398-7
           eBook   979-8-89676-399-4

Library of Congress Control Number: 2025920939

To my children. May this enrich our lives and get back our relationships.

And to Smitty, the only person who ever tried to help stick up for me in the workplace and never knew the truth until maybe now. I'll bet he regrets one thing he did to me as, without communication, no one could ever have understood the events. What a difference a cup of coffee would have made!

Thanks for saying people said I was crazy!

Also to the writers' group of mine—you rock. May you continue to inspire those who seek it! You were my rock against writer's block. May the gardens act as a steady usage for meetings!

And to one member of the writer's group who said I could use this quote: "If everyone likes you, you're probably not doing anything interesting." She made me feel good—I won't use her name to protect her.

But most of all, to Father John, who gave me solace when I found it hard to trust anyone. He simply said, "Trust everyone until they give you a reason not to, and then don't."

To all those who find solace in the truth and investigating to attempt to achieve it.

Work hard, and your dreams will come true! Maybe not the way you dreamed but the way it ends up!

About the Book

Intriguing events of life from one woman that will hold you captivated to find love, life, justice, and the pursuit of happiness and peace without abuse or jealousy!

She uncovered deceit, contempt, racketeering, hidden sex offenders!

She wanted to change America and the world to be kind and tell the truth!

She would fight hard to bring peace back to her life!

She sincerely writes this to help victims!

The author known only as *America*.

Writing started in 2005 until 2013.

"My *American Terrorists* is a powerful and eye-opening story that courageously sheds light on the devastating impact of family-based abuse and betrayal. America's deeply personal account takes readers on an emotional journey of survival, truth-seeking, and the unrelenting pursuit of peace.

This book is a must-read for anyone who values justice and resilience. Through her unflinching honesty, America not only shares her harrowing experiences but also inspires others to break free from cycles of fear and reclaim their voice.

If you're looking for a story that will move you, challenge you, and leave you with hope for healing after trauma, *My American Terrorists* is highly recommended."

—*Benji Cole, Host of the People of Distinction show*

Contents

The Beginning Again
A New Me
And New Life Too!
Sophia
Love Always

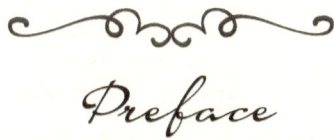

Preface

America's early life story through her childhood goes like this:

As my later years to the present day to 2012, when I finished this miniseries of my life, I was a woman who was very happy and fun-loving and went from a happy life and wonderful outlook to totally abused and unhappy, lied about and lied to; relationship of unknown boundaries revealed later when the story unraveled. I studied and lived life and found a way to get back to my enriched environment and hold it true to her beliefs; of course one that she would create herself. True but sad, the story unfolds and twists and turns and reveals through investigation uncovering of lies and betrayal, deceit, unfaithfulness, cheating, manipulation, verbal and sexual abuse, and, most of all, alienation of my children who were the love of my life; they were my life, and they didn't even know why I loved them and received love from them and not from the husband who was supposed to love me most. Later, after the birth of my grandson after his second birthday, I saw a boy playing at work and decided it was time to tell the children what I suspected and held tight because I had no proof, just my inner feelings to reveal. I suspected their father was gay, and I knew it would shock them, but nonetheless, they needed to know the final piece of the horrible puzzle that had ripped our lives apart in the far-fetched story which you are about to read. I had no proof to offer but still revealed what was true in my mind.

The story is told so that you understand, learn, and educate yourself, your children, and your grandchildren about marriage, betrayal, deceit, cheating, and most of all, twisted abuse and personality profiling that should be done. It just sometimes takes a twisted turn of events to happen before anyone believes what you are trying to say. This goes out to all who trudge through the mire to get to the truth. I say amen!

Within the story is also a great story of one American who was fired eleven times for being honest and who lost her home in 2010 to foreclosure after being promised a modification. It was happening in America, and it happened to me. You, too, will relate and read the horrible story that was happening to millions of people across what we used to think was the best country in the world—America.

This book is a tribute to all those who lost their homes and people like those who occupy Wall Street who are trying to speak up about corporate America and what it is doing to the 99 percent of us who work hard and get the shaft.

Let's get America back and fight for our right to survive in good condition with respect and a place of our own.

It is why I chose my author name to be a simple pseudonym… America!

Chapter 1

My Early Life—Age Ten to Twenty-One
Growing Up in the City of Springfield
Life Lessons Learned
The Important Ones Left Out?

There once was a girl with long blond hair who lived in Grove Manner, Springfield—a small community in the city of Springfield consisting mainly of German descent families. My father and mother were born in the States, but my grandparents were immigrants. My father worked in the factory seven days a week mostly, and my mother was a homemaker until I was in eighth grade. They met at my father's sister's wedding when she married my mother's brother. Two years later, he asked her out, and they began a courtship. My mother loved telling that story as it took him two years to get up the nerve to ask her out; he was shy. They were married and lived in a flat, and few years later and two children later, they bought a house. The house, my mother said, needed much work, but my father insisted on having a home that he could own.

My father was raised on a farm, and when he was young, they lost the farm, and he had to come to the city to get a job when he was thirteen. My father had definite views on working hard and money and religion. He was very religious, and for his reasons, he and my mother had ten children. I was the ninth child; there were eight girls and two boys. We had a six-room home, and my father did add a small family room off the back of the house years later when I was a little girl. As a young girl, I shared a room with my five sisters. We had two double beds, and we slept three in a bed when we were small. We had one small closet, and it was always jammed with this and that. We went to religious private school, and I started kindergarten and walked to school with my sisters and brother. We had family parties and got together on special occasions. My mother was an excellent cook, and my father

1

loved to cook too. We always had good food to eat, and my brothers and sisters used to say whoever ate the fastest got the most. We had food, but my father would only allow us to eat at the table. We were never allowed to go into the refrigerator or cabinets without asking. I guess with ten children, you can imagine why: so they would have enough food for the week for the family.

We always had chores to do, and my mother would see to it the house was always kept clean and neat. She was a very organized person and even had us embroider a special color dot of embroidery thread into our underwear so when she did the laundry, she would know when folding which belonged to whom. My mother sewed most of our clothes when we were young, and she would buy everything else at the store. My father did not allow her to go to garage sales; that was for poor people. I couldn't wear blue jeans as a teenager because my father thought they were for poor people as well because as a farmer boy, he only had jeans and the other children at school wore fabric clothing. He had views about life, and I think he did not like that he did not have money as a child and wanted better for his children and peace of mind for himself that no one could ever upset his life by taking his home away and that they would always have money to pay the bills.

For our birthdays, my mother would say, "You get to pick what is for dinner and what kind of birthday cake you would like." My mother made beautifully decorated cakes or whatever you wanted to make your day special with dinner ordered up to your specifications. She always made my birthday a very exiting day and one filled with love and good food and, of course, presents. She stated that my father never had a birthday cake before she made one for him. She stated that she would make a cake and he would eat the whole thing in one day. I think it was his way of saying thank you to my mother, but in his own way, he couldn't believe that someone cared that much about him. I think his mother was very disconnected from direct love, and I soon learned why my father was not the hugging kind of guy. He never liked us hugging him, and I used to wonder why.

Fun and laughter were always a big part of my life. I am a very happy positive person by nature, and I was always upbeat and happier than my other siblings for some reason, which I didn't even care to think about when I was young. Life at home was fun; even though at times I felt that I had a lot of chores to do compared to my friends, it was a happy home. My father, I felt, was a bit overly strict in his rules and disciplining us, but it was his way. We grew up with work ethics and religious ethics of an enormous calculation. My father never learned to have fun; therefore, he thought everyone in life should be thinking about work all the time. I, on the other hand, thought work should be a necessity, but fun was the spice of life which kept you happy and healthy. So my father and I had separate views on life, but I always respected his viewpoint and gave him direct respect when I was ever in his presence. That was important to him and to me as well.

I was very involved with friendships and went to the park to swim in the summers and loved the water. It was like a feeling of freedom in the water, from your chores, troubles, and anything else you didn't particularly want to think about that day. It was fun and great exercise. We would leave the pool, which was in walking distance from our home, and we would get a pretzel and snow cone to eat on the walk home. My sisters and I were very close when we were young, and we had fond memories of sticking our pretzel down into the snow cone, letting the flavor of the day soak into it and eating it. It was like one of those little things that stuck in your mind about how fun life was and how it should be as well later in your life. The simple things to do in life and friends just hanging out when you had nothing else to do or no money to spend either, which was the poor kids' way of having fun on a very small amount of money, and I became excellent at it. We did not get an allowance, but if we were going somewhere in particular sometimes, we would get an extra nickel to spend on penny candy on Sunday at the corner store if Dad was doling out the money. A nickel would get you pretty much candy, and they then put in a small brown paper sack so we would each have our own to eat out of on the walk home. It was like heaven in a bag.

In grade school I loved to play outside with friends at recess and was a very good student. At that time children began to call me teachers' pet and Goody-Two-shoes. I never could understand why, but I guess it was because I always did what I was told and was a good student. The teachers really liked me. I wasn't fake or phony, but I guess people took it that way; I was just one of those nice kids who did everything to please others. My friends at school were very special to me, and my best friends didn't think that of me at all that way. We used to have so much fun in the playground and after school at each other's homes. I played soccer, basketball, volleyball, softball, tennis, and any other games we would play in the backyard. Our neighborhood was full of children. My mother said that on our one city block alone, there were almost one hundred children; that was unreal to me. We used to play games in the alley way behind the house like freeze tag, kick the can, spud ball, Indian ball, etc. We were all so lucky to have fun and come from good families that cared about us. Even though we were middle class and didn't have much in the way of personal items, we found a way to have fun with whatever we had, including the dandelions that grew in the grass; my sisters and I would sit for hours and tie them together and make necklaces out of them to wear so we would look pretty. We were happy. We would take my mother's clothes poles from the laundry and make a teepee and drape a blanket around them and sit inside and pretend it was a secret place to meet and talk. In the winter we would build igloos out of the snow and have fun sitting inside. We always went sled riding and playing in the snow. My mother would dress us all up in winter coats, hats, gloves, and boots and send us out to play. We would come into the basement and strip all of the wet stuff off, and then she would make us hot chocolate.

My mother used to make homemade donuts. My sister tells the best story about how her friends used to wait under the kitchen window when they knew my mother was making them and my sister would throw a few out to them. They were that good. My mother was a very generous woman. Poor men who lived in shanties on the river down by the park not far from our house would come to the back door occasionally, and she would feed them because they were hungry. She taught me to care for everyone no matter what; she taught me to think of others before myself. Her father was an alcoholic and died when she was nine from it, and her mother raised the children alone. She knew how hard it was from watching people in her neighborhood and in her own family how food was probably scarce and the reason why everyone was so thin as well. She would state to us, "Don't tell your father about me letting people in the house and feeding them," as she knew he would be angry with her.

My father and mother were always helping everyone in the

neighborhood or up at school with anything they could help with. They were very giving of their time and talents even though they had ten children at home. My mother used to say that my father would help the neighbors fix this or that and paint. She said one day she finally told him to stop because he was always tired. He worked seven days and week and still found time to help people. He was a perfect example for his children in giving of himself. He was, however, hard on us and expected us to hold our own, which I never could quite understand; but if you ever asked my father for help, he would give it to you, but you might hear his opinion about it first if he thought you could do it for yourself. He wanted us to be independent, and we were.

My father was very strict in some areas, which I didn't agree with, but as a teenager I think that was natural.

My mother would take us for long walks to get us out of the house because my father worked shift work and slept during the day. We would walk to the park and spend hours swinging and playing; it was fun. She tried everything to keep us quiet. We would go in the basement and play games to be quiet. I got good at winning at games—cards, games, and darts, etc. We had fun together as children in the basement. They would teach me strategy and patience to win. The game of brain skill would be passed back and forth to each other without us knowing we were doing it.

It was no wonder my father would lose his cool often and get angry; he probably had sleep deprivation. Most of his life was spent working seven days a week and fixing things around the house. The man probably never had enough time to enjoy himself, and he was so unrelentingly strict because of his parents' way of parenting him.

By the time I was in fourth grade, I was very athletic and liked to do the things boys did, so I was a bit of a tomboy. The boys at school liked me, but I was unsure of the attention as my religion and father had definite views on relationships before marriage and interaction with boys as a young girl. I can remember telling my mother that I let a boy kiss me in the eighth grade at the school picnic; it was special, and I really liked him. He was Italian, and I thought of him as someone that would never go out with me since all the girls liked him. His name was James, and he was a cutie, and I thought of myself as plain. The kiss was a french kiss too. I remember thinking that I was going to hell after he kissed me tongue and all. We did like each other, and we kissed many times after that. I went with him—which is the term we used for a couple dating—for a while and then thought it best to stop because I felt like my father wouldn't approve. I knew he would not approve. The boys at that time had nicknamed me "Tallest" because I was so tall. I was tall about five feet and six inches in eighth grade. They made me feel unusually strange at times, but they used to do things to me that I thought were obnoxious, and only in my adult life did I know that they were doing these things because they actually liked me. I remember thinking, "What a bunch of jerks." James did ask me to a formal dance in eighth grade, and my mother bought me a new dress that was white and green with a double breast of buttons, and it was shorter than most of my other dresses. She fixed my hair, and I met him at the end of the block as my mother agreed to let me go, but my father did not know about it at all. She kept my secret, and I loved her for making me feel like it was all right to go to a dance with him as my date. I remember thinking I had grown up on that very day. He arrived on time at the corner and looked snappy and had an orchid corsage for me, which was very expensive at that time. I remember thinking that he really cared about me when everyone at school, especially the girls, all made over my corsage of orchids. We danced all night, and he walked me home, and we kissed many times during the walk home, stopping in the alleyways where it would be private.

By seventh grade, I had made lots of friends and then had the responsibility of watching my sister's seven children every day after school, which definitely put a crimp into my social interactions with my friends. She was divorced and worked nights. My mother appointed me as the one to go and watch the children. I never did ask her why she picked me since I had older siblings who would have been much better suited to be the babysitter than me, but nonetheless it was me she told to go. I did it because I was told to do it. I never disobeyed my mother ever, but I do know that I had Cinderella syndrome and did everything everyone asked of me. I never gave excuses or responded by saying ask someone else to do that. I would soon learn later in life it would be endearing to some people, but some people would use me in that respect to get what they wanted and then treat me bad and discard me or abuse me.

I watched my nieces and nephews all the way through high school, and when I had to get a job after high school, then her oldest daughter was old enough to watch them after school as she was a freshman in high school. I must admit, after realizing that I missed out on a lot of my youth watching the children, they became close like they were my own. Later in life, my sister never really thanked me graciously for watching her children, and I always wondered if my mother sent me instead of my older sisters because maybe she didn't like me and wanted me out of the house. I don't know. At times I'm sure I could be a challenge. I was very strong-minded. Maybe she thought I could handle the job. I think it was later in my life that I wondered which reason it was as it appeared to me that she did not like me very much at all. I guess my strong opinions were a lot to take for some people. I did not do everything she said once I became an adult and definitely did not think like her on some topics. Maybe that added to the aloofness that I felt from her throughout my adult life. My mother wrote many letters to the editor in our local paper.

In high school, I was happy as a lark. I loved school but was not the best of students and ranked about in the middle of the class. Getting home late might have had something to do with it. I think I was interested in having fun because at night I had to be a mother to seven children. I never thought much about it, but I think that is why I did not take high school as serious as I should have because I was missing out on the fun after school because I had seven children to take care of. I had to cook dinner, help with homework, give baths, read bedtime stories, and then do my homework and walk home at 11:00 PM once my sister got home—not to mention if I had a problem with my homework, I had no one to ask so I would possibly understand it. I'm amazed I learned anything, but I was a B average student, and I did like school. I was on the yearbook staff, and senior year, I was the editor of the yearbook and photographer as well. It was fun. I wanted to be in the plays at school but couldn't because practice was after school and I had to babysit. So the nuns let me be in charge of painting the scenery for the plays since I was a good artist and loved art class. I enjoyed painting the scenes, but in the back of my mind, I wanted to be on the stage in the play with a part so I could sing and dance. But it was not to be. On my birthday when I was a senior, my friends at school wrote up this beautiful parchment paper that stated I would be an actress and bought me a pair of blue jeans. I thought it was the best day of my life. They were the best of friends and always cared about me and my dreams; sometimes I know how lucky I was to have such good friends. They were the best but not later in life when I needed them the most. Later though in my life, I was shocked at how my friends steered clear of me after my divorce as no one believed what I had to say and looked upon me as if I was really crazy as my ex-husband and one sister were stating. I remember being so hurt by that; I wanted to move away after that realization hit me and never look back. "Thoroughly humiliated" is putting it mildly—an assassination of my goodness and loving character.

I started to realize in high school that I would get attention from boys but didn't really know what to do with it. I think it offended me because I didn't know what to say. I did ask one boy I liked to go to the prom with me as the principal of the school told me that I should find a date. We did go out many times and kissed a lot in the park in his car. I asked him to go to the prom with me but then thought that it was kind of unfair as he didn't have much money and he would have to buy dinner, rent a tuxedo, and buy flowers, etc. So I told him that my father said I couldn't go. A few months later, he married one of my best friends across the street, and they are still married today and live not too far from me now. I like seeing them so happy. When she drives down the street in her convertible Corvette and waves hi, I know she's happy, and that makes me happy for them both.

Friday nights in high school were spent at the Bentley's house. The girls and guys would meet and watch TV and eat and talk and laugh and have fun. I loved going to her house. Her mother made Chinese food, and I loved it. It would be the first time I had eaten it as my mother did not make it at all at our house.

My church was a cathedral-type church that was a historical site in Springfield, and attached to it was the monastery full of priests who ran our parish. We would all meet up at church and sit on the stone wall that went all around the monastery and talk about what we would do for fun that weekend. The monastery had underground tunnels that went from the monastery to the church and back; we thought that was cool and used to talk about how fun it would be to break in and wonder around the tunnels at night.

We had bicycles and would ride down the lane to the park and have fun the whole day just riding and talking and looking through the Civil War history museum there. We would wait till the end of the day to go to the museum because it was air-conditioned and we would cool off before the long ride home. I remember that quick rush of cool air on my hot, sweaty body feeling so good. We didn't have air-conditioning at home, so this was a real treat for me, especially when I was hot and could cool off. So maybe that is why I took an interest in history as I got older. Who knows; but in my life thus, far I know that psychologically, things we partake in make us part of that genre—perhaps forever or perhaps for a short time we take interest.

By this time sports were a big part of my life, and soccer was my favorite. I played soccer as often as I could, and it was my source of fun. I was not the greatest player, but the team of girls I was playing with was so good, and we had been playing together for so long that I loved it. It was our way of being stars, even if it was just on the soccer field; we won quite often. We have been coached by one of the best coaches who later was inducted into the soccer hall of fame in Springfield. He made the game so much fun along with being a good coach and expecting the best from us. Soccer was big in my area, which it was not in most parts of America at this time. One of the local bars sponsored our team, and we would meet there for meetings and have fun. Oh, what fun we had.

I had many boys who showed interest, but I did not return the interest; I guess because I didn't know what to do with the feelings I had when I did have a boy in my life. I guess it scared me. Maybe it still does, now more than then. Older and wiser, I guess.

I did date a few boys after high school, and I always felt that since I did not sleep with them their interest declined quickly, or I cut the relationship short, as in one date. Therefore, I became very picky about who I would go out with. After one date, I could tell if a guy was right for me or not. I guess to some that seemed cruel to cut off a relationship before it got too far, but to me it was the nice thing to do. I felt very awkward at hurting someone's feelings; I know I cried a few times and hated how it felt to have someone rip out your heart and leave it on the floor. In high school the principal came to me after she found out I was not going to the prom and said, "You have to go, you have been voted into the queens court for prom, so please pick a date and attend."

I really did not know what to do, so I told Sister, the principal, that I was not going. "I don't think my dad would like that idea."

I had asked a boy, but while we were seeing each other, he said to me, "I'm going to come to your house one night to see you."

I said, "Please don't. My dad will throw you off the porch."

He came one night, and oh, how he surprised me. I was upstairs and had a towel around my head as I had just washed my hair.

My mother yelled up, "Julia, there is a young boy on the porch for you."

I could hear my father coming from the family room through the kitchen and to the front door.

He stated, "Young man, my daughter is too young to see a boy, please leave."

I was mortified, and he got the message and left. I had asked him to the prom but after that incident told him that my father said I could not go. I really felt it was best as he did not have the money to pay for the tuxedo, flowers, and the dinner for prom; he was such a nice guy. Maybe I was not ready for a serious relationship either at that time.

My high school graduation came, and I was one of the tallest girls, so of course I was in the back of the line to await the long walk down the aisle in church to accept my diploma, and I cried to be leaving school as I walked out of church that night. My father did not allow the girls in the family to attend college, and I remember feeling it was not fair. My two brothers had gone and became engineers; why couldn't I go? I couldn't even get a school loan because my father made too much money, and he would have had to cosign for me, and he wouldn't. I remember feeling so angry at him and my mother, who always told me, "You can be anything if you want, just get a book and read." I guess that was really for boys only in our house, and I wanted to be an artist or a gym teacher. It was only my little sister and I at home; surely, they could afford to send me to college. But no, they said no. I thought to myself, "I guess it's up to me to get a career on my own that will help me to survive and live a life that would have enough money to have fun too." I loved to have fun and do things and go out. It was important to me. I remember thinking that I would succeed. I don't know what I would do, but I would do something that pays well.

My first year out of school, I took a job at a shoe company as an assistant to the salespeople, and they were nice to me. I thought to myself, "I'm a slave, making not much money." Then I took a government test and got the job. I remember thinking that I was so poor and living on little money but still had to pay my dad rent money of $50 a week to live at home. I still had to do chores for everyone else, including ironing everyone's clothes.

I thought to myself, "This it, the last straw, they aren't ironing my clothes, and I pay rent just like my siblings."

Once again Cinderella was being used, and I was not going to put up with it for long. I felt like Cinderella, and I know that I continued to feel that way for two years until I moved out as I had enough and stood up to my father.

At nineteen, my father and I had a disagreement about something I bought and gave to my sister. He was mad at my sister about being with a man who was previously married and divorced, whom she married later, and he said I shouldn't send her a gift at Christmastime as she had moved away with a man whom my parents did not approve of as he was married once.

I said, "It's my money, and I will buy and send whatever I want." He stated that I was in his house, and I had to obey him.

I said, "No, I'm working now and paying rent, so I should not have to listen to your rules about my money."

He stated that I should leave if I could not obey him. I left. I told him that I would not speak to him until he apologized to me. Love was important to me, and my parents taught me to love my sister. And I did.

I moved into an apartment not far from home across the street from the little park that my mother used to take us to when we were young so my father could sleep in a quiet house, and it was a long walk. The apartment complex was old, but I could afford the rent. It was a studio apartment and had one large living room that also was my bedroom. It had an eating area and small kitchen, one bathroom, and a hall with a closet area. I did paint a mural on the wall by the kitchen table; it was a garden scene and made the room look bigger, and it made me seem as though I was out in the garden eating every meal. I loved the outdoors and loved to eat outside or be near a window when I was eating. I had a balcony and could sit outside and eat when it was warm—the view from the window was the park, and it made me happy thinking of all the days I played there and had fun shimming down the hill and watching the river rolling by, its muddy waters so rich with history and stories of all that had traveled it. It would be my serenity on days when I needed peace.

I made the apartment a bit nicer by painting it up with bright colors of blue and green and putting a mural of a garden scene on the wall in the eating area to make it look like I was eating outside every day. My friends thought it was great and told me how talented I was, which made me feel good. They were good about making me feel that I was good at things and had talents. I needed that at this point of my life.

When my friends came over, it was fun having my own place, as we could all do what we wanted and stay up late and goof off. I didn't have a car, so I took the bus to work or rode my bike on nice days, but then I met a neighbor who had a car that worked down the street at the government aircraft distribution center. She would let me ride with her. Soon, one of my high school friends asked if she could move in with me. She had a big fight with her mother and was crying. I let her move in, and she was fun. She was so different from me, had mud mask in the bathroom, and makeup and stuff that I never had at home. She was fun to have in the apartment, and she was grateful that I let her move in even though I didn't want to, because for the first time, I did what I wanted to when I wanted to. We had fun together. She was dating a boy at the time, and he and his friends kind of hung out a lot. Sometimes I wasn't happy about that, and sometimes I was.

One of my friends from grade school got married, and I was asked to attend the wedding. Lisa married her grade-school sweetheart Tommy. The first boy I ever kissed was also invited, and Tommy was one of his best friends, and it was hinted that I should call him and ask him to go with me. So I called James, and we went together. We had so much fun. He came back to my apartment with me, and we made out on the bed. I cared about him very much but could not do what he wanted me to, and I think he thought that meant I didn't care for him, but I did. I was raised as a young woman that I had to wait until marriage, and at that time, I thought that was what I should do. I disappointed him, and I feel bad about that today, but he had to understand me too. Maybe we just weren't right for each other after all.

I then bought a horse and had fun riding and taking care of Star. My mother said I couldn't buy a horse when I didn't even have a car yet; she thought the idea a bit irresponsible with my money. My Aunt Essie, her sister, told me that I could use her car anytime I wanted to ride my horse, so I bought him and had fun. I was naive about horses and picked one that was used for racing but didn't know it. I felt they should have told me that but didn't. Anyway, he was spirited and would bolt as soon as your foot was in the stirrup. I had to pay someone to teach the horse to walk. After that he was better, but most of my friends and family were scared to ride him. I loved him.

I moved into the upstairs of a home that belonged to my cousin and was across the lawn from my Aunt Essie, who was my best friend as well. She loved me living there as we were very close. She and my sisters and I used to go shopping every Friday night for fun for years. She never had any children of her own and was like a second mother to me. When we were children, she took me to the YWCA in the winter every Friday family night to swim, and she always had special ways of showing how much she cared. She worked in a bakery and cleaned offices at night. She was fun, and we got along like mother and daughter, and I respected her so. She was just like my mother in so many ways, but being that she was not my mother, I would tell her things that I would not tell my mother, and we became close. Later I moved into a house and rented the upstairs part from one of my cousins, and my aunt lived just across the lawn, and we became even closer. She was fun, and we would share our views about the world and people. She lived alone for years after her first husband died, but then she met Tim, and they married when she was eighty.

She used to watch the men who would come to pick me up for dates from her porch. The next day she would say I saw that handsome guy in the little red sports car tell me about him. It was endearing. My best friend Louisa moved in to live, which made the rent a breeze, and we had fun living in our apartment together even though it was not in California. We always said we would go to California and find Steve McQueen and be stars! Young girls' dreams. It's fun to think back about what we thought about at that time of our lives. I wanted to be an actress but could never get the parts in the plays at school because I watched my sister's seven children after school. I was always understanding of my duties, but I remember especially hating the fact that my mother made me watch my nieces and nephews at that point of my life. I wanted to be like all of my friends and hang out after school. "Dream on," I used to think to myself.

Later, I would learn that my mother wanted to be an actress. I never really understood my mother's lack of communication about herself to me, but I guess it was her way of leading her married life. She never talked much about what she wanted, only obeyed what he wanted her to do. I thought she missed out on life altogether, but that was my point of view.

Later, I would learn that I made decisions in my married life that would be similar to my mother as I didn't trust people to watch my children. I became a stay-at-home mother as well and missed out on my career too. I did teach my children that they needed to have a career of their own and go to college. That was very important to me since I did not get to go and later in life learned that you go from worse to worst sometimes working and searching for a job when you are over fifty and have no college degree.

Chapter 2

Age Twenty-One
Air Traffic Control School
All Guys Interested—Met Husband
I'm Still Not Aware of My Effect on Men

I found that at this time in my life, I needed to make more money, and without a college education, I needed a job with a future and money. The aeronautical engineers that I worked for at the aircraft distribution center in the aeronauts department came to my desk one day and told me I should take a test to become an air traffic controller as they opened the test up to women and minorities, which was the first time ever in history. I asked how much the job paid, and they told me, and I said yes. I took the test to become an air traffic controller and passed the test and then had to pass a very rigorous first-class pilot's physical where for fifteen minutes, the machine was running and recorded your heartbeat, and then you had to go up and down three steps over and over for fifteen minutes. The doctor came into the room and asked me what I did for a living, and I stated I was a clerk; I sat at a desk.

He then said, "What do you do for fun?"

I said, "I play soccer."

He stated, "No wonder your test was so good, and there was no difference from the first strip and the second when you were walking up and down for fifteen minutes." I laughed. I passed.

Then I had to pass a psychological test; I passed. I then had to spend one year in training at the tower and flight service station in Springfield. I spent four months first at the Springfield Airport Flight Service Station learning all about weather and pilot flight briefings. I had to record weather briefings, help pilots file flight plans, and take weather observations as well as other duties. I then went to the tower, whereby I was to receive the training for separation of air traffic per federal aviation regulations. I spent hours in the training room in the basement learning about each different aircraft consisting of air speed, rate of climb and decent, etc. I had many hours of learning the separation regulations and spent hours at home studying. I then was placed in the TRACON, the radar room, to learn how to separate the traffic on a radar scope, at the same time spending days up in the tower learning ground control, arrival and departure control, along with taking pilots flight plans. It was so interesting, and I loved the job. It was very hard for someone without a pilot's background or previous controlling experience, but they were trying to get women in the position as they were probably told that they did not have enough minorities working in the position.

I was placed on a team, and that team in the office worked on a rotating schedule. The schedule was first day, 8:00 AM; second day, noon; third day, 4:00 PM; fourth day, 7:00 PM, and the Friday or last day was a midnight shift. This rigorous schedule was because the tower was a level 4 station, which meant heavy traffic load at a major city. Level 5 was the busiest towers like O'Hare in Chicago and Kennedy in New York. The changing weekday schedule was so that you would not be working peak traffic all week long at the busy hours for a week stretch. Very smart on the part of the office staff, making decisions about stress levels, but I would think that it played havoc on the people that were married and had children as this schedule was very hard on a normal lifestyle. The first week on my team, I was introduced to the supervisor and then to the other controllers on the team. I was told I would spend one day up in the tower and the next down in the radar room as the team rotated those stations within as well.

The tower was awesome taking the elevator to the top opening to a winding narrow staircase, which ascended into the top of the cab of the tower. It was a small octagonal room encompassed with windows all around from desk top level to about six feet over your head so you could see the traffic and the airport ground surface. They placed me on the FDEP a machine that printed and spit out strips that stated each flight plan for every plane flying, which consisted of pulling paper strips from the printer and sliding them into the plastic sleeves that fit into the metal stack for arrangement of time and place to pass off the ground control position in the correct sequence of departure times. The ground control position, I would learn, was the busiest and the place where most controllers washed out of the Springfield Tower because it was extremely difficult. As a ground controller, you could not see the entire airport surface, and so some airplanes you were talking to had to be carefully viewed on the radar screen above their heads for accurate separation especially when the weather was bad. Sometimes it was all in your head when you could not see certain areas or the radar was out because of equipment failure.

The airport had two parallel runways; one was intersecting runway at that time in 1977. It was so awesome to see the guys work this position, but better yet to come was the training and viewing the controllers on arrival and departure positions when it was busy. It was like watching men in a bar who were playing foosball trying to beat each other at a game that was fast, fun, and the adrenaline got up and pumping like your heart was on the run. It was so fun to watch them draw names to see who would work the busy times. It was like watching little boys say, "I can do it better than you, so step aside and watch me." It was all about loving the job they did and proving to themselves that each day they still had what it took to do the job right and keep everyone alive, go home at night, and know that the skies were clear and safe because of their hard work and dedication to the job. I must say, though, I realized that part of the screening of personality was so that they could see beforehand if you had what it takes to say, "Yeah, I can do that better than you, just watch me." You had to be strong-minded and confident that you could get the job done. Hard work and heavy traffic would at times be even worse when bad weather, and of course, radar malfunction nightmare would occur simultaneously, and you were working about twenty planes on your radar scope. You had to have the mental capability to remember in your mind what the scope read because now it was *black* and you still have to stay calm, talk, and get everyone safely to their destination handoff. It happened more than once in the TRACON while I was in training. It was the controller nightmare, and I saw if firsthand. I had great admiration for those gentlemen once I really saw that they, indeed, had what it took to do the job and get Americans home safely. They were, of course, in my mind very underpaid for what they did. Later, in 1980, we would see what happened to them when they stood up for their work rights telling the public in a PATCO strike that they were not being treated fairly, and the rest is history with the firing of all the controllers who struck. I hated watching it; it was so unfair. I remember thinking to myself, "Is this America?"

It was a very busy place, and the men that worked there were very skilled in their jobs. It was made known to me by one controller who stated to me one day in the break room, "No woman had ever checked out at Springfield Tower!"

I said, "Why is that?"

Someone stated, "It's too damn hard," and some of the men laughed.

I said, "Well, I'm going to Capital Tower," which was a level 2 low-stress tower. "So you all have nothing to worry about."

I could feel in my bones that they were telling me that no woman could do his job. I didn't like it much but kept my mouth shut other than to let them know I was not working with them directly after school in Oklahoma, so they had nothing to fear from me, but the idea that they would even say that to me was arrogant and hurtful as a young woman trying something new because my country asked me to be a part of a new training process for women and minorities who had not been an air traffic controller in the military. Then about the third day with the team, we were in the radar room, and I had my headset on and was plugged into the position next to one of the controllers as the supervisor had instructed me.

After a few minutes, the controller assigned to me turned to me and said, "You know I can't train you because the union states that we have to have special training before we can train you because you are a predevelopmental and have no experience in separating air traffic."

Keep in mind that I had already had seven children, which were like my own by the time I was in seventh grade, so this was like a low-level challenge to me.

I said, "Well, go tell the supervisor because he told me to sit here and monitor you while you explained things to me."

I don't think he liked that, but I didn't care; I was hired to do a job, and as far as I knew, he was supposed to be training me. The controller just simply stated go sit next to someone else. I got up and went to sit next to another controller and plugged in my headset; he stated that he could not train me, etc.

I just said, "Okay, fine, I get it and took my headset off and threw it up against the control panel."

I walked across the TRACON to the supervisor's desk and told the supervisor that I guess he would be training me because the guys were telling me that they had not been trained by the union PATCO to train a predevelopmental in this TRACON.

I was hired with no experience by the Federal Aviation Administration, and most people got hired because they were controllers in the military, but the fact that I was a woman was evident without the words actually being said. I was really upset as I had transferred out of my old job and was excited about becoming a controller and making some really good money as I was single and living on my own. My supervisor said that I could monitor him until he got it straightened out and apologized. The guys did finally train me, but I don't think they liked it one bit; in other words, they were hired to be air traffic controllers, not trainers. Later I understood their dilemma, but at that time, I was angry. When I was up in the tower one day, I was on the arrival position, and it got pretty intense, and the guys amazed me as they would vie for the arrival position as it was the most stressful position; it was like they almost got off on working the busy, fast-paced traffic; no, they did get a power trip no doubt about it, and I likened it to parachute jumpers. Most people wonder why they do it; they do it for the rush, plain and simple. They say it's a good thing, and for them it is.

After I was on the job for a few months, I could see why they felt that way; it was a job, but it was fun and exciting to work when it was busy, almost like pushing the envelope to see how good you were. It was like playing a Nintendo game, and you wanted to get the best score you could and win. They were so good at their jobs and took great pride in doing it well but had fun in pushing themselves like a brainteaser to stay on top and push the traffic without legally offending the regulations. It was so exciting to see them work, and they were the most professional people I had ever seen on the job. The break room was this big room with lots of tables and chairs and TVs. We would take breaks and go and get something to eat and bring it back and sit and talk about the day's traffic. It was fun to get to know them all.

I was twenty years old, and a few of the single gentleman were showing an interest in me. I did date one gentleman for a few months, but he wanted me to quit my job and not go to school, and I said no. Another gentleman asked me to a concert one night, and of course, it was one of my favorite groups, and he had front-row seats for Fleetwood Mac. He picked me up in his little red sports car, and my Aunt Essie was watching across the lawn; it was cute. He owned a jazz bar downtown called Jazz Pines too, and we went there after the concert. It was hoppin', and I had fun and danced and met all his friends, and he was fun. We just didn't match up for a reason I won't state, but he was very nice.

I think the other guy I had dated a few times was pushing me pretty hard, and I was young and didn't understand the push of a personality that well yet, as well as a sexual action he wanted that I wouldn't give and a night of regret of things he did instead to me. Later, I would know all full well what the pretty girl with the long blond hair—remembering that one of my sisters said at that time that I looked like Kristy Brinkley—had still yet to learn about manipulative people who lied to get what they wanted, even if it's a pretty girl who's as nice as pie. I was smart and streetwise but had a lot to learn about men and why they said what they said to get what they wanted sometimes. Later I would learn the hard way.

I spent a week at the control center in Olathe, Kansas, and it was a big warehouse room like a factory full of radar scopes; it was an unending sea of darkness with only the light from the massive amounts of radar scopes in rows all connected to each other, almost like being in a movie theatre but this would be the real thing baby. The center controller handles all the traffic once the tower handed it off out of their airspace, which was so many miles outside the TCA, or terminal control area, usually around fifteen miles. The center talked to the aircraft and handed off to other centers until the aircraft reached its destination, and then it was handed off to the tower where it was landing once it was in its radius of airspace and altitude.

When the years training was over, I was to then attend the FAA Federal Aviation Administration School called Aero Center in Oklahoma City, but first had to report to my first duty station in Capital Tower, which would be my tower duty station once school was over. One of the new guys starting with me in Capital said that the guys were taking bets already on who would get a midnight shift with me.

I laughed and said, "I don't have to worry about their dreaming of a sexual night in the tower, they can dream all they want to!"

He laughed. I remember thinking that was really nice of him as a man telling me what the men had planned for the pretty new girl. The school in Oklahoma City was an intense four-month training setup for a refresher for controllers coming out of the military and working for the FAA. The girl that I started training with at Springfield tower, Glenda, was my roommate at school. She and I shared an apartment that they set up for us and drove our cars down separately to spend four months in Oklahoma. The school was set up as test labs with radar scopes to simulate the tower and radar room and instructors who were air traffic controllers on time off from controlling to teach and taught separation of air traffic and preparation for testing of the written regulations and procedures.

The first day was overwhelming as they gathered us all in a rather large auditorium theater–type room, and we took a test and most of the guys were pilots or controllers in the military, and they were all talking about their experiences one after the next, and I was the silent listener. I had been a clerk in an office but nonetheless was not intimidated by their experiences and loved hearing their stories. I passed the test, too, just like the men.

We spent many hours in labs separating traffic. I was proud of the fact that I never crashed two airplanes together in the four months that I was there, which was outstanding for a rookie without military experience. I would be at school all day, and then we would hit the bar for happy hour and talk about the day and get something to eat and dance and goof around. Then we would all meet at our designated study group apartment for the night for group study. We were all very interested and study group was really good for me, and Glenda, the girl who came from Springfield, as we were not controllers before and offered each other the solace of being new at this task. There would be one other girl, Lori, who was in the Navy as a controller who was also in our class.

My friend Glenda and I were doing quite well. We adapted and were having fun yet spending most of our time studying. By the second month, I had become interested in one of the guys in class, and he was also interested in me; he was in our study group. We were swimming in the apartment complex pool, and he asked me if I wanted to play tennis the next day.

I said, "Sure."

He was fun and always smiling. We played tennis, and I had a wonderful time. He was funny and nice and smiled all the time just like me. He didn't mind that I was good at tennis, and he was very good as well. We played for a long time, and then we went somewhere for dinner with the group. It wasn't long before he was coming over to my apartment, and we would sit and talk after study group, and one night he kissed me and we began a love affair. He was charming and sweet, and I was definitely interested in him and very taken by him. He had a way about him of making you feel very special. Christmastime came, and we all went home, and he stated that he lived with his mom and was going home to be with her, and his sister and that he had a brother, too, that was getting married. He didn't have a car at school; he stated that he left it at home with his mother. He showed me pictures of his car, and it was a hot sporty gray-silvery sports car.

My sister Sophia that I bought the Christmas present for and got into trouble with my dad over it stopped to see me while moving from Nebraska to California with her husband. I was worried about her as he had cheated on her multiple times thus far, and she had become very upset by his unfaithfulness. I had gone to see her twice when she was upset in Florida, and I hated the way he talked to her putting her down as she was not full chested and he joked about her all the time calling her flat-chested. I hated him for it. Later, we talked but only on the phone about her situation. I would not go again to see her until she moved to Colorado. While she was in New Mexico, I had moved to River Bend and began a marriage and children and didn't have money to travel any longer at that time other than to go home and see family. I did miss seeing her, and she eventually moved to Colorado and left him and had no money to come and see me either. We wrote and talked and realized that life is not always what we wanted it to be. I knew she deserved more in life and was glad finally to be rid of him once and for all. She was not what he wanted; she would never be what he wanted you know the bad girl in a leather corset.

I went home for Christmas and was telling my family about the wonderful man in my life. They were excited that I had met someone as

I hadn't dated anyone seriously at all since getting out of high school. I dated a few people, but no one that I felt strongly about. He was on my mind the whole time I was home for Christmas, and I told my family about him, not saying that I was in love.

We returned to school, and he was very happy to see me. We talked a lot about each other's families, and he knew that I was from a big religious family, and he, too, was religious. He talked a lot about his mother and that his father was dead; he had passed away a few years prior while he was in the military. He seemed close with his mother and that pleased me. He said that I was just like her; I could walk into a room and in five minutes everyone was talking to me. He said that his mother was the same way, very friendly and warm. I did have that personality and felt like I was very blessed to have such an outgoing personality and good outlook on life and myself. He made me feel like I was special, and we became very close. One night we did sleep together. I was shocked at myself; I was always waiting for marriage because of my religion, and that was when I knew for the first time I was in love and all his talk about being together made me sure this was the one I would spend my life with.

This was the first person that I felt that way about, and I was very happy; I was twenty-two. We still had school to deal with too, and I was doing great in labs and class work. He and I would spend many hours on the weekends together, and we would go dancing and having fun. We were perfect for each other and liked to do the same things. He liked sports, and so did I.

He said that he didn't dance, and I said one day, "Well, if you are going to be with me you have to learn to dance, because it is what I do for fun on the weekends!"

We would all go to a place called Glitter and dance all night to disco music with the lit floor all different colors changing as the music sang out and smoke machine era that puffed smoke into the room across the floor, making it seem as if you were dancing in the clouds. It was so much fun and a stress relief for me and great exercise as well. I would dance all night and never stop, so once the music started, I would only stop to get something to drink and get back on the floor.

When Paul said he did not dance, I said, "Well, if you are going out with me, it's what I do for fun, so with or without you, I dance for fun," and he quickly learned and had fun.

We would go to the lake and fly kites and run and talk and eat out and play tennis and swim on the weekends together. I was for the first time suited perfectly to this man who had won my heart. He liked to do everything I liked and loved sports as well and didn't mind if I beat him at tennis either.

The guys in the class seemed happy that we were happy together, and my friend Glenda thought he was nice too. Like a slap in the face that you weren't expecting came the words from a friend one night just weeks before the end-of-the-school session and graduation when one of the guys, Brandon, who was Paul's best friend down at school, came up to me in a parking lot and said, "Julia, I have something really important to tell you, and I know that it is going to upset you, but I need to tell you."

I said, "Go ahead, what is it?" not having a clue what he was about to say to change my life and break my heart into shredded pieces in an instant. He stated that Paul was married and that his wife was pregnant.

I remember it felt like someone ripped my heart out and stomped on it. I began to cry, and Brandon hugged me. He told me to let it go and break it off with Paul. I went to Paul's apartment, and he did acknowledge the fact that he had lied to me and was married and that his wife was pregnant. He stated many reasons for not telling me, but I was extremely upset and asked him if he loved his wife, Jane, and he began crying, and he said, "Yes."

I said to him, "Well then, you need to go home and work things out with her, even if you didn't know, I am not the type of woman who would break someone's marriage up, and I am not happy that you lied to me either. What the hell were you thinking?" And I walked out. I never told him that he broke my heart, and I wanted nothing to do with him. I just told him to go home to his wife and work things out and leave me alone.

I drove home crying the whole way, and I couldn't remember when I stopped crying, thinking to myself, "How could I have trusted this guy and been so wrong about him. How stupid was I about people?" I remember thinking that he probably wanted someone to sleep with while his wife was at home during school. You know, I was used for sex.

I was upset as I was a virgin and thought I had waited my whole life for the perfect boy, and now this. It was horrible for me and upsetting.

The last big written test was coming up as the final grade for the classroom part of the school. I remember that I did not study as I was crying all the time since I found out he was married, and I hadn't studied before that since I thought I was washing out of the program to move to River Bend to marry Paul. I could not believe that he could lie to me so convincingly and that I could not see the liar on his face or hear it in his voice. I was in love and all the rest was a blur.

I failed that last big test and therefore failed to pass the course and was phased out of the program. I was humiliated and went home and didn't tell my parents why. Glenda, my friend and roommate, and the other girl who was an ex-military controller did not pass the course either. It was upsetting for all three girls in the class. At least we didn't get taken out in a stretcher; one day in class one of the guys had a heart attack while we were practicing a lab separating traffic. I felt bad for him because he was married with children and lost his job in one instant, not to mention he had a heart attack.

So I thought I found the love of my life, and instead I found a liar and didn't pass the final big written test at school because of him. I was willing to give it up to move with him and marry him. I guess he forgot the important part that he was married. How could he ruin my life and my career? I guess he wanted what he wanted the beautiful fun blond girl whom everyone wanted, and he wasn't thinking about me or the long-term effects of his bad adulterous behavior.

He talked with me like he wanted to marry right away and have me move to River Bend and get married, so it was a great shock to hear he was married. How could I have not known? How could I have let myself give myself up to this guy who was nothing but a liar?

It rushed through my mind about all the things he said about living with his mom and this and that about home and at his mother's house. He had fabricated the whole thing. None of it was true; he would prove later to be something that I had really no idea that one mind could accomplish in fooling and duping others into the manipulative life he wanted to not only have but very carefully control to get what he wanted.

He was a manipulating, pathological liar who was obsessed with me, and I wanted no parts of him after that. I did fall in love with him and cried many nights and days alone about my foolishness of falling in love with a liar.

I moved back home and instead of moving to Capital as planned, I had to move back in with my parents as I had given up my apartment in Springfield. It really shook me up, and my mother was very supportive, but I did not tell her about Paul, only that I did not make it through school. We had many talks, and my mother and dad were supportive of me living with them until I got a job with the FAA, only this time in the flight district office out by the airport; they were very nice in seeing that I got a job even though I did not make it through school. The office investigated airplane crashes and gave written airmen exams. They hired me as the receptionist, secretary, exam issuer, and other tasks.

I did go out one night with friends dancing one night to a large disco, and we had a ball. I met someone and danced with him all night long. He was foreign, and I was having fun, and he was a great dancer. He asked for my number, and I said, "Sure," and gave it to him. He called at my mother's house, but I was not home and hadn't called him back.

The next night I got a call from Paul, and he stated that he was not in love with his wife but in love with me. I stated that he had to try and work things out, but he said he did try, and she was not the woman for him.

I said that I was sorry that it didn't work out, and he asked me if I would still be interested in being with him and marrying him if he got a divorce, and I said yes. I was happy that he called but felt sad for his wife as she was pregnant. That wasn't fair to her on his behalf, but I could not control how he felt, and he told me that she was not a very nice person and she was not in love with him. He was very shy and insecure at times about himself—or so he led me to believe.

Nonetheless, I was elated that he called and that he would be in my life, and we seemed perfect for each other. I was happy to be thinking about being his wife and moving to River Bend. I told him that I wanted to wait until he was divorced to move up there, and he wanted me to move now as he was lonely and missing me.

I remember one night when I called him at his apartment in River Bend, the desk person there put the call through, and I could hear him talking to his wife, Jane, on the phone. I just listened for a few seconds and then hung up. It was like someone did that on purpose. I wondered then if he was lying still to me. I wondered so much about what was happening in my life. I didn't know what to think. Emotionally, I was crushed for the first time. It was an extremely sad time of my life.

Many calls later, I realized that he did love me. Or I should say, he convinced me of that, and it would be twenty-three years later that I realized that he never loved me either. Did he even know how to love someone? Did he even know what love was or what it meant?

He called me and asked me if I was going to the wedding in New York as I was invited to go from one of the guys in our air traffic control class who had graduated and returned home to marry his fiancée. So I said yes but didn't ever tell him that Brian told me at school, if it didn't work out between me and Paul, I should call him; I remember thinking how could a guy who was getting married say such a thing to someone, but I guess I was not emotionally intelligent about men yet to understand that some men marry people they are not in love with or lust with but just are getting married for many other reasons but not love.

I met Paul at the airport, and we spent several days in New York, walking around seeing the sites, and of course, attending the wedding of the Buddhist girl and our friend Brian from school. It would be the first Buddhist wedding ceremony I attended, and it was lovely and so quaint and beautiful. Later, he and she did divorce, and I guess it would be the first sign of a real man stating to me months prior that he was about to marry someone but would take me over her now if I was available if things didn't work out between me and Paul. Seemed sad to me but nonetheless a very important statement in my life about people.

While in New York, we left the hotel one day and were going to walk to the Empire State Building. While outside we asked for directions, and a police officer told me to walk down Fifth Avenue as there was a parade that we could see as well. We walked over to Fifth Avenue, and the parade was coming down the street, and much to my total surprise, it was a gay-pride pot parade to legalize pot and sustain gayness in America by a public display of many of them walking together with signs.

He said to me, "Let's stop and watch."

I just wanted to keep going, but he wanted to watch. So we stopped inside a storefront, and sure enough, one of them tried to sell pot to us, and I just laughed and said, "No, thanks." The gayness to the parade would later make me wonder if that was why he wanted to stop and watch. Who knows, and at this point of my life, I don't even care either?

I told my parents when I returned home from New York that I had fallen in love with Paul and was going to marry him in River Bend, that I had met him in air traffic school, and he was married but separated and about to be divorced. My parents did not approve, and it was hard for me to tell them, but I did it anyway. My mother the next day told me I was stupid. She never said much else, and when the time came for me to move, I would not understand that it would be three years of silence from parents to let me know of their disapproval of the person I had chosen to marry. They never tried to talk me out of it and never once said, "Please bring this man to our house so we can meet him." They simply let me leave and go my way. I was in love, and they would not be at the wedding years later. I thought to myself, "Why would my parents not care enough to help me with this decision as I had listened to them in the past?"

I waited for a few months and then decided to go ahead and move up there as he stated he was living in a small one-room apartment which he called the dump. I visited him once before moving, and the place was run-down and dumpy. I felt bad for him, and that was when I decided to move up and help him as he looked so miserable; I did not realize that he was playing on my sympathy. As I look back on it, he was manipulating me to move up and help him because he had little money while getting a divorce. I wonder if it was about loving me at all. I would learn later after twenty-three years of marriage that it was not about loving me. He needed someone to replace his wife to state to everyone that he was a normal white male heterosexual who was hiding his homosexuality.

I gave notice at my job and moved with all my belongings in a truck by myself. I never thought I would be moving by myself somewhere for somebody, but there I was.

We had an apartment across the street from the airport where he worked in River Bend Control Tower at River Bend Airport. We didn't even have a bed, just a mattress on the floor. I did bring a kitchen table and a few other items. We gradually found used furniture and had the beginnings of a wonderful relationship and a home.

He got a part-time job at quick shop just a few miles down the street from our apartment, which was directly across from the air traffic control tower. His main boss was very gay, and he always worked with him. I remember it was weird when I was out in the parking lot one day trying to learn to drive his motorcycle, he asked me if I thought he was gay.

I said, "No, why do you ask me that?"

He said, "Well, my first wife told me once that she thought I was."

I said, "Well, you don't seem it to me."

He said, "Good."

That was the last time we talked about it, but between his working in that store and being gone a lot from home made me start to wonder a bit, and then on our fifth anniversary he took me to Toronto, and he asked at the front desk about a place to go dancing at the hotel, and we wound up at a gay bar dance disco, and when I realized it was full of men who were gay, I said, "I want to leave," and was laughing.

He said, "No, let's stay and dance."

I thought to myself, "Was his question to me six years earlier to have me rule out that he was gay and his first wife was correct in that he was gay?"

I would learn later with a new friend from work that I thought he was definitely gay. What a realization to have in your mind when you were married and thought your man was straight and loving, and he had this dual life that he evidently was hiding for his reasons.

"Why screw up my life," I thought, "when you are something else?"

At that time, I blocked it out of my mind and kept my feelings all to myself. Maybe I was afraid it was true. I should have told someone at that point, but I was embarrassed, I guess, that it might be true. How could I marry a gay person? What does that say about me? I would find out later I was stupid—just plain, old stupid about men. But in my defense, some people never truly reveal who they are to anyone. Like an actor on a stage performing day after day like a routine.

I tried to stay in the government and found a job at the VA hospital in River Bend as a temporary secretary, but it didn't work out, and I found myself looking in the paper for a job and came across a position opening as a security guard in a department store. It was so different from all of the work I had been doing, but I thought I was ready for something new. I liked the job and training at the main store in California before starting at the Boyton's store at River Bend Mall. The department store was a little up class and had some very nice things. I could not believe the number of people that thought stealing was an everyday occurrence and sometimes even a way of life as a profession. I caught everyday, one-time lifters to professional groups to employees, which of course was the hardest for me as I did become friends with some of the employees. We were trained not to become friends with the employees, but it was hard as it was a small town and a small store with a small-town environment. I caught people young and old from all backgrounds. It was a time of my life whereby I was doing something good but felt bad about it some of the time. I carried a badge and handcuffs and mace; I would make sure I had the evidence of what they had stolen, where they placed it, and would ask them once they were outside the store to please take the earrings out of the left pocket and place them in my hand and then would read them their Miranda rights and place the handcuffs on them and take them to the office whereby I would question them and then write a report. The police would be called to pick them up. If it wasn't a felony, they would be released and not prosecuted, but if it was, they would go before a judge, and I would have to appear and testify.

I remember one day catching two women in our remote location not the main store, whereby they had on booster girdles, and they would lift their skirts and shove the items of clothing into the oversized girdle that was open in the front and stuff the merchandise into the girdle and drop their skirt back down to cover it up. I was shocked at how quick they did this as a pair one would stand and the other would lift the skirt and place the items into the girdle without anyone seeing it. I admit I was amazed and shocked but nonetheless arrested them both, and while inspecting their car, lo and behold, inside the trunk were numerous bags of items from other stores that they had stolen all day long. It was a way of life for them, and they made a living doing it. I was certainly impressed by their expertise and more impressed with my ability to catch them both and handcuff them and arrest them.

There was one time also where I arrested a young female outside the store at the mall entrance, and she ran into the maternity store adjacent to our front doors to the mall, and she tried to resist me and started to throw me around the store; we fought for a few minutes, and then I realized that I was not able to detain her by myself, so I screamed to the sales clerk in the maternity store to call the police officer at the information booth. She did, and two police officers came to help me, and it took all three of us to get her down on the ground and put the cuffs on her. She was a wild cat and was only about twenty years old and about a hundred pounds—I being much taller and heavier was amazed at how strong she was and suggested that she might be on drugs. She did go before the judge, and it was at that time that I realized that the people I was arresting knew my home address, and I was not happy about that at all. I remember thinking that they could come to my home and hurt me if they wanted to. I made me feel uneasy.

Anyway, that day after being thrown around the store, I called my boss in California and said that I was not going to continue to work at the store because they were not paying me enough to get knocked around and hurt. They, of course, talked me out of it. The next time I can remember the feeling that I needed to quit was one evening in the store; it was winter, and a lot of snow on the ground, and I had a go code announced overhead to go to better dresses. I was about six months pregnant at the time, and anyway, the salesclerk was yelling. He grabbed the fur coat rack and took the whole rack of fur coats and all and went out the door. I ran out the door and down the sidewalk after him, but there was snow on the ground, and I was pregnant. I was running as fast as I could, and a man in a car said, "Hop in and I'll catch you up to him." Well, he did, and I yelled outside the car to drop the coats, and he did drop them but kept running. I did recover the coats but made no arrest. I thought to myself, "What are you doing?" I knew my family would not believe that I was carrying my first child and running down a street pregnant to stop a shoplifter carrying a rack of mink coats. I felt like I was in a movie or something as this could not be happening to me.

The job also entailed check fraud, building security, purse employee inspections, etc. It was a very interesting job for the little pay I received, and I had no idea that so many people stole things. I can remember that, but the friends I made in the store were invaluable as I had no friends in River Bend, so they were my friends. I can remember that I had a Pollyanna life and had no idea how many people stole things every day. Kind of like later on how I would learn how many people lie every day and think nothing of it. Unreal to me in this world I grew up in.

I made one good friend in the store, and her name was Sloan, and she and I spent a lot of time together. We had a lot in common, and her boyfriend worked at a computer and television, camera, and electronic store where later Paul would work part-time. We did things as couples, and Ernst and Paul became friends. Paul then took a part-time job at the store working the nights I was working nights, and he seemed to enjoy working there and made lots of friends. Everyone liked him as he would always joke around. He would always tell me that he would make up bogus things wrong with the equipment people would bring in, and he seemed to take pleasure in that, stating to one lady, "Your remulator is broken!" when there was no such thing or part.

I remember thinking at the time that he was dishonest to people, but he laughed about it and said he just said that because he did not know what was wrong as he was the salesperson, not the technician that would fix it. I didn't realize at that time that he was a pathological liar and lied about everything probably, and he seemed to take pleasure in it as well. At one time he entered a contest the electronic store was having: take a movie camera home and make a movie and whoever made the best movie got the camera. He made a movie about chili and a man who had Haitian chiliosis, something he made up which was a man obsessed with chili. He was making fun of our neighbors who one day was barbecuing *chili* on the grill, and he made fun of them; they were trying to save money as the man was in medical school. The movie was weird, and he shot himself in the end with a shotgun in the head because he couldn't find any chili in the stores. But he won the contest, and we got a free movie camera. Was this a warning sign I missed because he was laughing about it all the time? I guess so at the time; later I realized how screwed up this person was.

The sales staff at my store Boyton's gave me a baby shower, and they did give me a wedding shower too. The only baby and wedding shower and gifts I received were from friends; no family member did anything for me at all at home. It was hard for me to accept, but I guess I realized at that time that my family did not care about me much in a way that I thought they should.

The day when we were married in our home, we had a few friends and family over for the ceremony. Only two sisters and one brother of mine attended, which I was very excited about, and Paul's family was all there—his mother, sister, brother, and sister-in-law. Our friends in River Bend were there too, and it was a nice day, and I remember it being fun and happy. He drugged our two dogs so they would sleep while we had the ceremony and the crowd in the house; later this was crucial to his manipulation by drugs to get the result he wanted on a given day. My sisters and brother stayed at our house while visiting, so since we were not going on a honeymoon, we spent the night in a hotel. We spent the night at an inn. I remember the night was fun, but we had no heat in the room, and it was so cold I remember thinking, "How much did we pay for this?" It was not my dream honeymoon night for sure. He put no thought into this night at all. I was so disappointed but said nothing to him at all. Just remember being happy though.

My sister was my maid of honor, and our friend Ernst was the best man. I thought it odd that he did not ask his brother or our friend Barry. Ernst only knew us for about a year and a half and was my friend from work Sloan's to-be husband. Later, Ernst hung himself in the house that he and Sloan lived in after they were married for a few years. It was really sad. I remember thinking how I wished someone had loved Ernst better. People only kill themselves when they feel no one loves them. Or did he kill himself? Did someone maybe do it and make it look like suicide? I later had thoughts that maybe Paul killed him to shut him up about the fact that possibly he was Paul's gay partner in life away from me. Of course, I did not figure that out until years later. How sad if that is true; my gut says yes it is true, but will I ever know for sure? No.

One year later, I quit my job a few weeks before giving birth to my daughter. It was a happy time, but I was glad to finally be off my feet because walking and arresting people while pregnant was not advised. Alexandria was born, and my life at home was happy just taking care of her. We had decided since we did not know anyone well enough to trust someone with our child, I would stay home and take care of her myself. It was a big decision, but I think with the work schedule sometimes being nights, that was a part of it too. I would never regret our decision to have me stay at home and take care of our children. I was very fortunate that my husband made enough money to do that. But I do remember that one month before I gave birth to my first child, my husband stated that his best friend from home was dying from prostate cancer, and he needed to go and see him right away. I was not happy as I was afraid of being by myself if I delivered early, but he seemed upset, so I said, "Go ahead and go." That friend is still alive. I would wonder later in life to myself where he went that weekend? He hated that I was fat as I had gained fifty pounds with child, and he called me Momo, and I hated it. He made fun of his pregnant wife who was about to give birth to our first child. I guess it was his way, as I would learn later in my life; he didn't care about me at all. Life for him was all about his image and what was hanging on his arm and the impression he gave to others about who he was with. He was a phony, you know one of those people I hated but didn't realize he was that way as we were never around his friends or family that much. It would take me years to realize that part of his screwed-up personality.

A few weeks later, my husband found out the air traffic controllers were going to strike against the government because they had told the controllers that from now on, they could be personally sued if they crashed two planes together at work. Up until that time, if they did have a midair crash, it was the government who would get sued unless the airlines were at fault. I was so nervous that we could lose our home if someone sued us if Paul put two together at work one day or night. I didn't see that happening as he was a great controller, but it could happen; people are humans. Because of that, I was in favor of PATCO—the Professional Air Traffic Controller Union—backing the strike. All of the wives were on the picket lines one day in support of our husbands, and I had my two-month-old baby Alexandria in a stroller, and someone in a passing car threw a tomato at me and screamed out, "I can't go on vacation now that you screwed up my flight! Get back to work!"

I was amazed that this person gave no consideration to the needs at hand of the controllers, nor did he stop to ask me why I was picketing along with my husband. The national news, of course, was lying about the reasons the controllers were striking, and so I guess the public was not ever informed of the reason they actually went on strike, which was bad public relations for PATCO, the union, as they should have been informing the public of the truth and their need for the public to help out the situation by supporting them. Instead, Gabby Greg on the National News Station told the public that it was about controllers wanting more money, but that was only one part of the contract dispute, and the major part about being personally liable was never told to the public. The truth was being withheld from Americans. I don't know why. I guess President Reagan wanted to show his strength and break a union that they hated in the first place since it was a federal government job union, and they hated unions and wanted to break them down. Republicans hate unions, and they want employers to have the upper hand and make money off the backs of workers who they control. They don't like controlling efforts of unions, which we all know from history.

The first meeting in a bar in River Bend with the PATCO union guys from out of town said the wives had to be at this meeting. In the meeting, the organizers in charge that night threatened us with baseball bats in their hands as they hit them up and down in their hands that we were to do as they stated and support the strike and demand that our husbands strike against the federal government and stick up for what PATCO was upset over, and the president had decided to stop negotiations with PATCO, so their only option was to *strike*.

I remember driving up to New York and going to a bar with my baby for a meeting in New York that the union called and stated that the wives had to be there. The noise was so loud as the men were screaming and chanting loudly, "STRIKE, STRIKE!" that I had to go outside with my baby. These men realized that the government was selling them out, and they had given their lives to separate traffic as professionals and now were being sold down the river by the government who was trying to break union power at the time and give way to a personal tragedy for every family of a controller who would or may one day at work put two airplanes together in the sky. It was a sad time in America and a sad time for these professional men and women who had spent countless years of long hours, hard and stressful times, unhealthy working hours to protect the public and ensure the safety of the public while flying, only to have the public turn and point a finger at them when they were trying to say, "We are on strike because the equipment is bad and outdated and unsafe, and now they tell us we could be sued personally if we put two together because of equipment malfunction or otherwise." It was unfair of the government, but the public never heard the real story on the news, TV, radio, or otherwise. I will never forget seeing the reporter who was in charge of the storyline every night, Gabby Greg, giving the bogus baloney that was probably being fed to her by government officials. It was a cover-up. The controllers were, of course, fired, as it was said they took an oath to never strike. Well, the government officials took an oath to tell the truth, and they did not. It was unbelievable to me, and they said that President Reagan was either going to fire them or the US postal workers, whichever struck first to send a message and start union-busting in America.

I remember my sister in Springfield who worked at the post office and was so worried about the strike. She would never have to worry further because they usurped it with PATCO and destroyed those guys.

My husband was not allowed to collect food stamps or collect unemployment, and we were financially being destroyed. We were lucky that we didn't lose our home as we had purchased a middle-income home and did not have too much debt. We did suffer and ate potatoes and hotdogs for a long time just about a year. It was awful, and of course, two months before the strike, I had my first child and quit work. Finally, after months, they said we could have food stamps, and then it eased up but, it took a while for Paul to find a job.

The controllers stayed positive initially and thought for sure they would get hired back. A lawyer came to represent the controllers in Springfield in a class-action suit against the federal government. I testified, and so did all the controllers and their wives. The lawyer came from Raleigh, and he stayed at our home. He was very nice, and I thought for sure he would win, but of course, he did not. The guys were devastated, and, luckily Paul had already found a job selling cars but never gave up the fact that one day he might get his job back. He kept saying they couldn't do it for long without all of us.

What he didn't know was that at that time they were hiring anybody who once was a controller because they even contacted me by letter, stating I could have a job as a controller at Whiteman Air Force Base in Pennsylvania. I didn't even have a controller's certificate; they were hiring people that were let go for age and medical reasons. It was a sad time to watch professionals of such importance get destroyed and to watch the president of the United States deregulate the airlines and put them into the worst financial state that I as an American had ever seen. It would be the single most personally devastating event that I felt from a direct decision of the US president's office. I was ashamed of the decision. People said, "They took an oath not to strike."

I said, "The government promised the truth to the employees, yet they did not provide it." Some would say we made the wrong decision. I still stand strong in stating that they made the right decision. Hopefully, the office of the president learned something as well.

The FAA did send me a letter telling me they would hire me back to work at a military tower, and I turned the job down as my daughter was my job now. We had chosen that I would be a stay-at-home mother. I gave birth to my second daughter a year and half later, and she was so beautiful. My older daughter was so happy it was a girl, and she helped me take care of her; she was a good big sister. It was fun to see them react with each other, and they became best of friends as they played and laughed and loved each other. We did everything together, and they were with me all the time. We cooked and played outside; they helped me with the garden, and we put up a swing set, and they had many hours of fun swinging. Our dog Bud, a border collie, was a constant companion for me and fun for the girls too. They loved him and talked to him all the time. The girls would help me plant flowers; we had many flowers, roses, and tulips in the yard. I think one summer I planted over one hundred bulbs in the main flower bed in the middle of the yard. They were spectacular under the tree next to the largest rhododendron I had ever seen about eleven feet tall and a fountain made from stones that didn't work, but it was unique. They stated at one time the property was part of a park. The yard was oddly large for the neighborhood, and there were hedges all around the way around the yard about five feet and in the back of the yard about fifteen feet tall. I had to trim them on a ladder. I do not have fond memories of that task, but they were beautiful and hid our boat we parked in the back.

Our lives went on; I had started a women's soccer league because I had played soccer in Springfield most of my life, and it was my favorite fun and exercise all rolled into one. I called around to see if there was a soccer team I could join when I first moved up there, but I was told that there was only a men's team, and I could join them, but I stated that I was not up to playing with men. I started a women's soccer league for fun, and at first, we had a few teams. I started by asking the people at work, and my coworker Saddie who was a security guard too, and she said that her husband would coach so I could play.

I said, "Yeah," and we found more players to play.

The women were mostly older mothers, and we had so much fun practicing and playing. Then the colleges in town found out we had this women's soccer league and infiltrated the teams, and the play became much more intense and faster-paced. I then dropped back to playing defense. I played soccer a few more years and then quit when my youngest daughter would scream, "Mom, I need you!" as I was on the field in the middle of a game. All this new young blood on the teams made me feel as though I was going to have a heart attack from running so fast to catch up to them, my face beet-red after running a defensive play on one of the girls. I knew I was outplayed. I told the girls I was quitting, and they said that I couldn't since I started the league, but I did anyway. They were so nice and flattering, stating that I started the whole thing and couldn't quit, but it was time to take care of my family and think about my children and what their needs were. Not to mention my red face from over exhaustion from running too fast and my daughter Bella who would cry out, "Mommie!" and crying it out while I was playing the game. It made me understand that I needed to stop playing at that time of my life. I am a realist, as you will see throughout my life.

As a stay-at-home mother, I learned to concentrate on cooking more and became quite a great cook, trying out new recipes quite often and liking it. I canned and made my own baby food as well. We had a big vegetable garden, and I enjoyed planting, hoeing, and picking as well as eating the food we grew. Our yard was large, and I planted many flowers and enjoyed being in the yard with the children and the dogs and having family and friends over in the summer for backyard barbecue and just plain, old family fun. The dogs we had loved the yard as well and had a good home. I learned how to quilt from an Amish woman inside an Amish country store sitting around the potbelly stove, and it was so fun to learn her way of quilting as it was totally different from my mother who did cross-stitch and appliqué in a different way. I was becoming a mother and even sewed handmade dolls for my children and my nieces and nephews.

We had an older 1960 Thompson wood boat, and we would go in the summer to Lake River Bend, which wasn't far, about five miles, and we had a good time with the kids on the beach and skiing with the boat and having friends over and boating and fishing too. It was the best of times, and we were having fun and in love—or at least I was in love.

My sisters Lenora, Wendy, and Brunhilda would visit a few times, and finally my parents came with one of my sisters. They took a vacation to Canada and passed through River Bend on their way home and stayed a few days. My parents stayed longer and then took a train home. My parents seemed to finally approve of my life—I hoped anyway. My friends from high school came, too, on several occasions, and it was nice to see them and think that they were thinking about me.

I can remember Paul stating that my one friend was so pretty, how could she be divorced? I can remember that I didn't like that comment too much.

Maybe it was his way of making me think one thing when he wasn't even interested in me at all as I was the cover for his gayness and no wonder why everyone used to say, "How do you get him to do everything with you?" He was not the normal guy at all now, was he? Here I thought he cared about me so much he didn't want to be away with me. Hell, to the *no* as he loved being a woman and doing everything with his woman.

The tomboy who became the ultimate woman and mother picked a homosexual male who was hiding his sexuality from everyone close to him. Of course, except probably his male mate, which was never revealed to me if my suspicions were correct. I never caught him in the act; he just acted like it.

The snow in River Bend was overwhelming at times for me. I used to remember we would get twenty-four inches on Thanksgiving Day, and it would not stop until Easter. I used to shovel the sidewalk, and the snow would just come right back down as the pile had become too high to throw it up onto. I remember crying one day sick of shoveling and being stuck inside. The snow was beautiful, but I had just had two small children, and the house had become like a jail cell. I could not get out of since most days it was too cold to even take the children outside.

Some days you could not even drive your car when the snow had fallen so deep and so fast the plows had to have time to clear everything before you could drive on it.

Paul grew tired of the car sales job and took a job at the post office as a letter carrier and used to work long hours and overtime all the time. He would come home in the winter with icicles on his beard, and I said, "This is ridiculous, we should move, either to River Bend or Springfield, where we have family and not so much snow." He picked Springfield as he stated he wanted to get more pilots licenses and become an airline pilot. He had a private pilot's license but needed more to apply for a job with the airlines.

I, of course, was surprised by his pick of cities to move to as his widowed mother and sister and brother's family and his son from his first marriage were in River Bend, but he chose Springfield. We had a garage sale, and his mother came up to handle it for me as I had never had one. She was sorry to see us go to Springfield, and I could not understand why he picked Springfield, but he said it was because there was bigger airline possibility in Springfield for a pilot job. So he transferred with the post office to Springfield, and we put our house up for sale.

Chapter 3

1987–1992
Children, Home, Family

He went first to Springfield to look for a home and found a flat and bought it without me. I was upset as I wanted a house; we were used to a big home. The flat had three rooms and a small room that just fit a twin bed, and both the girls had to sleep in it together. I was not happy but didn't say much as I was happy to have moved home, and we were only blocks from my parents' home. I did, however, still continue to look for a home. Paul wanted to live in The Groves, an upper-class neighborhood, and I stated that we did not have enough money to buy a house in The Groves. They were all very expensive, and we did not have any money except the money from the sale of our house in River Bend, which at that time in 1985 was about $40,000.

I remember thinking, "Why would he move to Springfield when his life was in Raleigh only two hours from where we lived?" I guess he wanted his privacy for his own reasons, I would learn later. I remember how odd it seemed that he did not want to live near his widowed mother, and his own son from his first marriage lived there too. No wonder why she never wanted Paul to have Joe when he was little; she knew down inside, too, that he was gay but never told me or his family. Shame on her, I was going to try to, but without her help, he had already manipulated to everyone that I had mental problems. No one believed anything I had to say about him, and they were stating that I was crazy, even people at work who didn't even know my past or my private life. How this was getting spread to people, I did not know yet, but I was sick of it. I wanted a normal life now as it was my turn to live normally once and for all, and I would find someone to love me. I would find someone who would believe me and not all the lies.

The houses in Springfield were much more expensive than River

Bend, and we could not afford as large of a house as we had in River Bend now in Springfield, which I told him before me moved, and it was his choice to move to Springfield. I suggested that we buy a big house in the city and renovate it; that way we would still have enough income to send the children to private school. It was decided that it would be the best financially and for the family decisions we had made for our children. At that time, Paul was going to school nights while working at the post office in the daytime, and I was taking care of everything while he worked and went to school. He studied over at Area College and rode his motorcycle to school every other night, it seemed, and then the actual flight time was in addition to the classroom, so he was not home much. He seemed to like living in Springfield, but I know he was uncomfortable with my parents and used to think they did not like him. He always talked about my family and commented on what they had thought and things they would say. I would always just say, "Please have your own thoughts, and don't pay attention to what they think, that is what I do with my family. They have very strong opinions, and my opinion is my own and always has been." But I could tell that he never was comfortable about just being himself around my family.

No wonder he wasn't it was a regular topic of discussion with my family about how much they hated homosexuals at times we were together for holidays. So much so that my children even hated them for it, since they were beginning to make gay friends in school. I would just tell my children that our religion stated that it was against our religious beliefs that someone act upon the sexual nature of homosexuality. In other words, they could be gay and feel gay, but our religion stated that they couldn't act upon the feelings. Now I myself am not God, and I don't judge anyone. I don't judge homosexuals and never would judge anyone at all. I only can tell what the Bible says. People either do one thing or another depending on what they believe. That is what I told my children. I can't believe that God really intends for people to hate anyone who sins. He didn't.

While he was in school studying to be a pilot, I was asking him to have another child. He was not receptive to it at all and said, "I don't want any more children."

I said, "Could we please just try one more time for a boy?" as I had found this article about having a boy or girl and things you could do to make the outcome more hopeful.

It was not 100 percent proven, but I thought it would be nice. I wanted a boy and a brother to my daughters as well. He gave in to me, and I did all the things I needed to, and of course, later I had Shaun, an almost-ten-pound boy. It was exciting and not just because he was a boy.

But at the same time, just months prior to that, his ex-wife called and wanted her new husband to adopt his son Joe, which they had together. He said to me that he was going to do it as then he would not have to pay child support.

I said to him that it was a horrible thing to say and that it was his son. He clearly did not want contact with him because he hated her, and I would learn later why. She knew he was a homosexual as she was married to him for five years while they were in Europe while he was in the military and played baseball for the military. She knew something I didn't. Years later, I would call her to see if she would help me with my children as he had custody of my teenage son and would wreck his life to get back at me. She said no.

I would not let him give up Joe and let someone else adopt him. We paid the child support for the next ten years, and we hardly ever got to see him. But I didn't care. Rule was his birth name, and no one should change a boy's birth name so he knows who he is and who is relatives are and that he would never marry someone that was related as well.

We found a house a few blocks away from the flat we lived in; it was a grand home, almost a hundred years old that I had admired as a child, and it was the biggest house in the neighborhood. It was three stories and had an atrium window in the roof. The yard was twice the size as the rest in the city and had so much potential. It needed everything, but we were willing to invest the time and money so that we could have a big house and still send the children to private schools. We could spend the money as we had it to renovate the home that would become a home; we were proud of and worked hard to fix it up back to its original splendor. The home was breathtaking once we had finished it.

We started by putting in a new bathroom before we moved in as we had put the money aside to pay for this room only, totally gutting the room and starting from scratch, including new plumbing as the house was almost a hundred years old, and it needed it. I was pregnant with my third child, and it was a time of excitement and looking forward to a home that we could make our own to our expectations. The bathroom was beautiful when we finished, and we did all the work ourselves with my brother Jerry's help too. Paul and my brother decided to gut the kitchen too when the stack from the bathroom fell out of the wall below in the kitchen and fell on the kitchen floor. We didn't have the money for a kitchen at that time, so it took a while for the money to be saved to do the total kitchen renovation, which was expensive, of course. In the meantime, we moved in, and I had to do without a kitchen. The refrigerator and everything were in the dining room, and I cooked in the microwave. My father and mother lived across the alley and they came over often to help.

The whole house was wallpapered even the ceilings, and it would take much work to get the paper off and because I was pregnant my father did all the ceiling removal of wallpaper as keeping my hands above my head was tuff while I was pregnant. The gas lights were still in the basement on the wood pillars that kept the house standing; it was amazing to see them still there. The house was so beautiful with stained glass windows on the north side of the house in the staircase to provide privacy from the house next-door seeing into the stairs. The house had original pocket doors in the living room and between the living and dining rooms. The original hardwood floors were there under a few layers of old carpet and linoleum, and the house had grand wooden fireplaces with wood columns in almost every room except the bathroom and den throughout the whole house. There were three rooms downstairs, four upstairs, and the third floor had two rooms—one unfinished and one finished somewhat, which was really old. The third floor had boxes of medical books when we moved in; there must have been a medical student there living on the third floor at one time, renting the space to live while attending school. Oh, if those walls could talk.

While working on the house, my pregnancy advancing to the stage of yes, it's time to go. I delivered him at St. Ann's, the hospital I was born in, and the battle began in the morning. I came in as my contractions were five minutes apart. Then they seemed to slow down, and I asked if I could walk, and they said yes. That did seem to help, and soon I was in the birthing room. His birth was to be natural same as the girls; even though this was a different doctor and different hospital, it all seemed right. The doctor put me on a Potosin drip after promising that she would not, and I was not happy about that at all. Then when I was breathing in the birthing room. Paul was my coach with two other children, and he was telling me breathe too late as the contractions were starting by looking at the machine.

I called the nurse, and she said, "No, the machine is operating fine."

I said, "No, it's not, the contractions are beginning long before he is seeing them to tell me, and then my breathing is too late, and these contractions are hard and they're killing me."

She sent the doctor in, and they gave me an epidural, which is a shot in the back in the spine to numb me. It went easy, and the contractions got eased up, and everything seemed better. Then it was time to push. I pushed for hours every which a way you could imagine, and nothing was making this baby come out. Finally, after four hours of pushing, the words rang out, "It's time for a C-section."

I was mortified. Yes, my precious son had to be cut out, and they wheeled me to the surgical room, and while I was awake, they cut out my son while I watched and listened. I was shaking so bad and was in such a state that I difn't think it was good for me to hear and be awake, but nonetheless, I had no control over anything. Paul watched them cut me open. I remember shaking so bad I couldn't even hold my baby after they cleaned my son up—my darling little Shaun—as I was afraid I would drop him, so I held him for just a few seconds only until I got into my room. I was crying inside. I remember this was not what it was supposed to be at all. There was nothing natural about this birth compared to the girls. But he was healthy, and that was all that was important. His head was very large, and that was why he would not come out normally. I used to tell him it was because he had so many brains. He was very smart, and later in life when he was about three, he had a make-believe friend he would call by name. I was at first worried about this event but read that extremely intelligent children had make-believe friends. I felt better about it, and I would include his friend in things we would do at home. When he was around eight, this imaginary friend disappeared as quickly as he came, unless he just quit talking about him.

The house was starting to come together, and when my son was born, we were still not finished with the kitchen. I had to carry the dishes and bottles for the baby up to the second-floor bathroom to wash them as I didn't have a kitchen sink yet. My mother told me I should write a book about living in the past with no running water and call it *Little House in the City* like the prairie. I laughed but should have written the book as I learned how to do a lot of things by doing without the everyday things we all take for granted. My brother was helping Paul, and soon the kitchen was done as well. It turned out beautiful and was a large room, and I spent most of my time in the kitchen as I liked to cook, and the children were always in there with me. We spent hours cooking and doing homework and learning and playing games in that kitchen. Soon we worked on the backyard and made it a showplace with flower gardens, a patio, a vegetable garden, and fruit trees. It was a show place, and people were always commenting on how beautiful the house was when they would come over. I worked for eight years on the house and took care of the children and the home. The house was a dream of something nice at a price we could afford, and we could fix it up as we had the money to spend on it. We had fun fixing it up the way we wanted it. I was a labor of love, sweat, and hard work, and I was proud of it.

We had stripped all the woodwork back to the original state and stained it natural and put a few coats of polyurethane on it. It looked like a million bucks, and I was proud to have restored this fine home that was built with such skilled carpenters and builders, this kind of work rarely seen in new construction at the time of the day due to cost incurred. It was a timeless piece of art, and I had restored it to its original splendor, and it made me feel so good. Not to mention that we would have such a treasure for years to come, and we could afford to do all the other things we wanted and send our children to private schools.

I designed a heavenly serene side flower garden for peaceful resting and entertaining friends and family outdoors. That year for my birthday, my mother and father gave me fifty bucks. I took the money and bought bricks for a sidewalk patio that I drew up and spent time reading on the best way to lay the bricks to make a straight walk that rounded in the middle and then went straight again. It was so beautiful, and all around the outer sides were flowers of pink and white. It was a work of art, and it aroused many wonderful comments from family, friends, and neighbors that they were impressed with my talents. I was happy with my peaceful place to rest and have fun; it was important to me to rest peacefully in life while living it. We built a wooden privacy fence that had rounded tops that we cut and had newels atop the posts. It was without a doubt a heavenly spot for peaceful moments of life.

Later on the patio, we placed a small steel pool for the children to swim in when they were little. They had a lot of fun in that small pool. Our yard had become a family fun place as well as the vegetable garden to be enjoyed by us and my mother and father, and I told the neighbors to help themselves. I enjoyed putting in two dwarf Fuji apple trees for my husband's birthday present one year, and we had banana trees as well. The yard was fun for our dog Bud to run in as well. He had so much fun in the yard with the children and the animals that would wander in from the wooded area across the street from the backyard of a retirement home that faced the front of our house. When looking out our enormous rounded-top picture window, you thought there was a park across the street because all you could see were trees. It was a great view for the city, and we were lucky to have found such a gem ready to be loved and restored. I made it the best I knew how, and people were very impressed by my work and love of this old house. We had redone our home in River Bend, and I had refinished some pieces of antiques, but this house would be fun for me as an artist, and I remember thinking to myself that God drew me in to buy this house to fix it up for years to come.

My husband was starting to stay away more frequently. He was working part-time selling insurance for a friend of ours, and he went to the office on Tuesday nights, and then other nights would be on calls to people's homes. I remember thinking that he used to talk a lot about a very pretty girl at work and would help her on her route as she was pregnant. We went to a wedding for someone at the post office, and he sat across the table from her. I got up the nerve one night to ask him if he was having an affair while we were lying in bed, and he didn't say anything, nothing to me at all. Not one word. He just turned over on the other side and went to sleep. I remember turning out the light and then crying very quietly all night long until I fell asleep. I had just had my third child, and my son was about one. It would be the last of children that I would have with him. Shortly after that comment, he told me one day that he decided to have a vasectomy done. It was against my religion, but I told him if he did not want any more children, then it would be his decision as I was not doing anything to stop a pregnancy. He had the procedure done, and I did have to sign the paper giving him permission. It was sad for me as I had wanted many children; he had originally agreed to six when we first married. But I'm glad we did it now that I know what he had in store for me later in my life.

A year later, he said to me that his brain was going dead and he needed to change jobs as the post office was not challenging for him. I told him to reapply to the government position that I told him about when we moved to Springfield, but he decided to become a private investigator, and he said that the pay was to much lower to start, and I said that I would watch children in our home for a few years to make up the difference. He stated that would be great and applied and took the job as a private investigator. I watched several children of friends of mine in my home for a few years so that he could go get a job that made him happy. Imagine that I worked hard so he could be happy. Did he ever do this for me? The answer to that would be *never!*

My children attended the same grade school that I went to, and it was fun seeing them go off to school to the same place that held so many special memories for me. It was a time of great happiness, and they loved the school, and we became very involved in the workings of the parish and the school. I was asked to be on the preschool board as my second daughter was attending it and was voted in as president. We painted the old kindergarten room that I went to in kindergarten, and my father helped with that; we had fun painting it, and it was blue with other colors as well. I was asked to be the school board president of the grade school and said yes. It was a volunteer position for the church, but I was willing to help, and my children's education was the most important thing other than their happiness that I felt strongly about. I did not take my schooling seriously as I think I was always tired in high school because I watched my sister's seven children every day after school, nor did I get the chance to go to college, and I wanted that for my children very much so, it was number one on my list of things I wanted so their lives would be better than mine.

The children were busy now with piano lessons, dance lessons, an avid reading schedule, and trips to the library and bookstores in the mall. The girls were dancing in a performing group that danced around Springfield. The group kept getting bigger and bigger, and soon it consisted of sixty dancers.

Alexandria, my eldest, would become quite focused and loved dancing; she was a natural at it, and the dance teachers were asking if she would do a solo, and she said yes. Her first solo was a tap-dancing number, and she danced to a song called "Leaves Falling." She was so excited, and the rehearsals began. She rehearsed many hours for months. I made a custom costume, and she helped design it; she was only about nine. I made a pattern out of a paper grocery bag, and Alexandria said, "Mom, I want it to look like the ice skaters with the nude front *v* and the back a nude *v*."

She would talk, and I would design. The hat was very small, consisting of a small fob that I totally hand-beaded and had a puff of green netting out the back. The body costume was Kelly green with a nude material in the front and back in a vee shape and the back had a gold sequined vein of tree vines and then at the bottom was a spray of green and gold leaves made from sequins sort of set on top of each other in a spray. The costume was amazing, and she designed it herself while I sewed it up. She looked so beautiful, and the dance was a winner. Her first performance won her the top trophy, and she was elated. It was a fun time to see her hard work put such joy in her heart, and it was an extreme pleasure for me as her mother, for I wanted to take dance lessons as a young girl but did not. Bella was very good but only danced in groups and never did a solo; she felt at times maybe her sister was so good, but she was just as good as far as I was concerned, but I never pushed her at all. Alexandria would go on to perform many dances, and she and Bella performed all around Springfield and in dance competitions. I made many costumes, and we also bought many of them too. Costumes cost almost as much as the lessons over a year.

Bella was becoming more confident that she had talents, too, all her own. She was an excellent dancer and was picked to be the front line of her dance numbers too. She was loving it but did not want to do solos at all. Just wasn't ready for a single thing or even a duo. I asked her, but she said no, so I let it go. I wanted it to be fun for her, and she loved it. Bella sometimes thought her sister was better, but I told her that it was because she was older.

At one point, I took them out of everything they did the same so that Bella could see that her talents where her own, and she did not have to compare herself with her older sister, which would help her self-esteem. It worked, and I was happy to see Bella much happier all around in her own talents. She had so many and just needed to realize that for herself. She did, and she bloomed like a new blossom, and I watched so proud as her mother. I loved her so much and wanted her to believe in herself, and finally, with some work, she did.

Alexandria was a hard act to follow. I know that because she is just like me, and my little sister had shared with me that she was always jealous of me growing up, and I never realized it. So some personalities just need a little tender loving nudge to make them know that they have so many talents just waiting to come out if you believe in yourself. I don't think my sister ever got that from our mother. My sister has many talents; they are just different from mine. Different is fine, different is good, different is just that—different. No one person is better than another, and no person's talents are more important, and that includes intelligence as well. People are so jealous of the wrong things, and I was never jealous of anything or anyone.

Bella was never jealous but just felt badly about herself. She fixed it quick with just a little loving help from me.

The whole dance group would then get invited to come to Disney World and dance there. We were all excited and saved our money for one whole year. The whole family was excited. I volunteered to make the costumes for the sixty dancers. It was an undertaking in my dining room where my sewing machine was and turned into a factory, with many mothers helping. I remember what fun we had, all of us pitching in and making many costumes of all sizes and shapes and of course for six boys as well. We spent a lot of money on that vacation, but it was worth it and the children and my stepson and mother-in-law all had a great time. A vacation to remember where Alexandria danced with Mickey Mouse and taught him to tap dance and Bella found new friends, and my son got to see the Ninja Turtles and of course learned to swim by going down the gigantic pink dragon water slide at the swimming pool. A trip they would always remember. What kid wouldn't?

Years went by, and I was not happy with the decisions that were being made for the school. I looked around for a new school and found a principal that I liked in the county and transferred the children to the school even though we still lived in the city. I was not happy about moving the children to another school but felt it was best for them. The new school was great and, it was the start of years of happiness for the children. My oldest daughter, however, was under great pressure as she was liked by several of the boys since she was so pretty and outgoing and the girls were jealous. Bella had some attention, but because she was quieter, her beauty would be admired but not forming jealousy of the girls at school because she would make friends with them first. But the girls at the old school treated Alexandria the same way, so I helped the best I could. One day a boy stabbed her with a pencil in the leg. She threw up, and I was not called by the teacher or the principal to come and get her at school. I found out about it and was upset. They said the boy didn't mean it, but I said he owed her an apology. They never made the boy apologize, and it was not right. My daughter was liked by many boys, and it was hard on her. My second daughter was very pretty, too, but much quieter, as I stated; she was liked by many, but she was quiet about it. Watching the attention that my daughters received, I remember thinking about how boys must have viewed me as well. I had no idea that I created such a commotion and that my beauty, which was never talked about at home at all, would soon be realized by me when the boys started to pay attention more personally with me, but I had no idea how pretty I was at that time of my youth, just didn't even think about it.

My son was adjusting to the school very nicely, and I was asked to be the president of the school board again at this new school, which I accepted quite nicely as I was so happy with the school and the principal. Mainly, this meant I was to chair the meetings and take all of the complaints from parents so the pastor of the parish and the principal of the school could focus more on the tasks at hand. The board was needed to get accreditation of the state. The pastor really made all the decisions. I just wanted people to be happy; it was maybe one of my gifts to give, and I never gave it a second thought. I loved helping people.

I was also asked to coach soccer for my son in kindergarten. The teams which were co-ed both boys and girls consisted of K through second grade. It would be four years starting to coach who would become one of the best soccer players in Springfield—my son Shaun who would be on the Olympic development team and play later for a select team, which was the best select soccer team organization in Springfield. I coached the first year, teaching the children the basics of foot placement on the ball and the idea of what the game field consisted of and how they needed to stay in position on the field to pass the ball to each other and score a goal. It was fun for me and for them. We would win every game, and I would become the topic of discussion amongst many men in the parish. The next year I inquired at the select soccer complex what it would entail for my son to start playing select. Well, turned out one of the guys in my neighborhood who played pro soccer in Springfield for the Stars, Danny, whose sister Joan and I played soccer with, was in charge of the youth soccer. He spoke with me, and unfortunately at that age, they played early mornings on Sundays, and I told him that he had to go to church with the family at that young age still. So he did share his coaching sheets with me, and I thanked him for them and used them. We won every game, and the children learned so much from me and Danny's coaching sheets.

After the third year, Shaun was now going into third grade, and we only had five boys in the third grade, and it was no longer co-ed but CYC soccer rules. So I had to find more boys, and they said I could ask the players I coached from second grade as well if I wanted to call them. So I picked up the phone and called the boys. Of course, they all said yes because they liked me.

Well, little did I know that even though we would almost win every game, parents who had nasty in their lives would come to an athletic association meeting and accuse me of stacking a team and not including the other boys from the second grade because they were not "good enough" for my team. And that CYC rules stated that every boy got a chance to play.

I was outraged. I stated that I nearly had enough to play and that I was told directly by CYC to call the second-grade boys whom I had coached the year before to see if they wanted to play up for me on my third-grade team.

I was so upset that the next year my son went to play in another league, and I was through with their insults. My son was excellent, by the way, and anyone would want him to play for them. I was not one of those moms that talked the talk about their perfect child but only stated when they shone in one area of talent that made me proud.

We changed parishes when we moved to the county, and a boy in the neighborhood asked him to play soccer, and he played one year CYC with them, and they took the team to a select league and lost every game, and my son hated it. He decided to switch over to a different prominent select team and played for them instead. He was picked to play on the team after a tryout, and he was really happy. It was a day to remember with joy in our hearts.

I was happy for him, but once again all his friends' parents treated me angrily because he left the team. I was once again being treated horribly because my son was good and was making decisions that were good for him.

I could not believe this at all; this was fifth-grade level. Unbelievable as it was to me, again nasty people treating me nasty. I thought to myself, "I think I need to get out of my religion and stick to my own beliefs and just go to church and stay away from people." New parish and the same old nasty junk that people just do everywhere in the world, and I was so sick of it. Christian?

I did not volunteer at anything at this new parish. Nothing at all. I did work at the school picnic, and that was it. I resolved myself to relax and enjoy a bit of life of my own with my children, and I did even through the emotional torture of my ex-husband.

More money meant people were more stuck up. Wanting you to do what they wanted you to do. So in control these people were, my husband would learn much from them. He became even more controlling of me.

Oh yeah, by the way, he was on the parish council the night the parents accused me of stacking a team, and he never got up and defended his wife, the coach. I guess it was embarrassing for him the baseball player to have his wife coaching and winning games. He even took away my whistle one night at practice, and I said, "What are you doing? You don't even know soccer rules."

He was so abusive to me, so controlling. I didn't know but suspected that he was truly gay and had found a new partner, I suppose, and a new woman they could share. I was out of his plan for sure, but he would torture me for years, making me unhappy and punishing me for what my family was saying about homosexuals. He hated my family, and because of them, he came to hate me in his twisted life.

Why didn't he have the guts to just leave me, walk out the door, and never come back? I guess the weasel with no balls liked to verbally abuse women. Homosexuals usually didn't like women, especially their mothers. He didn't like his mother either; he just pretended to in her presence so he could keep his secret life just that—secret.

We had moved to the county when Shaun was in third grade, but before that when he entered kindergarten, I volunteered in school in the computer room while he was at school and then the next year when he entered first grade and was in school full-time I went back to work.

At first, I tried to get a job at aircraft distribution center as I had worked there prior to moving away and I could work there and have a career again. There was no job offered.

I applied to one of the universities here in Springfield after someone told me that if you worked there after five years, your children could go to college for free, and I said, "Okay, where do I get a job?"

I applied and was interviewed for a receptionist job at the medical public affairs office, and I got the job. I remember thinking that I didn't even know how to use the fax machine and felt so stupid, but I didn't let it affect me too long. Soon, I was feeling good, and I really liked the job. It turned out the vice chancellor was a brother-in-law of one of my good friends' sister. He was a very nice man and was religious too. The job would soon get me promoted without asking to be to administrative assistant to the vice chancellor, and I would assist seven science writers with getting out stories to the press about the entire new up-and-coming research at the university. It was impressive to see what the office would write about and what the doctors there were accomplishing—such outstanding work and dedication was realized by the press releases I would mail out on a daily basis.

Soon, I would come to realize that my boss's main secretary, who was my supervisor, did not like me at all. She was eighth-grade thinking and was out to get me and hurt me. One day, I proved after suspicion that someone had accessed my computer and switched documents, making them have mistakes in my computer that would have been printed out and sent out to the press. It could have gotten me fired. The next day I took a floppy disk and copied all my files, and then I took the disk and taped it to the underside of my desk where no one could see it. Sure enough, the next day I had the proof to myself that someone was messing with my computer files. They were public files, and she had access to them. I was so upset I didn't know what to do. I could hardly sleep at home, and I began to hate coming to work. Some days I was so emotional on my lunch break I would go in an empty office and lay my head down on the desk, unable to move or think.

I began to search for another job and transferred to another department. I remember thinking that my past thirteen years as a stay-at-home mom loving people and thinking about the lovely world had all come crashing to a screeching halt with the hatred of one jealous woman and more to follow in her footsteps of intentional actions to hate me so much so that I could barely handle the emotional stress of ugly jealousy at work. It was so hard to deal with and with more to come a time would come when I was unable to cope any longer.

Chapter 4

1992–2001
Jobs
My Family Life
Against My Will

I transferred to the performing arts department. The chair was aware of the situation that I was leaving, and he assured me that it would not happen in his department. He would make sure that if anyone mistreated me that they would be fired. The office manager that interviewed me with him left before I started, and the position was open. I started, and he hired a different woman, and she arrived, and we were friends. The position was perfect for me and very hard as I was really doing the job of about three people. I was the chair's secretary, the department secretary, and the receptionist. I enjoyed the job anyway and never complained. The professor was happy to have me there as I was very organized and whipped his office into shape. He was now on time for things and had a reputation for always being late. His past secretary was not able to keep up with his fast-paced life in the department. He was not only the chair, but taught classes, held rehearsal for shows in the evenings, and was writing a book.

The office manager he hired was not the right person for the job. The girls and boys at the college in the performing arts department did not like her. She was ridged and always stated to the students; that was just the way it was. Performing people were very expressive and need encouragement, and their lives changed on a dime daily. I had a child performer, and so I knew this and related to the kids very well. They liked me, and so did the chair, but the office manager did not; she was jealous, so what else was new. She began to harass me just as my previous supervisor. She accused me of having an affair with the chair and would outright hassle me on a daily basis. She would make me cry, and I would state that I was a happily married woman. My husband had met her and had come to plays in the department with me. I don't know why she did that, but the professor stated that he thought she had a tough life and maybe somehow had grown to like him, and she was jealous that we had a great working relationship and she took it for something other than it was.

He used to ask me on a daily basis, "Did she quit, or is she talking about it?"

I said, "No!"

At Christmastime, she came up to my desk and slammed a gift on it and said, "Here, put some pictures of the family in this, and place it on your desk, you need it."

I opened the gift, and it was a collage picture frame. I took it home and placed some beautiful pictures of my family and children in it. My husband was in the pictures also. I placed it on my desk, but this did not stop her harassment. I then went to human resources and talked to them. They stated that there was nothing they could do. The professor said he couldn't fire her because she had been with the university for fifteen years. I was crying daily, and my husband was meeting me in the park close to the university at lunch to talk with me and try to calm me down. I begged him to please go into the office and tell the office manager that I was happily married to him and not involved with the professor. He said that he would not do that and that it was like that in every workplace and I needed to just adjust to it. I told him that the workplace should not be that, and I resigned.

He was upset at the fact that I resigned, and he was yelling at me all the time. He constantly would scream at me about how we needed the money and the children were going to attend the college there and I had screwed the whole thing up. I would sit and cry, and he made me feel so bad about myself. Every day I would become more depressed by the situation and by him yelling at me. My happy life had ended. He daily abused me verbally and started to put me down every chance he got verbally, and it upset me on a daily basis. He would scream, and I would cry. I didn't tell anyone as I was embarrassed because we had been so happily married.

I remember thinking that he didn't love me anymore. He was always bringing me little gifts and was very thoughtful and bought me flowers all the time. He would give me gifts for every holiday and Valentine's Day was always special even for the children. He always made me feel special and used to tell me all the time that I was the prettiest girl in the room every place we went. Now he was screaming at me all the time, and I was crying.

The crying became worse, and I was in a deep depression. I didn't want to leave the house and didn't feel like doing anything. I was isolated and stayed in my room. He would come home from work and yell at me because I had not done anything that day. I felt unloved and worthless.

One night we went to church to get our family picture taken for the directory at the parish, and when we came home, I was sitting at the kitchen table, and we were playing a game, and I started to say weird stuff, and I didn't know why. I think my brain was so stressed, and I had no one to help me. He would just yell at me every time I tried to talk to him about it. Anyway, he kept telling me he was taking me to the hospital as there was something wrong with me. I told him that I was not going to the hospital, and he couldn't make me go; I was fine. My sister was in a mental institution twenty years prior for a week, and I went to visit her, and it was a mess, and I told her I was getting her out, and she left. I knew that was what he meant, and I said that I was going to pack a bag and go stay with my mother. He was yelling at me as I was packing my suitcase and my children were downstairs, and my oldest daughter says she remembers us fighting as she was listening on the steps outside the bedroom door. I was about to get in the car when he took my keys and said I could not leave.

He said, "I'm calling the doctor," and he picked up the phone.

I ran out of the house, not even pausing for a second, as I knew he was going to take me against my will. I knew I was depressed, but I was not insane. He himself was making me depressed by yelling at me all the time and not helping me at all. I think he wanted to get rid of me because I had started to question his honor and faithfulness to me.

He called a doctor, and I ran out of the house and hid in the neighbor's yard. He then called my sister and my brother and told them that I had run away and was sick. They came and looked for me, and I could hear them calling me, but I did not answer. I was waiting to sneak back in the house and get my keys and go to my mother's house. They found me and dragged me back to the house.

Once I was in the house, my sister, my brother, and his wife started to grill me and tell me that I had to go to the hospital where they would make me better. I told them that I was not going. They told me I was going, and my husband and my brother took my arms, and I was fighting them, and my husband hit me in the back of the head and then slapped me across the face, and I fell to the ground. My husband and my brother dragged me out the front door, stepping on my hair and pulling it out. They dragged me across the front lawn to the van and pulled me into the van; I broke my toenails off, and they threw me in the seat.

I remember crying and telling my brother and sister-in-law, "How would you like it if I did this to you in front of your children?"

I was so worried about my children, and I was crying. This was a complete emotional trauma event that would be the key factor in the rest of the manipulation of my ex-husband telling everyone I was crazy. A psychotic episode from extreme stress was making me blurt out things that made no sense, like the dog had chip insert and was part of the plot to hurt me. A psychotic event is a one-time thing induced by abuse. Period. No more episodes happened, and it does not make you mental. It makes you cry. Or did he drug me with hallucinogenic medication? Remember, he drugged the dogs at our house during our wedding. What? True—who does that? No one I ever knew. I thought it strange at the time but dismissed it. Wouldn't you put the dogs outside in your big yard during the ceremony? I know that was what I wanted to do. Never happened.

At the hospital I was placed in the emergency room, and my husband was not happy. I had asked for a police officer once they told me that I could not leave even though I was brought against my will. The police officer arrived and said there was nothing he could do.

They said they were admitting me, and I said, "I don't want to kill myself, and I have not harmed anyone, why do I have to stay?"

He said, "You just do."

I remember my husband looking at me and saying, "You could have gotten me fired from my job. Why did you ask for a police officer? I could lose my clearance at work, Julia!"

I was shocked at what he said, but I was mad and knew that he should not have done that, especially in front of my children.

The nurse came in and said that I was being admitted to the mental ward of the hospital for observation. A doctor came to see me, and it was almost midnight. The doctor said after hearing that I was brought against my will by my husband and family and that I had asked for a police officer in the emergency room, he did not want to get involved and another doctor might be assigned to my case. The next day he came back and said, after the blood tests, he could find nothing wrong with me and was ordering a brain scan at a later date to make sure I didn't have a tumor or something. He stated that he would let me go home the next day and prescribed some medication. The nurses then said that he placed me on a high-dose medication that made me like a zombie. It was called Haldol.

My family came to the hospital to visit, and I was not happy that I was there. It was nice of them to come. My father even brought me flowers. My sister Devilia, who had taken me there, sat on the bed and said to me, "You're my favorite sister, I hated doing this to you."

I didn't know what she meant by that at all. Later, I will reveal what I think she meant as time went on, and I learned what she was doing to me and why, to help with the crazy stuff because of a family mess that did not exist in my mind but in hers and one of my sisters. It was twisted and horrible and not true for me. Lies of my sisters to destroy my life. Why?

I was released the next day and went home. I was so drugged up that I felt like a walking zombie. I couldn't even get dressed by myself. The children saw me this way, and I remember feeling embarrassed by it. I kept asking my husband if I was going to get off the medication, and he said, "No."

One day I called the doctor and talked with him, and he changed the medication. I was on medication and was also seeing a counselor. Every counseling session, my husband went with me. He would tell the counselor how my family was bad and that my father was very strict when I was young. She would ask me about it, and I would tell her that yes, my father was strict, but it did not affect me. She once told me in a session that I was never to take my children around my parents ever, and I was to stay away from them. That was the day I decided to never go back. I stopped counseling but stayed on the medication as my husband would not let me stop. Every time I tried to talk about it, he would state that the doctor said I had to stay on it forever.

I said, "That doesn't make any sense." I was feeling great and had found a job and wanted to get off.

He said no.

I had taken a job working at a hospital for surgeons in their academic office. I was the administrative assistant or medical secretary for three surgeons. It was a fast-paced job with many responsibilities, and the main task was to type the clinical notes from the office visits of the patient with the doctor on a daily basis with a twenty-four-hour turnaround time. I did not mind the hard work because after three years of working, my daughters and son would be able to go to the university affiliated with the hospital for free. So I never really thought much about the hard work and little pay because it was going to pay off in the end. I never got a chance to go to college, and it was one of the most important things that I wanted for my children. An education for my children doing what made them happy in life. How sweet would that be! I remember my first job working for a bunch of salesmen, and the work didn't seem to suit my personality. Sales probably would have, but not bookwork and accounting.

For six years, I stayed on medication because my husband said I had to. I tried to quit several times, but he started to count the medication in the bottle and would yell at me if he caught me not taking it. I started to throw it in the trash can and wasn't taking it. He didn't know that either; I did that for a long time.

Things were getting worse between the two of us. He had been placed on an important job at work, and the assignment was many hours of overtime, and he was never home. He left the house at four in the morning and didn't come home until five. I got home at six, and he would make dinner, and that was nice. The job consumed him, and it was all he talked about. I remember thinking to myself that since we moved into the new house, I never heard him take a shower in the morning, and our bathroom was inside the bedroom with an open atrium-type ceiling between the bedroom and bathroom, so you could hear everything. I remember that I could hear the automatic sprinkling system in the summer that he would set on a timer for four in the morning to conserve water. The windows would be open, and the noise from the sprinklers would wake me up almost every morning. I could not understand why I never heard him leave for work with shower in our room. It was a mystery to me, and later I thought maybe he left without taking one and took one at the girlfriend's house. It was all so sad and deceptive, and I was perplexed and bewildered.

He would yell at me continually and say that we did not have enough money to pay the bills and that he had taken his retirement money and now his retirement was gone. I stated that he was wrong in yelling at me because it was he himself who sold our old house that we could afford and he bought this house that we could not. He said that was not the case and said that private school was so much money.

I said, "Well, we live in the county now, and the public school system here is great. Let's put the kids in public school."

And he said no way, he was not doing that.

A few years went by, and he obtained a promotion and was placed in charge of a very large well-known personality investigating job, and he was doing a lot of work. It consumed him even further. It was all he talked about in the house or out of the house. He was working all the time. I was taking care of the children and running them everywhere they needed to go. I was home all the time in the evenings and weekends when the children would have their friends over. I was the one they would come to when things were bad, and we would talk.

Chapter 5

Separation—Divorce
More Junk
Financial Destruction

We had been talking to the priest at church for years about getting married in the church as we did not because he was married the first time in the church and did not want to get an annulment. But now he said yes, and we were planning a church wedding and a reception. I remember thinking maybe he did love me the same as he seemed happy about it. We had about 150 people at the reception. The church ceremony was so nice, and friends sang, and my son was the best man, and my sister was my maid of honor again. He gave me a beautiful new ring, which was a surprise as I had said, "Why don't we go and get new rings?" And he said, "No, we don't need that," as I was trying to get over the bad years. He seemed to be weird, and later I knew why, as this was just some kind of show to him; he really was on his way out of my life. But he got me one anyway to keep up his image. It was a big diamond, which I had never had, just a band the first time. I wondered where he got the money, but later when I saw the ring was from Raleigh, I figured his mother bought the ring; she was a millionaire. I remember, too, one sister who would not come as she thought it was not right that the church was allowing us to be married. It was all my family was talking about before the ceremony, and it ruined it for me as they were not talking about my happiness finally, but about my sister Devilia not coming as if she mattered more than my wedding ceremony. My family was not making me happy as their focus as usual was on gossip about Devilia not coming to the ceremony and this and that about her and nothing about me.

It was their way; they gossiped about everyone and everything and did nothing positive about the moments in life that meant everything.

At the reception, my husband got up and made a speech and toast. I remember thinking that he was joking and laughing; I thought he would have wonderful romantic sappy things to say after twenty years of marriage, but he did not. I felt like crying but laughed. My one sister Sophia from out of town later told me that she knew that night that he was not in love with me by the way he was acting. I guess time would tell.

My husband talked to me one night about how angry he was at work because they would not let him be a consultant at a company that was doing business inside as a subcontractor. He was angry because he needed the extra money and thought they were just not letting him do it. He did do some contract work with a software company for a video game about good guys fighting bad guys, and they let him do that up in Chicago. I couldn't see why they would not let him do this in Springfield, but I did not question it. I think they wanted him to spend all his time on the special project.

I was now starting to sleep all the time. On the weekends, I was sleeping until two in the afternoon and was wondering why.

I called the doctor and said, "Doctor, the medication is making me too sleepy, and I have gained over a hundred pounds, can't I get off the medication?"

He said, "No."

I didn't understand why I could go to work every day and be fine, and on the weekends, I would sleep until two. It really upset me, and it was embarrassing for the kids and me. I never dreamed he was behind that as well. Not ever getting the proof but suspecting that he put something in my food and perhaps had injected something into my thighs when I was asleep.

My husband was not making love to me much anymore. I think being overweight was a turnoff to him. He was always turned off when I was pregnant and would joke about how fat I was, and I remember feeling really bad when he would say that. But that wasn't it at all; later I would wish that it was for other reasons that you will surely come to know.

Anyway, then one day I caught him in a lie; he said he was going out of town on business to one city, and I found out he was in another.

A coworker reminded me of this recently, and she said, "Don't you remember you found, out and he made up some story and then sent you flowers to work?" I didn't recall that until she told me. She knew us both very well, and I got close to her personally at work, and she as well got close to me. I was in denial and wanted a normal marriage but knew I had a mess. I was scared for my children as I wanted most of all for them to have a normal, happy life. That would not happen.

So one day he came home and told me that he was going to quit his job and go work for an investigative company here in town. I was surprised but happy for him as I was always telling him to start his own company and get the contracts for the work from the government. He would plan it for some time before I ever heard a word about it.

The people he worked with gave him a party at a restaurant. I remember he didn't talk to me at all that night, and as soon as we were finished eating, he ditched me and didn't come around me at all. They gave him gifts, and one of the gifts was a Harley Davidson Doo Rag, which he placed on his head, and a condom in a giant wrapper that said, "World's Biggest Condom," in bold letters.

I thought to myself, "They must know something that I don't." Anyway, it was apparent to me that he had no desire for me anymore in any way. They were all bragging about him, and he would smile, and I wanted to say, "So what, Mr. Big Shot, are you happy now?"

He took the new job, and it was months before he asked me to come to the office. He took me there on a weekend, and there weren't many people there. He had my picture on his desk. He gave me a gift card to Glamour Shots for Valentine's Day one year, and I told him that I didn't want it and was not going to go.

He said, "Yeah, go, and take the girls too."

He insisted and made me feel bad about it, so I went and took the girls. We had our pictures taken together and shots of each of the girls alone and shots of me alone. He wanted a picture of me all dolled up, and I didn't like making a big deal out of myself at all, so I did not want to go. Anyway, to make him think twice, I let them dress me up in fashionable clothing and then said, "What do you have that has a little zing to it?"

They said, "We have a leather jacket and hat."

I said, "Yeah, that will do it."

So I put on the leather jacket and leather hat and let them take a few pictures of that too. Well, to say the least, the pictures were great, and we had fun, and he got the pictures he wanted and more. Maybe his fantasy was to have me in some dressed-up fashion for himself. I guess I thought he was one person, but he was actually hiding who he really was from me. He was not the picture of ethical behavior for a married man, and he gave off the perception that he was. I remember when the priest at church asked him to be on the parish council, and he said yes, and Father assigned him to Christian concerns. His comment was, "Wait till my mother hears this, she won't believe it." He laughed devilishly as if to say to me what a joke. I guess that tipped me off as to who he really was and not the loving, devoted father who went to church with me on Sundays.

They had a big celebration over contracts for him, and his partner at the new company at a restaurant one day and the children were invited too. It was a family place, and it was very nice with lots of food and fun. Anyway, I remember some women saying to me as I was being introduced to several of the employees, "We didn't know Paul was a family man."

I thought to myself, "Well, who is he talking about at work?"

He started to talk about Mia at work all of the time and how much Art liked her. Turned out, it was he himself who liked her, and later, I will tell you about that. But I knew that night that my husband was not interested in me anymore for sure.

He started to not be around me, and we made love seldom instead of all the time as we used to. Our sex life was extremely good and always pleasing, but now it was not. He was purposely not pleasing me in bed, and I knew it, and I remember crying in the dark in my bed without him knowing it after we made love, and I never told him that as I knew he was purposely doing things to stop me from climaxing during lovemaking.

I started to think for myself, and he did not like that. I started to make decisions again, and he hated that. I had grown to let him control me, and it became obsessive, and I was going to bring it to a halt. I was tired of his controlling mess with me. I had lost myself somewhere along the years, and I think staying home with my children had helped to contribute to that happening to me. I was half brain-dead from controlling, narcissistic husbandry.

I decided to go to Florida to the beach for vacation. Every year we went on vacation with his mother and family to Nags Head. The children said they wanted to go to Florida, and I believed we should be able to go. Alexandria was a senior in college, and I thought it might be our last family vacation since she would be off to who-knows-where after college and maybe not wanting to go with us anymore. I didn't know.

Anyway, he was angry at me, and I said, "I don't care, we are going to Florida. Why don't you tell your family to meet us there."

His family said that was too far for them to drive. We drove two days to Nags Head every year, and I never complained we drove to Raleigh all the time. They never came to see us. I think his brother came once the whole time we lived here, and his sister only came once alone with his mother, not with her husband as he said we lived too far away. I wasn't judging them just wanted to go to Florida with the children. We did go, but he was not happy. We went with friends, and I remember it was the unhappiest trip I had with my husband, but the children had fun and even drove in their own car behind us, and he wouldn't let me eat in the car and was a pain in the neck. I think he did it just to get back at me for not letting him make the decision like every year to go where he wanted to go with his family. His mother could have come with us and was invited, but she chose not to come. She had gone with us there twice before but didn't this time. I think he was mad at me, but at this time I didn't care. I remember one of the days I said, "Why don't just the two of us go shopping or do something together?"

He said yes. Then the next day, he said the children were going with us, and I was mad. They followed us in their car, and then we got to the beach shopping area, and they all wanted to go eat ice cream. I said I didn't want any and was going to walk the shops, and he got mad.

I said, "I'm going," and left.

He caught up to me later. He knew I was not happy, and I didn't talk to him the whole way home. I went to the pool when we got back, and he came and apologized and said he was sorry for acting so obnoxiously to me. I, of course, told him that I didn't like how he was treating me, and that was when I knew he did not love me at all. He was trying to make people think I was difficult and the problem when really, he was creating the problems to make me look bad especially to my children.

The next year my son was in high school and came to me and said, "Mom, I don't want to play baseball but don't want to tell Dad."

He was afraid to tell his father because he knew he would get screamed at, which was pretty much the reason why he didn't want to play, because his father was his baseball coach and yelled at him at every game. It used to make me sick; he was a good coach and my son an excellent player, but the degrading tones and comments of, "You let me down," were too much for my son, and it took the fun out of the game for him. So I told him to just tell his dad that he didn't feel he was good enough to make the baseball team in high school.

He did tell his father and played soccer in his freshman year. He was picked to play varsity as a freshman, which was a big honor, and he played many games as a freshman and had a great season. He was doing great, and then his father announced that he was moving out of the house as he needed time to think about how he felt about me. I believed him but did ask him if there was someone else, and he said no. The children were very sad about it, but the girls were in college— Alexandria, a senior, and Bella, a sophomore. It was a hard time for me, and we had been going to a counselor where I worked, and I remember one session she asked if the whole family could come and talk. We did, and I remember my son putting his head on the table with his arms cradling his head and crying for about a half hour straight. My heart was aching, and I couldn't seem to stop him from crying. That was one of the hardest days I can remember as his mother. His dad did nothing. I remember we didn't get much accomplished, and then in a consecutive session, he stated outside after the session when he told the counselor that I shouldn't be home when he moved his things out as it would be too upsetting for me, and she agreed and told me to not be home. We got outside, and he commented on her talking about marriage vows, and he stated, "Marriage vows, huh, they don't mean crap." That was the final moment when I knew he was an asshole. I couldn't believe he said that but knew that was it.

He moved his things out while I was at work. I told the counselor that it would be better for me. What she didn't know was it was his way to take what he wanted, and he did the same thing to his first wife; only she was at work, and she knew nothing of it. He just drove down to the apartment and loaded up his things and left; she was pregnant too. Caring, huh!

He had asked for his dresser to our bedroom set and the living room furniture so he would have something to sit on. I told him that would be fine. When I got home that night, he had taken those two items, his daughters' dresser out of her room, out of which he took her clothes and threw them on the floor. It was an antique dresser that his mother had given to us. He took the stereo system and all the records, which were mine too, not to mention all the tapes and CDs. He removed items from the dining room china cabinet, including half of the crystal that I bought before we were married. Half of things—now that was making a statement. What would one do with half a set of crystal when setting a table for guests? It was his way of saying, "Screw you," to me. He also took many pictures off the walls and off the end tables in the house. I was so upset and crying when I saw that he had taken so much more, and the children and I then knew that he was not moving out for a short thinking period but was abandoning us for his new life. He was lying and making me feel bad that it was not working out, but in fact he had met someone else and was purposely making me crazy and depressed.

The thing that hurt the most was that when he met me and said he was unhappily married, he told me that happiness was his most important thing in life and gave me this saying called Deserterata on a hanging parchment type paper, and I hung it up in the apartment. It was a beautiful saying, and it touched my heart like no other. I had asked him to please never leave me this way but tell me up front if he ever did not feel love for me and found someone else, and he promised that he would tell me if there was ever a time when he didn't love me anymore. So the way he left me was so hurtful and against everything he had promised me. He couldn't even keep one promise I asked him—the father of my children. Asshole.

He said he had rented an apartment in the flat next to our old house in the city that a friend owned. He told me that was all he could afford, and he needed to get out and think for a while. But after the counseling session where he told me that marriage vows were a bunch of crap, I knew. It wasn't long, and he called one day and said that he wanted a divorce on the phone.

He said, "You need to call a lawyer, and I will call one too."

I couldn't understand what had happened to such a loving couple whom everyone talked about because we were so happy all the time. What happened, I didn't know, because he was not telling me the truth about anything. But I was soooo happy he was finally gone. Party on.

My attorney was very nice and was referred to me by my nephew who had gotten a divorce. I didn't know any attorneys and had never even spoken to one before other than the air traffic control job situation. I can remember sitting in his office as he asked me questions, and I would cry half the time in between questions because my whole life was destroyed and my children's happiness was being destroyed. He asked me many questions, and one was if I knew if he was seeing a woman and having an affair.

I said I didn't think so, and he had stated to me that he was not seeing anyone. One of my sisters told me that a nephew had seen him out with a woman at dinner one night. It was crushing to me, and so I point-blank asked him one night when he was at the house, and he stated it was a friend's wife, who was in town, and he took her out as a favor. I remember feeling so questionable and yet believed him when he gave me his answer. I had been brainwashed for so many years into thinking and believing that everything he said was the truth because I loved him. He had a way of convincing you of everything he wanted you to believe. He was a true salesman at his best and worst. He was for sure a liar. Later, I would learn he was a pathological liar.

We knew it was over, and he didn't love me anymore. He had thoughts about his life, and they didn't include me. He had reached his point in life where I was not important any longer; the work was and, of course, someone new he had met at work who probably made him feel important because of the work he was doing. I have never been impressed by someone at all because of the importance of their work, only by the person that they are at the time they are performing the work. If they are a nice person, then the work is important and shared; if they are bragging about it all the time and saying no one else can do it except them, they are delusional. He is delusional as he was when the air traffic controllers went on strike. He kept saying for years, "They

can't do without us, and they will hire us back soon, you wait and see."
For years, he talked about getting hired back. I was sick of that, too,
and said, "Let's just move on and focus on the life we have now, and if
you get hired back, great, but life moves forward, and so should you."
He never stopped talking about it and how important his work was, as
if he was irreplaceable. He had that mentality about himself, not just
pride but bodacious behavior about his importance and the fact that he
did something spectacular today that everyone should know about. In
his own right, he was a very smart person for a man without a college
degree and was very hardworking when placed on a project and the
project at work was very important to the world, no doubt about that.
But many jobs are important to the world, and you do it because you
are a part of the human race, but to him it became all self-importance,
and he was not like that when I met him. He was smart and one of the
best controllers in class but never bragged about it all; that was what I
liked most about him, his humility about himself. But the years and
time had changed that one thing I liked the best about him and took
it away.

He became someone I didn't particularly like. I like being proud
and even bragging about little personal things you might do, but to go
on and on about your self-importance because of a job that you are paid
to do just got too much for me as it was all he talked about. We didn't
talk about life and love and things to look forward to any longer, just
about the project and how things were going to be bigger and better,
and he was in charge of it all and he was angry all the time because
they weren't paying him enough money to produce the product he was
doing for them, and I agreed with him and told him it's a government
job and he had to figure out that the only way he was going to ever
get the money he deserves for the work was to start his own business
and get the contracts from the government for the project. He said, "I
would like to but don't have the money." I guess he found a way to get
the money, but the project didn't include me, so he dumped the excess
baggage—me. He took the money from his thrift savings plan three
years in a row, but I didn't know about it till later.

We used to hang out with other couples and do things; the past
three years were pretty much him having over people from work and
sitting on the patio or inside making talk about work. I used to get sick

of it and leave and go upstairs or something.

I can remember when we first moved back to Springfield. He would not allow me to go to my best friend's house for parties and gave an excuse, but I think he just wanted to control whom I saw and what I did. When money was tight, he told me that I could not send cards anymore to my friends as it was too expensive. He had begun to separate me from my friends of forty years.

He would always take me shopping, and everyone talked about how wonderful it was that my husband shopped with me. He shopped with me because he wanted to control what I put on my body. I was very pretty with long blond hair and evidently turned a few heads. I always thought he just liked being with me; we did everything together. My brother said to me later, "How could he have been having an affair? You did everything together and were always together even at the children's functions."

I said, "I guess he was good at hiding his time away from home and lying about where he was even work."

I'll never forget feeling so weird at a party that one of his coworkers had at her house. One gentleman came up to me that I didn't know and stated after, introducing himself to me, "Now I see what puts a kick in Paul's step all the time, he's so happy all the time."

I just smiled and said, "Yeah," and turned and went into the other room. I felt so uncomfortable. I can remember that one guy from work had a party every fall at his house kind of out in the country, and everyone would come and bring something, and it was a big party. Anyway, he used to say, "I think I'm going, but I'm not sure yet." Then someone told me that he always asked if the controller I once dated from years ago who worked in the building doing what he did was going to be at the party before he would say that he was going to the party and bringing me. I laughed and thought I hadn't seen the guy in years, what difference would that make? I guess guys don't understand women, or my guy didn't understand his loving and devoted wife who had morals and standards by which she lived. Many people commented about me, but on the flip side, many women commented about him too. I'm not a jealous, person but many women could not be married to him because he flirted even though it might be innocent. He did, and maybe he thought I did too. Who knows?

The court battle would begin, and after almost a year in court, the judge ruled that I got all the proceeds from the house but that the family home had to be sold because Mr. Rule was stating that he was not making enough money and had to get a better place to live so that his son could come for weekends. He never had my son come over to spend a weekend ever since he left me two years prior. It was a lie, and I knew it. But the judge believed him, and I did not get maintenance or alimony as we used to know it because he lied about money and where he was really living.

He told many lies, but I did not know to the extent of the lies until years later. He was the master manipulator as I had stated to my eldest brother on the phone one day and made him laugh, but he was. He could make you believe anything he wanted to. People couldn't believe what they were hearing when I would speak to them about him. He was so deceiving.

It was a mask of deception that he wore his whole life. Maybe wanting to be something he wasn't. Many people do that; they want to be bigger or richer or make up something, so they sound important to others. It is all nonsense, and I used to hate it. I used to think that he was always mad that his controller job was taken away, and now he was back to being a letter carrier and was better than that; but without a college degree, it was hard to find something that paid that kind of money. It was hard on his ego, I suppose, but partly and mostly, because he loved the job. He did it in the military, and even though he didn't like the military, he loved controlling traffic and flying airplanes.

I came out of the divorce with the house but had to sell it, and the children did not want to move from their home. My eldest was out on her own in an apartment with friends, and the other daughter had made a decision to drop out of college after her third year and go to culinary school. She had always been in the kitchen a bit more than the other two with me and loved to cook with me and make all the things we enjoyed eating. I will never forget; she was in the fifth grade when I went back to work full-time. In the summer months, my eldest watched the children, and one day I came home from work and walked in the back door, and she had cooked a four- or five-course meal herself, set the table with placemats, candles, place cards, and flowers from the yard. She served the dinner and then cleaned it up. She was ten or eleven years old. I couldn't believe it.

She said, "Welcome home, Mom. Dinner is ready in just a few minutes, so please sit down."

I thought, "You are amazing, and I can't believe what I am seeing."

She was so happy, and she did have a few children's cookbooks and years later reminded me that once I made a whole bunch of peach preserves, and she remembered eating them for quite some time. We had a big vegetable garden, and I used to put up and freeze many items throughout the summer months, and she would help me. Her father liked to cook also, and we all spent many happy hours in the kitchen making old recipes and new ones too. Her father was the avid and consummate gardener and loved being outside. We always had a patio and ate outside and partied outside. I remember asking him what he wanted for his birthday one year. He said fruit trees. I saw a TV program that stated at the time that the Fuji apple was the best eating apple, and so I found two dwarf Fuji apple trees and gave them to him for his birthday. He was so happy. He had banana trees in the yard, and we had many vegetables and tried something new each year. I learned a lot from him about gardening and planting and soil preparation. My parents did not garden, which was odd since my father came from a farm in his early life. I always wondered why someone with ten children who lived on a farm in his youth for a while did not plant a vegetable garden. But I never asked him. My father wasn't very vocal about his youth other than it was a hard life. It seemed that this side of my husband was appealing to me as I did like flowers; they were one of the loves of life, and he had reminded me of how he used to send me flowers all the time when we first decided to go together. I still like flowers, just don't get them anymore unless I buy them myself since I have not found a special person in my life to share moments daily and get flowers. I will someday.

Anyway, moving my household at this time of life was not a happy thought or time in my life. I lost a husband, then I lost the house too, my children's family home, my home. The judge had ordered my ex-husband to pay a home equity loan that he took out to refinish our basement. He never did, but the money was gone. Anyway, in order for me to sell the house, he had to pay the loan off. He stated that the judge did not say he had to pay that loan but that the proceeds from the house were to pay off the loan.

I said, "No way."

I called my lawyer, and he said that the judge did not mean for Mr. Rule to pay that home equity loan and that I would have to pay it myself. I stated that it was clear in the divorce decree that he was to pay that loan.

He said, "No, you have to pay it."

So I could not purchase the homes that I was looking at because I didn't have enough money. So my daughter was upset that the house we found that was nice and in our price range was no longer available to us. I didn't tell her why, which was a mistake on my part, or so I thought at the time. I was trying to stay in the neighborhood where all of my son's friends were, but the only thing I could afford was a condo. I found one on the third floor, and it had two bedrooms and two baths and was very nice. I thought, I could buy a sofa bed and one of the children could sleep there. So I showed it to the children, and they were upset; my son did not want to move there and convinced his sisters to pressure me into not buying it. So after we looked at it, we went home and sat around the kitchen table, and the children were almost screaming at me, and at one point one of them pointed a finger at me and said, "You can't buy that condo." I was under so much pressure at the time to find a house and get a job as I was unemployed after the separation. I had very little money, and the movers had to be paid, the house I was selling needed a new roof, a new furnace, etc., which I was not expecting. It was a troubling time, and I was all alone and without daily support to help me through a tough time.

I remember once my ex-husband came to the house, and he let himself in the front door, not knowing that I was on the phone long-distance with my sister Sophia who lived in another state. He walked in without knocking and started screaming at me, and it was funny. I couldn't even remember what he was screaming about, but my sister, hearing him, said, "Julia, I can hear who that, is do not hang the phone up even if you start a conversation with him."

He screamed for quite some time, and it was usual for me, and I tried to ignore it, but I asked him to leave. My sister was quite concerned and said, "Please go and lock the door." I remember thinking that now someone other than my children have heard the way he talked to me; he never did that in public. Everyone always thought he was so nice and fun, but there was a side to him that was out of control and nasty. I didn't know why this appeared after years of happy marriage and hardly ever a fight, truly hardly ever a fight.

I remember thinking that day that this was a turning point for me and that he would never have my heart again. He had not only broken it but chose to come back and beat it to death for his own self-serving purposes. I remember asking him once inside the family room after he had left me and had come to pick up Bella to take her somewhere, and I said to him, "Do you ever feel guilty about what you have done to our family?"

There was a long pause, and he said, "Sometimes," very quietly and turned and left.

I found myself making a decision to buy the condo and asked friends, and they said it was a good decision because it would be something I could afford after the children had moved out, which would only be a few years after they were finished with college, and it would only be a few months.

I set up the closing, and they were supposed to pay the home equity loan from the proceeds, and they were to also pay half of the credit card bill that was on the MasterCard, in which my part was $8,000, and he was supposed to pay half too. I told him to please pay his half so at closing, my half would be paid, and I could close the account. He said he would take care of that for me and pay his half right away. I believed him. I got to the house closing that day, and they stated that the half he owed had not been paid, so they could not close. I stated to them that if they did not close on this house today, they would be in trouble. Mr. Rule, I'm sure, was laughing about it all the way home, maybe just maybe, he paid them off to do that to me. I remember crying in the realtor's office. I made a decision as I was crying quite a bit because of this man, and I swore to myself I did not want to see him anymore. He would be crying soon.

Before the move, my daughter decided for sure to move to New York and go to school in Manhattan at a culinary school. I told her that the community college had a culinary school, and she said that her father said it was no good. So I called her father, and he said that they only taught cake decorating, and he wanted her to go a very good school. So she made the decision to go, and I told her that I could not help her with money as I was so strapped for cash. Anyway, she moved, and I was happy for her. She was pleased and happy that I was in support of her decision.

I set up the move to the condo and began to pack. It was hard as I had so many things I had been saving. It was a hard time, and I had to be careful as I was saving most of them for my grandchildren to play with and my children to enjoy seeing their children playing with their treasures from their youth. It was a sad time for me, and I had to part with things I thought would be in my family for the rest of time. I had emotional hard things to deal with, and the children were not happy at all. They were mad at me—the one who got cheated on and left behind to clean up the family mess. I was doing my best, but they thought it was not good enough or not what they wanted to happen, so I was an easy target to blame. It was so terribly hard on me.

I tried to make it the best for my son. He would have a much bigger room now, and I told him he could decorate it any way he wanted to.

He said, "Great. I want my room to be red."

So I went out and bought new bedding and lamps all red. I bought red towels for his bathroom and all the accessories were red. He hung posters all over the walls and then made his room his little haven. He was a very private person and wanted quiet. I respected his wishes and hardly ever went into his room.

I received a notice from the condo association that there was a complaint about loud music and a party with underaged drinking and that I would be asked to sell if this continued. It was only a few weeks after we moved in, and I did not like it. It upset me, and I asked my son what happened. He said one night when I was out late shopping with a friend and then went back to her house, he had some friends over, and they got a little loud. It was something that I told him would not be tolerated. He got all upset, and I said that I could be asked to move and could not afford that.

He was rebelling from the sale of his home. He was used to a big house with a patio and swimming pool and having all his friends hang out on the weekends. I felt bad for him but had to tell him that he could only have four friends at a time in the house because it would get too loud. I didn't mean all the time, just at night when they would hang out, they would get rowdy, and fewer would be better and quieter. He hated that I said that.

Times were hard for him, and he was mixed up and troubled about life. He was spending so much time in his room and did not want to come to the table to eat his dinner and wanted to eat in his room by himself.

I said no because it was the only time I had to speak to him directly during the day. His grades were failing, and my straight A student was having a hard time, not with studies just with interest because of a stressful time.

The soccer coach at school told me that I had better get him into shape and get him to focus again, or else he would not get into a college that he wanted. I was worried and talked with my son and told him that he had to bring up his grades; he said he would. But a few weeks went by, and he did not. I didn't know what to do and called his father and told him and asked him to please come over and speak to our son and convince him he needed to study and get his grades up. He said he would, and he came over, and the three of us sat at the kitchen table and talked about it. I told my son his grades were suffering, and he needed to bring them up. His father said that his grades were fine, and he could eat in his room if he wanted too. He directly was undermining everything I was trying to do, and he did it on purpose. He alienated my son and made me the bad guy; he always did. I was the person who was always making the tough decisions in my children's lives, and Daddy was always saying, "That's fine." He never did that when we were married; the girls were always told by him to expect the best and give the best and work hard in school. Now with my son—he was letting him ruin his life and he was doing it to get back at me. Later my son would explode when I told him that his grades were bad and he had two weeks to bring them up and could not play soccer until that time. He got so upset with me and started to scream at me and pushed me so hard that it bruised me. He didn't mean to, but his anger with life was coming out with the one person who was loving him the most, which was natural. He had punched a hole in the drywall in his room and, then I told him that he should maybe go and live with his father as he was stating that Dad said he was doing fine.

I said, "Then go and live over there with him and the girlfriend," and he kicked a hole in the wall by the front door. I opened the door and shoved him out. I got a call from his father that he wanted to stay a few weeks, and I said fine. Then I got another call saying they were having fun, and he wanted to stay longer.

I said okay. He asked if they would come and pick up a few items of clothing for him for school. I said fine. They arrived together at my insistence, and his father had said they were taking a few things. They took everything and even asked me for the home computer. I said no, and he insisted that Shaun needed it to do his homework. I said no, I needed it, too, and said he could just use the one at his house. He said he could not use the one at his house because it was not hooked up to the Internet because of top-secret information from his company. I believed him and let him take my computer. It was a bad night, and then his father handed me a paper that said I was giving up all parental rights and turning them over to Mr. Rule. I tore up the paper and said, "No way." I did not want my son living with him permanently. Anyway, they took everything. He said he would no longer be sending me child support, and I should call my lawyer, and he would call his.

He looked at me and said, "I'm not giving you a dime." He never did either after that day. He actually got $23,000 from me in court. Amazing, isn't it?

The millionaire cheated the twelve-dollar-an-hour ex-wife. He was something to admire in your nightmares, ladies. Don't get in the dating line.

I called mine, and he said that he would get him on back child support since he stopped before the court told him to and that he would get him on the contempt of court for the home equity loan even though he had told me that Paul did not have to pay it he said he did not say that.

So I said, "Okay, let's do it."

When Christmas came, my children came for Christmas day and came to stay at my home. My daughters were talking with me about my life and how things were going. The conversation led to me and the medication I had been taking while being married to their dad. I told them that I did not need it anymore and was not taking any medication. They got real upset and started to yell at me. They said I had to be on it the rest of my life, much to my surprise.

I said, "Who told you that?"

They said, "Dad did."

They told me that they were taking me to the doctor, and I said, "No, you are not."

They did not like the person I had become, which was exactly what I was before their father had me medicated, and I was strong, and they were not used to me saying, "No, and you can't tell me, your mother, what to do."

They said insistently, "You are sick."

I said, "No, I am not, and you are not even around me, so how would you know?"

They insisted that I was, and I said, "Well then, call my sisters, they are around me and talk to me all the time." I said, "My sister Sophia in another state talks to me regularly."

They said, "Get her on the phone."

I called her and they yelled at her and hung up on her. They said she was rude, and my sister said my daughters were out of line, yelling and saying that I was sick. I guess I had become a wallflower of sorts being married to a control freak, and the children had come to know me as such. It was sad for me, and they did not respect me or treat me with parental respect at all because they had been brainwashed by their father and he had been brainwashed by himself or the doctor into thinking that I needed this medication for the rest of my life. It was hard for me, but I told the girls to get out and not come back until they apologized. Bella was home from New York and was staying until after New Year's. My son was going out of town on a soccer tournament in a few days. I had him pack his things, and then he went to the airport with Scott, our friend. They were going to take care of him on the trip. I told my son I would pick him up at the airport when he arrived back home.

Stan called me to say the flight was delayed, and I said, "Okay, I'll check before I make the ride over to the airport to pick him up."

A few minutes later, my ex-husband called and said that he would be picking my son up from the airport and would bring him to my house. I had left a message for Bella that she had left a few things at my house and needed to pick them up before she flew back home. She said she would come to get them with her dad when they brought my son home.

I said fine. Later they arrived, but it was with my ex, Bella, Alexandria, my son, and Bella's boyfriend all at the front door. I was surprised and did not know they were all coming over. They all were invited in, and they sat down. We started to talk about the soccer trip, and then my son went into his room with Ray Bella's boyfriend. Mr. Rule then talked a bit, and I gave him a few items that his mother had given to me that I thought he might like. He said thank you and then said he had to go.

The girls then started to grill me about my medication, and I told them I would not talk with them until they apologized for the behavior they displayed toward me. They did not but kept asking questions. I told them they did not have the right to question their mother about anything. I needed for them to stop the questioning. They left, and I said that I would not invite them back until they apologized. They were adamant about their views and said that I had made a promise to them that I would stay on this medication for life. I don't recall why we agreed to that, but we did, and I told them the story had changed, and I was fine and didn't need any medication. They stated they would not have anything to do with me until I got back on my medication.

It was a very hard time for me as I was alone now and they were upsetting me constantly and not giving me any support at all at this very hard time in my life. I cried about it all the time. I missed them and missed my home and family. My sisters were my source of family life, and they were very supportive at first. They helped me and gave me advice. They were very concerned as I had so much sadness in my life, and I used to cry, which was natural; they just saw it as maybe I was sick again since for years they were told by my ex-husband that I was mentally ill with a serious mental illness, which I did not know he was telling people. He even told my neighbors this, and I was devastated when I found that out. He was a devil and had spread a rumor that was untrue to hurt me. He, as you will read as the story broadens, is a very deceiving manipulating person who wants something and doesn't care who he hurts to get it. He never used to be this way, and I don't know what happened to him. He was always kind and generous and thoughtful and romantic. It was a complete personality change from the man I met, which people say happens when they become successful in the business world and feel self-important and no longer feel the need to look for love in their life they have replaced it with something else and, of course, a new woman and quite possibly a man as well. He always was materialistic and loved to have nice things and buy nice things. I liked nice things but in a different way. My father brought us up to believe that you buy a quality product and save the money so that you have something that will last a long time. He believed that you buy something so you have something nice to look at most of all. But he also had this other side of spend thrift and was cheap at times about different things; it was strange. People said we were the perfect couple for years, but one of us had changed, and the relationship took a turn.

He had brainwashed my children into thinking that because I had one personal problem with depression because someone had berated me at work, and I was working in a hostile environment for many months with daily ongoing battering and accusations of an affair, which had me morally crying all the time since it was not true. This person would never come to know how she had destroyed my life and a wonderful family with it. She, I hope, learned a lesson because she did send me a note a few months after I quit, and I should have saved the note, but I threw it in the trash because at the time, she did not even remotely get one thought of mine in any direction of any kind, and by putting the note in the trash, it was telling myself that this person did not even deserve a reply; she had destroyed something very special and later had destroyed it all like a world war with all casualties reported. No one left alive as a family unit, but we are struggling to bring a few back together and will succeed despite her efforts for total destruction for her own purposes. So sad it is for my children as their youth can never be changed, only made better through much discussion as adults. It is my quest.

Chapter 6

Custody Battle
Crazy, Crazy Crap
Police Take Me by Ambulance to the Mental Ward at a
Hospital
Life Would Never Be the Same for a Few Years
Goodbye, Dad, However It Happened

I spent months with the attorney working on the wording for the contempt of court document and child support. I was scared and worried because when I filed the protection order the attorney told me to drop the charges or he would kill me.

I wanted to think about what Paul had said to me about Mia at work. One day while we were still together, he told me that Art, his best friend, liked Mia at work. I thought to myself, *That is good.* Later it would be that Paul himself liked Mia and left me for her. Was this a statement as a gay man that he found a new woman that his gay partner liked better than me? Gay men, I would learn later from a gay friend, marry a woman that their partner likes as well so they can do things together yet still remain normal living style as being with a woman yet they are gay.

Art had started to come to our house for holidays. I included him in dinners and cooked him special items as well to take home. I guess if I was right, they had both replaced me for her. It was interesting, but I would never know if that was the absolute truth as I was sick of the whole thing myself and at this point had not told anyone the truth about what I thought. If Art was not his gay partner, then who was? I would have to follow him to find that out, and I did not want to. Art did keep an apartment just a few blocks from their office when he had a house, and Paul and Mia had a house of their own. Was this apartment the gay-play place? I don't want to know. But Art kept the apartment long after he bought the house. Why? When I went to serve them both a subpoena, Mia told me they were both shopping together for office supplies, and in the back of my mind, I thought, "Are they just down the street at their gay-play place? Who knows? I don't care either." I did later tell my children of my suspicions of their father as my grandsons reached the age of three and one. I thought she should know in case he was a deviate about it as well; some of the gays are, as I would learn from a friend that sex between homosexuals at this time in America is sex with about fifteen at one time all sharing the experience. I was mortified by his statements.

I was working at the time at a college in the clinical trials office as a regulatory coordinator. I was let go at another college after six years of very dedicated service and was told that they were outsourcing my job to India, which came to me only weeks after my ex-husband had announced to me that he wanted a divorce. I was devastated after twenty-one years of marriage and now was left without a husband and no job, which also meant that my child in college lost her benefit of free tuition because I worked at the college. It was heart-wrenching and financially put me in a place that I could not survive on unemployment monies and pay the attorney for all of the services that were needed to prove my ex-husband's guilt in court. The lawyer seemed to be taking forever to get a hearing and get things accomplished.

The job at the new college was very difficult, and I was doing a great job. I was preparing the paperwork for clinical trials studies on humans in the radiology department at the center and also for children's hospital in the oncology division. It was a very nice office, and the staff was all women, so I liked that very much other than the doctors that I worked for but only met with once a month. There was a bond between myself and my coworker as her children played sports, so we hit it off immediately, and we shared an office, but she was part-time, so I had a private office three days a week. It was nice, and I put paintings up and a lamp on my desk and pictures of my children in the bookcase with glass and wood sliding doors. I loved it. Quiet and busy but interesting to me as well as challenging.

One day my husband called me on the phone at work and was yelling at such a tone through the phone that I held the phone out from my ear, and my coworker said, "Who is that?"

I said, "It is my husband, Paul," and she stated that I should hang up.

I was really upset, and she said that I should get a recorder and record his voice. He was always yelling at me all the time and made me feel awful about myself for years, even in front of my children. He was out of line to call me at work like that. My sister had also overheard his conversations with me one day while still in my house when he came in without knocking and I was on the phone with her.

He was shouting so loudly that she asked me, "Who is that? Is it Paul?"

I remember saying to her, so afraid inside, "Yeah."

She said, "Don't hang up the phone, whatever you do, don't hang up the phone!"

I was scared and wanted him to leave as I was there by myself; my son was out of the house. My son had heard him scream and yell at me for years, but this was the worst, and I was glad my son was not at home.

My coworker was remarried but told me of her divorce story, and she had a lot of great advice. She would help me on occasion with decisions and would overhear my conversations with my attorney on my lunch hour. She was worried and told me I needed a different attorney. My attorney was friends with the doctor that I worked under, and he kept telling me I had communication problems. The problem was with him, and I didn't know at that time that attorneys made deals with other attorneys. He was not doing what I asked him to do, so I asked him if I could bring someone in on the conferences with me, and he stated that it was not a good idea.

I said I thought it was as the case was very upsetting for me. So my friend came, and she stated after the meeting that he should not be talking to me in that way and that he was, indeed, not doing what I had asked him to do. She and her husband advised me to e-mail him and give specific things that I wanted him to do. I did, and he became belligerent with me on the phone. It was apparent that I was not being represented by an attorney that was working in my best interest. My friend at work overheard me ask him to call the government office to see what my ex-husband's retirement account would be when he retired so I would know what I would get as his ex-wife I was entitled to half of his retirement. My attorney stated to me that he could not inquire with his Social Security number as it was in violation of his rules as an attorney to use someone's Social Security number to find out information. This didn't sound right to me as how else would you search for assets and such in a divorce without someone's Social Security number. He was lying to me, and that was when I knew I had to get a different attorney for sure. I asked him if I could get a copy of my file since he had not been sending me anything through the mail except for bills. He stated that I could come in and pick up a copy of the file, which I did.

There was a big hearing on Monday in which I was going to testify in court against my husband, and I told my attorney, "You just get me on the witness stand because he is going down."

On Thursday, my supervisor came into my office and told me that someone had called from the IRB and told her that I was rude to them on the phone; I was not and told her so. She stated that this was policy and that I could be fired, and she was writing me up.

On Friday, she came into my office and told me that this was my last day and that I had two hours to finish up what I was working on and clean out my desk and that I could write a letter of resignation if I wanted to. I told her that if I resigned, that meant I couldn't collect unemployment, and she stated that this was not true.

I said, "Well, I'll call HR and ask them."

I called HR, and they stated that it was always not true that if you quit, you could not collect unemployment benefits. I stated that I was not quitting.

My supervisor came into my office five minutes later and said, "You have two minutes to get your things and leave."

I stated that she told me I had two hours and that I had important person things that were in the office and on the computer as I used it on my lunch hour since my ex-husband had taken mine from home. She stated to get my things and leave immediately. I told her that this was not right and I was going to call my attorney.

I called my attorney, and he stated that they could fire me for any reason. He did nothing to help me. He might have even got me fired because remember, he was friends with my doctor's boss.

She said that if I did not go immediately, she was going to call security on me.

I said, "Go ahead and call them."

I left but did not get to take all my things and the files on my computer that were very personal information about my divorce. It was never stated at anytime that I could not use my computer at work for personal things at my lunch hour; everyone there did, including my supervisor.

The next day, Saturday, the phone rang early in the morning, and it was my attorney. He stated that Brian had given him a call while he was at a seminar at the college and told him that the hearing on Monday was canceled. I started to cry and told him that it was not fair and that I had been waiting a long time for that hearing, and he stated that there was nothing he could do about it.

I said, "Well then, you're fired."

My sisters had been telling me for months to fire him as he was undermining my case.

So now I was without any money and without an attorney at a very crucial point in the case. Only later did I figure out why my sisters had been undermining my every move as well. You might say I got backstabbed by everyone in my life at that time. I kept thinking this was a dream and I would wake up one day and everything would be normal. That never happened. Except for one sister who is still the only person who has proven that she truly loves me. I'm hoping that a man will do that someday in my life as well. I can dream on.

This was a time when I was upset anyway about all of the lies that my husband had told me and that he was not truthful in anything and could not be the person that I thought he was all along. He did lie to me when we first met, so why should this day, month, or year be any different? I was not smart enough emotionally to realize this at that time.

How was I going to represent myself? I didn't know how to, so I started to call friends and family to get a name of an attorney that I could trust. I could not get any help from anyone; it seemed that everyone was giving me names but nothing was panning out. I did consult with an attorney that my cousin gave to me, but he just stated that it was going to take a lot of money and that his attorney would just keep continuing things to drag it out and make it cost as much as he could. Which was great advice since that was exactly what he was doing thus far.

So I had no choice but to represent myself and see about going through the case fighting for my son and the monies that were owed to me along with his government retirement and assets which he did not reveal in the divorce.

It was a trying time for me as I remember walking into the file room on the fifth floor after talking with the judge's clerk and asking her what I needed to do. She was so nice and told me that I could go to the fifth floor and write a motion and set a hearing. I had no idea how to write this motion, so I went to the law library and asked the person at the desk what book would have in it how to write a motion to set aside. She pointed to the shelf with about over fifty books on it and said, "It should be on that shelf somewhere."

I laughed and said, "Thank you."

I, of course, thought to myself, "You have got to be kidding me."

I looked at the books and then decided that it would take me forever to figure it out. So I took the paper and wrote what I thought the motion should say and gave it to the judge.

I asked him if he would accept it, and he said, "We'll see."

I left his office not knowing whether to cry or laugh, so I chose to laugh and then went to my sister's house for lunch and was telling her and her husband the story. She said she could not believe it and said how unfair the system was that no one would help me. But the ladies on the fifth floor did help me, and they were so kind and generous with all my questions. I did not realize at that time the files in a courthouse were public record and that anyone could come in and see my full recorded file of my divorce. In that file was all of personal information, including Social Security numbers, address, bank accounts, assets, and all the personal bills that I paid. I found this to be a direct invasion of my privacy and said that I could not believe this. They could not even tell me who had made a copy of my file or who had looked at it as they didn't keep a record of that. I was outraged.

It would be a long time before I had the knowledge that I could seal the file.

The next few months were very difficult, and I was in and out of court and on the phone with his attorney trying to settle this mess and get my son back and get money for me to live on, but his attorney was always yelling at me outside the judge's chambers, and it made me so angry as he kept stating that I did not need maintenance and that I could live on what I made. It was even more upsetting because I had PTSD (post-traumatic stress disorder from verbal abuse). I just didn't know yet that I had it.

It was time to see that I was not winning, and he was not letting me see my son, and I was crying all the time about it.

Then I received a letter from his attorney stating that they had subpoenaed my employment records from the college where I had worked and from one other place of employment. In the employment records was a note written by my supervisor from a phone conversation from my sister telling the college that she would like for them to hire me back and that I had a severe mental disorder called paranoid schizophrenia and would they please consider this and hire me back. I was shocked as this was not true. I called and asked my sister why she would say that, and she told me that my ex-husband had told her that. I told her that it was not true, and she stated that she was trying to help me. I asked her if she thought telling my old employer that I had a mental disease would help me; on the contrary it would only hurt me and had come to hurt my employment as they were passing this information on to other employers even though it was not true. He had not only destroyed my employment history but also destroyed my chance in court as now an attorney told me that once the judge heard mental disorder, whether it is true or not, he would believe it until it is proven otherwise, and proving otherwise was tough. So I decided to cry and go to sleep and think it about it later. It had put a screeching halt on all of my plans in court. It was clear they had done this intentionally and his lawyer was a big part of the nasty puzzle.

I started to ask around to other people if my ex-husband had been telling people that I had a mental disease and my very close neighbor at my old house where we lived assured me that he, indeed, had told her that I had a very severe mental disorder of paranoid schizophrenia and that I would have it for life. I told her that this was not true and that she could believe that I, indeed, was very sane but at one time just had depression because of a woman at work that was lying about me. This was hard for me to hear, and I was so tired of people saying this about me. I was a very smart, intelligent woman who had her life finally back and now this. As if I didn't have enough problems to deal with, I now had to talk about this too. I had too many big problems to deal with and was on my own as my family believed him too. I cried myself to sleep many nights and wondered how this man could make so many people believe all these lies about me. Wasn't I a person that they believed in? Could they not believe me just because I said so? His personality was so persuasive, and later on it would be hard for me to convince people of this behavior of his which was very controlling. My neighbor who taught at the police academy told me after telling her that he had a personality disorder of pathological liar with an obsessive personality with control issues. I remember listening to her, and even though I did not want to hear it, I knew she was correct. It was after that I would spend many hours thinking about his behavior and how everyone used to comment to me, "How do you get him to do this or that with you?" He was controlling me without me knowing why; I thought it was love and endearing, but it was just his way of controlling where I went, what I did, and even the clothes I wore. It was hard for me to deal with the fact that the man I thought was so loving was really just watching me for his own jealous reasons. It was hard to take, and for a while I used to think about it all the time, but now I have learned to block it out and just think of him as someone who was messed up.

I called the doctor who treated me years prior, and it was stated that I did not have a severe mental disorder. I was relieved and thought to myself, "How he dare tell people that about me?" He would never know how this sffected me, and he would pay later for this.

It was September 8, and it was my son's birthday. He had a soccer game at a high school, and so I went as usual, and he would not talk to me after the game. So I followed him to his car and asked him if he wanted to go out and get something to eat with me, and he stated no and got in his car. It was as if he hated me. I cried the whole way home, and as of this writing nine years later, he is still not talking to me. How gut-wrenchingly sad this was for me and will continue to be, but it has gotten better as I don't cry about it any longer on a regular basis.

I left that night and cried so hard. I could not believe that my son would be so insensitive to his mother who had raised him to not even talk to me on his birthday. I guess I'm making a big point of this to show how my children were in a complete emotional disarray.

I went home that night, and I had been planning on taking a trip to the Grand Canyon the next year with my children, but on the spur of the moment when my life seemed as though it could not get any worse, I just decided to pack my bags and drive to the Grand Canyon and spend some quiet time by myself. I was in between jobs and was not having any luck finding work, so I made an executive decision, and westward-ho I went, happy like a teenager.

I drove by myself three days to get there. The first day I stopped in Oklahoma City to spend the night. This was the city in which I had met my husband and thought I would stop and sit by the lake where we used to run and fly kites when we first met each other. We were so happy and so deep in love. How could that strong a love and relationship end so badly? I sat on a bench and looked at the lake trying to figure out what happened. I had talked with one of the girls he worked with at another office, and she said this to me, "He never said one bad word about you." I was one of those nice people that hardly ever said a bad word about anyone and always wanted everyone to get along and be nice. Now came a time when he was making me feel that this was all for nothing and not worth saving for his reasons, which were not clear to me at the time purposely configured by him.

I remember thinking that maybe I could let it go emotionally, getting rid of him there, since that was where it all started and also take time to understand how something so right had turned so bad. But it would not be until a year later that I realized that it was his selfishness that led to the demise of the relationship.

The second day I drove to Albuquerque, New Mexico, and spent the night. It was such a beautiful drive, and I had never driven west of Oklahoma City before. The country was so different than the East. Looking at all the desert and the painted desert was unbelievable.

The third day, I was anxious to get to the Canyon. I drove into Flagstaff and got gas and something to eat. I then continued up the mountain, which took some time, and the drive through the forest was so beautiful. By the time I got to the park entrance, it was almost dark, and I had to find a place to stay.

The hotels outside the park were all booked that night, so I had to drive back a few miles to stay the night. The next day the hotels had an opening, so I booked a room and then went into the park. I remember just as if it were yesterday my first view of the canyon; it took my breathe away, and I remember standing there and thinking, "This is why my dad said that going to the Grand Canyon was his best vacation ever," as he hated to travel anywhere, but when I asked him what his favorite vacation was, he stated very quickly, "The Grand Canyon." It was unlike any experience I had ever had other than looking upon the ocean for the first time. The awe of how great God's creation was right in front of me, and I was feeling that I could now understand his great power and glory of the world, and I was at peace with myself. I spent the whole day walking the south rim from end to end and was exhausted by the end of the day. I had taken so many pictures and was so happy that I had come to spend the time and think about what was really important in my life.

I marveled at the greatness of its beauty and the vastness of its, depth but most of all realized for the first time how much of the earth I had been missing while raising my children and working. I saw my father more at this time in his life because he had retired and spent most of his later years just sitting in the house, futzing as he would say. I remember thinking to myself that I would rather spend the money and time now while I was younger and could do some of the things like travel than to wait until I was seventy, but most of all, I learned that when things became overwhelming, it was time to have fun.

I ate at the hotel the first night, and the dinner was so sublime. I went back to my room and called my oldest daughter to let her know that I was out of town, and she stated to me that I shouldn't have gone by myself across country. This was my daughter who traveled to Spain by herself and stayed for two weeks while in college. I laughed and told her that I was fine and she should not worry, but I just wanted to let her know that I was not in town. She sounded surprised, and I told her that my mom and my sister knew too. I laughed to myself that my daughter thought her mother could not take a vacation by herself, but I think it was more about the fact that she was worried about me driving in a car by myself if something should happen to the car. She was being endearing.

I took many pictures and visited the hotels, galleries, gift shops, etc. I had lunch at one of the hotels called the Bright Angel Lodge. It was so rustic yet warm and comforting. I had the time to spend looking in the museum in the hotel too, learned about who built it and how it came to be. It was nestled into the path near the rim's edge and fit into the scenery like a tree planted amongst other trees in the forest. It was picture-perfect for log cabins in the woods.

The bright angel trail, I was told by friends, was very steep and that when you walked down, it took twice as long to walk back up. So I thought I would be brave and at least walk a short distance down. I walked down for twenty minutes and then decided that the slope of steepness of the hill, it was better to turn around and come back. It was amazing to see all the people that were on the trail, some professional and some like me, first-timers. They also had donkeys you could ride down the trail, but you had to make a reservation, and I was told that this was done a year in advance.

I bought some books and a recipe book as I like to cook too. I bought a musical CD of Native American Indian music for the ride home and wanted to listen to the music of their culture. It was peaceful and great for the long ride home. Coldplay would be my other favorite to listen to, and the songs from that CD would become my favorites for sure. Music for me is also about times of my life and relating to memories of each time in my era.

I had visited the welcome center, and in it was an IMAX theater with a show about the canyon. I did see the movie, and it, too, was awesome, and I bought the CD of the movie for home. This was a time of enjoyment that would never forget. I was ready for the trip back home.

I drove home down the route through Flagstaff and into Sedona where I spent the end of the day walking through Red Rock State Park and then went into town to eat and look at all the shops where the local artists would sell their wares. It was recommended by a friend that I not miss stopping in Sedona, so I did. It was beautiful to see all the artists who would present their creations. I was sorry I did not have more time to look through the shops but needed to get back home for money reasons. I had not planned the trip, and my credit card would show that. As an artist myself, I was in artist heaven. Maybe I should stay.

I thought about moving back there to live a life of creativity amongst creators.

I did drive through the Painted Desert and the Petrified Forest on the way home. The Painted Desert was so beautiful, and the Petrified Forest was something that I would never forget either. It was so unbelievable, and I bought some petrified rocks from the gift shop one for me and one for my parents. My dad liked green, so I bought him a green piece.

The ride home was long, but I purchased a few CDs along the way, and it made the ride so fun. I remember getting into Springfield late in the evening and unpacking the car and walking up the three flights of stairs with all of my stuff, and when I got to the top of the stairs, I looked at the door and thought to myself, "Is this where I live?" I didn't want to open the door and go in, but I did. It was a moment of strong feelings I shall never forget.

When I sat down overlooking the Grand Canyon and wondered how my family had become so messed up and wanted my children to have a normal life again, I remember thinking, "How could my family be so good and then so torn up?" The court's very own system which had a sign atop, "Family Court," in the hallway was not about family at all. It was attorneys making deals and tearing people apart. It wasn't about what was the best and fair. It was who has the most money and who was on top that won. Not what was just and fair but who had the most money to pay people to get what they wanted. I didn't know that this happened, and my attorney was not working to get what was best for me but for the best for him because he was being paid by my ex also. It was hard news to hear as I had been searching for a new attorney and spoke to over fifteen attorneys and finally found one that was going to be a judge soon, and it was stated to me that attorneys made deals with the other side for money and say, "I'll let you win this time, and next time you let me win." I remember listening to these words and saying, "No wonder, I was right to think that I was being screwed in court." Just didn't know that attorneys would do this. So unethical.

So being tired of fighting in court and getting nowhere, I was not able to get my son back as the judge said, at age seventeen, he could not make my son do anything; if he gave me custody and my son left and went somewhere else, a sheriff could pick him up, but he could just leave again. He was telling me it was hopeless. My heart was crying for my son because I was so worried about him. His father had brainwashed him, and I could not convince him otherwise. It was heart-wrenching for me to watch my son ruin his life. His father was using him to hurt me. The judge, of course, was paid off too, I would find out later. True.

I had told his father that if there was a trial, and all his lies came out his children would never speak to him ever again. I think this was his incentive to get even with me through the children. He was like that: you piss him off, he'll get even and doesn't care who gets hurt.

I called his lawyer and said, "I wanted to settle this matter out of court." He stated that he would draw up papers for me to sign with the settlement offer and that I could come to his office and sign the papers, and then we would go to court and submit them to the judge.

It was not something I wanted but could no longer go on with the fight without any money and no one believing in me that I did not have a mental disorder. I was completely giving up, but at this time, I was just plain tired of no happiness in my life, and I needed to find a happy place to be and needed to for myself get happy and then figure how to fix things later, even though I knew I was right I needed to be happy in order to deal with all the bad emotional stuff that was emotionally tearing me apart day after unrelenting day.

I learned this through years of unhappiness and sitting and figuring out why. It was because I was listening to other people; the very thing they said was that the reason why I needed to get rid of my husband because he was making all the decisions and I had lost who I really was and became someone else. Which I had. They were correct, but now they were all trying to make my decisions and making me feel bad about myself.

I now knew that only I could change myself and make my life what I wanted it to be.

The hearing was in a couple of weeks, and I still did not hear from the attorney about getting the settlement papers signed. I called, and he told me that we still had to show up in court and have a hearing about custody of my son.

I said, "What? You told me there would not be a trial, just a meeting with the judge about signing the settlement papers in chambers."

He stated, "No, we still are having a trial."

I was upset and said, "Fine then, I'll prepare for a trial."

I had one week and spent many nights all night with no sleep preparing. I was ready.

I arrived in court ready for a trial, and the lawyer said, "Come into the judge's chambers."

I said, "What is going on?"

The judge stated that I should take the deal offered and not have a trial because everything I had was just hearsay and would not be admissible in court.

I was shocked and said, "Then why didn't Brian draw up the papers to settle? I have spent the last week preparing for this trial because he said we still had to have one."

The judge said I should still consider the deal and go out with Brian and try to work it out.

My brother, his wife, and my sister were in the courtroom. Brian came out and said, "Let's go across the hall and talk about this."

Mr. Rule was nowhere to be seen. We went across the hall to another court room, which was empty, and I saw Mr. Rule sitting in the hall. He wasn't even in the courtroom. He was such a sleaze. Anyway, Brian started to talk about all this settlement stuff and the way he had it worded was not the way I thought it should be worded at all, and I did not want to sign. I went to get my sister and asked her what she thought; she said she didn't know. We went back into the courtroom, and I showed it to my brother and his wife, and they said to me, "I don't know, why don't you just get this over with and sign the settlement papers?" They didn't really come to help me, and that was clear. They just all sat there, and later I knew why. Such hurt I thought I would never feel from family.

I decided to sign the papers now and get it over with. I was completely stressed out.

The actual paper that I signed was handwritten on a tricolored empty form paper that Brian prepared evidently that morning in court because otherwise, he would have had it typed up and ready to go for signature, but he didn't for a reason I will reveal later. The form stated that I was forgoing the payment of $24,000 in lieu of payment from me to Mr. Rule about college money for my son of 25 percent of the local state college, books, and room and board and $300 a month for four years of child support for my son until he got out of college. This was a large sum of money, and the judge knew I could not afford to pay $300 a month in child support on the income that I had. It was not fair at all since I was in need of maintenance myself, and the judge said I had to pay child support and come back at a later date for maintenance. My ex had lied about his income, and I had no way to prove it.

I was exhausted and weary. *Weary* is the word that I had come to know and use often. It was a word I had never really dwelt on before. I was always such a strong personality and always knew what to do and how to achieve what I set out to do.

This was a way for me to find out how to accomplish things and still keep my sunny personality. Little by little, he had stripped that away from me, and it was the one thing that drew people to me. I am strong and have a high self-esteem; it is not self-achieving, but I do come by it naturally. I do not brag, but if someone asks me about something, I do not hold back and always tell the truth.

He had kept me silent about the family mess because it was apparent to me that he would find a way to punish me or the children if we did something that he did not like. It was quite apparent to me that his smile was a front to his twisted way of getting what he wanted without you knowing that he was manipulating me. I now call him the master manipulator. It is true and sad at the same time.

Things had been going wrong in my life, and I could not figure out why. I was beginning to think that it was on purpose.

I had trouble with my phone bill as it kept coming wrong, and then I tried calling numerous times and kept getting the run around. I must have called about over twenty times to straighten it out. They turned off my service one day, and that was when I knew that someone was doing this on purpose. I knew it was him getting someone to do that for him from the phone company. We had friends, a couple that both worked there in the office downtown, and it was his wife that was going to my lawyers with me. It was apparent to start with them. She was retired, but he still worked there, never thinking that it might also be another friend of his. I asked the customer service supervisor to please check and see if this person had anything to do with my file or with the people that had been talking with me. She said she would call me back and did not. I called the security department of the phone company and asked for them to do a security check on my account to see if he was talking to the people that I had been talking with. They called me and said that they would check on it for me but that I should send him an e-mail of all the people that I talked with. It was suspicious of me; I asked if I could come down and talk with them.

My checking account at the bank had bounced, and I was upset and figured out it was electronic withdrawals from things that had been ordered online, but they were things that I did not order or place an account with. There were about five things in one-month period. I called the police as I suspected that he was getting into my apartment and doing this on my computer. Because someone would have to have know my passwords and been on my computer to send the e-mails and generate an e-mail back to my address.

The police arrived and stated that they could not investigate because there was no break-in and that I should just be careful and change the locks on the house. I told the officer about the phone mess, and she suggested that I get a city police officer to go along with me into the meeting with the security person as I was scared to report the incident. She said I could just call them when I got down there in the morning and requested that someone go in the meeting with me.

I was scared but left in the morning for the meeting at the telephone company and parked by the police station and went in to talk to someone about getting an officer to come to the meeting with me. The officer at the front desk said that they were not a station and that I would have to call 911 and ask that an officer meet me there.

I said, "Okay."

I left the building and walked down the street a few blocks and then called. They said to wait outside the building and an officer would come in with me.

I walked down to the building and went in to tell the information desk to let him know that I was here but was waiting for a police officer to come up to the meeting with me. I waited outside the building, and an officer came and we went inside. The man from security was standing at the front desk and stated to me and the police officer that I did not need a police officer to be in the meeting with me and that he could go. At that time, another officer arrived and stated that he was called because there was a disturbance in the building.

I stated, "No, there is no disturbance, just this officer who is going into a meeting with me."

The first officer who arrived stated that he could not go into the meeting with me as he was not allowed to do that. I stated that a county officer told me to call him. He stated she should not have told me that. So the second officer who arrived on a bike in shorts stated that I did not need an officer in the meeting. The security person from the phone company said that I did not need anyone in the meeting and that I should not be afraid of him. So I told the officer to go ahead and leave. And they both left. The security person and I then proceeded to the elevator, and we went up to his office. We were in his office for about a few minutes as I began to tell the story, and in walked the police officer in shorts that showed up in seconds and stated that he felt that he needed to be in the meeting as I seemed upset.

I said, "I am not upset, just worried about who is doing this to me."

He said he needed to be there, and then I said, "No, you don't."

He then made a statement as to my mental state, which I knew then that someone had sent him for him to ask that question of me. I then looked at the security person and said, "You just write me up a letter today stating that the person I am inquiring about has not tampered with my bill."

He stated that he could not do that for me but assured me that no one had tampered with my bill. I knew he was lying since he would not type up a simple note to state that for me. The officer kept badgering me with questions. I stated that I was not staying for the meeting and left. The security person walked to the elevator with me, and I told him that my ex told everyone that I have mental problems and that I was suspect of why this officer would say that, and I left.

I went home and called the county police precinct and asked to talk with the officer about what happened, and they stated that she could not help with that problem that I needed to go to the city and report the incident to internal affairs. I drove back downtown and asked to speak with an internal affairs detective, and they stated that I could just wait.

I was then approached by the IA detective, and he said, "Come upstairs and we will talk."

We went up the elevator and he took me into a room, and we went into a conference room, and he asked me to tell him the story. I told him the story, and he said wait here for just a minute and left. He then came back into the room and started to yell at me and said that the officer did nothing wrong, and I almost started to cry, and I left.

I was so upset and drove home and cried.

I had suspected that someone was getting into my condo, and I couldn't sleep and was putting furniture in front of the doors, including my bedroom door, when I would go to sleep at night. Then one day, I went into the spare bathroom that my son used when he lived with me. I had totally cleaned out the bathroom, including emptying the cabinet under the sink. I opened the cabinet to get something, and there were some porn pictures that shocked me out of my life. I picked them up and started to cry. How could they have gotten there? The only people in the condo were my daughters and my sisters. I was upset; someone had put them there, and if it was not them, then it was someone else who got in with keys.

My car kept having problems, so I finally went to the dealer to have them look at it. They said the car needed a battery, and they would fix it. I waited, and they fixed the car. I got in to drive to a job interview, and the red light came on again. I went to the interview and called them to say that the light came on again. They said, "Bring it back in." I took it back in, and they said that it needed more work, and I said, "How it could need more items when I just had it in here and the service person began to treat me incorrectly?"

This was the first time that happened there. I was upset and asked to speak to a manager.

He said, "Please wait in the showroom, and I will have someone talk with you."

I waited for a long time, and then someone came in. He stated that he was the general sales manager and that he would straighten out the matter. He said that my car needed more work and that it needed to be left and that they would fix it no charge.

I said, "Okay."

He said I could just wait in his cube and we could talk while my car was being fixed.

I said, "Okay."

He was very nice, and we talked about an hour or so. He had just lost his wife and was talking about her so endearing. I told him, "I was just recently divorced a year or so, and I know what being alone does to you." I told him that I was sorry about his wife. He put his business card on the desk and said, "You can call me anytime if you want to."

I said, "Okay."

They said my car was ready, and we walked back to the service area. I told him we should have dinner and talk one night. He said okay, and I gave him my number. My car was ready, and he said, "I'll call you, and we could go out Thursday night."

I said okay. I drove away and went down the street to see a movie. The car seemed to jump into gear oddly. I saw the movie, and when I got out, the car was shifting hard and jumping all over the place. I called him back and said that the car was having problems, and he said, "Just bring it back in." They said they would have to keep the car and hook it up to see what was wrong. They gave me a loaner car, but first he tried to talk me into buying a new car and junking the old one.

I said I could not afford it.

He said, "Okay."

I drove away with the loaner. We went out to dinner the next night, and we had a great time. We hit it off right away, and we both knew it. The next day they called and said that my car needed a new transmission and it would cost $3,000.

I said, "You have got to be kidding me."

They said, "No, we are not kidding you."

I was upset and called a friend about the car.

He and I went out again on Saturday, and we were having fun. It got serious real fast, much to my surprise, as I was not looking for serious at all. I did have trouble this way when I was younger. Guys go out with me and get serious real fast. I was not prepared for this, and being the first man I went out with in three years since my ex left me, I was not ready for serious that fast.

I talked with my sisters about him, and they seemed to think we were sharing too much personal information with each other at this time. But I guess at our ages, that was just what we did.

Anyway, the car was upsetting to me, but I didn't want him to get involved with it because it was where he worked. So I found someone else to put a transmission in it, my best friend from high school whose husband owned a sports car mechanic shop. Anyway, it was upsetting.

We went out to dinner and to a casino one night as he liked to gamble. I did not but had fun watching him. We then came home to my house, second date, and made love. It was a surprising thing for me as I am religious and do not sleep with someone that quick ever. I was falling in love with him and told him so. My friends said I should not have told him that, but I did as we were in an embrace, and I looked at him, and he said, "Just go ahead and say it," so I did. He didn't say it back to me though, which was upsetting to me. He would leave the condo after we made love and would not stay the night. He would say he had to get home because his granddaughter lived with him.

I was starting to wonder about all the things he was saying to me about having money and things and talked with my daughter, and she said that he was lying and all guys lied to the girl when they first met.

She said to me, "Did you check this guy out?"

I said, "No."

He was not the person I thought as I used an Internet service and checked him out. He had liens against almost every property he owned and had moved many times. He had filed bankruptcy, and I was upset to read this as he touted a few times about how much money he had when we met.

I then looked up his address in the phone book and drove by his house. It was not the house he had described to me. He was lying to me, and it hurt as badly as he knew I was upset about my ex-husband lying about many things to me. He said he would never lie to me and that I could ask him anything.

We went out to dinner one night, and he stated again that night that I could ask him anything and that my nephew had even been in his house so there was no need to doubt him. We ate dinner, and the whole time I was thinking that he lied about his house to me. We went home, and he kept talking about how he liked the package. Referring to me as a package while he was looking at me sexually really upset me. I thought this was so insulting and told him that the package was my heart pointing to it. And the body was the bonus from God. He laughed, but I was dead serious, and he did not respect me at all. We went home, and he made love to me, and I felt like a hypocrite. Anyway, I needed to confront him about my suspicions. So I did. As he was leaving, I told him that I drove by his house, and it was not the house he had described at all and asked if he would please explain that to me. He said very sternly that his house could not even be seen from the road (which it could be as I had driven by it—another lie). His cell phone rang, and he answered it in the middle of this conversation. He stated that it was his son and he had to leave. The next day was my birthday, and I had asked him to come downtown with me to celebrate as I had gotten a room at a very expensive hotel as a gift to me on my fiftieth birthday as a gift for not being paid as my own attorney for nine months, laughing to myself, but it was true.

He just said, "I have to go."

I said, "Well, are you coming with me in the morning or not?"

He said, "I don't know." He left. I noticed in the morning that he had left his watch and ring on the nightstand in my bedroom.

I called him as I thought he might need it at work in the morning.

He said, "Okay, I'll pick it up."

I asked him if he was going with me downtown, and he stated he didn't know.

He arrived in the morning of my birthday, and I went to the door and opened it. He was on his cell phone talking and came in and gave me a kiss while talking. He was in a heated discussion with his son about his son's friend who evidently got a girl pregnant. I was upset that he was talking and not saying, "Can I call you back I'm at Julia's house?" It was my birthday—no flowers, no nothing.

He talked about ten minutes or so, and I tried to go into the other room so I couldn't hear him. He sounded upset. He got off the phone and said he did not know if he could come with me today as someone had called in sick at work and he had to go into work today. I was upset and asked him if he thought he could come late in the evening just to at least dance with me.

He said, "I don't know, I'll call you!" And he left. I could not believe it.

I was so upset and called my girlfriend. She said she would go downtown with me and walk around with me. We went and walked around a bit. We ate dinner at the buffet in the hotel, and he still hadn't called. I was really upset. My daughter Alexandria called to wish me a happy birthday, and then I and my friend went up to the room. He still had not called me. Then the room phone rang, and it was him, and he stated that he was not sure if he was coming or not and was almost yelling at me.

I said, "Then forget it, as I wanted you to come down and have fun with me, but you must have other plans."

He said, yelling, "Do you want me to still come?"

I said, "No, forget about it."

My friend needed a ride home as she came with me, and I thought maybe he could take her home and then come back. But he was a nasty man. I took my friend home and then came back, but it was too late to go dancing by myself, and I went to bed. What a birthday on my fiftieth. I was so upset but got up and ate breakfast and drove around downtown taking pictures of all the places I used to go.

He called me the next day, and I said I was upset. He said there was nothing he could do about it.

I said, "I know you were busy."

He said that he was moving, and it was taking a long time.

I said, "Go ahead and move."

He had asked me if he could move in with me after four weeks, and I said no as I didn't even know him that well, much less move in with me.

I liked him very much, but he was lying to me. I didn't trust him. He called me once more, and I screamed at him, and he said that no one had ever talked to him that way before.

I said, "Well, maybe they should, you're a liar," and I hung up.

That was the end. My sisters kept telling me I should call him back and just be friends, but I said no. The man never brought me flowers and did not even get me anything on my birthday. He was not interested in me at all. Just wanted someone to sleep with, I guess; he said I was easy to hold. I guess I was. It was over.

My sisters kept telling me to call him and go out and just be friends. I said I couldn't be just friends, and so I didn't call him. I did not like the way he treated me or talked to me.

It was a time of learning for me, and I guess I wasn't ready for someone to start lying to me as I don't lie and don't quite yet understand why and how often most other people do lie on a regular basis. The liars would later become an interest of study for me.

It would be later that I would challenge the lies that people tell and dealing with coping with the lies and know how to deal with letting them know they lied without getting upset toward them. I'm learning at this point because I don't understand it. I never lie about anything at any time. I think everyone should be that way. The world would be a better place wouldn't it.

I don't trust people, and I guess I am learning to trust again in my own way. I guess it's taking longer than I thought.

I was glad the court stuff was over.

I went to one of my sons soccer games at the soccer park, and it was there that I started to talk about the case and proceedings in court and wanted to help my children to understand who their father was and help them to understand that they should not be in his life as he has serious problems with life and lying was a normal thing for him.

I sat down next to one of my neighbors, and she and her husband's son had played soccer with my son for years. I started to tell them what had been happening in my life and that I was worried about my son and started to tell them how I had been fighting in court for nine months to get my son back. They were surprised at what I told them about Mr. Rule as everyone thought he was such a nice person. I knew I needed to start talking to my children's friends' parents. It was time for me to figure out a way to let my children know who their father was. But as the night went on, we talked, and when the game was over, we walked down the bleachers and waited for our sons.

I wanted to ask my son if he was going to the baseball game with me as I had bought some special tickets to go on Easter Sunday. I had not seen him or been with him in a long time. As I tried to approach my son, I asked him if he could go with me, and he said, "No, Mom, I can't go," as he kept walking.

Then, out of nowhere, Mr. Rule came up behind me and started to yell at me, stating, "Who the hell do you think you are, and what gives you the right to talk to people about me?" He was yelling loudly.

The look on my sons face was one of extreme embarrassment. This was the soccer park where he spent most of his life playing, and all his friends and parents heard this.

I just replied, "You're going to hell," very softly and walked away.

My friend I was sitting with was surprised and said, "Are you okay?"

I said, "Yes!" but was shook up. I turned to walk up the stairs, and on the stairs was my nephew Gray.

He said, "What's going on, Aunt Julia?"

I said, "Your Uncle Paul is out of control."

He said, "Are you okay?"

I said, "Sure, but I am very worried about my son."

He had for the first time humiliated me and my son in public. He had done this regularly at home but never in public. I was, indeed, worried for us both.

I thought a lot about what he did and why he did it. It was to intimidate me and keep me away, just as I had left cookies on the porch for my son at his girlfriend's house as this was where he and my son were living. He called me up and told me I had to get permission to come on the porch if I ever needed to drop something off for my son. He was controlling me and scaring me at the same time to stay away from my son. What an evil heart he had become and quite possibly had always been but hid it from me until it was needed.

The next soccer game I went to, he was sitting in the car by himself, and I was determined to see why he was treating me the way he was. I walked up to the car and knocked on the window; he rolled down the window, and I told him that if he ever embarrassed my son and myself again in public, I would take care of it.

He pushed open the door, which knocked me back, and he got right in my face and screamed at the top of his lungs, "You need to be on your medications!" He said it like a wild man. I knew right then at that time that he was doing this to me on purpose with malice. He was out of control and was yelling at me to intimidate me in ways that he was good at. He is a nasty man.

I then knew why, "You need to be on your medication for the rest of your life," was coming from his mouth. By medicating me he could control me and my actions much better than before. He liked it and needed it to feel superior. I often wondered why I would always say, "I am feeling much better," and he would say, "You can't stop taking your medication, you need to take it forever." I was depressed and didn't understand that. I knew many people who had been depressed in their lifetimes at one time or another, and then they would be fine a few months later, no big deal. He kept insisting that this was a lifelong thing for me. I just didn't get it. But he would watch my pills, and when I stopped, he would know because he was counting them all the time. Once I realized this, I couldn't stop. I didn't think to just throw them in the trash, which was what I should have done. It was a hard time for me, and he was always so persuasive. Ask anyone that knew him; he had a way about him.

I never knew before that he would be so conniving to someone he had said he loved for twenty-three years. It was at that moment that I knew that he was never capable of giving real love. It was all phony and fake and just for show to get what he wanted for his image.

This would be a monumental day for me as up, until that time, I did not know that he was doing that to me on purpose. Someone asked me if I was scared of him, and I stated in some ways, but I was glad I did what I did to know for sure once and for all.

It would be a long time before I would tell anyone that, and it would be a long time before I would get someone to believe me.

I went to the police and told them of the action, and a female officer told me that he was obsessing after the marriage and that I should stay away from him and any friends that we had mutually while we were married. She said that I should file an ex parte protection order against him so that when I went to soccer games, he could not come up to me and embarrass me or my son ever again.

I told her that I wasn't sure that I wanted to do that and went home with the information booklet that she gave me. I went to bed and was reading it in bed. I fell asleep. When I woke up in the morning, the information was on the floor upside down, and my hand was sliced in the middle of the palm of my hand. It scared me so bad. I didn't know what to do. I called my sister, and she said, "Are you sure you just don't have a paper cut?"

I stated, "No, this is not a paper cut."

I didn't know what to do and was crying. Someone for sure was in my condo. I didn't understand it, and I was so worried. I would not get a good night's sleep for years to come after this day. Sad but very true. It is important for victims to get safe.

About two weeks later, I decided to go ahead and file the order. I went into the closet where my legal divorce files where, and they were all mixed up, and some were missing. This was a clear-cut yes to me that, indeed, someone was in my condo. No more doubts about it for sure. I stood their frozen, knowing full well that someone had violated my privacy, my home. It doesn't get any worse than that, and the many nights of lack of sleep would come to wear me down to the very core of being so unhappy some days I wanted to end it.

I spent the night reorganizing the files and putting them back in place and then putting them in files with punch holes in them. The files were different colors. I placed them on the kitchen table and then went about getting ready to go to court.

I knew without a doubt that I was actually going to file the ex parte protection order and now had a reason besides the yelling in public to present to the courts—or so I thought.

I left the house and went to the courthouse to file the paperwork. I got there and went to the fifth floor where the files were kept, and sure enough, the last entry paperwork for the settlement of the divorce was different than the one I had been presented with in court on the last day of the trial. I knew for sure who had taken the documents and why.

I filed the ex parte protection order and had to go home to get more paperwork to completely fill out the order for the judge to sign. I then went back to the courthouse but first went into the building that houses the jail and the public defenders and asked to speak to one. The receptionist asked why and told me that if I thought someone had tampered with the files in the courthouse that I should go and tell the judge. So I went over to the courthouse and filled out the paperwork for the ex parte protection order and the judge signed it on the spot. I then filed for a hearing.

I went to the second floor to tell the judge in my divorce case that the file for the case had a document in it that was different than the one that was presented to me in court. The clerk pulled up the court records in the computer for that day, and it stated that the case was over and the contempt of court had been dropped by me. My eyes got large, and I stated that I did not and that I would have never dropped the contempt of court on Mr. Rule as he was in contempt and that I lost my home and the home I was going to buy because of his lies. She then told me that I could write a motion to set aside the judgment and get the case reopened again. I took the paperwork and was going to fill it all out at home, and the judge told me to go and tell the police on my way home that someone had gotten into my house.

So I stopped in the precinct and asked to speak to the officer whom I had spoken to before. They said she was not available and that they would dispatch someone from Clayton to come and talk with me.

I sat for half an hour waiting. An officer arrived, and he was not happy looking. He stated that there was nothing he could do as there was no break-in. I stated that my ex-husband was the one and that I had just filed an ex parte order on him. He stated that he wanted to call my ex-husband.

I said, "No, you can't do that, or he won't answer when the sheriff delivers the order!"

He said, "What is his phone number?"

I stated sternly, "I do not want you to call him!"

He said again, "Give me his number!"

I said, "Okay," and gave it to him but said, "Please do not call him."

I left the station and came home. It was a trying day, and I was upset.

A few minutes later, the doorbell rang.

It was the officer, and he said, "Can I come in please?"

I said, "Yes, but why?"

He said, "I just wanted to look around a bit."

The officer said, "Let me see your computer area where you said you think someone was on it, and let me see the area where you keep the files from your court proceedings."

So I took him back to the bedroom office, and I said, "Here is the office and my computer."

He was looking all around and then went into my bedroom also and looked around. He said everything looked secure. As he walked past the stereo, his walkie-talkie made this screeching sound, and he said that maybe someone had bugged my condo, and I told him that another officer had instructed me to get a hidden camera put in my home to see who was coming in.

He said, "Did you get that?" and I stated that my friend was going to buy that for me.

He looked up at the air vent and then looked at the pictures of my children on the wall. He stated that they were very nice-looking, and I asked him if he called my ex-husband, and he said, to my surprise, "Yes."

I stated, "Why did you do that? I specifically told you not to call my ex-husband" and with that, he took out his flashlight from his back belt loop and began to slap it in the palm of his other hand as if to intimidate me. It scared me for sure, and I just looked the other way.

I then went to file the paperwork from the courthouse in my files and noticed that the paperwork that was missing in my files was now back in it. Somehow someone had gotten back in my home from morning until 5:00 PM to replace the missing document. I was upset and called the police again to tell the officer to please come and look at the file.

The same officer was dispatched, and I met him outside because the day before he stated that someone might have bugged my home.

I said, "Would you please look at this file and fingerprint it for me and tell me who put this paperwork and also I think that someone has drugged or poisoned my food."

He said, "Well, let's look at the file."

I said, "Please help me figure out who is getting into my home."

He stated that he could not fingerprint the file as there was no break-in.

I said, "I know there was no break-in, but someone is getting in!"

He said, "Show me the file."

He put his fingerprints all over the file and then was flipping through the paperwork and I said, "Please don't touch the file as I want it fingerprinted."

He said, "No, I can't do that," and he bolted out of my house and set the alarm off as I had armed it when he came in this time.

I shouted out to him on his way to the front door that the alarm was still on, and he bolted out of the door anyway, clearly to upset me. It worked.

I immediately called the precinct to tell them of this officer, and they said the supervisor would be in the office in the morning. I went in to talk to the lieutenant in the morning, but he said that particular officer's supervisor would be in at two o'clock and I should come back then. I went back then, and they said wait just a minute and I would get him. I waited for about twenty minutes and then was thirsty, so I left to get something to drink and came back. Two officers came out of the back and sat at the table with me. One was the lieutenant, and the other said he was an officer. But after speaking with him, I knew there was some type of psychological counselor officer by the way he was asking the questions.

He said that someone was playing mind games with me, and I stated, "Yeah, so then let's get them to stop whatever it is they are doing, in and out of my home."

They began to state that I have been coming to the precinct too many times about things and that I needed to stop doing that. I told them that the officer in my home the day before acted inappropriately, and they began to talk as if I had a mental disease. They stated that I needed to go to the hospital and get evaluated.

I said, "No, I don't," and I said that I was leaving.

They stated that they were going to take me to the hospital.

I said, "No, you don't have the right to."

They said there was a law that stated they had the right.

I said to them nicely, "Show it to me," and they stated that there was not enough time to do that and I was going.

I said, "That is not fair, I am not hurting anyone. I just came here to complain about an officer and get your help."

Later I would come to know that one should *never* complain about a police officer unless you have witnesses. *Never*. Trust me on this one thing the most. *Never*.

I opened the door to leave, and there were ten police officers standing in the hallway waiting for me, and I said, "Let me see the law that states that you have the right to take me when I don't want to go."

They said to me, "You're going, and that's that."

I thought, "Well, I guess I could go out screaming." But I guessed they would beat me and then throw me in a car and take me. Well, there was an ambulance waiting to take me; they said they had called my mother and my sister and that they had signed affidavits to take me, and they escorted me into the ambulance and the officer whom I had come to complain about, then got in the ambulance. I stated that he was not to ride in the ambulance with me. Then another officer got in with me. The ambulance attendant then asked me to lie down, and she strapped me in and took my blood pressure. At that time she asked me some questions, and I answered them all. I was not upset or anything but stated that they did not have the right to take me.

When I got to the hospital, they escorted me into the emergency area. I was asked to wait, and again my vitals were taken. The officer that I complained about was outside my door; I could hear him telling the doctor that I said the CIA was following me, and he was lying about everything. He was a liar, and it was clear I was being set up.

A counselor came in to talk with me, and she asked me what was going on in my life. I stated that nothing was going on just that I went to complain about an officer, and they took me here against my will. I told them that I was not paying for this either. They said my mother and my sister said I needed to be there. My mother and my sister had not even talked to me at all. My sister Devilia, whom I had not talked to in six months—how would she of all people know that I was in need of anything? I was not speaking to her because she told me that I was wasting my time and money with lawyers and that my children were awful and I should stay away from them; my mother was saying the same thing. My father had passed away a few weeks prior, and they didn't even ask me to be involved in the ceremony or my children either, even though other family members were asked. My mother had pushed my daughter away from the casket in the funeral parlor. I was not happy with my family.

The counselor they sent into the ER room said, "You have a lot of stuff going on."

I stated, "I know, I have for quite some time. My life is quite complicated, and people aren't helping with it, in fact they are damaging it further."

She stated that she thought it would be a good idea if I stayed the night.

I said okay, and then they came and took me to the Dylan Center by escort van. I was clearly not just spending the night. I was not even given the opportunity to go home and get a bag of clothing and stuff before they took me.

It was midnight, and they took my shirt and shoes and gave me a paper shirt to wear. I walked around with no shoes, just paper hospital booties. No family member came in with me nor asked for my keys to go and get my things. No family ever came to see me ever the whole week I was there. Clearly, this message was enough for me. They cared nothing about me.

I was clearly not making any upsetting statements so I could go home the next day. I was pleasant and then went to bed. The next day I woke up and ate breakfast and used the phone to call my lawyer and call the police internal affairs and the FBI. I asked them to please get me out of there as I was taken against my will. They had no right to take me there, and I was not sick, just that I had complained about a police officer and was not ill and wanted to leave. The attorney said that he could not get me out as they had the right to keep me there for so many hours by law.

I was asked by a person on staff, "What are you doing here?" She went to high school with my sister.

I said, "I had complained about a police officer and was taken here."

She said that she was surprised I was there and said that I should call her brother Dick that I went to grade school with when she found out I was single still.

She said, "He's still single."

I said to her, "Tell him to call me."

She said, "I will."

The doctor met with me and said, "You don't seem sick at all, why are you here?"

I said, "I complained about a police officer, and they brought me here to shut me up."

He said, "Well, your mother and sister said they thought you should be here."

I said, "They were wrong, I have been crying about things, and I'm depressed, but I'm not mentally ill. The police told me they had signed affidavits from my mother and sister, and so they had the right to take me there because I was bugging them too much." I cried internally. Betrayed by my family in the worst way I could have ever imagined.

The doctor stated that I could leave tomorrow if I could get two people to say that I was all right. I told him that my sister in another state would vouch for me, and I had lunch with a couple of high school friends who could say I was all right.

He said, "I will have the staff call them, and you can go home tomorrow."

I said, "Great."

I gave the staff my sister Sophia's number and my friend JoJo's number. They said okay and then took the numbers and said they would call them.

Later that afternoon, I was eating my lunch, and the doctor that I saw for six years for depression came into the lounge, and I said hello. He said hello back, and he left. I wondered why he was there, and it seemed suspicious to me. Was he paid off, too, to lie about me to the staff? I think he was and have no doubt about it, but no proof either. Who knows? I do know he did not return a reply to letters that I wrote to him.

The next day the doctor had me in the room and told me that I was paranoid and had to stay for another week.

I said, "What happened? You said yesterday I could go home, and now today I have to stay and I am paranoid?"

He did not give an answer; he just turned his back and walked away.

Later that night, at 10:00 PM, three males came to me and said that risk management told them to come down and inject me with medication since I had refused the meds.

I said, "I do not want this and don't need it."

They said they have to, or else they would hold me by force and inject me. I was upset and said that they were abusing me and allowing the continued abuse by my ex-husband and others, including the police department.

They said, "We have to do it."

Inside I sank down to the floor even though I was still standing, and I walked to my room remembering it felt like my body was floating up and I couldn't stop it, and I was horrified that my ex-husband had won again. I lay down on the bed, and they injected me in the hip. I fell asleep immediately, and the next day, I was so drugged that I could not even get up out of bed. They had heavily drugged me, and I was out and almost comatose. I did not attend any meetings that day or the next days that I can remember. The paper file of evidence was under my pillow, and now heavily sedated, another switch could be made, but it wasn't. I was relieved. But no one ever did anything with it anyway in the years to come. True.

No family member at all came to see me. I had ninety-one people in my immediate family at that time, and I knew then and there that no one loved me at all ever, not the way they should have. My sister out of town did but did not know what exactly was going on so far away.

I was talking to my sister Sophia, and she said that she could not believe that I did not have any clothes or incidentals. She said she would ask my sister Brunhilda to come and bring me items. She brought me old clothes, a toothbrush, and a book. I thanked her, and she went home. The book was about some woman who wanted to kill her ex-husband. I thought to myself, "My sister is the one who is sick and trying to get me into trouble." I hated her. I knew at that moment that she was not my friend.

The next day the doctor came in and said I could go home

tomorrow. I called Brunhilda and asked her if she would come and pick me up as my car was at the police station. The whole time I was in the mental ward, they put my keys and personal belongings in the house safe, so they said. I was uncomfortable since the police brought me there, and now they had access to my keys too, and my car was in their parking lot at the police station for a week.

They were not helping me because they did not want me to complain about the police officer. They actually find ways to hurt people as well that do. Believe me on this fact.

Not one of my family members called or came over to see if I was okay at all, and I was very angry, and my family had let me down once again. I called my mother to see what officer told her I needed to be there, but she would not tell me and hung up on me. It would be the last time I would hear my mother's voice on the phone. I did not trust her anymore, nor did I want to see her ever again.

I was now aware that people in the world did not care about me, most of all my family.

I received a bill from the hospital for $5,000 or more, so I sent a letter to them stating that my sister and mother and the police were responsible for the payment of this bill.

I realized that my children had been brainwashed by their father, and now my family was also as my one sister had made statements that she knew that I had a mental illness because that was what my ex-husband told her. She was screwed up and didn't really care about me at all. She was the worst of the worst in the world. She had placed such a burden on me and had done nothing at all to correct it. She was satisfied with her life and did not have to straighten out her mistakes; but it wasn't a mistake as she did it on purpose. My older brother had tried to tell me this about her for years and other siblings. She controlled what she wanted to in any way that she wanted to. She was like my ex-husband. An awful person manipulating people to get what they want. Her soul was ugly, just like my ex-husband's.

Now it was up to me to make my life what it was and live it the way I wanted to. They would miss me, and if not, that was okay too. They seemed to be doing fine without me anyway. I haven't heard from any of them. They don't care at all. Fine by me. Seven years later, it is still the same. My life is much better, and I am finally happy.

I am in a situation that I thought my family would rally around me and help me, but it is just the opposite. They do nothing but give all the reasons why everything is wrong and blame it on me making me cry daily. I guess that is how they lead their lives, not me.

I now learned to live life, and I don't regret anything I have done or have tried to do. I failed to help my children, and for that I can't beat myself up about it too much. For you see, they did not try back to help me help them. So it failed all the way around, and I have finished crying about it seven years later. I have gone on to lead my life and live life. People and new friends and counselors say I should see them. I say I tried, more than anyone could. They don't want to see me. They don't return my calls. I love them, but I now need to learn to love myself just as much.

I finally had to accept that, and with a big inner sigh of discontent, I do. It is eternally saddening at this moment in time, but I will get by with that and live my life the best I can and without them for now.

Chapter 7

Jobs Terminated, and It Turned into an EEOC Extravaganza

I have been fired from two jobs now—one, a college, who of course fired me for crying when I got some bad news about my ex-husband and the girlfriend seeing each other for six years while I was still married to him, who at the time six years prior to my divorce was one of his bosses. The another company was where I worked wherein they were a drug-testing facility, who fired me for three reasons that were not true because a janitor who was interested in me didn't like that I didn't pay attention to him at my desk, so while in the break room eating my lunch, he began to the put the dirty chairs on the tables while I was eating, and I said to him, "If you put one more chair closest to me on this table while I'm eating, I am going to tell on you." He did it anyway, and I walked out of the break room and told a supervisor. Guess what, I got fired from my supervisor who lied three times. I later called back to tell the HR person what had really happened, and she thanked me.

Now, here came the third job in a row where I'd be fired again. It was a consulting company that represented people trying to gain Social Security disability benefits and needed an attorney to write a medical brief proving disability. I was hired after an interview where the officer manager liked the fact that I had an extended medical background and that I was very detail-oriented and organized. However, she did not tell me that I would be working for an attorney. I did not even meet the person while interviewing. I would know later why.

The first day on the job, she walked me back to my desk and stated that the attorney would be in soon.

I stated, "Attorney!" to my surprise.

She said, "Yes." Oh my!

Anyway, the attorney was a woman, and she was nice at first but then very difficult to work with. She was always in late and liked things done exactly the way she liked them, which sometimes weren't exactly neat and tidy. She did not like change evidently. Anyway, weeks into the job, she told me that she does not like perky as we were talking about a local car leasing company. I told her that my daughter worked there and she was very perky like her mother.

She just said, "That's why I never use that company when I need a rental car."

I thought not only was she insulting my daughter, she was also insulting me, as everyone told me how perky I was and how I had a wonderful smile all the time (maybe not all the time!). Anyway, as time went on, she became more difficult to work with, and I began to think that she had emotional problems or alcoholism as she was in late all the time and very angry about things. She was a good person with the clients, and I would begin to see good things in her as well as the ones that were apparent to me that she had not fulfilled herself in her work or something was not right in her life. Maybe, just maybe, it was just the way she was, and she liked it that way. I never asked her. I didn't care either.

The attorney in the next cubicle, a male (who happened to be Black, which was fine with me), started to hit on me one day in a very smooth, cute manner. After about fifteen minutes, I'm sure other coworkers told on him as two supervisors came to my desk immediately. I was just sitting there doing my work when he came over and sat down next to me, sliding a chair over and started asking me how things were going. He was very nice, and I felt comfortable, and I said, "Fine," and we talked. He called me one night at home, and he caught me off guard as I had just changed my phone number as people were calling me leaving nasty messages, and I stated, "Is this Mark from work? How did you get this number?"

I said, and I must have alarmed him and made him think that he was in trouble, and he said, "I have the wrong house and hung up."

So I thought maybe it was a wrong guy, and I just let it go. He never said anything at work either. I just let it all go and then later would learn he was a nice person who liked me. He was an A-type. His desk always neat and clean, his attire very nice and always clean. One day he came in with a suit on as he had to be in court.

I said to him, "You're looking very dapper today."

He looked at me with a big smile and said, "Thanks."

Anyway, he kept flirting at work, and so one day, I asked him if he wanted to go to my son's graduation breakfast at the Plaza Hotel.

He said, "I'll see if I'm available, and I'll let you know."

I didn't want to sit across from the devil (which I was calling my ex at the time sarcastically) or my ex-husband and the girlfriend by myself. Anyway, it was nice that he was interested, and he was very nice about it. He did not go with me because his daughter was graduating from eighth grade that day as well.

He said, "I have your card in my pocket, and I'll call you sometime," pumping his hand on his pocket as he smiled at me.

I thought, "Well, I did not hurt his feelings or intrude in any way in his personal life as he was separated from his wife." He was a parole officer at one time, and I thought to myself, "Great, he could whoop up on the ex if he got out of line at the breakfast." I remember thinking to myself that he could take care of me if I was afraid, and Lord knows I was afraid of my ex-husband at that time in more ways than one.

My father died, and even though he was ill, it came unexpected on that given day. I got a call around 9:30 AM. It was my sister, and she said, "Mom wants to talk to you."

I said, "Okay."

My mother got on the phone, and the words came out, "Julia, your father has died."

I remember hesitating and then sighing, and I said, "What happened to him, Mom?"

She said, "I was getting ready for church and your father fell out of bed, I could not pick him up by myself, so I only had a few short minutes until my ride was coming."

My father was quite ill, and my mother did not drive, so my sister's friend Pam picked her up weekly for church services at the same time 7:30 AM each Sunday. This particular day was no different, and my mother made a choice to just let him lie on the floor and she would call someone later.

She said to me, "I just decided I didn't have time to call someone to pick him up, so I just put a pillow under his head and left, and he told me that would be okay."

I being my father's daughter did not like that my mother made such a choice, but you have to know my parents. You did not miss church on Sundays unless you were personally ill and could not get there yourself. I guess my mother assessed the incident and did what she thought was right at the time.

I said to my mother, "Mom, I'll be right down to the house." And I hung up.

I put on my coat, got in my car, and drove very carefully to the house that I grew up in, knowing that I would never see my father again inside that home that he lived in and raised ten children in—one of them being me.

When I arrived at my childhood home, my brother and sister-in-law were on the front porch.

I said, "Hi," very solemnly and thought it odd that they were on the porch but left it alone and went inside. I saw my mother straight away down the hallway sitting on a kitchen chair and the one my father had sat in most of his adult life in the kitchen. I gave her a hug and sat down next to her. She was very calm and dead like a fish in a bucket just lying there.

Right about that time, my sister Devilia came through the front door and was running up the steps wailing in a very odd tone that was surprising to me, almost like she was putting on the biggest act in her life. "Ohhhhh, Dad!" It sounded like drama 101 with all the fake, phony junk she could throw in.

I turned back to Mom, now wondering what the heck was going on, and said, "Are you okay?"

She said, "Yes, I'm fine."

I said, "Mom, are you going to get an autopsy performed on Dad?"

She said, "No, of course not, your father died of old age, and we don't need an autopsy to prove that."

I had my suspicions, of course, since weeks before my mother and I had conversations about my father's pills in the plastic daily pill separating container. Weeks prior to his death, my mother was stating that my father could not sleep and was up all night.

I said, "Doesn't he take a sleeping pill?"

And she said, "Yes."

I said, "Let me see the container."

She took me to the dresser in the hall, and there atop the dresser, was his pill container with the days of the week on them. She opened the tops of the compartments, and inside was multiple pills for day and night for each day of the week.

After careful inspection of the pills, I said, "Mom, you have the sleeping pills in the AM container, that is why he is not sleeping at night, which puts these pills in here."

She replied, very upset, "Devilia does this for me."

I said, "Well, tell her to stop it, and you get someone else to do it or do it yourself."

She said, "Okay."

The next few weeks were weird. Dad told me that he couldn't talk to people because the phone was downstairs, unless Mother brought the portable phone up to him.

I said to him, "Do you want me to put the regular phone up here on your nightstand?"

He said, "Yes, that would be so nice, then when I am lonely, I can call someone."

I said, "Okay."

Well, that would be easy for me to do, and it took only minutes for me to get the phone plugged in. He was so happy, and I loved seeing him smiling.

However, the next day, I was back at the house, and the phone was on the other side of the bed, opposite of his side on the nightstand.

I said to him, "How did the phone get over there?"

He said to me sadly, "Devilia, your sister, moved it on me, stating that I was calling her too much, and now I can't call anyone again."

I was really upset that my sister had moved the phone, so I moved it back.

When Devilia came later, she said to me, "I moved the phone because he was calling me all the time and even late, I don't want him calling me all hours of the night!"

I thought to myself, "How cruel can you get?"

I didn't say anything else to her other than, "Except I moved it back so he can get in touch with someone if he needs to, please don't move it on him again."

She went right over to the nightstand, unplugged the phone, and moved it again right in front of me. She was older, of course, and we called her the Popess! She was God, and she ruled, don't you know. I remember sitting there thinking to myself that she had done that to me all of my life. I remember thinking that I would not be a baby, and after she left, of course, I moved the phone back where it belonged, next to my father, where he could call if he wanted to talk with someone, so he would not be alone.

Later, on another day, I went to give him a foot massage and took my foot bath and tools. I had gotten the hot water in the tub and walked it into his bedroom. He was excited about getting the foot massage. Well, wouldn't you know who showed up—Ms. Devilia Popess herself walked up the steps and came into the bedroom spouting off how she had gotten Dad some tight leggings to help his leg circulation and was going to put them on him.

I said, "Please wait until I am finished giving him a foot massage, we are ready now, and the water is hot."

She said to me, pushing me aside, "I'm doing this right now, and Dad needs these on."

I looked over at my mother, and she said nothing. I just emptied the massager and set it in the bedroom, telling Dad that I would come another day when it was convenient and give him one. I wondered at that time if my sister was just being her unusual self or what was going on here; she was scary to me. It was weird. It was almost like she was trying her best to make me angry for some reason. Maybe Mom had told her what I said about the pills. I wasn't sure just yet, but I knew I wanted to get away from her. Far away from her, forever.

On the following week, Devilia asked me to sit with Dad while Mom went to her son's new baby's baptism.

I said, "Sure, but that Sunday, I have already promised a neighbor I would help her move that night and take her out for a goodbye dinner."

She said to me, "Sure, we'll be back by five o'clock."

She didn't come back till 7:30 PM. I was angry, and Dad kept wondering what happened to them. She didn't even say she was sorry, but it almost looked like she got pleasure out of screwing up my promise to my neighbor. I just left and said to myself, "She is being her usual self and 'I get my way and don't care what is important to you today' kind of day."

So after all the events and the one included when my dad was in the hospital and she lied to the nurses saying that my mother had dementia and then later abusing my dad in her home right in front of me, I was very suspicious of my sister's behavior yelling out at the top of her lungs, "Oh, Dad," while climbing the steps on that day that he passed away to get upstairs. I had begun to get that gut feeling that my sister might have killed him. But what would be her motive? Did she hate him and I didn't know it? Was it his money? What? I didn't know, and I was certainly not going to ask her.

At work the next day, I remember telling one of the girls as we walked at lunch that I think my sister might have killed my dad and I didn't know what to do about it. She was very nice and said that if I thought she might have, I should tell someone. I thought to myself, "Without proof, what would I say?" So I held off being in grief for my father, and not knowing what to do about it, I did nothing. I was in such a conundrum of emotional upset, and I hated it.

I attended the funeral, and I was so preoccupied by my personal strife in court with my ex-husband and my friends who were all asking me about the situation to see how I was holding up with both things happening. I remember that my daughter was not happy either that night with my family. The funeral came and went, and of course, I was tired.

I was told at work to take time off. He died on Sunday, and I came in on Monday, and the attorney that I worked for said to me, "What are you doing here?"

I said, "Well, I didn't know if I could have time off since I have only been here a few months."

She said, "You can have time off without pay."

I said, "Okay."

I took Tuesday and Wednesday off as well. Wednesday night at the funeral parlor, Val and Barb from the office came in and stated that I should not worry about work and to come in when I was ready. So I called in and said that I would not be in to work until Friday or Monday. I thought that was okay, but when I returned to work, no one had been helping with my work; there it lay, and it was all time-sensitive, and I felt bad and asked why no one had pitched in and completed my work while I was out. Tori said she was too busy and couldn't get to it. People relied on the work we did, and I was appalled by that statement. They clearly did not like me and did not do my work on purpose to make me look bad to the boss. That's okay, I'm sure she knew.

I made the mistake of telling one of girls in the office that I had asked Mark to come to the breakfast, and then she reacted in a very odd manner. We were washing our hands, and as we left the bathroom, she said, "You need to see a psychiatrist."

I was really upset that she would say that. I just walked away and came back into the office, and as I was walking down the aisle to my desk, she told me that he was a pervert and that I should not have anything to do with him. She said this in the aisle at work by my desk.

I said this to her, "He could sue you for that, and I'm a big girl, and I can take care of myself."

It seemed as though she said this because she was friends with another girl who I think liked him too; she was another attorney in the office. Young and pretty, and I think they knew Mark was interested in me. It was a nasty situation that I knew all too well. Well, I had a bunch of stuff going on in my life, and someone had access to my condo even after I changed the locks, which were messing with my head again. I felt so unsafe and always on edge. I was scared at work and at home. I went into work one day and asked the supervisor if I could take a long lunch as I was going to speak to the FBI about my personal stuff.

She said, "Yes," and I did.

The next day I came into work, and they said that I was fired for no reason and that this was my last day and I was not to talk to anyone on the way out. Well, I did, and I told them that I was being fired because I said I was going to the FBI. It was crazy. I never heard of such a thing—fired without any reason? How could they do that? The "at will doctrine," which is not a law but a doctrine—that's how. The doctrine that I think would later wreak havoc on Americans who no longer had job security if the company wanted to downsize; this would be their ticket to get rid of the old and in the with new, releasing many company dollars to put back into their pockets while working our youth for less and of course without benefits because they would still be at home and on their parents' health insurance. You know that kind of business thinking, and I hated it. I watched this for years and finally just looked the other way when people would lie to me. I hated it and would write a few stories and poems to get me over the hump of emotional madness. I spent a lot of time being mad about people.

I went into the Career Center for the Employment of Springfield and told them that I was fired again. They told me that I should just check in and begin to look for a job again. I told the gentlemen that I did just take a class on interviewing and worked with the job searcher as I was exhausted from what had happened and that I was fired again and asked them all to please help me. They told me that I should just get back to looking for another job. They told me that maybe I should go into sales.

I said, "I have no sales experience." They said that was okay.

I said, "Well, I will think about it."

I was also told by the community college counselor that I should take what was called a fast-track business class, which was one week long, and crammed into it are all the things you needed to know to start up your own business.

Anyway, I spent a long time looking for a job, and it took a while. I had gone to several employment agencies who said that they would not hire me because I had been fired a few times. I remember laughing inside to myself stating that I was the very one who would need the help and they could not give it.

One day a call came to come and interview for an insurance company. I did not know who they were or how I got the interview as I had not applied directly to them.

I went for the interview, and they were very nice. A woman owned the company, and her husband, son, daughter and nephew worked there too. At first they seemed to be a happy family, and they said they were a soccer family too, which pleased me since I played and coached my son, and my son was playing in college then as well. I told them that my son played soccer and I was his soccer coach when he was real young for four years.

They said, "Well, that's great."

I was curious why she would want to interview me. She wanted someone to scrub applications that the agents brought into the office. I told her I could learn that but had never done that before. I was a bit surprised that she would consider me. Later, I found out that it was easy just time-consuming, and you had to pay attention to detail, which I was excellent at; no wonder she hired me. I think at the time she wanted her office to be a little bit more professional as well, and I certainly had spent many years in professional offices in Springfield.

Anyway, I remember during the interview that her son winked at me. I felt uncomfortable about it and told my sister when I came home. She said it sounded a bit weird but told me that salespeople did stuff like that.

I said, "Okay."

Her ex-husband was a salesman who, of course, cheated on her multiple times before she divorced him. I would learn later that sales and lying would go hand in hand for many a salesperson, but not me.

So in a few days, she called me to tell me that she was offering me the job.

I said, "Great!"

She said, "Can you start in two days?"

I said, "Yes!" even though it was the middle of the week.

So on Wednesday, I started and met Lesal, the office manager, and Mandy, the receptionist-slash-secretary to Mr. M., her husband. He ran a small accounting business from an office behind the reception desk. There was one other woman, Ally, who worked directly in the office part-time as well. Small office, and I thought to myself, "This will be easy, not too many people to please." Well, little did I know that these people were not the churchgoing soccer family that I had pictured when first meeting them.

I asked Penny to please write me a letter stating my salary and benefits that she was giving to me.

She said, "Why don't you write it and I'll sign it."

I said okay and wrote the letter, but she never signed it nor gave it to me. I had no letter stating what she was going to give me as pay or benefits and that she had promised me a raise in a few months if I did a great job.

The second day on the job, Lesal was training me, and she made the statement that I was very sharp. I thought that was nice. While I was training with her, a gentleman came in to put his work in the basket and reached across me and stated, "Hi." I said, "Hello," back as he was very cute. A smile you could not forget. One of those wow smiles, and he was quite handsome.

The job was nice, and the people were very nice. The boss lady seemed to be very easy going yet expected a lot and was pleased that I could start late and stay late. I had an office of my own and liked the fact that my work was in one area. The door was always open, but I was in my own space and liked it. After a few weeks, the boss liked the fact that I would talk with her about ways to make the office more efficient.

She talked with me one night about how she was trying to figure out how to scan items in the copy machine to the computers in the office so that she could have e-files and no more paper files to save space. I told her I knew how to do it as I had been in an office that did that. She listened to me and stated to me that I just earned my salary for the year, and she was quite pleased. I remember thinking to myself, "Finally I'm not going to get fired as the boss really likes me and my work ethic." As I worked there longer, I realized that she would get information out of people and did some pretty unethical things to people to somehow punish them for the things they said or did that she did not like instead of just coming out and saying something. I never did anything else or told her anything else after that to help the office. She was clearly using me. I did not like her manipulating punishments and her phony agendas.

All the while, it was clear that the other women, especially Lesal, was not happy that Penny liked the job I was doing. I was trying very hard to keep a low profile, but it was hard on a daily basis as Mandy and Lesal would make fun of me and make me look bad. Maybe they had told Penny things about me that weren't true, and she believed them, and maybe that was why she began to treat me bad too. Nasty women can be very nasty to a point where no matter what you say, people will believe them if they want to and don't bother to ask you questions anymore. They don't believe their instincts; they believe who they think is a friend when in fact they were doing everything to undermine her and the company. When she would be on vacation, Mandy and Lesal would be gone for hours, and I didn't say anything, just showed up on time and did my work. I guess they thought this was acceptable because maybe she didn't pay them enough for what they did for her and the disdain among all of them was evident to me. The boss was abusive, so the workers didn't care any longer, and I was stuck in the middle. It was awful. What I thought was going to be a small family business turned out to be a nightmare. The worst place I ever worked.

Penny's husband, Mr. M, had come into my office and handed me a printout of an e-mail he received and handed it to me and said, "Read this." It was a joke about the elderly and orgasms. I didn't find it funny but stated that my father said he was happiest when he was asleep and handed it back to him.

I thought to myself, "You weird freak, keep away from me."

A few days later, when I had time to look over the hard drive on my desk computer, I had also found some pictures on my hard drive that were in a file someone created and were of children and animals, and it was porn referred to as child pornography or animal bestiality. I was really upset and went straight to Mrs. Penny M's office and told her of these items. She said they must have been the girl who had my job before me, Carrie.

I said that she should have erased the items from her hard drive before someone else got on the computer. So I went straight to my office and deleted all those files. I told her later that I dumped the files and that her computer man could search to see when the files were placed there, so she would know the exact person who did it.

I also found an e-mail from Lesal's husband going to Carrie, the girl who had my job before me. The e-mail was a dirty joke, and I put it upside down on Lesal's chair and didn't say a word to her as I knew she would be embarrassed. I don't know if they were an item, but it was none of my business, and later Lesal just looked at me and said, "Thanks so much."

After that, Lesal asked me if I could be her sister. We talked a lot about my sisters and how much fun we had together. She said she and her sister did not get along at all.

I said that she could certainly be my sister and I would love for her to do some things with me my sisters. I told her my one sister was going to have an art showing and that she could come with me, and she said all right.

She just looked back at me and said, "Some people have time to write such junk, huh."

I just said, "Yeah, I don't know when they would have time for that."

I was not impressed by her husband at all. But maybe they were good friends, but Lesal never talked about Carrie at all at work, so I think that might be why Carrie didn't work there any longer. I didn't know and didn't ask, but later it would be revealed that on the other computer in the outer office that I would be moved to that Carrie had emotional problems that also I could not believe was not erased from the computer after she left. Also, personal information about her and her children after divorce and seeking medical help. Divorce is nasty, and people who haven't been through it don't understand.

Mandy in the office started to call me Doris Day jokingly, but she did not like the nice comments I was getting in the office, and she started to make dumb blonde comments, too, when I would do something wrong. She was tormenting me in her own nasty way but was insecure about herself, which was the reason why she was treating me that way. One day I brought in some dessert items as Penny asked me to bring some things in for the Friday meeting.

Mandy's comment was, "Oh, the guys are going to like you for this!" She also said, "You are just trying to impress the guys."

I said, "No, I'm not."

I never did anything to impress anyone; I am quite happy with who I am and have been my whole life. I think it's why people liked me sometimes. I was always confident about myself but not in a bragging way. I do things because I want to, and sometimes it has nothing to do with anyone else.

Mandy was divorced, and we would talk about our problems and talk about being alone and responsible for everything. She still had two children in high school. One day I asked her if she wanted two tickets to Six Flags that I got for free for her teenagers. She said yes, and I brought them to work and gave them to her. She said to me that she and Mickey used them to go and that he wanted to thank me for the tickets.

I was in my office, and she brought him in, and he said, "Thanks so much for the tickets. Mandy and I had a good time, I could just kiss your toes."

I was very surprised by what he said looked up and saw Mandy's face in disarray and stated, "That would be her department."

And Mandy looked very upset, and they both left the office. Later, Mandy came into my office and stated that he was just kidding and didn't mean anything by it. I could clearly see that she was upset. After Mickey left later, I just stated that no one had ever said anything to me like that directly at work and that if he were my boyfriend, I would kick him to the curb if he said something like that to another girl in from of me. She stated that he was just goofing around and didn't mean anything by it. She said salesmen just talked like that.

I said, "It's all right, Mandy, and I let it go."

She made me feel weird, and I knew that it was not going to be smooth sailing with Mandy any longer, but little did I know, she was out to get me fired.

Then a few days later, I was talking on the phone with Albert, that cute guy that won me over with just his smile and nice demeanor, and told him that he had errors on his work.

He said, "Okay I'll be in to fix them in an hour or so," and I said okay.

Mandy came into my office and grabbed his work off my desk and said that she would take care of it.

I said, "What are you doing?"

She said that she would handle his work. Clearly, something was going on with Albert and also with Mandy. I was upset and didn't say a thing. I thought this was too weird. I guess because I had told her that he was cute. When I said that, she made this horrible comment to me, "Oh, you like 'em young!"

I just walked away from her. She was nuts. I just commented on how cute he was, and she said he was twenty-eight, and I said, "Oh my god! I didn't know he was that young, he didn't look it or act it."

I thought to myself, "Would it be awful for me to date a man that was twenty years younger?" I don't know, but at the time, I personally did not think so. Later, I would learn that people don't look upon that as something wholesome. I don't know why. I think most people are twisted and I'm liberal-thinking and never would rule out anything that seemed right with both people. I guess I don't judge people or situations either about people. I do know that Mandy was making fun of me, and it was ugly.

I asked Mandy and Lesal and Penny if they wanted to go to the Botanical Gardens one night as there was a Chihuly glass blowing show.

Mandy said, "No," and Lesal said, "Yes."

Penny said, "I'll see."

Anyway, I went home and purchased my ticket online. Lesal was the only one who went with me, and we had a great time. We walked and talked, and I took pictures of all the glass displays, which led to a magical night of wandering around into the dusk looking at this splendid display of intricately twisted colored glass into shapes that would wow your eyes, camera, and many books of his works. We finished up the night with a light dinner in the garden restaurant, consisting of appetizers, sandwiches, salads, wines and drinks. It was fun, and we sat and talked about life and our families, and Lesal asked me if I had a special someone.

I said, "No, but I am interested in someone a lot younger than me." I asked her if she thought that was a good idea.

She said, "Sure, why not, if both of you are in agreement with it, go for it."

I told her it was one of the salesmen at work, and she said, "Which one?"

I said, "No, I better not say which one."

Then she began telling me of how she and her husband met and how happy they were. I was happy to see her happy about a marriage since she had been married for quite some time. She was clearly in love with her husband, and I was happy that she had a special someone for so long. I did not tell her that it was Albert I was talking about until later in the office when I first called him about doing something sometime.

He said, "Sre, your number is in my cell base, and I'm with a client right now, but we'll talk."

I said, "Okay."

Lesal told me later he had a girlfriend, and I was a bit crushed that he didn't say anything. I did not know, and I never approached him again in the office. I did call once to see if he wanted to ride to Springfield so I could ask him questions myself, as I didn't believe what people say at work about others. But it got weird with Kenny and I decided I had better not drive anywhere with him since he told me he was friends with Kenny. Oh, I wish I had just so he would have understood me and what and why I think the way I did. Later I would learn that he thought I was old enough to be his mother. It hurt like a knife to the heart, which would later be twisted in for the kill with the things he did and said about me, which eternally made me cry inside for many years to come, perhaps until my death as I had never been publically personally humiliated before about my feelings. I would think later that this is how movie stars must feel when people lie about them and yet it's too late already in the public reading arena with no recourse but to let it lie.

Then Mrs. M. told me one day that she wanted me to switch offices with Lesal and I would do the work that Lesal was doing and vice versa. I was shocked, and she did not ask me if I wanted to—just told me. Lesal did not look happy about it. She told us to move offices on Wednesday. On Wednesday, Lesal came in all dressed up and looked upset and said she had a lunch date.

I said, "I thought we were moving offices today," and she said, "I'm busy today."

So Mrs. M. and I moved all the computer stuff and set things up. We had a good time, and I remember how I felt bad for Lesal. Anyway, Lesal from that point on definitely gave me wrong information about everything, and I knew it, but I didn't complain, just did my work and kept my mouth shut. But the weeks went on, and Lesal got worse, and she and Mandy were making my life horribly miserable on purpose. It was clear the woman in the office were at war with me. One day it got really bad, and I knew I needed help.

I called Albert one morning from my cell phone on the way to work and asked if I could talk with him and told him that the women were at war with me and were screwing things up on purpose for me. I asked him if he knew Mandy was going out with Mickey and that Mickey had said that he wanted to kiss my toes with her standing in front of me and that I thought that she was mad because of that and I was not interested in Mickey at all.

He said, "No, and Mickey is a married man."

I said, "I didn't know that!" and asked him if he had ever gone out with Mandy as she ripped his work off my desk. I thought at the time maybe she liked Albert too.

He said, "No, I haven't gone out with Mandy, and I have a girlfriend, and she's the one, so please don't include me in on the office gossip."

I said, "I was not gossiping but looking for some help," as I did not have friends at work and only talked with him about this issue.

He said, "I don't like gossip," and hung up on me.

Later I would learn that he was personal friends with Lesal and Mandy and never told me that. He made a fool out of me in the office, acting like he cared about me, when all the while he cared nothing at all about me. It was all a joke on me.

I also left a message on Penny's phone that the women in the office were at war with me. When I got into work, Penny came up to my desk and stated that the women at work were not at war with me real loud. Lesal was in her office and could hear everything.

I was surprised that she would do that to me and stayed at my desk.

Mandy immediately started to treat me with disdain and make obnoxious comments to me like, "Your desk is so clean, you are always so nice to everyone, you're trying to impress the guys with this or that." She was clearly jealous or was told to do this to me to get rid of me. After all, Mandy had been there for nineteen years, and I was getting tired of her nasty comments and juvenile behavior. It was unbecoming and made my work environment an awful place to work. A hostile work environment gone bad again—I couldn't take it. My tears came nightly, and I wondered where the good people were.

Kenny was constantly making me feel uncomfortable every day, and it was not good for work, and I felt as though I was in a hostile work environment.

One day, at lunch, Mr. M. ate with me alone at the table, and we talked, and he was very nice, but I did feel comfortable at the end of the lunch as he was asking me a lot of personal questions.

My sister told me that I should stay out of the conference room and eat my lunch out of the office and make sure that I am not alone with him again. He made me feel very uncomfortable as he was making statements like, "You don't really know who your soul mate is when you are young and you get married." It was clear to see he was not happy with Mrs. M.

I just said, "No person is perfect and divorce is the worst thing that could ever happen in your life."

I was starting to get to know some of the salesmen, and Albert was by far the apple of my eye; I had no idea he hated me. He was so handsome, but I was seeing if he was nice too. After a few weeks of talking with him, I knew he was. He seemed very interested and would talk so sweet on the phone all the time and when he came into the office. I did learn later it was just him being nice; he was not interested in me at all, per his statement to me months later and in writing that he filed a stalking order against me for coming to his house to try and get the story straight and tell him what was going on in the office as well as how I really felt about him after I got fired since I pretty much ignored him in the office after my call to him saying to forget about driving to Springfield. But it never happened; he was lied to and just didn't care about me at all for either the reason that people scared him off, or he just was in love with someone else. I never did get to ask him, but he did say my love letter to him was weird and his friends said it was weird. Maybe that was a guy statement; maybe it was just truth. I don't know, and it will make my mind wonder till I die, unless of course he reads this story and wants to call me. I guess the only way of knowing the truth is by words of response, even if they are years later—that is if I would ever believe anything he had to say. But it does not matter anymore anyway, since when someone is interested, they know right away and tell you about it. I knew that but loved him anyway and stayed to myself at work.

One of the salespeople in the office Jenny was getting married, and everyone was talking about going to the wedding, but I was not invited. I think she handed out the invitations before I started working there, but I did want to go and thought about how fun it would be to dance with Albert and get to know him and see if we had anything in common as I never asked him any questions of a personal nature at work at all— you know, loving imagination which I had not had much of in my lifetime. I guess I was lonely and really never wanted to be with anyone really, just happened upon him. He only gave little items of personal use as we would talk. He was always a gentleman. I don't go out to look for men, just think you meet them here and there. Maybe you meet the wrong ones sometimes, maybe not.

I said to Mandy one day that Albert was kind of cute as she was telling me that she was dating Mickey in the office. She stated, "Oh, you like 'em young." I thought this to be very unprofessional, but she was just that.

I said, "I think he is a nice guy," and walked away.

I remember thinking, "What kind of person says such a thing about another person?" I was young at heart and never even questioned his age. He didn't look twenty-eight to me, and I guess later I would learn that I didn't look fifty to him and everyone else in the office.

After that, it seemed that I was smitten by him even more, as I usually don't talk about personal stuff that much at work anymore. He was the only man who was not hitting on me but would just talk sweet and spend time asking me about my children and my weekend. He was special for sure and a gentleman. I guess because he loved someone else and was not interested in me that way at all. He made that clear.

So one day on, my lunch hour, for the first time ever in my life, I called a guy from my cell phone. I called Albert and said, "Hi, It's Julia from the office, and I was wondering if you would want to do something sometime?"

He sounded happy and said "Julia from the office, yeah, I'll put your number in my cell base, but right now I am with a client."

And I said, "Okay, I'll talk to you later."

When he had talked with me in the office and told me that he was from Springfield where my son was at college, I thought to myself that maybe he could drive down with me one weekend and see his friends and family, and on the drive down, we could get to know each other as I was driving down there by myself all the time and maybe he could use a free ride home to see his parents. I thought I could see if he would be interested in someone older than himself, like me. But much to my dismay, we never did go because I was afraid Kenny would fire him since he had a crush on me.

I told Lesal that I asked him to drive to Springfield, and she said, "Oh, do you think he is handsome?"

And I said, "Yes."

Then she said, "Well, he has a girlfriend, it will be interesting."

I didn't know what she meant by that at all, but I let it go. I did not know he had a girlfriend, but I thought he would have said he wasn't interested in doing something if she was a special person, right? He would have said, "Thanks anyway, but I have a girlfriend right now." I guess guys are different from girls, at least this girl. I always tell the truth and expect that others should as well.

I would see Albert only on Fridays pretty much unless he came in for something else. He tried very hard to talk with me at my desk, and he would always get messages on Fridays while in a meeting, and I would go and give them to him at the end of the meeting. We would smile, and I would say, "How are you doing?" and he would say, "Fine," and that was it. Maybe I would imagine in my mind that he had people called on purpose. I guess it was just him forwarding his phone number to the office number while in the meeting. I guess I wanted to feel special in my mind, and I was funny in love. Funny, isn't it? In love with someone who didn't even want anything to do with me. Everyone thought I was the girl with tons of boyfriends, when in fact I sit home alone all the time. I used to shake my head and think to myself, "Why do they think this about me. Is it because I'm pretty and outgoing, is that why? I guess they don't know me that well and I guess I give off that persona for some reason." I had no clue why!

The office situation was getting harder for me, and I was not comfortable any longer at all. So I called Albert from home one night and left a message that said, "Would you like to drive down to Springfield on Friday afternoon with me?" Then I hung up and thought it was probably not a good idea. So I called him back and said maybe we better not do this as I was afraid he might get into some kind of trouble or get fired at work. I regret I did that; actually, I regret I made any call to anyone at that office. Or tried to be friends with anyone; they were the most evil people who gossiped and manipulated along with being dishonest to their clients. Clearly, not a place for me to work ever.

But one week I had asked Kenny if I could get off early as the soccer schedule had changed for my son and now the game in Kansas City had been changed to a later time and if I left at noon, I could make the game.

He said, "No."

Anyway, that Friday at the meeting, Lesal came up to me and said, "Take these cards of Luke's and put them in the box after he initials them."

I said, "Okay."

And the meeting was going, on and I had nothing to do, so I initialed them for Luke and put them in the box. In the meeting, Kenny asked who was going out of town this weekend, and Luke said, "I am going to Kansas City."

I could hear the conversation from my desk. As soon as the meeting was over, Kenny hauled Luke into the office and fired him. I could hear them in the office, and then Mrs. M., who was out of town, called me and asked to speak to Kenny. I stated that he was in her office with someone, if she wanted me to interrupt them, and she stated no. Then the door opened, and out they came, and Lesal came to my desk and said that Kenny had just fired Luke. I thought this was weird, and at that time, I knew Kenny had it bad for me for sure, even though he was married. I in no way gave him any inclination that I was interested at all in him; he was married very unhappily but married, and I am not ever interested in married men, ever!

Anyway, I told Albert on the message that I would be very professional in the office. The next day, he came in and came to my desk and said, "You are the bomb."

I thought, "What does that mean?" Looking up to him, I said back to him, "So are you."

That was all that was said. I wanted to tell him that I really cared very much for him. I hated that I made that decision and will regret that for the rest of my life. Later on, he said things and did things and so maybe not.

I had told Lesal that I bought concert tickets and was going to ask Albert if he wanted to go with me back before I knew he had a girlfriend. When he said that he had a girlfriend to me, then I didn't ask him but asked Lesal if she might like to go instead. She said, "No." The night of the concert, Lesal kept saying to me to call Albert, and I would reply he was on vacation. She said, "Call him anyway."

I said many times no, and she then was stating that her secret boyfriend was calling her, too (I thought she had lost her rocker), so I finally called him, and he said to me so angrily, "I'm still on vacation, Julia. I will take care of the office problem when I get back in town."

I hung up and told Lesal what he said.

That night too, Kenny had on blue jeans for the first time in the office, and he was hanging around the conference room by my desk at the end of the day, which he never did; he always left an hour or so before me, and I was feeling weird about it. Lesal must have told him that I was going to ask Albert, and she must have told Kenny. The fact that he wore blue jeans that day made me wonder if he was waiting to see if I would ask him, since Lesal knew I did not have a date for the other ticket—who knows at that point. That was the impression that my mind had at that very moment. I was upset and left work and went to the concert by myself. It was a wonderful concert by James Blount, and I wanted him to sing to me my favorite song he wrote, "You're Beautiful." It was my favorite, and that night he would sing like I never heard him on his CDs or the radio; it was new kind of sound for him, and I liked it. This young Englishman had certainly made it worth my while to sit alone by myself at a concert even though the baseball playoff games were going on just down the street. I am a big baseball fan and love to watch them play and win. That year in 2006, they won the World Series, and that year was the year they built and finished the new stadium, and it too, indeed, was awesome. It was a wonderful night even all alone without a date or someone who cared for me. I was finding that I could go out on my own by myself and be perfectly happy with that as well for the first time. I didn't like being alone, but I vowed that year I would not sit at home and not go somewhere because I did not have a date.

After that night, I did not tell Lesal anything about my personal life. She was manipulating things at work to make me look bad, and I told her that I knew she was doing it one day and asked her if she wanted me to tell Penny, and she said no. She kept talking about prearrangement dating and how her daughters had that done.

I said to her one day, "I don't like anyone picking anyone for me."

I said that to try and get her to stop talking to the other sales guys about me as I knew she was. She was underhanded, and I'm sure the guys were asking her to find out everything she could about me, maybe even Penny asked her to for her son, Kenny, who knew what these people were doing at this point, and I didn't care any longer. I needed for her to stop whatever she was doing. The guys were waiting for me at lunch outside the door and questioning me. She had guys showing up late at night at six when I went home. One night Saul was hanging around all week long late, and by Thursday, I was feeling very uneasy. I think Lesal knew it. Janet got on the overhead and said out loud, "Saul, it is time to go home, please leave the building now." I felt like I didn't even want to leave at all but go to my sister's house not too far from the office.

One Friday night, I had nothing to do, and so I was going to go to the movies after work. Lesal told me to go and see *The Illusionist*. She said it was a very good movie for me to see and that I would take interest in it. She kept going on and on about it and that I needed to see it. I didn't know what she meant at all. It was weirdo.

So I said, "Okay, I'll go and see that tonight." And I went to see it. The movie was about a woman who worked for a man who was obsessed with her and would follow her around and have people watch her. I think she was trying to tell me that Kenny was doing that to me at work, possibly having people follow me. She was really not nice at all to me, and I felt like she was using this to upset me. She stated all the time when the phone rang, I would answer and someone would hang up, that it was my secret boyfriend. I never had a secret boyfriend ever. She was weird. She stated all the time that her secret boyfriend would call her at work.

When her mother passed away, we all went to the funeral and then to Lesal's house afterward, and I bought her some flowers and brought them to work. She stated that one flower arrangement was from her secret boyfriend. I thought this weird for someone her age to be talking like this. At her home, she barely talked with me and only introduced me to a few people. She seemed weird, and I just went into the other room and sat down at the table and ate and then left. Her mother-in-law, Posey, talked with me, and she kept asking me questions about other places I had worked; it was odd, and I knew that she was questioning me for Lesal or someone. It was strange, and I was being interrogated at her home. These people were not nice, for sure. Cordial and phony, but not genuinely nice to me.

One day, there were new people starting, and they had lunch in the conference room and said that I should come too. There were three or four new people. One was a woman named Angel. She was very nice and said she had worked in a restaurant in New York. My daughter worked as a pastry chef in New York, and I thought that was weird. She also stated that she wanted me to bring in some items that we had been talking about in different recipes. So I said I would. We all sat down to eat, and everyone was nice. We talked, and Henry the trainer from the insurance company paid for the lunch, so I said, "Thank you very much," and went back to my desk to work. One of the new men came in to talk with me and was nice, and he stated that he was going on vacation and would start in a few weeks, and he would see me then.

I said, "Okay."

There was talk in the office of a Halloween party. Mandy kept talking about it, and the guys would talk about what costumes they were wearing. I, however, was not invited. Jeff was having it, but I guess he didn't feel I was a person he wanted to invite, which was okay—just seemed odd that everyone was invited but me. Again I was not included in the outside work fun. Work seemed to be that way for me for various reasons. I never get invited to go out with the gang or to parties. I guess I was too nice, too cute, too everything that men liked, so they didn't invite me so their wives didn't meet me and women at work didn't like me either. At this point in my life, I really didn't care any longer; I lived life and was finally happy with myself.

It was boss's day, and Lesal was still out because of her mother's death. I asked around at work if they gave Penny something for boss's day, and Mandy said, "Yeah."

I said, "I'll get something as Lesal is out and we can give it to her."

I got a flower arrangement at my local florist and brought it in.

Lesal was back by then, and I said to her, "Why don't we take Penny to lunch on Friday for boss's day?"

And she said, "Okay, I can set that up since you got the flowers, and I'll pay so you don't have to pay anything."

I said, "Okay."

She asked Penny, her husband, and her son Kenny to go along with me, Mandy, and Kelly. Mandy did not go, but the rest of us did. I was not happy that she asked Kenny and Kenny Sr. to go along. But she did, and there was nothing I could do about it. I went, and when we got into the restaurant, it was clear that Lesal and Sally and Penny arranged seating so I would be sitting next to Kenny Jr. I was quite uncomfortable and wanted to throw up. I was pleasant and ate and then went back to work. I asked Lesal why she had asked the men to go to lunch too.

She said, "Well, it is boss's day."

Mr. M. was not my boss, nor was Kenny. I was upset, and she knew it; most of all she knew why as I had told her how one woman at work had really messed up my life and said I had an affair with the boss when I had not. She knew and was doing it just to piss me off and upset me. That was clear, unless someone told her to do it. At that point, I didn't know and didn't care.

The next week, Lesal asked me to go to lunch with her.

I said, "Okay, where would you like to go?"

She said, "I don't know?"

And I said, "Your pick!"

Then I got my coat on, and she stated that Mr. M. was coming along too.

I said, "No, Lesal, I do not want to go to lunch with Mr. M.," and I left the building.

She came out shortly after and got into my car. She stated that she did not know why I was upset. I told her that she knew perfectly why I was upset, and I drove to Bread Company. We ordered lunch, and I began to talk to her about what she was doing. She said that she was not doing anything.

I said to her, "Yes, you are, I specifically told you that I will not go out to lunch at work with any man in the office because of what was said about me in previous jobs."

She said, "Well, I didn't know this would upset you."

Knowing full well that it would, she made me want to drive off and leave her there without a way back to the office. She was lying. I told her that Albert was the only person I liked at work, and she got all upset and said I didn't tell Penny about Albert. I didn't know what she meant. Nothing happened between Albert and I other than he didn't want to go out with me, so I said to her, "Okay," and I told Lesal that I was not interested in anyone else at M. and that I wish that she would pass that along to everyone as she was the office gossiping with the guys. She said to me that she was not and said, "I have to go and pick up my dry cleaning, and I'll meet you in the car."

Albert and I never had any relationship at all other than talking on the phone. He never did anything inappropriate at all and was always a gentleman on the phone. Lesal was manipulating everything to make me look bad; she was mad at the boss for switching our jobs and offices, and she was doing everything in her power to make my life a misery while employed there. I think she quite enjoyed it; she and Mandy liked friends manipulating someone else's demise in the workplace. Her daughter was an attorney, and she knew how to make my life miserable. Lesal always talked about psychology and how she was good at it. She was friends with Jeff in the office, and they talked all the time.

Jeff used to hang out on Tuesday afternoons, and I never could understand why. Then I realized that when they switched jobs with Lesal and myself, they were watching who was hanging around on the days that sales leads came in by FedEx. I had the suspicion that either Mandy or Lesal were giving leads to some of the salesmen. I was watching who was not making the same money as before and the names of the people whose income decreased after I was put in place to watch and distribute the lead cards. The company paid big money for those leads, and the salesmen got them on a pro-rating as to how they were selling. If Mandy and Lesal were giving them out to boyfriends and friends, it would cost the company and be showing favoritism in the office amongst the sales staff.

One evening, Penny had me in her office, and she said to me, "The lead cards will now be your job to dole out when I am gone or on vacation," as she went often.

I said, "That's fine, I would be happy to learn that job and be in charge of those as well."

Lesal was in her office sitting on a chair at the filing cabinet in front of Penny's desk, filing something, and the look she gave to me when Penny gave those instructions to me was not good; she looked like she wanted to kill me for sure. I now knew without a doubt that Lesal hated me.

Lesal was also friends with her daughter, Janet. Janet was always in my drawer in the money box where the petty cash and stamps and gas cards were kept. The box was not locked, and I told Penny one day that she was helping herself to the box and if that was okay.

She said, "Of course, that is my daughter."

I said, "Okay, I was just making sure since now I'm in charge of keeping track of what goes where, just to make sure that was all right in the office."

Earlier Janet stated to me one day that I was so honest.

She said, "I'll bet you are the type that doesn't even sneak popcorn into the movies."

I said to her quite frankly, "Yes, you are right, I don't sneak anything into the movies."

She said, "I'm not surprised," and kept on walking.

She was so arrogant; I couldn't believe it. Was she making fun of me, or just trying to find out if I was honest? I had no clue at this point in time, but I did not like the comment.

She was friends with Mandy. I saw them talking all the time. For Jenny's wedding, they both went out and had their nails done together and talked all the time at work about the wedding and the shower that I was not invited to. Janet sat at my desk one day, asking me all kinds of personal questions about being with someone that had children from a previous marriage.

I said to her, "I've only been divorced once, and I know that I would treat anyone's children as I would my own as that is the kind of person I am."

I wondered if this was the truth about her relationship with someone else or if she was snooping. Her older brother was interested in me, and he had a son, but he was married, and so I was not interested at all for that reason.

One day she said to me, "Is that your car out front with the Pro Life stickers on it?"

It was a few weeks after I had started, and the sticker said, "If you are religious, then you can't be Pro Abortion."

I said, "Yes, that is my car out there!"

Mandy came walking into the conference room and said, "I know the M's will like that, you got balls, don't you?"

I just laughed back at her and stated, "I have tennis balls at home, Mandy, yeah, I do have balls!"

She made me laugh, but clearly, she herself did not like the stickers on my car; maybe that would be the reason why she treated me so badly. I would never know, nor later did I care. I would learn later that she did not like religions, priests who molest, and hated the religious church for its stance on ignoring priests who molest as if I was a priest or molester; little did she know that I myself was a victim of molestation and abuse. She revealed this point at lunch one day. She was mad at my comments about how I only believe what I know to be true, and if someone was found guilty in court, then I guess I could say I guess they were guilty; otherwise, I don't know. She and Lesal were ganging up on me on this topic at lunch, and finally, I said, "Let's change the subject." They both left early, and I finished my lunch and went back to the office.

Mandy was supposed to come to my house to play tennis one day but didn't come; instead she called me up and stated she was drunk after going to Jenny's bachelorette party and called me to say she would not be coming over after all. I had planned lunch and everything, so it was disappointing, and it upset me.

She said, "We'll just play at Mark's house some night after work."

She never came to my house or anything ever again, nor did I invite her. I think she just wanted to get my address and phone number for her own personal use to give to others and see where I lived. She was a devious person, and that was clear in the first few weeks. When she told me that she was going to Jenny's bachelorette party and we went shopping to get some things, she kept talking dirty in the store and picking out some pretty racy lingerie. I, on the other hand, picked out some pretty romantic things and said to her, "I'll give you the money for this, and you can take it to the party for Jenny."

She said, "No, you don't have to do that."

I said, "Yeah I want to!"

She said, "No."

Lesal and I finished walking around the store, and Mandy slapped her hand on her butt and said she had a thong on.

I said, "Yeah, my daughters call them butt floss, I don't have any."

And we all laughed. We all went to lunch and then back to work.

It was clear by the things that Mandy would say at work that she was not conservative about anything—which by the way was her choice—but I felt that she was giving me a hard time because I was. My bumper stickers said, "Pro-Life. It's a child not a choice." This was not me judging people, just me making a personal statement for people to think about. But some people view this as a direct attack against someone that had another opinion. We in the religious church who believe what we believe because of our beliefs should not be discriminated against nor should we be fired because of what we put on our cars. I never discussed religion at work unless someone else brought it up.

Mandy always brought it up and said that Lesal was Jewish and that Mr. M. was always asking her questions about the Jewish religion. Lesal had worked there for six years and Mandy for nineteen years. Mandy and Lesal were friends, and I didn't realize how close until Lesal's mother died. Mandy was manipulating me about that too. It was apparent that Mandy did not like me or what I stood for and was constantly trying to undermine me and had Lesal coming right behind her to help in her efforts. The night we all went to Lesal's house, Mandy made sure I went on the night that the other salesmen were not there. She did not want me to be around any of them or maybe just her Mickey.

One day, Lesal said to me that Mandy was not upset until I went to talk to Penny about Mickey. I stated that I never talked to Penny about Mickey until long after Mandy started acting obnoxious. Lesal looked surprised and gave me a weird look, like someone had told her otherwise. This office was clearly gossip-central and full of unhealthy sexual innuendo that I would not nor could I ever approve of. At this point, I didn't care who did what in that office; I just left after work and went home.

There was so much lying going on at the office and so much gossip and not much work being done. No wonder the guys were complaining about the girls in the office to me.

Mandy and Lesal would tell me to not complete anything on an application because the guys were just lazy and they would make the same mistakes every week and I was to call them and get them back into the office to correct something. They were working on commission only and did not need to come back to the office every day to fix minor things that could be done by me. That was how I felt about it, and they were giving the guys a hard time, especially ones they did not like for whatever their reasons were. I always treated everyone fairly and justly even if they don't happen to be the kind of person I think they should be. I would never show favoritism not even for a child of my own in the workplace. My work ethic is above reproach and would never be compromised by anyone or anything. I am a strong and honest person, and my parents are to be commended for this personal trait; it doesn't exist too often today, and I am quite proud that I can say I am hardworking, honest, and above all will do the best job I can do for everyone. But I will not lie for anyone.

My honesty, I feel, had been getting me into trouble in the workplace. Especially at this business office, full of whatever. The word *whatever* stands for horrible moments at work.

Many people were making big money on insurance. Their top salesperson, who was a woman named Judy, made $120,000 a year or better. It was October, and we had two months to go. She was outstanding, but this was a great deal of money for a black woman with no formal education. She was nice and said, "People either need it or they don't. Insurance is easy to sell."

Penny knew I was not comfortable at work anymore. I asked her if we could go to lunch and talk about things.

I said she could fill me in on the guys at work as they were getting out of line, but I didn't tell her that all; I wanted to talk about Mandy and Lesal.

She said, "Okay, we'll go on Thursday."

Then she came to my desk and asked me if Lesal and Mandy could come too. I was shocked and said okay. So we went to lunch, and Penny set up Mandy and Lesal, asking them what they did with the guys work that were turned in wrong, and they answered honestly and said they gave them a hard time and told them to come in and fix it even if they had to call five times. I think Mandy and Lesal thought I put Penny up to asking them that question, but I did not. I wanted Penny to go to lunch to see which guys she thought would lie to me about stuff and who were always honest as I felt some were using me and I knew it. I hate being lied to. The gas cards were one area where they were lying to me, and someone was taking them, and the drawer was not locked, and the names were kept as to who won the cards on Mondays and Fridays. Some of the guys came on strong, and I think Lesal used to give some of them things even when she shouldn't have because she made friends with them. It was hard, and I know I didn't judge anyone as I saw people be abused by Penny, but maybe she had reasons that I did not know about. I knew she didn't like Mandy dating Mickey because she told me so. I was surprised that she would talk about Mickey and Mandy that way as Mandy had worked for her for nineteen years.

Penny said to me one day, "Mandy will do anything for money, anything."

I thought this was an awful thing to say about someone she had running her front desk for so many years, so I questioned her loyalty to her employees but later learned that maybe she had good reason to believe that because Mandy, I think, was stealing from her. Cash, gas cards, and possibly getting money on the side from the guys for leads that she would take out of the FedEx folder and keep to give to the guys and her boyfriend instead of giving them to Penny.

One day Penny asked me about her credit card. She said someone had been using it erroneously. I told her I had a similar incident in my life with someone using my debit card online, and so I stopped the card. I think she was trying to tell me that Mandy used her credit card for things other than food for the meetings on Mondays and Fridays. I told her if she thought that, she should stop the card and change the number and never give her card out to anyone. If she wanted a card for Mandy to use, she should get on card just for that and give to Mandy when she needed to and not to use it for any other use herself. It was great business advice.

I was doing all the customer service work for the company, and many days I took calls from people who would cry that salesmen were selling elderly people insurance replacing there Medicare and Medicaid. The social workers were yelling at me that someone had sold them the wrong thing and took away their benefits, and now they had bills coming in that were not being paid because it was not covered under the new insurance plan. It was unreal what I was hearing. I approached Penny, and she said that the salespeople knew exactly what they were doing and that everything was fine. I had senior citizens calling me up daily and crying, and it really upset me very much at work, as I had just lost my father months prior, and I thought to myself this would have been such a horrible thing for one of these salespeople to have done to my parents.

Penny said one day that she wanted me to go through the Medicare drawer and organize it.

I said that I would and began the task. Near the end of the task, I was working on the file drawer with the *W*s, and lo and behold, there was my mother's name showing she held a policy with M. Insurance Agency. I did not know that; my mother never said a word after I took the job there. Anyway, I just glanced at it in curiosity and found that my mother's birth date was wrong, which of course put her in a lower bracket to be charged less for the policy. I thought to myself, Would my mother lie to an insurance man? I thought this was weird. I didn't think to make a copy of it but later said something to my sister Sophia about it, and she said, "No, Mom would not lie about something like that." I told her it made me feel bad, and I was upset and didn't say anything to anyone. Would my mother lie? I guess I would know later that yes, indeed, she would. It would shock my world, and of course, make it one world that I never dreamed for myself. I thought differently of my mother, and I guess at the time since I just broke up with a liar, I was astounded at the fact that mother was just the kind of person that my ex-husband was as well. Was my father always antagonizing my mother because she treated him in a way which we never saw? She sure revealed her true self to me after his death, which I never, ever thought my mother was that kind of person, or was she just upset at my father's death? I don't know, and at this point of my, life I don't care to think about it anymore.

One day I had a gentleman call me at work, and he stated that he wanted to cancel his insurance because he was not doing business with a company that was not honest.

I stated, "What do you mean?"

He told me of the undercover interview on the TV that was done about the insurance company. I knew nothing of it, and Penny did not tell me about it either. I was shocked and went home to watch the news that night. Sure enough, the company was under investigation for selling policies to the elderly that took away needed benefits that they already had with Medicare and Medicaid. The undercover camera caught it all on tape, and there it was on the news. I couldn't believe it; someone actually caught these criminals on tape and put on the Nightly News, and of course, I was overjoyed at this viewing and the aspect that someone was going to stop them and put them out of business. I was so upset that neither Penny nor anyone else at the company said anything to me at all of the incident that aired on the news. I just had people on the phone crying, and I didn't know what to say to them. Penny not saying anything to me led to be certain that she was not an honest person. She was underhanded and didn't care. She had the big house and a house in Florida on the beach to make her happy; she didn't care about other people that she would hurt as long as she was making money. This was my conclusion as she never spoke to me about it. Never.

One day a few days later, something unusual happened. I received a fax that some paperwork for the company in Florida that we did business with was saying that a whole bunch of forms were not filled out correctly by our office, which was one of my jobs. I called the agents and told them, and they were surprised and stated that they would come in a fill them out again. I called Albert first, and he sounded upset. Then I called Erol, and he said, "I know I filed those out, something is wrong," and I agreed with him and pulled the files, and sure enough, the agents had filled out the forms, and the fax was a lie. I called Rennie in Florida, who worked for the company in question, and he stated that it seemed that someone was trying to set him up; it was a weird statement, and he was friends with Lesal in the office as she even visited him in Florida when she visited there. Maybe this was her secret boyfriend I did not know about.

I said to him to please investigate this as it looked like I didn't do my job and the agents didn't do their jobs. He never got back to me, and Henry was in the office and said, "Can I help you with this?" as he overheard my conversation.

I said, "Yeah, help me out, someone is setting me up and making me look like I didn't do my job."

Stan in the office came in, too, to look at everything. Kenny Jr. just turned around and walked away; little boy surely would not tell on his mother, or maybe it was him. I knew then that they had set me up it was clear. Kenny Jr. should have been the one to straighten out the mess, but he probably created it to make me look bad. He knew I was not interested in him but in Albert; it made him mad, and he probably wanted me out. At that point, I really didn't care any longer. I just was tired of being fired.

Then there was a luncheon in the conference room that Kenny Jr. set up with Mandy because I overheard it. I was not invited, and so on that day, I left and went to my sister's house and sat in the rain in her driveway. I was upset and crying but had nowhere to go. I went back after lunch, and everything was gone, and no one offered anything to me. Mandy had gotten what she wanted. They were making plans to get rid of me.

The next Friday, I had checked the work submitted to me. I went to lunch, and when I came back, some of the applications I had checked already were missing. I know because I checked them and put the totals on my total sheet, which they didn't know. I told Penny that someone had taken items off my desk, and she stated that no one would do that and that I had just misplaced them. I told her, "I don't misplace things on my desk. Not much to get in the way, my desk is so clean." She was nasty to me and walked away, stating, "They will turn up."

I got on the phone to the agent Angel and told her that her work was missing. Kenny Jr. overheard me do this and came to my desk and said, "You shouldn't have done that, it makes the company look bad. You should have just told her that somehow, they were misplaced."

I said, "No, I don't lie for anyone."

He gave me a dirty look and walked away. The next few hours, I left to go the bathroom, and lo and behold, they were back on my desk.

Penny said, "Somehow they must have gotten misplaced."

I said, "Yeah, you're right," but I knew then that she herself had done this to me. I was upset, and later, I must state, that I was surprised that I could hold my temper and not pull this woman's hair out.

The next week, Lesal asked me to go to lunch.

I said, "Okay, but I have to make a couple of personal calls in my car, and then come out, and we'll go."

She said, "Don't go outside, just do it at your desk."

I said, "Well, there is no privacy at my desk."

She said, "Just lock the door between your office and the conference room."

I said, "Okay."

I locked the door and sat down to make some calls, and Penny came in and opened the door, and Jeff was standing on the other side of the door, I guess listening to my calls. She didn't say anything but just looked at me. I had to finish my calls as they were important. I was on the phone with the cable company, and Janet came in and started to yell at me to get out of the office and to not make any calls at my desk. I hung up and stated to her that I was on my cell phone and had to make a personal call.

She yelled at me and said, "Go outside and do that."

I went straight to Lesal's office and said, "Lesal, Janet just yelled at me about making a call on my cell phone at my desk, and this was unacceptable behavior to me in the workplace." I left and went to lunch.

I came back from lunch, and Janet and Mandy and Lesal and Kelly were all in the conference room and stated real loud, "You came back!"

I said, "Yes, I did!" and sat down at my desk and began to work.

Clearly, the office staff and the boss were having fun with me. I thought to myself, "I'm not going to get disrupted at all, I'm just going to work."

Penny came back from a late lunch, and I said, "Can I talk to you please about Janet, your daughter?"

She said, "Sure," and pointed to the chair and said, "Sit down."

I told her that Janet screamed at me at lunch about making a phone call on my cell phone at my desk.

She said, "Oh, you know Janet, she does stuff like that, and don't pay any attention to her." She said she was sorry that she did that, and she would talk to her and tell her to please not do that again. Janet never came and apologized at all. She was clearly doing it on purpose; they thought they could get me to quit.

I said to myself, "No, I'm not going to quit."

The next day, the boss's nephew Tony came into my office after weeks of working with him one-on-one to straighten out some mess with his area and the applications. He had stated to me on the phone one day as I was helping him with the questions, and he told me to go to the website and gave me his password, which was "I Love Women."

I just said, "Okay."

He said, "Thanks so much for helping me, I love you."

I just changed the subject and kept talking. Then he was in my office, and Penny was standing there, and he looked at me and said that he went away for the weekend with his wife to Branson, and he was asking me if I had ever been there, and I said, "Yes, I had been there many times." He in talking to me said something about it and then stated as he was pulling his cheek out that some people were just too fat for some people.

He was giving that look like, "I'm too fat for you, huh, you not interested in me."

I said to him, "I'm sure your wife thinks you are special."

Penny did everything to get him out of my office. Penny knew the situation was getting weird as all the guys were coming on to me. Drew was at my desk all the time, and Mark was always there, saying something about QT and stuff like that. Mandy was always asking me to go to Mark's house to play tennis, and I said no on several occasions. Lesal was always trying to get me to go to lunch with the guys. I always said no.

Only one day I was tempted when it was Albert who was going to lunch, and he was out in the hall, and Lesal was at the front desk, and he looked at me and said, "I'm going to lunch, a man's gotta eat." I so wanted to go to lunch with him, but I knew Lesal was setting him up as Kenny Jr. had a major crush on me for sure, and I didn't want to get him fired, so I said, "Have fun." I wanted to say, "Yeah, I would love to go to lunch with the most handsome guy I have ever met, and you are so nice on top of it too." I was totally into him, and I don't think he knew it as I did not share that with anyone. I wish I would have not cared if he got fired and went to lunch with him. Maybe he would have gotten fired, and then we could have dated for sure. I was not sure if he knew what was going on in the office and felt that Lesal was using him to get him fired and possibly get me fired. I was not going to do that to him because I loved him. I loved him very much and was in love with a man that I totally did not expect to fall in love with at that time of my life. He was twenty years younger, and I didn't see him that way at all. He was so much of a gentleman and never made a pass at me or said something stupid or inappropriate. I had found the perfect guy for me; I knew it, and I didn't handle it very well at all, and he was not interested in me at all. One day he came into the office to get a pad of forms that I ran out of because Lesal didn't tell me I had to order them; she did stuff like that to make me look bad. Anyway, he looked so mad when he came into the office, and I wanted to tell him that Lesal did that as he looked mad at me, as if I would do that purposely because he did not go out with me. I wanted to shut the door and kiss him so he would know that I loved him and no one else, but I was always professional in the office and so was he, I guess. I thought if I could do that, he would know that I did care about him but respected his statement that he had a girlfriend and that she was the one for him. I was being just a silly woman and kept it all to myself. I didn't know what was what in that office. Everyone was so hell-bent on Mandy and Mickey and this and that, and I just worked when I was there.

It was the day after Lesal was supposed to go to lunch with me and pulled a last-minute change, stating that Mr. M. was coming, too, after I had my coat on.

I said, "No, he is not, and I am going to my car and you can come if you want but he is not!"

She did that on purpose to make me mad. She came out to the car, and when she got in, I said, "Why did you do that, I told you directly that I did not want to go to lunch with any men from work, especially the boss's husband."

She said, "I don't know what you are so upset about, that does not mean anything."

I said, "You know perfectly well why I am upset!" I let her know at lunch that she was out of line and that she was not a friend of mine as she was manipulating things and people, and I did not like it. I asked her why she was doing that, and I said to her, "You know that I was interested in Albert, and he told me he has a girlfriend, and that is that, there was nothing going on ever with me or anyone at work."

She said, "I didn't tell Penny about Albert."

I said, "Lesal, nothing happened between Albert and me at all for you to tell Penny anything. What are you talking about?"

She said that she was sorry and that she was not talking to the other guys about me, but I knew she was lying to me the whole time. She was not a very nice person and was manipulating people because she was probably asked to by the Ms, who knew at this time, but she was my workplace Salieri. Salieri was a character in the movie Amadeus who purposefully manipulated and undermined Amadeus to his ruin and eventually to his death. She was their little spy, I guess, but little did they know she was stabbing them in the back too. It was a nasty situation, and I was in the middle of a very unprofessional mess and an office that had more sexual stuff and gossip going on than did work. More blatant dishonesty than I had ever seen before at work.

Albert and I would have been perfect for each other in my mind if everyone had left us alone. Maybe he never would have gone out with me, and that would have been fine. My big mistake was telling Lesal about him and that I had called him. I'm sure now that she used that against me. She was an awful person. Imagine at one point she wanted to be my sister and said I was so nice and that my stories told to her about my sisters and what we did together sounded so fun, she wished her sister didn't hate her. I guess she found out why her sister did, and so did I by now. She did not communicate but judged and was hateful. Many people are, and they would rather not communicate and have things said and done rather than just talking about what they are doing and why. This is a basic lesson of life; communication is the key, and when people don't want to talk, it is because they are guilty and don't want to talk about their bad behavior. This is universal for every person or any place in time that conflict begins. It is the way people misbehave and then don't want anyone to know of their bad behavior; they just shut you out and don't talk and then behind your back. They lie and connive to get what they want by convincing everyone that you are something that you are not. It is the worst thing ever, but people do it every day. The Lord above will take care of punishing them; that's what I say to myself. I do know this one thing: I sleep good at night, and I'll bet they don't, for if they do, surely, they have no conscience.

Albert quit coming into work, and I knew Lesal was lying about me to everyone. She was a nasty, dirty person. That was clear.

Penny pulled me in her office the day after Lesal had lunch with me at the end of the day when everyone was gone.

She said, "Please come into my office," and Kenny Jr. was there. She began to tell me how it was not working out and she was going to have to let me go because Mandy could not get along with me and she had been there for nineteen years.

She said, "What do you want me to do, fire Mandy? She had been here for nineteen years and is like family to us."

I wish now I would have said, "If Mandy is like family, no wonder why this place is so screwed up. There is more sexual innuendo going on than work in this office." It was the most unprofessional office I had ever worked in.

She went on to say that she was not going to fire Mandy and that Lesal had told her that I had been talking about the younger salesmen. She said that no man twenty years younger would be interested in a grown woman who had three grown children. I remember thinking that she was so mean to me at that point; clearly, she felt she was my mother or something, I suppose.

I said, "What makes you say that to me? Has Lesal been talking to you, or have you been observing the behavior of the people in this office? Lesal has some sort of dating matchmaking things going on here, and I told her I didn't appreciate it, and that is when I decided not to tell her any more personal information about me at all."

Then Kenny Jr. said, "Well, the guys are also making complaints about you."

I said, "Well, who is saying what? And I will respond."

He said, "I'm not going to tell you."

I said, "Well, if you believe them, then that is up to you, whoever is complaining."

I was sure it was Mark as he was so angry that I would not go out with him and it was clear by the way he looked at me and talked to me. He was getting back at me by complaining, and I think Mandy was helping him and vice versa as they were friends, and I'm sure he was friends with Mickey too. It was awful, and they gave me no credit for my hard work.

I just said in final response, "Look, I'll bet it was Mark he has been asking Mandy to get me to come to his house to play tennis and I said no. So if you say that you won't fire Mandy for acting like an eighth-grader and you want to listen to a jealous man, go right ahead as I can't control others, I can only control what I do. I can tell you what I haven't done, but you don't want to hear that, do you, Kenny?"

At that time, I knew Kenny was pretty upset that I was interested in other people and not him. His childish ways would not only make the company lose a very excellent employee but possibly later an excellent salesperson for the company as well.

I just simply stated, "Mandy is acting like an eighth-grader and instead of firing her for her behavior, you're firing me." I was so mad and I just said, "It's not fair, I work hard, come in early, stay late, and yet you fire me!"

She said that this was her busy season, and she could not fire Mandy and Lesal, so she had to make a decision and fire me.

I told her as I was packing my things that she was making a big mistake and that she was firing the wrong person and should be firing Mandy and Lesal. I was ready to prove to her that the two of them were stealing lead cards and giving them to select salespeople but did not have the absolute proof yet to present to her. I was just about there, and I think they knew it too. Her daughter, Janet, too, was participating, but I was not sure at that point; it was just my hunch as she was close friends with the two of them.

I walked out and was not even given two weeks' pay, just shown the door. I just packed up my personal belongings and went out the door. Not of course without making just one simple statement.

"You're firing the wrong person!" I said firmly but nicely, and I left.

I was devastated, and now this would be the fourth job in a row that I was fired from. How was I going to get another job? My résumé looked like crap—little did I know it would get even crappier. When I was given a retention specialist two weeks before I was fired, I e-mailed her to tell her what was going on. I think back now and resolve that it may have just gotten me fired; I would never make that mistake again. I think at that point that she e-mailed the owner, Penny. What a stupid thing to do, because instead of contacting me, she told Penny about what I had said. Such stupid people, they don't have a clue about the workplace, yet they are put in charge of helping people stay in their job.

A few weeks later, I was summoned to the community college to talk with my retention specialist, and instead of meeting with her, I met with someone named Hattie. She was dressed professionally with a scarf around her neck, and she looked across the desk at me and stated that I was having continual problems with people at work, and since I was getting fired over and over, they thought that she should have a chat with me. She shoved a stapled packet of papers across the desk at me and said, "I think you should look these options over."

I looked down at the desk onto the papers, and the content was about mental disorders and mental health. I looked back up at her and stated that I was not in need of a mental health person; I needed someone to back me up in the workplace. She just responded by stating again that she thought this would be a good option for me.

I left her desk quickly and wanted to tear the pieces of paper up in her face and throw them at her. The professional that I was, I just turned and left and went to the desk of my retention specialist and said to her, "I thought I was coming here today to talk with you?"

She said back, looking up at me, "Sit down and let's chat."

I said, "I have been treated very terribly, and I know why, people hate me because I am good at so many things, also I'm nice, I'm pretty, and I work hard, and now I'm single as well, and people get jealous."

She looked surprisingly back to me and stated firmly, but condescendingly, "You think you're all that!"

I wanted to rip her hair out. I stated very firmly back to her, but matter-of-factly, "No, I don't think so, but other people do!"

I held my tongue that day and didn't say anything I really wanted to say to both of them. I wanted to say, "How dare you accuse me of a mental disease when these people were so horrible to me. Don't you care about me? Maybe I should rip your hair out for sure, and I could get incarcerated and never have to work again. How great would that be for me." I knew I could not handle jail, so I opted for the safe option and walked out, as I did always. The good little Cinderella.

I went to the career center and told them I was fired again. They felt bad and told me to just start looking again. I was tired of job-hunting and getting fired. I had never been fired from a job in my life. This was unreal. It would be the start of a line of firings and my self-esteem dropping to an all-time low at times that I wondered if I could even go on living.

I was so upset and went home and thought about it over the weekend. I went down to the EEOC office on Monday and filed a report. It was a hard thing for me to do. I felt so mistreated and felt as though I was wronged again, and I was not going to stand for it this time.

I was asked by the EEOC to help in participating in the investigation, and the Commission on Human Rights also asked me to help them in their cross-examination. It would soon prove to be devastating for me. Lie after lie about me. I was not emotionally ready for the horrible events that would occur.

I got another job at the Public Protection Agency of Greater Springfield as an inside sales representative. I was hired by a person they hired from a marketing company who used to work for the public protection agency. He was smooth and talked all about how wonderful it was to work there and how the benefits and salary potential were unsurpassed. He told me that I would be making of upward $50,000 a year or better, and I would be buying beautiful clothes and a BMW to drive, new hairstyles, etc. It was the most underhanded lying scheme of hiring I would come to ever know.

Later I was told the Public Protection Agency that they did not know that he was saying that to people and said it was his entire fault for the lies. I knew better. The president of the public protection agency is certainly knowledgeable enough to know that people were being lied to; she just wanted to make money as they had moved into a new office and the rent was probably more than she had bargained for. He took me to the sales floor, and all the salespeople sat in cube desks that faced each other, and you could hear everyone talking. It seemed a bit odd, but every time someone signed a business up as a member, they would ring a bell, and everyone would say, "Congratulations." I thought this to be somewhat baby-ish, so when the man they trained me with came out of the two-day training, which by the way the other salespeople said Jo and I sounded like we had been doing this for years, we would make a lot of money doing it. We sat across from each other, and our desks faced each other. Every time we made a sale, we would high-five by slapping each other's hands and kind of giggled, and it was all so weird. This was much harder than they made it sound, and the leads were not good at all as they were mostly beauty shop owners who had no money. We would have to call over one hundred businesses a day (cold calls) and pitch the sales script. It was really long, about twenty minutes or more, and most businessmen would be angry that you took up that much of their time. It was unbelievable how they had us lying to businesses and telling them that we were calling about the reporting language that we used on the website. Later, I would learn that they were doing nothing with that information that I was taking down, and it was not on the website either. Not even for the businesses that were members. Turned out it was nothing other than the name and address, and if they had any prior complaints and whether or not they were resolved complaints.

It was clear to me a month into this job that people had lied to me; I was lying to business owners, and once I knew that, I could no longer pitch the script the same way. So of course, my sales went to almost nothing with my paycheck looking the same—a big fat zero!

But before I even got to get to the point of being good, the sales manager who used to be on the sales floor and had friends that she went out with at lunch with and partied at night with would soon reveal that she was giving them preference over me. I hardly ever got a ticket to call someone that called in and said, "I want to be a member." In other words, the easy sales of members who called in wanting to join were given to people that were her friends. I do believe that my callbacks from companies where I left a message were also being routed to others when they called back and not to me. The sales leads that I worked on at home and at work were kept on my desk. I asked one day if I could have a lock for my desk, and she said no.

I said, "While you are out, someone could take leads from my desk if I am at lunch, do you realize that?"

She said, "No one would do that!"

"Bullshit," I wanted to say, but as usual, the Cinderella held her tongue, sat back down at her desk, and began to work.

It was obvious to me that no one could care less about me and my leads. All they wanted was for you to sell hard and make money.

So once the manager knew I was good and was getting sales, she started to strip away the training technique that the trainer used to train me. He was more upbeat and positive, and she kept harping on me to change this and change that messing with my head and sales pitch. It was intentional. She was a rat or a super rat who was undermining me to help her friends who worked there. It was horrible. Every day I had to hear, "You are an overachiever, aren't you?" "You are arrogant." "You are this and you are that." "How much money does your family have?" "How rich are you?" They were the questions they were asking me. I found them to be out of line and very personal and of course none of their business. I could not believe what I was hearing from these people. It was a hostile work environment again. Oh, when would I be rid of that issue? I was exhausted from the last place and would now be crying in my car at lunch some days tortured by them and wondering if I could go in and work.

Mind you, I was educated in rats and super rats from the movie *Breakfast at Tiffany's*.

Well, I received a call one day from the unemployment office. They told me that Penny M., the owner of the insurance company I left, told them that I never worked for her.

I was shocked and asked them for a copy of the paperwork.

They said to me, "No, we can't give that information to you."

I said, "Are you kidding me? I can't have a copy of the paperwork that someone said I did not work there?"

They said, "No, that is confidential information."

I thought to myself, "Confidential that they had proved that she lied about me and won't give it to me. Was I living in America?" I said this to myself as it did not feel like it.

At the same time, I was talking with Albert about how to better my sales pitch, and I was using the pay phone at Dier's a local grocery store as he seemed to be willing to talk to me when I called from there and not my cell phone. I did not realize that his girlfriend actually lived with him and not in Montana. I'm sure she checked his phone, and such a possessive person didn't trust him for a reason. I would call him from time to time from a phone booth so no one could trace my cell to his as I guessed that they were watching the salesmen's cell phone calls maybe at work too. I thought that was nice. He told me on the phone one day that I could be his mother, and it hurt my feelings really bad, and I hung up on him. I guess he was telling me in his own way that he could never be interested in a woman of my age. I was crushed. I would cry from time to time thinking about his words to me.

Later I would come to understand that people in America in general think that people should not be interested in someone twenty years junior or senior as this is out-of-the-box thinking, and I would never think this way, never.

I was calling him at this time as a friend since he told me he had a girlfriend. I did not know that he was not even interested in being just my friend. I was emotionally inept at the time to understand men. I decided at that time I needed to educate myself a bit before I dated again. Little did I know, it would be five years later before a man asked me out on a date, and I still don't understand certain people at all because of my family moral values.

One night I asked him to meet me and go out dancing at a club. I didn't hear back from him, so I got dressed up, and while I was driving in my car, my cell phone rang. It was him; he had called me this time.

He said, "Where are you going?"

I pulled over to talk. I told him I was going to a club called Mickey's and asked if he wanted to come along and get out of the house (at the time, he told me his girlfriend lived in Montana). I thought we could chat about work events and have fun; that was all. He said that he could not go and wanted to know something.

I said, "What do you want to know?"

He said, "The people at work are telling me that you are crazy."

I said, "Well, I'm not," and he went on to say, "Why then would they say that?"

Those words crushed me, and I only said, "I am not crazy, but

Mandy and Lesal are the crazy eighth-graders, not me," and I hung up on him. I sat in my car and cried and felt so bad that I drove home and got drunk—plain, old, nasty drunk alone. He purposely did that to me to hurt me.

Later, I would learn that he was friends with Mandy and Lesal and not me. It was a feeling that I will never forget. I will never make friends with anyone at work again; I had learned my lesson. I would, however, be hounded by this statement, and it affected me, so much so that almost five years later, I have not gone out on a date or even interested in doing so as someone might say that again. I don't care anymore who says what about me, but I will say they will receive a challenge if they do say it about me. I would later see a doctor who would document a diagnosis contrary to the lies that were spread by my ex-husband and family members too, if you can believe that. I would come to know just how hurtful people can be to a nice lady like me.

I called an attorney once I knew that the insurance company backed out of the mediation process. I was talking to him at lunch even about the Public Protection Agency as they were treating me so badly once they found out I had filed an EEOC action against the insurance company. I think they called them for a reference weeks after I worked there, and they were lied to about me. I know this for a fact as Penny M. and Albert would do something to me that was so devious to get the EEOC to not believe a word I said to them.

One night, while I was supposed to go to my high school reunion, which I didn't go to because the planning committee consisted of four people—myself, Sue, Dick, and Ronnie. Sue was in charge and was starting to get obnoxious at the rest of us who were having so much fun at the restaurants talking about old days and what we did when we were kids. Sue made the mistake of telling me that Ronnie got one of my friends pregnant in high school. I thought to myself, "What kind of gossiper are you anyway?"

I said to her in an e-mail that maybe her husband would not like it if he knew how she felt about Dick. Previously, one night before we met, she stated that she had a crush on Dick when she was little.

I said, "Well, I never knew it." I didn't pay much attention back then about who dated whom. I was a tomboy pretty much of my youth and only had genuine interest in two boys from grade school and all through high school. But I sent the e-mail to her and Dick. She sent me back the nastiest of e-mails and said that we would no longer be having any meetings at all.

I said, "Great."

Dick e-mailed me and said that he still wanted to meet.

I said, "No, I think I have had enough of this anyway!"

I remembered what Dick had said to me one night in the restaurant he looked over at me and said, "You look really great, every guy in the place is going to want to go out with you!"

I said, "Thank you," but in the back of my mind, I was, and I was thinking, "What does he mean by that?"

Surely the married men at the reunion would be without their wives, of course, since the planning committee decided that spouses were not allowed! I don't go out with married men; I don't go out with people attached either or living with a girlfriend. I will if the woman is not someone, they are willing to marry and are searching still for someone to marry; otherwise, I stay hands off to anyone with a girl or wife, period.

I went to Albert's house a few weeks after I was fired, and I put a note on his door and just rang the doorbell and left; it was the night I was supposed to be at the class reunion, and instead I said to myself, "Would I rather be in a room full of married men thinking about going out with me, or tell the man I really cared about that I was indeed in love with him all along at work?" I was careful to just leave the letter and ring the bell; it was dark as I walked to the back of his apartment complex and turned back a bit and saw a young silhouette in the dark following me, and he had a piece of paper in his hands. He watched me get into my car, and I said nothing as he got into a car as well. I drove off.

The note was an explanation of the events at work and how I was afraid to tell him about how much Kenny was jealous of me, even though I gave him no reason to like me at all. In fact, I couldn't stand him. Anyway, I put the note on the door and left. I saw him come outside and walk behind me, but he didn't say a word. I just got in my car and drove away. This was on the night I was supposed to go to my grade school reunion and didn't go because the guys who were planning it with me said that every guy in the place would want to take me out now that I was single. I was devastated by this statement as many of the guys were married. I didn't know what to do; I was in love with Albert, so I thought I should at least explain that to him and let him know in case that would make a difference somehow. I didn't want to put it off maybe wondering my whole life, did he care for me or not? So despite my eldest daughter's advice to never give a man a love letter, I chose to do what my heart was telling me, and I took it and left it on his doorstep that night. Well, it didn't make the difference I wanted it to. Turned out he had no feelings for me that way and was in love with his girlfriend.

I went back the next day after coming home and put a note on the door that said, "I'm out in the parking lot, and if you want to get a cup of coffee and just talk, please come out in the next five minutes. Otherwise, I will just leave." I had no idea at the time that I was sitting outside the eyeshot of his back bedroom sliding door and his girlfriend lived with him, and they could probably see me sitting there. I was such a fool in love and thought she was in Montana and it would be harmless to have a cup of coffee and just let him know why I did and said the things to him at work.

I left the note and rang the bell and went to my car. He never came out, probably for the obvious reason stated above.

I thought okay and went home very sad. I never heard from him either by phone.

I called him from the phone booth, and he told me that he was not interested in me and I could be his mother. I hung up, of course, and never called back again other than to talk about the case with the EEOC. I would later learn that everything I was telling him was going back to Penny as he was friends with Mandy and Lesal. It was the harshest feeling of betrayal I had ever felt besides my ex-husband and my family members.

I think at that time, I was just ready to give up on everyone and just stay home and be by myself the rest of my life. That was what I thought, of course, and five years later, I'm still sitting at home by myself, but did lend myself to one date after a man who talked with me on the phone about his problems said one day while talking, we should meet, I said sure, he said later in conversation that it had been a long time since he was out on a date.

I said to myself, "Oooo, he said the *date* word." I went, anyway.

One night when we were talking, and I was trying to get Albert to help me so that it would never happen to anyone else that worked at the insurance company as they would be punished and it would be documented.

He said this to me, "I'm not in love with you, and I'm not helping you, so quit calling me, or I will call the police as you are harassing me!"

I said, "I am participating in an investigation, and I need your help," I started to cry.

He said, "I'm not helping you!"

I said, "Won't you even help me as a human being?" while crying.

He said, "If you call me again, I will call the police."

Little did I know, at this time, that he had filed a stalking order on me to protect Kenny and the company. True.

I went to his house only one more time to place a Christmas thank-you gift on his doorstep in December around the second week to say thanks and apologize in my own way, not knowing he had done such a horrible thing already to me. He came out his back sliding glass door with his girlfriend and was screaming to me, "This is my girlfriend!" He asked to please leave him alone. (What a show they put on.) I didn't even turn around, and I just kept walking to my car. He was screaming at me, and I just kept walking to my car and said, without turning around, "You have this all wrong. I was leaving you a thank-you gift as I do this for everyone during the year that has helped me in some way." I was crushed again and would never ever see him again.

But to my surprise, while I was in the attorney's office representing me in the EEOC complaint one day to discuss the case, the attorney was happy that the owner admitted the fact that the sexual statement was made and that Mandy got mad and was doing and saying stuff to hurt me. But then he went on to say that I had stalked a young man from the office, Albert, and he filed a protection order against me. I was about to fall to the floor and said, "No, he did not, and I was never served with anything like that." I said, "If he did it was only because he was lied to and they told him I was crazy."

Of course, at that time I never thought he did it on purpose to help the company, how sad for me. The attorney left the conference room and came back, and sure enough, there was the paperwork that he had filed a protection order against me.

I said, "I was never served."

He said, "Yes, you were."

I said, "No, I wasn't, and I will go to the South City Courthouse and get the proof."

I went straight to the courthouse, and sure enough, there was the paperwork with my love letter to him in the file as evidence that I was stalking him. I would cry many days over this lie as I am crying right now again while writing this page. It was a lie, and they only did it to make the EEOC feel as though I was this crazy girl who was doing bad things to people at work and to him once I had been fired. It was the worst thing anyone had ever done to me and lied about me in such a way. I went to the sheriff's office in Clay, and sure enough, their records on the computer showed that I was served.

I said, "Can I see a copy of the paperwork?"

And she said, "It is in the file in the South City Courthouse."

I said, "It wasn't, and they told me you had it."

They said, "No."

I went back to the courthouse, and they said it was never served.

I said to the clerk, "Why then do you have this on record still when it wasn't served and there was no hearing?"

She said, "We will keep it that way forever as someone filed it."

I said, "It wasn't true, and that's why there was no hearing because it was all made up. I only went to the guy's house a few times to talk. I never stalked him in any way. He was lying to help Lesal and Mandy. He said his girlfriend would testify to it as I was trying to talk to him. I guess in this world I have learned, never talk to anyone once you have left work after being fired, they use it to make it look like you have done something inappropriate. I still had to talk to him later for the investigation, and it was very damaging to me psychologically and emotionally."

He would reveal to me after months of talking that he was friends with Lesal and Mandy. I read to him what the protection order said and said to him, "Did you say this as it is lies about me?"

He hung up. The guilt of his actions was only reinforced by his unwillingness to talk to me. He had damaged me in such a way that I would be very lonely for years because of it. Not willing to even put myself out there too much because of how he betrayed me. I had already been betrayed by two other men, my ex-husband with the ultimate cheating on me, and then a guy I dated for six weeks who lied to me also and yelled at me in the house after we made love because I asked him a question which he had lied to me about and he wouldn't answer. I would come to learn the hard way that people who don't answer questions are guilty and choose to not answer at all because of their bad behavior toward me. It is a hard lesson to learn but one that I would come to know is applicable in all of life sometimes. I would learn to know right away to trust but be very wary, to date but very carefully, to love always when I feel it.

He would always hold a special place in my heart as I knew he was lied to, but I thought to myself, "In the same situation where someone had lied to me, if I cared about that person enough to find out the truth, I would, and he did not." It was telling me the sad truth that he never even cared about me at all in any way shape or form. I was just another pretty girl who was looking for attention, and that's all. Attention I didn't need—I get enough of it that I don't want sometimes. It was love I was looking for and love I felt. What a shame for me, as love is hard to find for me. My sisters tell me I have too many expectations. I say better to have too many than not enough and wind up again with someone who doesn't love me but the way I look.

I do think of him often though and wonder, if the story had gone a different way and he had met me for a cup of coffee, would it have made a difference? I guess women in love always seem to think somehow someway it might have; sometimes if we are a romantic, we like to think that if we have feelings about someone, they, too, will have the same about us. It makes our feelings validated about love and how we feel when we find it. What a pity for me. I was so ready to give it again. It would be years before I would feel that way or have anyone even ask me out, even if it was to meet, but later he said it was a date. Seemed that he did not call me back. I called him the next night, and he said, after talking for an hour or so, "Let me plug in my cell phone."

I said back to him that I had to be in court early tomorrow and I better get to sleep. I told him I would call him the next day to let him know how court went. He said okay. The next day I called twice, and his answering machine was full. I called on Friday as well, and it was still full. I called on the following Monday, and finally, he answered in the evening, and we talked about twenty minutes, and he seemed a bit odd on the phone and said that he had to go.

I said, "Well, why don't you call me when you have time?" And I hung up.

Weeks later no call had come. I guess he did not like what he saw but liked me as a person. He seemed to be very into the way people looked as he talked very much about his wife's shape and breasts all the time. Some men are that way. Oh well.

Now while working at the Public Protection Agency, they started to ask me questions about my life, family, etc. I would not know until later it was because they were trying to find out what happened in my life with my children and ex-husband. I don't know why people are so interested in me, but I think my manager was asking for a gentleman in the office or the trainer who trained me if I was interested in him. I would never really know, just a feeling I had. She was always telling me to call the trainer. I would not. It was clear to me that he was smitten by me, but he was married, and I don't mess around. I am not that kind of woman, and it makes me sick to think that people sleep around while being married. I hated it as it happened to me in my marriage. What must they be thinking of me? At that time in my life, I really didn't care any longer what people thought of me.

Anyway, I went through the training and came out onto the sales floor to my desk and cubicle. It was the first desk and faced the front door. So when people came into the sales area, I would be the first person they saw.

I practiced my script at home for months; it was many pages and more pages of rebuttals. I was also trying to learn to get leads at home on my computer, out of the paper, and anyplace else I could think of to get them. They gave us lead cards at work, but most of the time, they had been called previously and were mad that you were calling them back again.

I was told by the top salesperson that I was really sounding good and she thought that I would be wonderful at the job and make lots of money at it. I told her, "Thank you."

I was not nervous, but it seemed it was a lot harder to get a sale of a membership than they made it out to be. It seemed to me that I was calling every small business that did not have the money.

I said, "Why aren't we calling the big corporate companies?"

I was told that the small business owners were my bread and butter. I was told that I should not try to call corporate businesses because it was too hard to get to the decision maker to get the membership. I thought to myself, "Well then, they don't know how to get to the decision-maker." I thought I would challenge myself and call some just to see.

When my supervisor found out I was calling corporate offices, she said, "You can't do that. That office has been called already."

I said, "Really? It was not on the do-not-call sheet or already-called or already-a-member sheet either."

She said to me, "We will give you a list shortly of the corporate offices you can call."

I said, "Well, what about the pending one I have out that is big and waiting for the decision-maker?"

She said, "Don't let that worry you, I will keep track of it."

I said, "Really." Seemed a bit odd that she didn't track any other ones; it seemed to me like she wanted it for herself. I was upset but didn't say too much.

I later learned that the corporate accounts were supposed to be placed for membership calls by the president herself and not the other salespeople.

I said, "Well, if she's not doing it, why the heck can't I?"

She said nothing back to me. Clearly, I had stepped in an area where they were not willing to let me take the high-commission sales after I had figured out an easy way to get to the decision-makers. Well, well, doesn't that beat all?

I then realized that while I was drowning with no paycheck, the boss didn't care. She was probably bringing in a big paycheck and I was scraping with nothing and couldn't pay my bills. I was now using my retirement money to live. Little did I know that later, it would be revealed in court by subpoena of business records that she was pulling in a mere twenty grand a month. Yes, twenty grand a month while I was going down the tubes financially. Nonprofit?

About four weeks into the job, I realized that some of the things that we were saying were not truthful. I could no longer say them. I was having a hard time getting myself to ask anyone for a membership, but I still made my hundred calls a day.

I was working hard, and it seemed to me that people were starting to treat me bad, saying nasty innuendoes to me that made me cry at lunch.

Long story is, they were all friends and didn't want to see me succeed. They were all talking about me, even asking me how much money my family had, and one day in the accountant's office, she asked me if I knew that Val was bipolar.

I said, "No." But I wondered if she was asking me that because my ex-husband had been telling people I was crazy as Albert had told me that at the insurance company after I got fired. I did not know it at first, but when he said it to me, I remember crying for a long time. I did not know if she was bringing that up because of me; surely no one would reveal such a personal thing about another employee, right?

Maybe I was just abnormally paranoid due to the horrible treatment and people stating that I was crazy just to get rid of me after I complained to a retention specialist that they had child/animal porn on my hard drive computer in their office and I was being retaliated against for someone's boyfriend saying that he could just kiss my toes. I did nothing, but it caused a major bunch of crap for me as it was Mandy's boyfriend after all, and she had been there for nineteen years. Big wup!

I remember crying. I sat in my car at lunch as they made me feel so horrible about myself. One day Dana, the boss's friend, called me arrogant.

I said nothing, and my supervisor was standing right there and did nothing. *Nothing.* Later while in college, I was tested and found that I had ideational fluency, and because of it, people saw me as arrogant because I was always making statements on how to make things better or giving ideas of new things that came to my mind. I hated her but later understood that jealous people say such things and don't care how it makes someone else feel.

I knew I was not getting support from my supervisor as she did nothing at all. She just stood there because maybe she, too, was jealous of me as well.

I called an employment attorney about the insurance company and started going to his office in Clay after work. I spent many hours telling him the story and giving him a large amount of a paper file I had collected about what happened in the office. I was feeling really bad about everything. My life sucked. I was fed up, crying some days about how I felt and how people had lied about me again. How could I go on?

I was in the attorney's office one day, and we were in the conference room alone together. He had spent many days with me, and I thought he was helping me prepare a case against them. Then one day when I came in, he said, "Go in the conference room." I sat down, and he started to go over the evidence that I had given to him.

He said, "M. is saying that Albert filed a stalking charge against you and gave it to the EEOC."

I said, "WHAT!"

He said, "It states here that you have a stalking order filed against you on Albert, from M. Insurance Agency."

I said, "I do not, no one ever served me with anything." I was totally embarrassed and felt that they must have lied to him or someone was lying about me and I was getting to the truth.

He said, "Well, hold on, and let me check." He left the room and came back a few minutes later with a print out from the courthouse stating that I was served with a protection order because I was stalking some guy.

He said to me, "Here it is, right here," and handed it to me.

I said, "I was never served." I told him, "I can go to the courthouse right now to get to the bottom of this."

But before I could do that, he said to me, "Is that your pen knife on the floor over there?" pointing to the knife on the floor.

I looked down on the floor, and there was a blue pen knife with the Star of David on it.

I said, "No," and knew better not to touch it or pick it up.

I thought to myself, "Are you actually trying to set me up in your office, you asshole?"

Surely, as an attorney, he would have gone to the courthouse to get that paperwork and found out for himself. He could do that.

But I got out of that conference room as quickly as I could. "WHAT THE HELL WAS THIS?" I said to myself driving there. I felt like Alice in Wonderland, and I was falling down the hole to nowhere to never return. People had gone wacky, and I didn't know why.

I drove to the city and parked and went into the courthouse. There was an attorney whom I had just interviewed with for a job. I waited in line and said, "I have this printout showing that I was served with a stalking charge, can you give me a copy of the service from the sheriff, because I was not served?"

She just looked at me and said, "You seem really nice," and pulled the file.

She gave me the file, and I could not believe what I was seeing. There was my love letter to Albert, my personal feelings of love for this man, taken and placed in a court file saying that he was afraid of what I might do to him and that people at work said I was crazy. What a moment in my life—he had trashed my personal words of love and made them into something dirty and filthy, called me crazy and made my heart weep beyond any feeling of weeping that I should ever know.

Clearly, I was aghast at what I saw and could not believe what he said about me. I was so nice and never would do anything to hurt anyone. I never stalked anyone. I was trying to explain things to him as people had lied to him. Clearly, he used me to make me look bad to the EEOC to protect his friends Mandy and Lesal (which he did not tell me he was friends with them till later), and the company, of course, since he was friends with Kenny. He made me look like the bad person—when really it was Mandy, his friend, that made my life horrible as well. It was a clear-cut filthy attack on my personage to help his friends. I'm crying years later about it as well; it made me feel so bad that someone would do that to me. I'm so nice and kind and generous. I wouldn't hurt anything or anyone on purpose, ever.

So I said, "Can I have a copy of this?"

She said yes. It stated that I was served, but I was not; there was no sheriff report in the file.

She said, "We send that back to the county."

I went to the county courthouse, and they said they had record in the computer that I was served.

I said, "I was not." They pulled it, and it stated that the sheriff did not serve the order.

So I went back to my attorney and showed him the evidence that I knew nothing about this, and clearly, they made this up to hurt me and gave a copy to the EEOC to help M. Insurance Agency. Albert was friends with M. Jr. and Mandy, who worked there. They could have been sued by the EEOC on my behalf, but Albert made sure that I looked like a stalker to the EEOC, and they believed nothing I said to them about M. and would not prosecute them or give me a paper saying that I could.

So after everyone at M. wanted to sleep with me (except Albert, of course), I got the shaft and looked like a crazy hooker on paper. How could he do this to me? Was I dreaming? No. This was reality; this was not a dream. It was a living nightmare. I stay in my house now and avoid men at work with a girl, with a wife, or any of the above mixture.

My attorney said this to me, "I'm not your attorney, and I never said I was."

I said, "What? You have been meeting with me for months on this case, and this is a lie, they made this up to make me look bad." I said, "Well then, I guess I'll have to go."

I got up slowly and left the office; I didn't even think to ask for my file. I was clearly being made fun of by this attorney at a point in life that would make me cry even as I write this down five years later.

I went home and cried the whole way while driving. I called his office and spoke with the lead attorney, and he said, "Well, if he gave you no contract, then he does not have to represent you."

I said, "He's been talking with me for months, he told me that we had the evidence to prove my case, which we did, even Penny M. lying about me to the unemployment office, saying I never worked there. Clearly, I was the girl who cried workplace harassment and got the screws put to me even further. I guess because I was also stating that the company had been ripping off seniors by selling them life insurance that took away what they had, they did not like me. My sister warned me as I was talking to her about the place, and she said, 'Don't sit at the conference table any longer and get out of there as fast as you can.'"

I remember thinking to myself, "Am I dreaming? Could this be happening to me again? What am I, some kind of target for abuse?" Abused by everyone any day they felt like it. It was exactly how I felt.

This would be the last time I would make friends at work. No friends at work.

I now had no job, no money hardly, and everyone stating that I—the abused woman—was an abuser myself. I cried for many days. I cried, and I'm still crying. Maybe I'll never stop crying about this as it was the last time I was going to let someone do this to me. Use me, lie about me. But it would not be the last time someone lied about me. For sure!

I thought, "My God, why do people do this to someone? They are all Salieri's." They do it because they are horrible people. They are the bad people. The good people try to protect themselves, but sometimes the badness in others can overcome the good people. It would be my start to understanding why I would later help victims like myself and start to stick up for people in the workplace and watch out for myself even closer. I feel like this time around it was at my breaking point.

So all the talks on the phone by Albert were just to get more information to hurt me as he never cared about me at all. How could I be that stupid again? How could I trust that this person was actually doing anything but hurting me? I was stupid but not for long.

I set a court hearing at the courthouse and sent Albert a letter at his new address in Montana. I also sent him information so that he did not think a crazy woman was stalking him. I was hell-bent on letting him know that he did this horrible thing to a very nice lady. I remember when the first time we spoke after I was fired, he was abusive to me with his voice and wording of words and sentences, and I said to him, "Never mind, I thought you were a nice guy."

He said back to me, "I am a nice guy."

"I am a nice guy," huh, well. I guess I'd have to be wary of guys who say "I'm a nice guy" now.

Because he was a monster who said he was a nice guy. I knew different but ignored the signs. Why? I had done it before—why again? I would soon learn I needed to take time to learn about people and about myself. So I would never do that again, ever. He said my love letter was weird; that said a lot about him. Anyone who took my sweet words of love and makes them into something horrible was in my estimation the worst kind of person that I would stay away from every chance I got. I would never want to see him or talk to him again.

He never responded to the letter either. I showed up in court that day, and he didn't show up at all. He didn't even have the decency to let me know that he would not be there.

The judge stated that I was never served but did not dismiss the charge so it would not show in the computer.

I said, "Well, I need the file to be sealed then."

He said, "I can't do that, I do not have the authority."

I said, "Who does?"

He said, "My boss."

I said, "Who is our boss?"

He said, "Why don't you find out and come back and tell me?"

Clearly, he was the Royal Jerk of the Year—a judge who was a smart-ass. The other cases that did not have a hearing were all dismissed, except mine.

I said, "Well, there was no hearing in the first place, and today he did not show up to state anything on the record about me. I will find out who your boss is and get back to you."

I remember thinking as I left the courtroom, "Now I have a stalking order against me for nothing making me look like a horrible person. How would I even get a job? How would I explain this to my grandchildren?"

Clearly, Albert didn't care, clearly neither did the judge. I guess men stick together and lie about anything they want to in this case. Clearly, I was going to have to work hard. I went to the Capital and found out I was the judge's boss and wrote him a letter telling him to seal the file because I was his boss. He did. Never was I ever so humiliated in my life. Never would I ever go into a man's house or apartment ever after that. It would be years before I would even have a date or something that a man called a date.

So now I finally realized how to act around men at work. Don't bring them to your house; don't call them; don't say anything about caring for them; or they will just stab you in the heart and make a public accusation about you that is not true at all. Weird—I'd say people who lie are weird. That's what I have to say about that.

I have to find another job. I do find one, but without a good reference, it ends up being at a marketing company working nights since I am still in court during the day trying to get my son back. It was the only thing I could find, so I took it.

Clearly, the world had gone crazy to me, yet they were calling me crazy. I just had to suffer through it all and end up being called crazy many times, maybe just not to my face. I hate those people, and I hate those who talk about others and say nothing but lies.

Things are better, and I have tried to hang on financially yet make my life livable to my reasonable needs as the judge has stated that my reasonable needs should be met.

Long haul—I'm smiling, but not liking it one bit.

You're not guilty until proven so. I've been guilty for years without even knowing that someone has stated that I am as I am innocent and kind, generous, and thoughtful to all. I have been stressed and lost control on occasion because of the wrongdoing, but only in my personal life, not ever at work.

But now I was crazy—how do you fight that gossip? After many years of tears, I later learned to embrace it and accept what you can't seem to change and go with it. Laugh all the way to the bank.

I would learn the best lesson no one at work is your friend. No ONE!

Chapter 8

My Emotional Workplace and Personal Life Intelligence Education

I started to investigate what people were saying about me and why. My ex-husband had told everyone who knew me, and of course my children, that I had a severe mental disease, which I do not. It was clear at one point that I did have what is called a psychotic episode, which I have learned is short-lived, due to extreme stress on a person's brain emotionally. There are no psychotic people, just psychotic events that happen and go away if the stressor is removed. My stressor was my ex-husband's verbal abuse and other things he did and some events in the workplace such as spreading a rumor that I had an affair.

He made it even worse for me after I quit and came home once, which showed me that he cared nothing about me at all. Of course, I did not know at the time he had a girlfriend as well, so he did not need me at all except to babysit his children until they got old enough that they could live with him and he would have to do nothing to help them with anything. Which was exactly what did happen to myself and to my children. When he said these words upon leaving me, "I'm leaving you do to something selfish for myself," he couldn't have been more right. He cared nothing about his children and his wife and was so bigheaded by this time about the prospects of his new business that he cast aside all those that he no longer needed—me, and of course the worst, his children. They could not see it, and he kept up the pretense with his children to make people think he was a good guy to other people and that I was the problem in the divorce. He was excellent at this manipulation.

This had all been a strain, and now I had to try and clean up the mess as my life was so strained. I couldn't seem to get a good job because I was fired four times because of this issue or because of other reasons as I get a lot of male attention at work. I told the Career Center where I lived that I needed to find a job working from home, and they said they couldn't help me as they hardly ever get jobs to work from home. I just knew that I was tired of this horrible junk in the workplace and I had had enough of it.

At last, I found a part-time job where I couldn't get fired—or so I thought. The pay was low, but I liked the job at the marketing company because I just log onto my computer in my cube and started doing online surveys most of the time talking to farmers and asking them questions about herbicides and chemicals seeds they used. It was fun, and I liked talking to people. The place had a few criminals, but I kept to myself and tried to ignore them. Talking to the farmers was interesting; I did find people very interesting and because my uncle had a big farm, I knew a little bit about farming as well as myself having a fairly large vegetable garden most of my adult life. I think the farmers helped me, too, as I needed to talk to people in America who had good values and cared about what they were doing at that time in my life. Farmers surely cared about the land, the people, the crops they grew, and of course I lent them an ear to also talk once in a while about what was bothering them. I called late in the evening when they were tired and finished with their dinners, and they would like it that maybe they had someone that would listen to what they were complaining about on that given day as well. People need people to talk to, who will listen to them. It was my job to listen to the farmers and then record answers but as well to be a listening ear to anything they wanted to say that night. The more comfortable they were with doing the survey, the more apt they were to complete another next time we called them back. The company made big money from a large corporation on the information we gathered, and they complied into marketing information. I later learned that the girl who trained me said to me after the third day when I had to take an agricultural test, "Are you trying to take my job?" because I got a 98 percent on the test.

I said, "No, why? Are you quitting?"

She said, "No."

I thought to myself, "What a jerk, is she just trying to get me fired already before I actually start working, or was she trying to tell me that she was the trainer and I was not under any circumstances going to take her job away from her?"

I could not understand why this person was so insecure; surely, I did nothing to her personally, just received a great grade on a test, which she should have been happy about since she trained me. She should have said to me that she was wowed by the grade and that I made her look good by getting such a great one! But she didn't. Such was my life at work up to this point. It used to be that being smart and accomplishing something would get you a raise; in the lower-paying jobs, I would find it just got you into trouble and made people want to get rid of you as you might take their job.

Later I found out that she, my old trainer, was a registered sex offender in my state and was hiring and training a lot of teenagers, coming and going. Then someone else at work told me, and then I told the corporate office as she stated that the other employees didn't know. Corporate office said nothing to me except to say that she was being switched to a different job. They took her out of the training office and put her in a different job with her own office. I then switched to sit in front of my supervisor's desk as I was in fear of losing my job. Later on, when my supervisor was on vacation, the sex offender and her friend fired me, saying that I was loud and abusive at his desk, which of course was a lie. He was best friends with her, and she was his supervisor as well. He was training to be a police officer, and I found it odd that a police academy cadet would be participating in such lying deceitful tactics, but nonetheless he did it for his friend to get back at me. Retaliation is what some people are into; I myself have never retaliated against anyone who did anything to me ever. I only have told the truth to stop others from being hurt or stop people from gossiping. It was why I found it funny that Albert told me while I was working at the insurance company that he did not participate in gossip when I tried to get his help with people who were lying about me but later told me that people at work were saying that I was crazy. So he believing and listening to some people gossip just made it clear that he did not want to hear about what the ladies at work were doing to me. So as you see, if you have no friends to back you up, then people can say anything at work, and it is only your word to refute what they say. No matter how much a long stretch or lie it is, some manipulators surely know how to do it. To me, they seem to take pleasure in it making it a fun part of their lives. I call them the ugly-hearted people. I remind myself on many days about the ugly-hearted people, and I stay to myself in my apartment writing for days. My peace space in my life is now the most important thing to me. Peaceful existence in my living area would be my salvation at times.

Things are better, and I have tried to hang on financially as well as make my life livable to my reasonable needs as the judge was setting many separate hearings because of the motions I had filed in court about my son and my needs after divorce. I needed the days off to attend them and try to get my son back and get some money for me and get things settled about the business he started before the divorce was final. This was all extremely sad for me in many ways. Never did I ever think that I would be the brunt of someone's nasty accusations, and never did I ever think that anyone would think because I was asking for help that I was then a gossip. I don't gossip, and it would be clear that it was because of gossip that a woman destroyed me in the workplace; it was gossip that would make my life miserable. Once I remember making a statement that I think the secretary was in love with the boss; I said it in a nice way as to say she spent so much time with him. I think she liked him more than her husband. Rightly so, from the things she would say at work about her husband and how he mistreated her and would flirt with the lady next-door. I felt sorry for her. She was implying interest in her boss, yet she knew he was happily married and good family man; she just admired him in a good way but showed her adoring admiration sometimes, with just a bit too much smile.

I was about to find out that I really did not like what was happening in my life workwise. I was fired for no good reason, many times, and it was clear that the workplace had figured out, "If we don't like someone, just say that they have conducted themselves improperly, and we can fire them, and they can't collect benefits, which is good for business." Then they denied my food stamps until I got a signed letter from the company stating that I was fired and they would not do it.

I said to myself, "How can they do this to people in America, keep me from food too?" They were sons of bitches for sure. I can't remember how I could keep up my great composure, but I went back to the car and called the police. I stood outside the office door and told them that I called the police to come since they would not sign the form. The police said this was a civil matter, and they could not help me.

I said, "I am supposed to get them to sign this form, but they won't, and I can't get food without it being signed."

They said, "Sorry, we can't help you."

I went back to the food stamp office, and they said, "Don't worry, we will try to get it for you."

I said, "I left the paperwork for them to sign, and I will put a copy in the mail as well."

Later on it would prove that my food stamp case worker had thought I was lying about how my bills were getting paid.

I went into the office after he called me and said, "I need for you to come in and talk with me about your expenses." I went in to the office to talk, and he said, "You can't really be paying all these bills since you make little money, right?"

He was laughing at me when I said, "People have been helping me with money, my church and my sister." While he was laughing, I said to him, "You think this is funny?"

He said, looking back at me really smug, "Welllll, miss, you can't really expect me to believe that you are paying your bills and are eligible for food stamps?"

I said, "Yes, sir, I am paying my bills with help, and yes, I should be eligible for food stamps."

He said, "Well, your expenses don't match up with your income, so I will send you a letter about your benefit amount."

I left the office and went home, thinking to myself, "This guy is such a jerk and a liar and enjoyed humiliating me." I received a letter, and the benefit amount went from $86 to nothing. In other words, while I was employed, I received $86, and now that I was not working at all, he reduced my benefit to nothing instead of increasing it.

I went into the office and asked to speak to another case worker. I went into the booth and asked her why my benefits were cut.

She said, "Your expenses lines have nothing in the computer screen."

And I said, "How could that be? My expenses did not change at all."

She said, "Well, someone changed them."

I thought to myself I should gather evidence of this fraud. I said, "Can you give me a printout of the computer screen so I have that for my records," very calmly.

Sure enough, she gave it to me, and I knew I had everything that it would take to prove what he had done to me on purpose committing purposeful fraud.

I called the case worker back and said to him, "I think I need to come in and talk with you."

He said, "Okay."

I went into the office. He sat across from me, and I was ready with the evidence but did not tell him that I had it.

I said to him, "Why were my benefits reduced to nothing?"

He said, "Well, it appears that you don't have any income and your expenses were getting paid, so we were wondering just how you were getting the money, so we assumed that you were not paying them, so I took them all out of the computer."

In other words, calling me a liar and erasing my expense figures, which would then make the computer calculate that I was to receive nothing in the way of benefit money to feed myself at this horrible time of my life. I now had a food stamp caseworker who was supposed to be helping me committing fraud against me in a state computer. And people said I was crazy. On the contrary, I was very smart.

I said to him, "Well, I told you that people were helping me, did you not believe me?"

Very smugly he said, "Well, miss, it is not about what I believe, it is about what you can prove."

Looking back at him holding back my anger, I calmly said, "I gave you all the proof you needed."

He was laughing at me again, and that was when I hit him with, "You removed all my expense information from the computer, didn't you? I think that is fraud, isn't it?"

His face became gray, and his jaw dropped a few inches, looking like he was going to pass out. He got very quiet and listened to me now.

I said, "You committed fraud, sir. Why do you have this job? Do you even like this job? You are supposed to be helping people, not hurting them, right?"

His face was now gray, and he looked as if someone was going to arrest him.

I remember thinking at that time how good it felt to be confronting this emotionally dysfunctional beast who took it upon himself to humiliate me, keep me from benefits, and laughed in my face while explaining how he went about erasing my information in the computer on the premise that he believed I was lying. What a complete asshole.

His reply was smug, but he was not laughing any longer, and he was sitting up straighter in his chair. I now had his attention.

He said to me, "I am not sure what you are stating."

I said, "You committed fraud and removed all my expense figures, didn't you?"

He said, "Yes, I did, you have no money, so clearly you could not be paying out any expenses either."

I could not believe that he admitted it to my face in the office.

I said, "Sir, it is not your place to say whether or not I am paying my bills. I tell you that I am, I gave you the proof, and now you actually have admitted that you erased my expense figures in the computer."

He said, "Yes," looking at me so cocky.

I could not believe I finally had everything I needed to fire this horribly uncaring inconsiderate jackass from his job and that it would be such a great feeling doing so. I could not believe I felt that way, but I did.

He would never make any woman, man, or child feel like dirt again. I vowed from that moment on, I would take him down and get him fired no matter how long it took me.

And I did a year later, writing many letters, talking to many people, crying a lot, and many sleepless nights thinking about how this horrible man laughed at me and committed fraud against me and laughed directly in my face and thought nothing of it; as you see, he was in control, or so he thought.

Finally, after many calls and letters to the USDA in Virginia talking to the top people, I was referred to a legal office in my state, and a benefits person was in charge of my case. He said he could not bring it to a hearing; he used to work in that office and said that since I did not schedule a hearing at that time, he could not do anything to help me. He said he could not help me but knew I was right. We became friends of sorts, and he empathized with me saying that this guy was a jerk. I set another hearing for another reason, and I was going to get him out of that office if it was the last thing I did. I was finally given a new case worker after talking with someone from the USDA in Virginia, but my supervisor in that office said no, I could not get another case worker after he did that to me.

She said, "Just file a sexual harassment case."

I said, "He committed fraud."

She said, "Just do it."

Well, what I would learn later from an attorney in the Washington, DC, office of the USDA was that they were not hearing cases for harassment as they were too busy and short-staffed this year.

I said, "Really, I guess that is why his supervisor said for me to do that way, huh!"

I was really mad then, angry that they were doing nothing to get him out of that office. What I did learn later from my friend at the legal office was that a state employee once fired from the food stamp office would not be replaced because of the recession. So the supervisor was only trying to keep her case worker so she would not be short another case worker. She did not care personally about me at all or what he had done to me; that was clear. It would be a sign to me that in America, people have changed and that they don't care about each other as I think they should. Maybe I don't like living here any longer for just that reason. I don't ever remember feeling this way when I was younger.

The more I read in the book *Lighting the Way: Nine Women Who Changed Modern America* years ago, I wanted to grab the phone and call them all up and say come back from wherever you are in heaven and fix this again because it's all screwed up again, and people don't care anymore about the little worker or the poor person who is being treated with disrespect, humiliation, and above all denied the very right to even eat. I needed divine intervention. I guess at this point, I didn't feel bad at all about the food stamps. I knew I had post-traumatic stress disorder and needed help from anyone who could help me. I was so stressed out just from talking to this jerk since I was a victim and the liars of the world would be part of my nemesis in my personal life along with being abused. I was lied to daily throughout my twenty-three years of marriage, or so it would seem to me after the divorce as I uncovered so many things that would make me cry on a regular basis for years. I stopped crying about all that, and right now, as I don't care the tiniest bit about that person any longer at all. In fact, I am very proud of myself that I could finally let go of any feelings whatsoever and begin a new life for myself. It is in starting over that we are set free from the past. Some people want to know what the past is. I say to them, "I can tell you, and you might not like it, but is it really important to us all."

One man whom I met years later is still working through his mess and does not realize yet that the past is there to be spoken. But if it keeps you from enjoying life, then let it go after you have done all you can do and have protected the people you need to protect. He was trying to prove to everyone that his estranged wife had poisoned him. She admitted it to his face two years later, and his life would never be the same. Trying to trust people for him would become very hard, especially a woman whom he may one day find to entrust his heart to. That was the hard part for me. I just decided one day to speak the truth when I need to, even if no one believes me, but move on and meet new people and learn new things to bring my life back to good place with peace in every day. Peace is what I strive for; in speaking the truth sometimes, people might not let you have a peaceful day. They may just take it and turn it into something ugly and make you cry. I say then cry and know that those people are just the very ones that I talk about who really don't care anyway. So forget about them, and continue your journey through life, and find some people that do care.

So I called the benefits person back. He said he was trying but could do nothing without a hearing scheduled. I found myself back into the same old situation, but I found a reason for a hearing after switching jobs again. The hearing was set; I was ready to bring this entire issue up, and wouldn't you know, I went in a day early and said that I was ready, they said the hearing was canceled.

I said, "Well, isn't that convenient for all of you."

I knew what they had done, and I was pissed at them all. Cover this up and then they can't be sued for anything or any treatment I had received. The next day I got a call saying that they fired him. Cover-up, you bet, but I don't care; he'd never do that again to anyone. I didn't want to sue them anyway, just wanted the guy out to protect others. I had done my job and would never have to look at that awful persons face again or let him make me feel like a jerk or cry after being made to feel that I was nothing in this world that mattered to anyone, not even a caseworker.

I remember vowing that at that point in my life that I was beginning to understand that if I did not give up, I would win. It would be a turning point in my life. Sticking up for yourself can be hard, but if you can withstand the pressure, stress, emotional upset, and work, you will win. It would make me stronger than I ever thought and make me stronger to help others as well. I remember at one time while I was talking to someone from the USDA in Colorado that I was crying and saying that I feel like Rosa Parks and I was not sitting in the back of the bus any longer. I would never sit in the back of the bus, ever, not for anyone. I was a white woman, who was feeling a bit of what Ms. Parks must have truly felt that day when she decided this was the last day someone was going to make her feel that she was less than someone else or not worthy of the simple things in life. Her personal story had always inspired me and on the highway by my house, there is a stretch of road dedicated to Ms. Rosa Parks. May everyone think of her often when certain events present themselves, even when they are not driving down that stretch of road on Highway 11 in Springfield.

I had started to read a book called *Lighting the Way Nine Woman Who Changed Modern America*, written by Karenna Gore Schiff; it sits on my nightstand. The book would further inspire me to stand up for myself and for others in the workplace. It is, indeed, and should be on everyone's best reading list to inspire us to become something other than ourselves and speak out for workplace injustice, no matter what the personal cost.

I didn't care at that point what anyone said about me previously. I was not going to let the crazy comments that lay dormant in my mind obstruct me in any way to get this person out of that office. Getting someone fired from their job was not my idea of a good day, but in this case I felt absolutely no remorse. I, on the other hand, was jubilant that my persistence had won over evil and that good people in the world can make a difference.

The benefits man from the legal office would come to have a genuine fondness of my truthfulness and my need to get a person out of job that was abusive to others. Even though no one ever apologized to me directly and even though there would never be a formal hearing, he told me that I could use him as an employment reference as he admired my ability to persist and tell the truth, but most of all stick with it until the proof was clear and then present it to the right person who could get the job done.

At that time, I didn't have very many good references to find a job since I was whistleblowing left and right for years, so his compassion for me and admiration would be the one thing that would be my most presented form of an apology. It made me proud that he thought highly of me, so much so that he would give a reference when he didn't know me personally and had never worked with me but understood that I had every moral fiber of my being entrenched in this investigation and I did not give up on the truth. He admired that in me and said that he would be happy to be a reference for me. I couldn't believe it.

Here I was again with no job, but I did remind myself what had happened in court at the time I was at the marketing company.

Chapter 9

Courtroom Journaling

Discovery of evidence and personal information continual tears to the truth, but did I really deep down want to know? It was hard, but I realized, without the truth, I would never be able to understand what happened and why. Why my envious relationship with my husband, as we were so happily married, would incur friends and family—especially my sisters who used to say to me, "Wow, he treats you so good and takes you on trips and brings flowers, with romantic nights at the fancy hotels with champagne and strawberries looking in the closet at new negligee and custom necklace he had made just for you with the birthstones of your three children draped over the hangar waiting for me to share a weekend of love"—how this relationship would go from so romantically wonderful to this horrible, abusive, screaming nightmare that my mind did not want to absorb and months later couldn't rationally. So I began to gather evidence about him and readied it for presentation in court, which is called discovery.

The general rules of the court were such; you will find it interesting to read this rule and understand what you have to do to gather it and submit it correctly to get the courts to accept it on the record. It is very detailed. Keep in mind that I have not been to law school or to college for that matter. I am intelligent, but the law is very hard to act pro se; the words they use for representing yourself in court. I tried my best, but reading things like this discovery rule in the law library on the fifth floor of the courthouse would make me weary most days. All I ever wanted, of course, was a happy life, and now this. The following below may be a recipe for insanity.

Rule 52.01 General Provisions Governing Discovery

(a). Discovery Methods. Parties may obtain discovery by one or more of the following methods: depositions upon oral examination or written questions; written interrogatories; production of documents or things or permission to enter upon land or other [property, for inspection and other purposes; physical and mental examinations; and requests for admission.

The party see discovery of the existence and contents, including production the policy and declaration page, of an insurance agreement under which any person carrying on an insurance business may be liable to satisfy part of all of a judgment that may be entered in the action or to indemnify or reimburse for payments made to satisfy the judgment. Information concerning the insurance agreement is not by reason of disclosing discovery shall bear the burden of establishing relevance.

(b). Scope of Discovery. Unless otherwise limited by order of the Court in accordance with these rules, the scope of discovery is as follows:

(1) In General. Parties may obtain discovery regarding any matter, not privileged, that is relevant to the subject matter involved in the pending action, whether it relates to the claim or defense of the party seeking discovery or to the claim or defense of any other party, including the existence, description, nature, custody, condition and location of any books, documents or other tangible things and the identity and location of persons having knowledge of any discoverable matter.

It is not grounds for objection that the information sought ill be inadmissible at the trial for the information sought appears reasonably calculated to lead to the discovery of admissible evidence.

The party seeking discovery shall bear the burden of establishing relevance.

(3) Trail Preparation: Material. Subject to the provisions of Rule 52.01(b)(4), a part may obtain discovery of documents an tangible things otherwise discoverable under Rule 52.01(b)(1) and prepared in anticipation of litigation or for trial by or for another party or by or for that other party's representative, including an attorney, consultant surety, indemnitor, insurer, or agent, only upon a showing that the party seeking discovery has substantial need of the materials in he preparation of the case and that the adverse party is unable without undue hardship to obtain the substantial equivalent of the materials by there means. In ordering discovery of such materials when the required showing has been made, the court shall protect against disclosure of the mental impressions, conclusions, opinions, or legal theories of an attorney or other representative of a party concerning the litigation.

A party may obtain without the required showing a statement concerning the action or its subject matter previously made by that party. For purposes of this paragraph, a statement previously made is (a) written statement signed or otherwise adopted or approved by the person making it, or (b) a stenographic, mechanical, electrical, audio, video, motion picture or other recording, or a transcription thereof, of the part or of a statement made by thirty and contemporaneously recorded.

(4) Trial Preparation: Experts. Discovery of facts known and opinions held by experts, otherwise discoverable under the provisions of Rule 52.01(1) and acquired or developed in anticipation of litigation or for trial, maybe obtained only as follows:

(a) A party may through interrogatories require any other party to identify each person whom the other party expects to call as an expert witness at trial by providing such expert's name, address, occupation, place of employment and qualifications to give an opinion, or if such information is available on the expert's curriculum vita, such curriculum vitae may be attached to the interrogatory answers as a full response to such interrogatory, and to state the general nature of the subject matter on which the expert is expected to testify, and the expert's hourly deposition fee.

(b). A party may discover by deposition the facts and opinions to which the expert is expected to testify. Unless manifest injustice would result, the court shall require that the party seeking discovery from an expert pay the expert a reasonable hourly fee for the time such expert is deposed.

(5). Trial Preparations: Non-retained Experts. A party, through interrogatories, may require any party to identify each non-retained expert witness, including a party, whom the other party elects to call at trial who may provide expert witness opinion testimony by providing the expert's name, address, and field of expertise. For the purpose of this Rule 56.0(b)(5), an expert witness is a witness qualified as an expert by knowledge, experience, training, or education giving testimony relative to scientific, technical or other specialized knowledge that will assist the trier of the fact to understand the evidence. Discovery of the facts known and opinions held by such an expert shall be discoverable in the same manner as for lay witnesses.

(6). Approved Interrogatories and Request for Production. A circuit court by local court rule may promulgate "approved interrogatory and request for production submitted to a party shall be denominated as having been approved by reference to the local court rule an paragraph number containing the motion by a party or by the person from whom discovery is sought, and for good cause shown, the court may make any order which justice requires to protect a party or person from annoyance, embarrassment, oppression, or undue burden or expense, including one or more of the following:

(c). Protective Orders. Upon motion by a party or by the person from whom discovery is sought, and for good cause shown, the court may make any order which justice requires to protect a party or person from annoyance, embarrassment, oppression, or undue burden or expense, including one or more of the following:

(1)   that the discovery not be had;

(2)   that the discovery may be had only on specified terms and conditions, including a designation of the time or place;

(3)   that the discovery may be had only by a method of discovery other than that selected by the party seeking discovery;

(4)   that certain matters not be inquired is not, or that the scope of the discovery be limited to certain matters;

(5)   that discovery be conducted with no one present except persons designated by the court;

(6)   that a deposition after being sealed be opened only by order of the court;

(7)   that a trade secret or other confidential research, development, or commercial information not be disclosed or be disclosed only in a designated way;

(8)   that the parties simultaneously file specified documents or information enclosed in sealed envelopes to be opened as directed by the court.

If a motion for protective order is denied in whole or in part, the court may, on such terms and conditions, as are just, order that any party or person provide or permit discovery. The provisions of Rule 61.01 apply to the award of expenses incurred in relation to the motion.

(d) Sequence and Timing of Discovery. Unless the court upon motion, for the convenience of parties and witnesses and I the interests of justice, orders otherwise, methods of discovery may be use in any sequence and the fact that a party is conduction discovery, whether by deposition or otherwise, shall not operate to delay any other party's discovery.

(e). Supplementation of Responses.

A party is under a duty seasonably to amend a prior response to an interrogatory, request for production, or request for admission if the party learn that the response is in some material respect incomplete or incorrect and if the additional or corrective information has not otherwise been made known to the other parties during the discovery process or in writing.

(f) Stipulations Regarding Discovery Procedure. Unless the court orders otherwise, the parties may by written stipulation (1) provide that depositions may be taken before any person at any time or place, upon any notice, and in any manner and when so taken may be used like other depositions, and (2) modify the procedures provided by these Rules for other methods of discovery. Any stipulation under subdivision (2) shall be filed.

Rule 72.02 Security for Costs

The court may require a party to furnish adequate security for anticipated costs. If the security for costs is not furnished as ordered, the court may dismiss the civil action or order other appropriate relief.

Rule 72.01 Costs Recovery in Civil Actions

In civil actions, the party prevailing shall recover his costs against the other party, unless otherwise provide in these rules or by law.

Rule 72.03 Plaintiff may Sue as a Poor Person When

If the plaintiff is a poor person, the court may permit the plaintiff to commence and prosecute the civil action without making a cost deposit or furnishing security for costs.

Rule 72.04 Offer of Judgment—Recovery of Costs

At any time more than thirty days before the trial begins, a party defending against a claim may serve upon the adverse party an offer to allow judgment to be taken against the defending party for the money or property or to the effect specified in the offer, with costs then accrue.

This is the end of the initial court recipe for insanity...

I started to make daily journal pages on my laptop so that I could remember since the facts of the days were getting very detailed, and I didn't want to forget anything. So I dated the pages and wrote short or long daily journaling of the events of the days.

This is somewhat like my diary of agonizing events that I would live and feel.

5/30/08

I called and talked with the office and got Help 111-115-4746

Prosecuting Attorney's Office

100 South Main Ave. 4th Floor

Springfield, Anywhere

We had talked months prior. He remembered me and had instructed me at the time, which until I proved there was a crime they could not enter into the case. Until I proved it?

I was calling to see if now that I have the proof can they enter the case and file the perjury charge. He stated that I had to prove it in civil court first and then the charge would be entered into a criminal court room. He told me to call the Chief Investigator at 111-222-7530.

I said thank you and called. See notes.

5/30/08

Mr. M listened to my story and said there was nothing he could do to help me with and asked me when the next hearing was and I told him June 12, 2008 at 1:30 PM.

6/24/08

I walked into the Prosecuting Attorney's office after receiving the letter from Mr. Kraft that the subpoenas would not be signed by Judge Unfair. I was really upset and did not make an appointment just drove down and walked in.

I went in to ask if they could tell me if that was against the law and show them the paperwork.

Michael an investigator came out to speak with me.

He took the paperwork back into the back office as I waited in the reception area.

He came back out and stated that an attorney in the back stated I should contact an attorney immediately. (I thought to myself wouldn't that be nice if I had some money)

He also stated the following:

1. Call Police and have them write a report.

2. Talk with Mr. Kraft and set up a meeting with him, the judge and myself to see about getting the subpoenas signed.

I went across the street to police headquarters as I thought that is where the investigator told me to go.

They instructed me inside that I needed Clay police and a dispatcher called them for me. She told me that she told them to meet me in front by the statues.

Officer named B showed up. He had spoken with me prior to that about investigating the court file. He remembered me.

He stated that they couldn't write a report and said my home subpoena copies that were stolen whoever the person was who took them probably wore gloves and it would only make me look crazy again if I reported it and they came to my home. I also told him about the court computer and the subpoenas sent back to me by the clerk and showed them to him. He said that would be an issue for the court house administration not him. At this point I could not believe this shit; I think they were doing this to me on purpose; you know having fun at my benefit.

I then walked across the way to the court house and talked with Mr. Kraft and he called me a liar and said I did not go to the prosecuting attorney's office and that I made a ruckus about the college subpoenas too. He yelled at me and I said, "If you don't believe me call them." He picked up the phone and I could see him talking and he stated that I was in his office with my arms folded. He hung up. What a big fat disgusting liar.

I said, "Did they verify what I told you" and he said, "No." I said, "Well, I was just there twenty minutes ago that's really odd" knowing that he was lying right to my face. I remember thinking how proud I was of myself and my self composure of calmness.

I asked him to check in the computer and he said your incorrect your case can be seen in file.net. I said, "No it can't." He printed out a sheet showing it. I told him that I just printed out the sheet at the front counter and nothing was there (I didn't know at this time that Mr. Kraft had the ability to hide my case in File.Net. And a few weeks ago, I did the same thing and nothing was there. I kept those printouts as evidence that they were covering up my case to the public online. They had the IT power to put it in hide mode so people could not view it. Later I would learn it's what they do when they seal a court file. Maybe the CIA had asked them to.

Then I noticed a guard from the front door behind me as I was leaving and I said to him Officer S, Mr. Kraft just called me a liar and stated that I wasn't at the Prosecuting Attorney's office.

He said, "That's not true Ms. you always make a disturbance. The officer said he was just there to see that everyone got out of the building safely." As I walked out, he was behind me and I stopped at the front counter where the computer was and picked up the sheet I had just printed out. I showed it to him and reported that I just talked with Mr. Kraft and he printed it out showing my case was indeed showing up to the public on the website but he was lying and or was able to remove the block himself as I had just tried minutes earlier and nothing came up. The officer stated he was not my witness. I asked the girl who witnessed the same thing a few weeks prior too. She said, "Yes I remember you and yes you could not see it in the computer weeks prior either, she is right." I walked out with Officer S. No one was doing anything about this cover up of my case on File.Net. I could not believe it but it proved to me that the connectivity was way deeper in that courthouse than I wanted to even dream about. I always saw movies about court corruption but thought much of it was sensationalism for the movies. This was the clear-cut truth and it was very upsetting for me as I thought that the courts were for justice of the innocent to prove crime; not cover it up. White collar crime as they have called criminals in business are the worst in my eyes, but this was men covering up for men in court while myself a woman married for 23 years faithfully to the same man and trying to get justice and get custody of her son was disillusioned by what she had figured out. They were all crooked and I would never get justice in this case. Not at this time.

6/26/08

Called Chief Investigator 111-222-7530

He said he is not getting involved in my case and that the investigator I talked with yesterday said what he said and he got mad and said I should quit calling him etc.

He stated that he had not prosecuted a criminal perjury charge in the 12 years he has been in that office.

I said, "Really why is that ok" and he hung up.

In May I entered a motion for clarification of the document for the final hearing date in the custody modification of my divorce.

Then I decided to hire an attorney and her name was Jannie who reset the hearing dates for November 5th.

She had written four or five motions and set them for the first of hearings on Nov 5th for the contempt of court on my ex-husband; I was very impressed by what she wrote and she used all of the information I had given to her.

Then, she set a hearing for October 1st which I did not know about. I only found out when I went to the court house on October 5th to look in the file and found that my ex-parte file had documents missing.

I went directly to Ana; the Judge clerk to look at my file. She handed me the file in her office and in it was a hearing set for October 7th which I did not know about. I copied the motions and also copied the ex-parte file.

I then walked down the hill to Jannie's office and I was told by her receptionist that she was not available. I stated that it was important but she stated that she could not see me because she had someone in her office. The receptionist stated that she could set a hearing without my knowing it. I said no, she can't; not representing me as she and I had a clear-cut understanding that I was to know everything in the progress of this case. She had me scheduled for a doctor's appointment on October 17th with a psychiatrist for an evaluation that she set up. The appointment had been scheduled earlier but was then rescheduled. I was upset about that too. Anyway, at that time I was unsure if I could trust my attorney because she had spent all of my money and we hadn't even gotten into court yet. She had informed me the $5000.00 that I gave to her only months ago was all used up by talking and meetings. I could not believe it, I worked hard for that money and she had done very little, except to write the motions which I gave her the information for, I was upset.

So I left and was upset. I drove out to the doctor's office and told them that I was canceling the appointment and that I wanted my money back. They had the check ready from the last time I was there. I felt like my attorney was making me pay $800.00 for a doctor's appointment because my ex-husband said I was crazy and by that time I was fed up and said maybe he should pay or prove himself that I am. Why do I have to prove that I am not crazy when I'm not. I guess I did not trust psychiatrists either as they want everyone to take a pill and feel better so they can make money. They concur with other doctors so no one get sued either. This I knew from working for doctors, they hate lawyers.

I then thought about my case and knew that I did not have any more money to give to Jannie so I went back to her office and asked for my file back. The receptionist said ok, and then Gina the other attorney in her office who was working with me on the employee case came out and said that for 400 years it has been a practice that lawyers can schedule hearings without the knowledge of their clients.

I said that Jannie and I had an agreement that she would not do anything without my knowledge and she said ok.

Anyway, I called the Bar Association and asked to speak to a lawyer and they stated that yes indeed it is not against the law for an attorney to schedule a hearing without the client knowing it.

I now was representing myself again. I had to refocus and get in gear again for the legal fight. I was up for it this time. I had no idea where to begin but yet here I go.

On October 17th, Jody did not show up for the hearing for withdrawal, but instead Gina showed up.

The Judge did not have time to hear this case and so it was continued to October 9th at 1:00. But when we tried to file it Brian wrote the order for November 5th. I of course caught the mistake and said no it is supposed to be before October 9th.

On October 9th I showed up and so did Jannie, Gina, and her receptionist. Jannie would not speak to me when I approached her to make a settlement offer and discuss her withdrawal. She would not speak to me.

The Judge took us first and I asked that Ms. Jannie be granted the right to withdraw. I stated that she had used up all of my money and never got to court. $5877.00 for writing four motions and this was not right. I said that she was billing me too much. The Judge said, "Well then you don't want her as your attorney, right?" I said, "No I still need her as my attorney to represent me until such time as I have the money to get another attorney." The Judge said denied and granted the withdrawal. This left me once again in a state of complete emotional disaster without an attorney once again. They take your money and use it up and no one does anything to stop them. I liked Jannie and I felt that if I had been able to speak with her that day in the office we could have straightened things out, but her receptionist did not care and maybe did not like me, I thought she was a bit rough with clients on the phone and not a very caring person. Although I must say, I did not like the pottery jar on the front counter which stated, "Previous difficult clients Ashes." As if they had some clients that got burned. Get It! I didn't think it was funny at all.

He never heard my motion for Pendente Lite for my son and myself; which is a hurry up hearing for money to help live and custody returned to me of my son which was the most important thing to me as I had not revealed to the courts a truth that I had kept secret as I did not want my abuser to further harm me or quite possibly kill me to reveal his secret life and why he treated me so horribly at the end before he left me. I will reveal it later for you and you will be shocked.

University journal page for October events:

This is the University where my son is attending college on a soccer scholarship. I needed the information that his father submitted to the college as to his financial years salary statements to prove in court that he had lied on court paperwork about what his yearly income statement was; I knew he was lying but wanted to prove it before I gave my ex-husband a subpoena for his income tax statements. That would-be clear-cut proof he lied to the courts about his income. I had no idea that the corruption of the courts and the connectivity of his lawyer in that courtroom would make all my hard work all for nothing; as not even the Judge held him in contempt for lying on the witness stand under oath, a direct corruptive move by a Judge in Springfield.

On October 9th I delivered a subpoena to the White County Sheriff's office in Springfield and then went to the University to see if Gene was in so that if they delivered it right away, I could go home with the information as the drive was 2 hours to get back to Springfield. It was 9:00 AM and they told me that she would not be in until 2:00 PM.

I then asked if there was anyone else I could speak to about my son and what it would take to get him back on the soccer team. They referred me to Mr. C in the athletic office and I walked over to speak to him. He told me that my son needed a 2.0 GPA to stay on the team. He needed to bring up his grades in summer school that he attended. What I would learn later was that he did indeed bring his summer grades up past the 2.0 but was kept off the team anyway, I did not know why, did my son opted to not play so he could focus on his studies more. At that time he was not talking to me so I did not know.

I drove home.

On October 7th the hearing in court was postponed and I never received the information I had requested from the school by subpoena.

On October 8th I called Ms. Gene and left a voice message as to the fact that I had not received the information from the University and could she tell me why.

She never returned the call.

On October 1st I drove to the university and saw the soccer games played by both the girls and boys. The girls won and the boys lost. My son of course was not playing

I spent the night Sunday and then woke up on Monday and drove over to the University and asked to speak with Gene. I was once again told that she would not be in until 2:00. I said fine I will wait and they told me to have a seat, I told Robin that maybe she should call her back and tell her that if I didn't get the information today she would be held in contempt of court as now the Judge has signed the subpoena also. I called in to work and told them that I would not be in to work that day as I start at 3:30. Not five minutes later

Rob told me that Gene would be in the office in twenty minutes.

Gene arrived and I was asked by an assistant to please go across the hall into an empty conference room and wait there for Gene. I said, "Of course, no problem." I waited about 10 minutes.

She came into the conference room and did not look happy. She did not say good morning or offer me anything to drink. Another words; no hospitality. She said that my son had not been gong to class again and she stated to me, "Where is your son, we do not know where he is, he has not been gong to class." She had me worried and I asked if she could have security run over to his room and see if he was there and she said she could not do that for me as it was against his privacy. She had me very worried as his mother; as he was not at the games the day before nor had he been at the games several weeks prior that I came down to watch nor was he answering my phone calls. I thought it strange that she would not check on my son for me.

She began accusing me of not giving her ample time to uphold the delivery of the information. She stated that there was a question about the validity of the first subpoena delivered by the sheriff and she was asking questions to the attorney as there was no date and she questioned the seal and the signature on the subpoena which I had gotten at the court house in Springfield. I asked her why she did not immediately call me and say that she had a problem, she said she did not know why.

I asked her why she did not respond to my voice mail I left last week regarding the subpoena. She said she did not have time and it was fall break; however, there was no message on her voice mail that she was out of the office on vacation. It seemed like stalling tactics to me.

Then she became irate and accused me of having the second subpoena with the Judges signature as a forgery. She kept saying, "How do I know that this is the Judges signature" in a very loud and degrading demeanor. She was upset as I had told her that this put her in contempt of court. She said to me, "This is all about money isn't it, in a very nasty manner." I politely said, "No it is not." She was out of line and clearly didn't care about my son.

I did not file the second subpoena signed by the Judge or take it to the County Sheriffs office to be delivered to her that day, so that she would have a chance to answer before she was in contempt from the Judge. However, she made matters worse and accused me of having a document that was somehow compromised. It was a direct assault on my character. So immediately I stated, "If you don't believe me, I'll just call the Judge's office and you can speak to the clerk Ana, she has the file."

I called information and got the number for Ana. The phone rang and I gave the phone to Ms. Gene to speak directly to her.

I heard her speaking and then she said she was transferred to the manager in administration. She talked for awhile and then I said, please let me speak to him when you are finished.

She handed me the phone and the manager stated, why did you interrupt her, I said, "I didn't sir I asked her to please give me the phone when she was finished speaking to you, so that she wouldn't hang up.

He stated that he gave his permission for her to give the information. I said, "Thank you" and he hung up.

Gail stated for me to wait there and she would get the information. She was clearly upset.

I waited for some time and by then I was thirsty,

so I got up and told the information desk person that I was going to get something to drink and I would be back.

Gene then came in and gave the information about my son's grades, she spoke with me only briefly and did not explain in detail and never sat back down with me. I had many questions, but she said she had to go to a meeting and left. I was not happy with her demeanor towards me as I was paying a lot of money for my son to go to that private University as he was not on a soccer scholarship any longer.

I felt very insecure about my son. I decided to go and talk with the Dean of Students. Dr. was not in her office and I was told she would be back at 1:00 PM. I stood in the hall and one of the cafeteria people came out and asked if I was being helped. I said that I was worried about my son and she told me that I should go down to the security office and ask them to check on him.

I walked down to the basement floor and into the security office. Diane was not there but someone else came out and said she would help me. I told her that I was worried about my son and sat a bit and talked with her. She said that she would send someone over to his apartment to check and see if he was there. So, Ms. G had lied to me, security could go check on him in his room. That was clearly upsetting for me.

We talked for a bit and then he came back and said that my son was ok and in his room. I said thank you and then drove home. I arrived back home and sat and read over the information that was given to me. I felt very uncomfortable. My son's grades from summer were 4.0 for session I and 3.3 for session II for the summer which was excellent; however, he was not placed back on the team. He had been asked to write a letter at the beginning of summer as to an appeal to stay at the university. He states that his co-curricular activities were too much for him and he would try to do better. Well, the summer classes definitely proved that he had done better and yet was not allowed to play soccer. I was not happy and I know that my son would not be either. I would never get to tell him. He would not return my calls.

I drove home and I rested and looked at my mail for the day and opened it. Low and behold was a letter returned from my son with his address on it from an invitation I had sent to him to come to Thanksgiving dinner that year at my home with his sisters.

I couldn't sleep much and decided to drive back down to the college again the next morning to ask more questions to my son since I now had his address. I thought God was helping me to make sure he was fine and talk with him about these issues.

I left at 3:00 AM and drove down again to talk to and see my son myself.

I arrived at 7:00 AM and went directly to my son's apartment. I could not see any numbers on the outside of the buildings so I wasn't sure which one was his. I walked around a bit in the dark and then suddenly one of his friends from the soccer team Sam came walking across the street. I said, "Hi aren't you Sam from the soccer team," and he said, "Yes." I asked him which building Shaun was in and he pointed to it. I went around the back side of the building and through the hall and noticed right off that there were broken beer bottles and alcohol bottles broken all over the ground. I was really concerned but because it was so early, I knocked on the door softly and waited. There was no answer. Then Sam came back and was going into the door opposite my son's and he said that Tom (another boy from the soccer team lived there and had a party last night) he was going into the apartment to get his keys as he said he left them there last night and asked me if I wanted to come in as it was cold. I said, "No, I'll just wait out here until Shaun comes to the door." Sam and I talked a bit about school and he said that he liked it there and I told him that I was worried about Shaun as he, too, was not on the soccer team any longer and must have been cut like my son. I asked him if he liked the coach and he said yes. I told him that they were not very nice to me yesterday here on campus and he said that's too bad and said he had to leave to get to work it was about 8:00 AM by then. I tried knocking on the door again and again but no avail. Then a boy came around with a leaf blower and was blowing out the hallways. He blew the broken glass while I was standing there. I then knocked harder on the door and Shaun's roommate Nick came to the door and said I don't feel good but come on in and Shaun's room is straight ahead. I went to the door and knocked on his door and said Hi Shaun it is mom Nick let me in I want to talk with you, please. He acknowledged that he was there but did not open the door. I then went to sit down at the kitchen table to wait. He came out and looked at me but then just turned around and went back into his room. I waited a bit and then went to his door and waited for him to come out. He did not. After a few minutes the front door opened and security came in yelling Ms. you need to get out of your son's apartment right now as you are trespassing and we will throw you into jail. I said, "What! I was let in by my son's roommate and I was not trespassing. They said I needed to leave now. I walked out of the apartment saying fine I will leave and the Judge will love hearing that you told me that my son was not attending class and so I came to his room and there are broken beer bottles and other broken bottles on the ground.

I then went to the main office and asked the receptionist at the information desk to please call the Dean's office and see if I could speak with him as I was just yelled at by security to get out of my sons room or they would call the police and have me thrown in jail. I was extremely worried about what kind of University this was.

She stated that the Dean would speak to me and that I could go to his office. I walked around the building and went inside and walked to the second floor. I was not greeted by anyone, so I said, "Hi I am Julia Rule and I have an appointment to speak with the Dean." They said have a seat.

The Dean came out and said hello and come into his office.

We sat down and talked for a while about the security people and about Gene. I told him that Gene had talked to me in an inappropriate manner and that I was very concerned about my son. I was not happy with the way he talked to me and he did apologize for the security people. We talked a bit about the broken bottles and I said that I understood how young adults did things such as that. I wanted him to know that my son was in trouble and that he needed to take care of the situation. He seemed very concerned and he stated you got what you wanted didn't you, meaning the information from Gene about my son. I didn't like that comment and so I said I was leaving.

I then went to the Dean of Students office and told the Dr. that the Dean asked me if I had screamed at Gene and I told him on the contrary, she yelled at me. She was surprised and I told her about what happened in my son's room and the broken beer bottles. She said she was sorry and I said well I guess he is yours now and left.

I am extremely worried about my son and this is why I have been in court for the past years trying to do the right thing for my children and myself so we can get back the family we had with the four of us and now a son-in-law and grandson. I need a home for them to come to and feel they are home and Mom will take care of them and their needs. That is what I always had at my mother's home and my ex-husband had at his Mom's home. He had taken away our home and for that I would never forgive him.

On November 5th I arrived in the court house at 10:30 AM to file stamp some of the items that I was going to give to the Judge.

I then went to the resource room to ask Fanny the attorney some questions. She stated that she could not give me legal advice. She stated that I could go to the law library, but that if I wanted to change Judges that I could.

I am not sure what to do. But I did decide to stay with the same Judge.

The hearing time was 1:00 PM and I went into the court room and sat down in the attorney chairs.

Brian was in there and he said that the Judge would be back at 1:30 PM. I had already had enough of Brian and his tactics so I just sat tight and waited as the Judge had informed me that I was not to go into his chambers without Brian.

I was not going to do anything wrong. Then the Judge came out and called everyone's names. Brian was not there but I answered yes. He told all the other people to come back to chambers except for me. I was mortified but said nothing, just sat and waited.

Brian came out of the chamber hall with a letter in his hand.

Then Ana came out and handed me a letter and Brian a letter. It stated that Ms. Jannie did not enter the motions of mine on time, etc. Clearly, they were full of shit.

Then the Judge came into the court room and said that we were next and I sat down at the table and Mr. Brian and my ex-husband sat on the other side.

The Judge began to speak on the record and swore me in. He never swore my ex-husband in. Then he stated that he could only hear the Motion on Contempt and not the other motions. I stated why not, we're here and ready to go and the Judge stated that there were other cases that were still to be heard. I stated that I wanted the Pendente Lite motion heard for my son first, he said it would have to wait. He said Ms. you look like you have a lot of papers there. I said yes, your honor; I do have many things to give to you and to Mr. Brian. He said go ahead and I gave them to Mr. Brian and to the Judge. Mr. Brian asked if they had been filed with the court today as they were file stamped and I said no, I just file stamped them before coming up to the court room today when I arrived.

He stated that was fine.

I was shocked and surprised and asked why. He stated that Ms. Jannie only entered the one motion to be heard on Nov 5th and not the others, I stated that the motion I filed Pendente Lite was supposed to have been heard on October 7 and never was. It wasn't heard on October 29th either. I guess I failed to ask for a continuance. This is frustrating.

Anyway, the Judge asked me if I wanted to only hear the contempt motion and I stated that they were kind of a succession of items and that they should be heard that way and that we could continue and hear them all. Then Judge said to reset the hearing for November 30th at 10:00 AM and everyone agreed.

I asked the Judge if I could file the motion for undisclosed assets at this time to be heard on November 30th also and he said yes, give it to Mr. Brian. I handed it to Mr. Brian and he took it and slid it under his paperwork as if it would be his excuse for forgetting to add it to the list.

Then Judge stated that Mr. Brian should write down all of the motions to be heard for hearing on

November 30th at 10:00. The Judge left the courtroom and went into his chambers.

Mr. Brian then began to question me about the clarification of document motion and as I tried to explain he began to badger me. I left and went into the clerk's office.

I waited for Mr. Brian and he did not come back into the Judges chambers, so I went to look for him and he was sitting at the table in the courtroom still writing. I went back to chambers and waited.

Then he came in and handed me the document to sign. It only had 5 of the 7 motions listed and I added the other two including the motion for undisclosed assets which he tried to hide by slipping it under his pad of paper. He clearly is purposely trying to deceive me again and the presentation of the documents to be heard on the 30th. Clearly the Judge would now know that Mr. Brian was intentionally doing this underhanded type actions, which would later be quite important to the fact that someone had replaced documents in the court files on the fifth floor and had gotten into my house to take he paperwork that was the original and replace it with the misleading forged copies he had placed in the file at the courthouse.

The Judge took the motion for continuance and we talked a bit about evidence and Mr. Brian said he may need a continuance for the motion to modify and I asked why. He would not state why and he said he needed more time to gather information.

I said we have to move quickly on these motions and gather the evidence; attorney's like to stall because they can continue and drag it out so their clients pay more money.

I needed evidence of this from the responses he gave back to Ms. Jannie from the motions we wrote.

I told him that he could have any evidence from

me that I had; pay stubs, etc. that he needed and I would give him copies. We walked back into the courtroom and I asked the question, does your client know about my son and what is happening at school.

Mr. Brian immediately turned the conversation into accusations that I did something wrong down at the University. I said on the contrary, the only impropriety was on the part of the University and I did not trespass I was let in my son's roommate, I did not trespass.

Mr. Brian then began to speak in a derogatory tone which he did earlier and has done in the past to intimidate me.

I left the courtroom to go down the escalator and he yelled this to me out loud, "I guess your son is worth $350,000 dollars to you huh that's your idea of custody." He was a pig; the money was to punish my ex-husband for taking away our house when he clearly had enough money to have kept helping me make the payments for the next 7 years. Clearly, we only owed $110,000.00 and if I had stayed in the house, I could have taken a loan out by myself and bought it as after the sale of the home I bought $95,000.00 condo. My children and I lost our home, so he could live with a girlfriend and take our home away from us. He got no money from the proceeds so it was a way to hurt myself and my children to have their home taken away. He was a monster in my eyes for sure.

I said, "No the money is for a house which was taken away from us." He said, "You don't need a house." I said, "Yes I do for my daughters, and my son; a son-in-law and my grandson." He said, "You just want the money!" and was speaking in a very intimidating way to me as if to imply that I wanted money for myself and not my kids. He was the scum of the earth divorce attorney who got plenty of money to harass me and intimidate me. The abused woman who could not bear much more now had to take this as well every time in court. I was growing weaker and weaker in my mind. My past verbal abuse had left mental scars which would haunt me and turn my brain to mush when I was stressed.

He continued even after we got off the escalator as I passed by the security area to go out the front door and he was going out the back way still badgering me and I stated, "You are going to be disbarred." Little did I know that he would not as they don't punish lawyers for such behavior so they do it and get away with it for sure. It would become one worldly evil I would wish to change.

I left and went to my car and drove home. I was very upset and sat on the couch all night long not even wanting to move or think. I had no emotions in my body at all. I was numb.

November 6, 2007

Today I went to the courthouse to get some subpoenas and to think about writing a note to the Judge about Mr. Brian's behavior in the courthouse the day before.

I got the forms I needed on the third floor and then went to Marcy's office to ask her a question about the subpoenas.

In her office was Mr. Kraft and he acted like he left and I introduced myself to Joan and asked her if I could deliver subpoenas myself if I am representing myself in my case and she stated very quickly yes of course. I told her great because Mr. Kraft said that I could not serve it myself and that I needed for someone else to take it in and hand it to the person.

He chimed in and said no I believe that I told you it would be best if you did not go yourself to deliver it because it would not be safe. I stated oh, I thought you said that I could not deliver them myself that the law for pro se states they do not have the right as an attorney does to deliver a subpoena. Clearly, he was lying right to my face and the Circuit Clerk.

He stated, "No that is not what I said." Clearly to me he was lying and he knew it and he looked me straight in the eye and said, "That is not what I said." He lied in my mind for sure.

I said, "Yeah I guess I learned at one place a few weeks ago, what would happen if you even go back to get the information; and I must say, I did quite well," as I bit my tongue when I was badgered.

I knew that I could not trust Mr. Kraft after that moment.

I thanked Ms. Marcy and I left. I filed out the subpoenas and thought about writing the note to the Judge about Mr. Brian and time stamped the form but thought I will see if I can go to his office. I thought to myself, I'll give him one more chance and go to his office to drop off the letters as I did not want to send the letter certified to save the money. I knew the subpoenas were going to cost a lot and I am not doing well with little money. So, I drove over to his office and took the elevator up to the third floor. The elevator opened and in front of me was a reception desk.

I approached the desk and said hello to the woman behind the desk. She said, "Hello." I said, "I am delivering this letter and would you please stamp the letter as received and make a copy for me." She stated that she was not able to do that and that she would give it to his secretary and would tell Brian that I was there. I stated, "No, don't tell him that I am here I don't wish to see him just stamp the letters received and copy them for me. Thank you."

She left and went out of the area. A few short minutes Mr. Brian came to the reception area and stated that he was not going to accept the letters. I stated to him, "You have to accept them I am dropping them off myself to save time and money." "I was going to send it certified but it costs $5.00 and right now I am tight for money."

He stated, "I will accept the one but not the other." I said, "You can't do that I am hand delivering them to you." He said, "Yes I can and started to get loud." I said, "You are going to jail," as I threw the letter at him and left.

I took the one letter he gave back to me about his behavior and went back to the court house to write the Judge a note.

When entering the courthouse at the security area I stopped and asked the guard if he knew who was on duty yesterday around 2:30 PM or 3:30 PM. He said that he did not know but gave me the number to call the officer in charge of scheduling. I said ok.

I called the number and Officer Albert was not in and I talked with the Officer and he said that he did not know and asked me for my name and number so that he could call me back. I said, "Ok."

I wrote the note and copied the letter and file stamped it on the third floor. I took the note and the letter and took it to the second floor and put it on the Judges clerk's desk.

I then took the subpoenas I had stamped and copied them and placed the copy in the file basket on the third floor.

I then drove to the Sheriffs office and paid to have the subpoenas delivered at a cost of $134.00. They were very nice and I paid by check.

I drove to work and stayed there even though it was early.

November 7th 2007

I had left a message on Tuesday after talking with Officer Walk and then Officer Al. Officer Al said that he could not tell me what officers were working at the front door station in the court house at the times between 2:30 PM and 3:30 PM but that I could call back and talk with Officer Albert at 111-222-5489 to find out the names of the officers so that I could question them about Mr. Brian's behavior as I left the court house on Monday November 5, 2007.

November 8, Wednesday there was a Message on my phone from Officer Albert.

Wednesday I received a message on my phone while at my sister's house from Office Albert letting me know that he checked will all of the 9 people that were working on Monday and none of them remembered a loud conversation between me and Mr. Brian on that day as we left the court house coming down the escalator.

He stated that the officer's remembered a woman from adult abuse had been coming down the escalator and having an altercation with her ex-husband and that was all they could remember of that day.

He said that I could call him at 111-115-5489.

It was time for me to enter the motion to ask for a change of Judge to bring Judge into another courtroom to testify as to Mr. Brian's behavior of the documents in court one day and the documents that had been switched in court and taken from my house.

I found the rule that applied and wrote the following motion. I thought you might like to see what it looked like since this does not happen very often in court.

IN THE CIRCUIT COURT OF SPRINGFIELD COUNTY
STATE OF ANYWHERE

Julia Rule,	)	
SS#XXX-XX-5556	)	
	)	
Petitioner,	)	
	)	
Vs.	)	Case
No. PC-003222		
	)	
	)	
Paul Rule	)	
SS#XXX-XX-2226	)	
	)	
Respondent,	)	

<u>CHANGE OF JUDGE PROCEDURE PER RULE 1.05</u>

STATES:

a). A change of judge shall be ordered in any civil action upon the timely filing of a written application therefore by a party. For purposes of this Rule 51, motions to modify child custody, child support, or spousal maintenance filed pursuant to chapter 452, are not an independent civil action unless the judge designated to rule on the motion is not the same judge that ruled on the previous independent civil action. The application need not allege or prove any cause for such change of judge and need not be verified.

I hereby request a change of judge in this case due to the fact that I will be calling Judge and his clerk Ana in this case as witnesses to the hearing on February 24, 2006 whereupon I am requesting immediately that Judge recuse himself in this case for the foregoing reason.

Petitioner has filed motions for emergency hearings in August that have not been heard about her juvenile son, she is in fear of his safety and loss of parental guidance and hereby emphatically requests that a guardian be placed immediately in his favor for the remainder of these hearings and motions before the courts. And that said, the guardian will contact him immediately.

A copy of this motion was given to Honorable Unnamed, Presiding Judge, Division 1 and in doing so the request of change of Judge placed on this case. Julia Rule the petitioner and pro see attorney is seeking swift and immediate action on behalf of her son Shaun Rule with the first immediate date for hearing in November as the next hearing in the case to her heard is November 30, 2007 at 10:00 AM.

Respondent's attorney has requested a hearing on November 8, 2007 set for November 18, 8:30 AM whereby he states that he has not had enough time for discovery and that I have filed amended financials that he wishes to discuss. The financials were filed by me and the earlier ones were made out by my attorney's secretary and were not correct. All Mr. Brian needs to do is call me to discuss them. He stated that he was going to bring me in for deposition on November 5th and never has as I had requested that he set the date as I was available any day and then have Mr. Rule, Mia, and Art also deposed at that time. He has not called me at all as of today.

Judge himself told Mr. Brian to get Mr. Rule's Financial Statement and Statement of Property which he has not even complied with as of this date November 21, 2007. He has continually requested more time when he has had months to get Mr. Rule's financials on the record. I do hereby request vehemently that his request be denied and my very urgent request for hearing on my son in this case be heard first and that a guardian by appointed to my son immediately.

STATE OF ANYWHERE   )
)

COUNTY OF SPRINGFIELD)
)

JULIA RULE lawful age, being duly sworn on her oath, states that she is the Petitioner named above, and the facts stated herein are true according to her best information, knowledge, and belief and is representing herself pending emergency monies for continuance of representation by counsel by which to provide a fair and just representation in this continuance case.

_____

Julia Rule, pro se

A copy of the foregoing was mailed to Mr. Brian, Attorney for Respondent this 21st day of November 2007.

SO ORDERED:

_____

Honorable Unnamed Date

SO ORDERED:

_____

Presiding Judge Unnamed Date

IN THE CIRCUIT COURT OF SPRINGFIELD COUNTY
STATE OF ANYWHERE

JULIA RULE,	)
SS#XXX-XX-2226	)
	)
Petitioner,	)
	)
Vs.	) Case No. PC-003222
	)
	)
PAUL RULE	)
SS#XXX-XX-2222	)
	)
Respondent,	)
	)

MEMORANDUM

COMES NOW Petitioner pro se and files Petitioner's Motion for Change of Judge to be heard if needed November 28, 2007 unless the Judge signs it without hearing needed.

Respectfully submitted:

By:_____

Julia Rule, pro se

2222 Cozy Lane

Springfield, Anywhere 30009

(111) 777-2222

Pro Se attorney for self

Certificate of Service

The undersigned certifies that a copy of the foregoing was sent this 21st day of November, 2007 via US Mail, postage paid to: Mr. Brian, Clay Road, Springfield, Anywhere 30009.

November 10, 2007

I received a letter from Mr. Brian that he had asked for a continuance in the motion to modify.

I was quite surprised as I thought that he would be sending a letter to inform me of the deposition of myself in his office as he had asked me what times were good in court on November 5th and I told him any morning of the week this month would be fine just call me or write and let me know.

I later had a subpoena taken to the County to serve Mr. Rule; Ms. Mia and Mr. Art on November 6th stating that they would all be deposed by me and Mr. Brian in his office to be determined at a time that Mr. Brian would set.

I sat down and wrote the response to his motion for the Judge to deny his motion on grounds that he was stalling and had ample time to call or write to me to ask me anything he needed in this case and we did not need a hearing for a continuance of the motion to modify.

I then wrote out the responses to there reply of my motions to him and was going to take it to the court on Monday and file it all and copy Mr. Brian but it is a Holiday Veteran's day and so I will file it all on Tuesday Nov 13th.

November 12th Veteran's Day 2007

Today I was going to go to the court house but then realized after stopping at the bank first that it was Veteran's Day and the court house would be closed.

I was also going over to the other state where my ex-husband lived to check on property assets and so I took this time to drive by the home of Mr. Art and friends Bees to see where they lived and to stop at the Sheriff's office to ask if the subpoenas had been served last week on Mr. Rule; Ms. Mia; and Mr. Art.

I spoke with Sheriff Bobbie and he stated that Mr. Art had been served but Mr. Rule and Ms. Mia had not.

I told the sheriff that Mr. Rule's business is Investigate U and is located on Gentleman road right off Pappies on the right side of the road in a new small office building and he is on the upper part of the building complex on the right side of the road.

Sheriff Bobbie said that he would deliver service on him today and that I could call him at the County office in his living area later in the day to check to see if he was served. His number is 111-222-6666.

November 16, 2007

I went to the court house to see if the Judge had granted the hearing on the 28th that Mr. Brian had set. I don't know what it is for other than what he stated about my financials.

I went to the Judges Chambers and asked the clerk at the desk Nan (Not Ana) if there was a hearing scheduled on the 28th by Mr. Brian.

Nan tried to pull up the file in the computer and it would not let her. She stated that the file number was not in the computer.

She said that she would have to find it and call me and when she said put your name and number on the paper, the Judge came out and said that he needed her in the court room as I was writing down my name and number and the day of the hearing and I had to stop because she went into the court room.

She said that she would call me.

She never called back that day; then I was eating in my car before going into work and the phone rang and I couldn't get to it. I looked at the number received because no message was left.

The number was the court house. I called and Nan said that she could not get into the screen about my file since it was sealed. She said Ms. Bury would call me back to let me know if there was a hearing on November 28, 2007.

I was not happy and went into work.

But also, on that day after I left the Judges chambers, I went out to the lobby and then sat in on his court proceedings for awhile.

There was a divorce case going on. The couple had evidently settled the matter but the Judge put them both on the stand to state what the agreement of the settlement was so there was no question as to what was settled and what was not.

Each man and wife had their turn on the stand and I found it interesting that this did not take place in my case at all either in the divorce in 2004 or in the Motion to Modify on February 2006.

I was astonished and then knew for sure that my case was not handled within the limits of the law ether with Mr. Zero or with the Judge.

I feel that this happened because Mr. Brian and my ex-husband were friends. I was told by other attorneys that Mr. Ponto was probably paid well for not handling my case properly because of a friendship and a good old boys club mentality and in the process myself and my children were screwed out of our home and our lives with each other as the whole thing was too much for all of us to take. It split us up and the bad feelings were so hard to handle and the lies of their father were too much for me and my children to cope with along with the perpetuating lies of the attorneys on the case.

November 17, 2007

I went to the Prosecuting Attorney Center and inquired at the front window about what they could do to help me in the matter of the case I had before the courts as the Judge, attorney and police officers involved in the case were committing criminal acts against me.

He stated that the case was civil in nature thus far and that I had to prove that the documents were taken from my home and the documents in the court file were switched by Mr. Brian.

I talked with Tom in a private room and he instructed me to go to the presiding Judge over Judge Essner. I went to the information desk and asked who the presiding Judge was over my Judge and she stated that it was Judge B on the third floor.

I went directly to his office and spoke with him in his chambers.

I told him of my concern and he stated that he could not do anything about the file situation until I made a police report and I should call the police.

I walked across the street to the police station and they instructed me that the file is in the county and the Clayton police station is located down the street and that I needed to go there.

I then walked down the street and went to the counter. I spoke with a young woman and she said she would have an officer come out and speak with me.

An officer came out and spoke with me his name was Brian. I told him the story and he said that they could do nothing because the file at home was not in their jurisdiction and that I should go to the county and ask to speak to who ever is over Lieutenant Bird and ask for an investigation they also stated that the file in the court house does not belong to me it belongs to the courts and that they would have to make a police call about that court file being tampered with not me. They said it would be hard to prove. I said yes it will but they have to help me. They said I should go to the county police and tell them.

I walked up the street and had not heard back from Ms. Bury and called again and left a message that I was outside the court house and would wait a few minutes to see if she would please call me back. I walked to my car and got in. Then my phone rang and Ms. Bury said that she could not give me any information over the phone that I had to come into the court house. That she was on the third floor in room 115.

I walked into the court house and up to the third floor. Her office was the last one down the hall in the back offices.

She was in her office with another woman at that time, who did not identify herself. I introduced myself and she said that she had the file. I stated that I had asked multiple times about the protocol for the file now that it has been sealed and she stated that she had the file now and that she just had not entered the information into the file yet. She said here you can look at the file and handed me the file. [Note—I did not ask for the file at all. She was up to something; I did not know what.] She simply stated that the hearing had not been entered into the system yet. She was not going to tell me anything else and asked for my identification. I gave her my driver's license and she took the file and said yes, she was entering the hearing on the 28th today. I was amazed and asked her if the Judge had seen my reply to the hearing. She said she didn't know and she held open the file and my request which was sent in before Mr. Brian's was in the file but Mr. Brian's was on top outside the file she said waiting to be entered. I said, how could that be since I entered mine after his. She said she did not know.

I inquired if she would be the one to have the file now since I was told that Mr. Kraft would have the file now.

She stated no that she had no idea why he would have the file. I said Fanny had the file and gave it to Mr. Kraft and he stated that I needed to come to him to get the file whenever I wanted it. It took me four hours one day just to get something and copy it from the file.

Then I told her that Mr. Kraft had accused me of being untrustworthy outside the Judges courtroom in the public waiting area. I stated how dare you, accuse me of the very thing that I am saying is wrong with this file. I asked him to sit down and speak with me. He sat down and I told him that I am saying that the file was tampered with and documents were taken out of the file by someone and it was not me.

There were words and she said I'll just give you the file and you can sit outside here in the outer office and look at it and she led me to the outer office and pointed to a couch and said you can sit here and review the file.

She then went back into her office.

I looked at the file and on top was Mr. Brian request for hearing and underneath were papers not even belonging to the file but to someone else's case. I immediately got up and told her of such and said when Mr. Brian comes to your office do you let him sit outside of your view like this and look at the file and she said well of course he is an officer of the court as an attorney I would trust him. I said well don't, no one is to see this file unless someone else is looking at it at the same time so nothing goes in and nothing goes out that is not supposed to go in and out. Referring him to an officer of the court was such a joke.

I was amazed that she looked upset but by this time it was clear to me that the file is floating about the court house in disarray much more so than a regular file. My sealing the file seems to have put it at more risk of even more hands touching it than before.

I don't know what to do so I asked her who would be the person over this file so I could go to the police and state that the file has been tampered with.

She said that Marcy would be the one to inquire about that. I said thank you and left.

It was too late to go the police station across the street because I had to get to work and didn't want to be late.

I was so weary and tired but wanted to leave anyway as I was sick of hearing; I can't help you or talk to you. I have been getting too much of that and it is tiring for me along with working at my job. Because I was not an attorney, they treated me with disrespect. Interestingly in the court room I was told I had to do everything like an attorney; what a two-edged sword they all wielded at me every day.

I am a bit stressed about money and the fact that I need to change Judges.

It is a long struggle and I grow weary on certain days but have learned how to deal with it.

I have never found myself so utterly interested in the truth and how to go about getting it. At this point I was determined to secure the file and tell them what happened so that it could not continue. They did not know that at one time I worked in a secret library full of files for the federal government and knew how to secure files and determine if the file could be tampered with and I had proved that it can be in that court house.

November 19, 2007

I went to the police station across from the county court house to deliver the complaint about the police officers.

I talked with Ham in that office in the Bureau of Professional Responsibility; this was the office that investigated the inappropriate actions of police officers.

He said that he could not do an investigation of my files or the court files as he could only check on the conduct and ethics of the officers involved.

I asked if he could give me a copy of the affidavits that the officers said they had when I was at the local police station when they took me to Dylan; they said they had them signed by my sister and mother and I had to go.

He stated that he could not get a copy of those. I should ask the hospital; as they were not in the copy of my file that I got from the hospital so I would go there to get them.

I gave Ham the copy of the request for an investigation of the files in the court house. He said that he could not do that and I said that the Courts have to call the police and have that done for themselves. I said that I was going over there right now to get it.

I thanked him and walked out.

I went to the court house and stamped the documents for Judge (presiding).

I went to the 3rd floor and Judge (presiding) had a sign on her door that she was in a trial for the next week and if anything was needed that it should be taken to Judge C as he was the acting Presiding Judge now.

So I walked across the hall into Judge C courtroom and sat down as he had criminal court being heard. I was sitting there and the bailiff motioned to me. I went up to him and stated that I needed to give the Judge something. He said are you an attorney and I said I am representing myself in a case pro se. He said have a seat and he will call you.

After he finished the case he was hearing; another attorney entered the room and went to the bench. He stated his purpose there and left. Then the Judge called me up and I told him that I was representing myself in Judge's court and had a request motion to have the Judge appoint a different judge in the case for the reasons on the paper.

He stated that a criminal judge could not be placed because it was not a criminal case. I said well it will be.

Then he stated you haven't given the reasons why you need a change in judges and I stated that the Judge and the clerk will be called as witnesses and the Judge cannot be a witness in a case in his court per the rules of the court.

Judge C then stated that it is not what is written and he denies the motion and said that I had to rewrite the thing and have Judge recuse himself. I guess at this point that I was not sure what to do. He stated that he would file the denial in the file and I should take the copy to Judge.

I then also gave him the request that the courts ask for a police report on the file in the court house. He stated that he would give the request immediately to the manager the Administrator for the court house. I said thank you and could you please give me a copy of the denial you wrote.

He said ok. The bailiff gave me a copy and I thanked him and left.

I then waited outside the court room and thought that I better tell Judge (presiding) that her name was on the paperwork with the phone number to call her but I had given the request to Judge C instead. I talked with her clerk and she said that was fine.

I then went back out into the hallway and sat down waiting for the manager to come back into his office as he was not there earlier. I wanted to ask what the protocol for the file sealed in the court house was as Ana Judge's clerk had not given me a copy of the protocol.

I had waited for over an hour and called his office number and left a message on Dorothy's phone to please call me when he gets into the office.

I waited until 1:15 PM and then the bailiff from Judge C's office came out and saw me and said did you not get what you wanted and I said that I wanted to talk with the manager and he said go in there he's in his office now.

I said ok thanks.

I then went into the office and Dorothy was at her desk and I introduced myself and stated that I wanted to talk with the manager. She said he is in his office and said please have a seat and I'll let him know you are here.

I sat for awhile and Dorothy didn't say much a friend of hers came in and she talked a bit with her.

I talked a bit too. But Dorothy just sat at her desk and read a book.

Then the manager came out and said hello and didn't introduce himself at all.

I said hello I'm Julia Rule we spoke on the phone before, he said yes, I remember. When I called from the university to talk with Ana Judge's clerk; Gene talked with Ana and then all of a sudden, she states that she is being transferred to the manager in Administration. She talked a bit with him and then I asked to speak to him. He then said I told her to give you what you wanted. He now remembered who I was previously in this case where he had direct action.

He said come into my office and have a seat and he sat across from me at a conference type table.

I asked him to please give me a copy of the procedure for the protocol for the sealed files in the court house.

He said that depends on how the file was sealed and stated to go into an explanation of it and it depends on the type of sealing of the file and I asked could he please tell me all the ways it could be sealed and then we would decide which way mine was. He stated that he was trying and went into this dissertation about the press getting access to the file in the case of the owner of the Springfield Post-Dispatch Pulitzer case and he pointed to the books on his shelves sand said that the press drew up a writ and stated that they had to give over the file. (I didn't tell him that this would not happen as I was also in a court case against the Public Protection Agency and they are one of the members and could not have access to the file as I had a case pending in court against them it would be a conflict of interest.

He then began to get angry when I again stated that I just want to know the protocol for the file as I have a hard time knowing where the file is when I come in to get something out of it.

He got belligerent and said that I was not going to get it and that if I was going to act that way I needed to leave. He was definitely acting that way on purpose to upset me and not give me what I wanted.

I could see he was purposely trying to get me to scream and yell or something but I just said well, if you are not going to give me what I wanted. I'll just go.

He made a derogatory statement to me and I said that was not nice and I left.

I went out of the office and to the elevators and went upstairs to the fifth floor to talk with Marcy. She was in her office but on the phone.

I waited till she was off and then went in.

I introduced myself to her again and stated that I was having a hard time getting the file when I came to the court house. She said just come to the fifth floor and get the file. I stated that on several occasions I did just that and then they didn't know where the file was and it was in the resource room, Mr. Kraft's office and then in Ms. Bury's office. She stated that she had to go to a meeting and that I could make an appointment to talk with her and she asked for my phone number. I gave her one of my cards and said please call me and schedule a meeting. She said she would and I left.

When I got home I called back to Judge C's office and left a message stating would he please reconsider the motion I wrote for the change of Judge as it really was not stating that I was asking for a criminal Judge and left my name and number and said please call me tomorrow. He never called.

November 20, 2007

Today is Tuesday.

I called the police station again to the office of the Chief of Police and talked with Carol. She asked me several questions and I said that I had talked with Officer Ham yesterday and she said that they don't have an officer by that name. I said it was a complaint and his officer was on the first floor. She said Oh. Then she stated that she was going to transfer me to the

Investigative burglary division and have me to speak to an investigative officer.

She transferred me and I talked with Rona and she transferred me to Officer L and his answering machine kicked on. I left a message and stated my name and number and that I had made a complaint yesterday and now needed an investigation.

He called me back about an hour later.

We had a very long discussion and he stated that my story sounded like it was too late for an investigation and that the file folder fingerprint was too old to get a print off of and determine what was up.

I asked what is the time limit for a finger print to be dusted? He said it depends on the kind of fingerprint. He was being so vague that it upset me so.

And I stated that so if the investigation was done at the very time I asked for it then the fingerprint would be there right, and he then said well, yes.

He immediately changed the story to the fact that I was delusional and hung up. Clearly, I was learning that the police will say anything once they know they screwed up. Clearly, he was attacking me since I asked would you find a finger print if it was done when I immediately asked for it when the dumb officer was in my home and acted like a jerk not helping me at all.

Then St. Ann's Hospital called me and said that the copies of the affidavits were not in the file but up in risk management. Michelle in medical records transferred me up the risk management and they said they did not have the copies but that the supervisor would have the copies in medical records and that I would have to talk to them and I said no. You need to call back down to Michelle in medical records so that she knows that she did not do the right thing so the next person who inquires will have the right thing. She said no you have to talk with the supervisor. I said no you have to get the copies and send them to me and she hung up.

I then called Officer Ham and left a message so that he would know that the Judge (presiding) did not get the copies of the complaint but Judge C did and left my name and number.

December 20, 2007

Today I received several letters in the mail.

One was a motion to quash the subpoenas of Judge's and Ana the clerk to testify in the case switched to Judge H's courtroom. I could not believe it. It was the whole reason why I had to switch Judges and I was so upset I remember sitting and trying to stay focused so I would not cry. But I did anyway. All that work and now the court house was fighting me too; to get to the truth. I thought how could they do that to me after all that I have been through.

One of the letters was and Order to Show Cause why my file is to be sealed by the court.

I knew I would have to research but the basics are already in the file I just need to put them into a motion I suppose.

I received a letter from Mr. Kraft, the courthouse's attorney, and Marcy the Circuit Clerk stating that they would not be meeting with me about the security and protocol of the sealed file. Clearly they, too, felt threatened by me and it was a conspiracy to cover up how an attorney in the court house on the fifth floor could at any time take a file from the fifth floor to the desk opposite it and sit at a table and take anything out and put anything into it. I proved it. They knew I could sue them but I did not want to as I was after the truth. I was so sad I cried even harder, thinking to myself if I had worked so hard to get to the truth and now, they had just undone everything I had worked on for months. They were so irresponsible as far as I was concerned. I was so upset and disillusioned. I felt like quitting and moving away which is what I wanted to do in 2005 but I felt I needed to get my son away from his father and that was my motivation. I decided in my worrisome state to keep up the fight and persist even further despite no help from anyone it seemed.

Journal page from December 27, 2007:

Pat called from the Legal Counsel for the Springfield Business Journal and stated that she still did not want Timothy the journalist who wrote the story about Investigate U starting business in 2003 to testify.

I told her that I got the envelope with the newspaper article stating that it was an error but the article about the error was just written this week.

She stated that since they printed a retraction that his testimony was not needed.

I told her that I had looked in the Rules of the Court and did not find any rule that stated that a newspaper reporter could not testify about an article. And that the Judge would get the original article in the paper that they printed from this week stating that there was an error.

She was very diligent trying to get me to retract the subpoena but did not win. I knew she was lying.

She even went as far as stating that I should just get the money I was asking for the kids placed in a trust for them and not worry about myself. I almost laughed out loud.

I don't know who she thought she was talking to but no lawyer would ever advise another lawyer about a client of such a thing. Or maybe she was trying to help in her own way I don't know; but for me to not get anything and rely on the kids giving me anything is just not a consideration considering the circumstances as they are today with the relationships with my children as unstable as they are but I know that will change for me in the future.

She stated that his testimony would only hurt me stating that the business was not started in 2003.

I tried many times to tell her but she would not listen to me. So, I said that he must testify and we ended the conversation. Clearly one lawyer still helping lawyers and not me, I could not take it.

She was not happy with me at all.

Also:

I received a letter from SBC Subpoena Service Center in Dallas stating that there were no phone records for 6333 Mississippi listed for Paul Rule.

I then called their number and he stated that I needed separate subpoenas for the two different states and that I needed a state subpoena for that state's records.

I then went over to the court house in that state and county and asked about filing a case in their court.

Diane the clerk was very nice and even found me files with similar cases for me to use as a guideline.

She let me copy two files and I took the paperwork home and stated that I would be back tomorrow to open a new case with them and apply for the subpoena to be approved.

Today December 26, 2007 I took the reply and denial of objections to the court house to submit to Judge H. I arrived at 12:00 PM and his clerk was not in the office; the door was open but she was not there.

I waited outside the court room and went back in at 12:45 PM and there was still no one in the office but the door was open.

I went into the Judge's (presiding) office and she was sitting at a table and I asked if Judge H's Clerk was there and she stated is she in her office and I said no she is not there but the door is open.

She said that the Judge would not see me without the other side being present.

I stated that I had a procedural question and she stated that I could not submit anything to the judge or ask him a question without the other side. This seemed odd to me as I saw attorneys ask questions all the time inside the offices of the Judges without another attorney being there.

I asked her if people would be in contempt if they did not comply with the subpoena and interrogatory information and that I had written a reply to the attorney's objection.

She instructed me to just file the reply and denial of the objection up on the third floor.

I took the denial to the objection up the third floor and filed it.

I then went into the law library and tried to research the instruction of the law firm of the Springfield Business Journal that they stated that their reporter did not have to testify because he had immunity and would not testify.

I stated to her that I didn't want the reporter to reveal a source or anything just testify that he wrote the article and that the date in the article of the business starting up that he did a story on was either 2003 as it stated or was it wrong.

I did check today with several book stores and could not find the book Rules of the Court.

Today I mailed:

Express Mail to ABC Services Subpoena Center— Reno, Nevada

Priority Mail to the States Health Office

Priority Mail to the attorney for the Public Protection Agency brief which came back in the mail because of lack of postage of 35 cents due.

December 28, 2007

Journal day for Friday December 28, 2007

I drove over to the court house in the neighboring state where he now lived and filed a new case for $95.00 and submitted the paperwork and 3 documents—1 Order—2 motions one with a rider.

I needed another states subpoena for the phone records for the business and the house where he lived. The phone records would prove that he had a phone at the business before the divorce was final and therefore the business would be half mine since it was started before the divorce was final and my ex-husband had listed nothing on the business expense forms that he owned a business or had started one or was in the process of starting one up. The start up of a business can take months. Clearly, I gave him the idea in 2001 to start up his own business when he was not getting promoted at work in the agency in Springfield. I said start your own company and get the contacts yourself; you do the work now almost completely anyway with Art except for the work the IT person does. He listened to me but started the business with his friend and of course the girlfriend who was a contractor coming into the business to consult. When my ex-husband asked the office if he could consult for another outside company to be with her, they said no and he was so upset at home; I did not know about her. That is the day I said to him I'm sick of listening about work, all you do is complain, let's just start our own business. I was only to learn later that the girlfriend was in the mix and part of his business deal in order to make sure that if he left and went to work for another company and her company got the contracts from the government office to produce his special way of investigating that he patented; he would then secure the contracts through her office and then the plan was for him and his best friend and co-worker Art to then leave her office with the girlfriend Mia (who by the way was the big boss that opened up that office in Springfield—I would later learn as my daughter told me she worked for a veterinarian's office when she met the girlfriend. I had no idea and would learn later that my ex-husband and the girlfriend were together for six years before he left me.

She stated that the Judge was not in today and I should call next week on Tuesday (which she didn't realize and neither did I that it was a holiday; New Years Day) I will call on Wednesday if I don't hear from her on Monday.

I need to fax the out of state subpoena with a check when it is approved.

I called Doctor Chia my psychiatrist and left a message for him to call me back and that I need to chat about the current situation.

I called the Geek Squad with Best Buy as I thought someone might have hacked into my computer as files were changed and they said it was past 90 days and they could not do anything for me, except a gift card for 50 bucks which she will mail.

Checked the Military records request and I only received one page. The page seems suspiciously incomplete as he was in the military for years. I will check on it later.

Department Store, I stopped by, Allie will be in the office on Wednesday and I will call her. I spoke with the cashier and she didn't know anything.

Court Reporting Litigation; I called to tell them that I did not receive a copy of the deposition and that it was not fair to have the deposition without a copy when I approved the errata sheet and now I don't have a copy. I said that I would strike it from the record since I did not get a copy of the approved sheets when I was in their office to approve it, immediately upon signing. Anything could have been changed after I left their office.

I called Security for his office and spoke with the people who will call me back next week.

I served the subpoena on the phone company at 10 Pin later in the afternoon. I walked into the building and the security guard at the desk said to have a seat and someone would be down to take it from me.

The security guard and I chatted for some time and he was very nice.

Then who shows up but Ben Still the guy who handled the mess in 2006 with my phone mess with the phone company where the police officer was shouting at me in his office and saying that I was crazy. I left the building by myself without finishing the meeting.

Anyway, as he approached me, I stated, Oh Hi Art and he said you know me. I said, "Yes, don't you remember me I came for a meeting with you and there was a big mess with the police whereby a south city police officer told me to take a city police officer into the meeting with me. I arrived and a city cop showed up and talked with me and then a bit later another city cop showed up in bicycle shorts and you stated that no cop was needed and they both left. Then you took me up in the elevator and we went into your office. Later the bike cop showed up and began to badger me and I said I don't need this and left. I went down the elevator by myself.

I did subsequently file an internal affairs report on the police officer per the south land police instructions.

Anyway, he was surprised I remembered him and I stated that I used to be a security guard years ago and would never forget his face or voice because of the nature of the meeting. It was a very stressful meeting for me as I was accusing one of his employees of tampering with my phone and my phone bills and had my phone disconnected twice.

Then he took the subpoena and put inside his coat and said he had to go to the bank. I thought this was funny but talked a bit with the guard and left.

I walked to Kinko's where I also faxed a copy of the four pages of the subpoena to Dallas. It seemed odd that I had to take that in there because the phone recording just said I could fax it.

Anyway, I then went to the State Court of Appeals downtown to see about my employee case against the Public Protection Agency because I received a statement that a female attorney was now the representing attorney for the state. It seemed odd because Tim Long was the attorney on record for the State. So, I wanted to see what was in the file. I asked to see the file but the document was not in there. When I inquired the clerk said it's probably not filed yet. I asked her if she could see if the document was submitted. She looked upset that I asked to see it. She went to the back and came back with the document. I asked her how could there be another attorney on record when one did not withdraw. She stated in a very upset demeanor that they are in the same office and its fine. I said I thought one attorney had to withdraw to have another attorney take over the case. She said no they don't if they are in the same office.

I then left and went to the Court House in Clay to file the subpoena and other paperwork.

I was only in the building for about 15 minutes and left.

I came home and parked the car in the carport and came inside and set my house alarm. I ate something watched a movie and then went to bed.

I woke up in the morning and leisurely sat around, did some cleaning and then I needed to get to the bank before it closed at noon so I got dressed and went outside.

Much to my surprise was my three-month-old sporty new convertible Mazda Miata soft convertible top all sliced up like someone had fun the night before playing slice and dice with my soft top. I was scared to death. I had to get to the bank before it closed. So, I got into the car and drove a few miles to the bank. I then came home and called he police. They showed up and took a report. I told them that I had just filed contempt charges on my ex-husband in court or maybe because I was in court against the Public Protection Agency I don't know who did this. I was really upset and I did not cry outside. I went inside and called my insurance company and they said that my policy was cancelled that morning.

I said by whom and they said they don't know. I said it was not me that called in. They said don't worry they would take care of it. I drove over the office where I took the policy out and my agent no longer worked there. I was upset.

I drove home and called the police back to ask if they could please finger print my car as someone had cancelled my insurance policy that morning as well and it was clear to me that someone did this on purpose to scare me and cause me money troubles. My deductible was $500.00 and of course I did not have it.

They sent out a police squad car but they said no finger prints were on the car.

I called the corporate office of the insurance company and they said don't worry we will keep your policy at our corporate office so you don't have an agent any longer in the field. If you need anything let us know. They fixed the top and I sold the car as I had no garage and I knew who ever did this would and could do it again.

I was scared for my life for first time ever. I found

it hard to go outside my condo or even take out the trash. Someone used a knife on my car. If it was my ex-husband would he now come after me with a knife and slice me up? I did not know and was scared as someone had been getting in and out of my home on a regular basis changing things and doing this to mess with my head. It was clear to me it was my ex-husband doing that to me. But who had done this heinous thing to my new little car that brought me so much joy? The only joy I had even though it only lasted for a few months was a direct source of fun for me driving around with the top down with the feelings I had as a young teenager on my bicycle the wind whipping in my hair. I hated whoever did this to me and it would change my life and I never parked in my designated parking spot any longer under the carport.

Sequence of events of the documents from file in Circuit Court Springfield County. Typed June 26, 2008, by Julia Rule:

Julia Rule versus Paul Rule

May 2, 2008—Friday, I filled out two subpoenas (one to HR and one to Savings Plan for my ex-husbands retirement issues) for Judge Unfair to sign and took them to his clerk Carry and dropped them off for him to sign. She stated to me that he would sign them either on Monday or Tuesday and I could pick them up after that.

May 6, 2008 I called and left a message for Carry asking if they had been signed so I could pick them up.

May 8, 2008 I did not hear back from her and went to the court house. I went to the court room of Judge H and called Carry the clerk on my cell phone as I am not allowed to come into Judge's clerk's office as stated in November by her that there is a law stating that I as a pro se litigant cannot enter her office or the Judges chambers. (At that time I challenged that and the Bailiff Eugene also stated the fact that Mr. Kraft told them both that there is a law stating that I cannot enter the office or the chambers of the Judge. Mr. Kraft said he never said that personally directly to me. I have it on tape Carry and Eugene saying that to me).

Carry came out of the office and stated to me that the Judge had not signed the subpoenas yet and I asked why. She stated that he did not know where to sign them as Judges do not sign subpoenas. I stated to her that Judge H signed three and showed her where. She said she would keep them and get back to me. Carry stated that the clerks upstairs sent them back to me in the mail.

May 9, 2008 I go back to the court house to file the subpoenas again with a note to the Judge on why he needs to sign them with the original letter from

HR with the mailing envelope attached. (That original letter was not returned to me ever). The Judge wrote denied on the note I sent for him to please sign them. I received them back in the mail. (Officer Walk from the front door went in with me after I called from the red phone and he witnessed the clerk not knowing that a Judge can sign a subpoena and he waited with me until I then talked with the clerk Kim and she stated that they had been mailed back to me again) He walked me out and was a bit surprised at the treatment I receive and I stated that it is usual for me and that's why I called because I was gong to file perjury charges and he would go to jail and they don't like it.

May 15, 2008 I received them back in the mail envelope stamped May 14, 2008. The subpoenas had been date stamped per the court procedure and the date stamps had been written over real big VOID CK. Making them unusable and the original filed in the court file removed as if they had never been submitted and clearly this was against the law.

June 12, 2008 I have a hearing set for maintenance. After the hearing I present the subpoena myself in person to Judge H. He stated that he could not sign them and I was to take them up to the Circuit Clerks office and that I should call the Prosecuting Attorney for the fact that Mr. Rule told people that I was a paranoid schizophrenia and that I was taken by the Police to Dylan Mental facility at St. Ann's Hospital when I was trying to tell them to investigate the court document dated February 24, 2006. The police did not believe me and my sister Devilia lied (she says it was because my ex-husband told her I was a paranoid schizophrenic which I will explain, too, but is a lie) Judge H very concerned gave me those two instructions.

June 18, 2008 I take the subpoenas to the circuit clerk on the fifth floor and was told that Marcy was in a meeting all day and could not meet with me. I asked to speak to Mr. Kraft and Gal the assistant to Marcy came out to the front counter and took all of the information and subpoenas from me and stated that she would look into it. I called her back and said that I would like an appointment to meet with Marcy and she left me a message later that day stating that Joan would not meet with me and Mr. Kraft would be sending me a letter.

June 18, 2008 I also filed 6 motions that day and one was the perjury charge and Kim the clerk said she had to check with Mary, Judge Unfair's clerk about putting them all on the same day. I asked her to please not and put the perjury charge first with the most current date she had open. She said no and left with them and took them down to Mary and said that she interrupted the court proceedings to ask about the date and putting them all on the same day. She set them all for September 4, 2008 as this was the soonest date after the she talked with Mary. I asked if the perjury charge could be separated and she stated no again. (so now it would be four months wait to hear a perjury charge and I thought to myself I hope I don't get killed before then.

June 21, 2008 I received a letter in the mail from Mr. Kraft stating that he was returning all my information and subpoenas and that the clerk told him that the Judge refused to sign them.

June 24, 2008 I went to the Prosecuting Attorney's office and asked if they could help me as I thought the clerk was lying to Mr. Kraft as the Judge had instructed me personally to take the subpoenas to the Circuit Clerk and that he would not sign them. Mic the investigator spoke with me in the Prosecuting Attorney's office. He told me to do two things after speaking with an attorney in the back.

1. Call the police and ask that a police report be written up about the documents being taken from the legal file in the court house and mailed back to me.

2. Meet with Mr. Kraft and ask that a meeting be set up between Mr. Kraft, the Judge and myself to rectify the situation and get to the bottom of it.

I left the building and walked across the street to the police station and asked to speak with an officer. The woman inside said I need a Clay Police officer and dispatched one to the front of the building where the two statues are. Several minutes later a police officer Brian arrived and spoke with me for 15 minutes or so. He stated that he could not write a report as it was not a crime. I said thank you and he left.

I went down the steps and into the court house and up to the third floor. I stopped at the computer and tried to pull up my file in the File.Net and it was not there. I had tried several weeks prior and was amazed that my case cannot be seen from File.Net. I printed out the proof again as I had done the week prior with a witness from the third floor at the desk next to the computer.

I then went to the reception desk and asked for Mr. Kraft's phone number and she said that she was not allowed to give it out. So I walked back to his office and he was on the phone so I waited in the hallway. When he got off the phone, I presented myself in the doorway and he said come in. He did not invite me to sit down. I proceeded to tell him that I came from the Prosecuting Attorney's office and he listened but his face got all screwed up. Then he busted out really loud almost yelling at me that I was a liar and that I did not speak to anyone at the prosecuting attorney's office and that I had been in there about other subpoenas and created a scene which is a lie. He then said he was calling across the street to the Prosecuting Attorney's office and he said. "Yes, she's standing in my office with her arms folded and is insisting that she get her questions answered." And then he hung up. "I said did they verify that I was there?" and he said, "No." Just about then a guard from the front door appeared behind me. I stated that Mr. Kraft had called me a liar and Officer S stated that he was only there to see that everyone got out of the building safely. On the way out I told the officer that my case can not be seen in File.Net and that the woman sitting at the front desk next to the computer could verify that and I turned to her and she said yes, I do remember her and she is correct. I had printed it out several days prior to this day and today also and my case was nowhere, yet when I told Mr. Kraft in his office, he printed it out for me that it could be seen.

I went back across the street and back up to the second floor to the Prosecuting Attorney's office again. Mic was not there but I told he receptionist that Mr. Kraft called me a liar and he had me really shook up. I had to go to work after that and the next day spent the day in bed because he upset me so much. (I have been verbally abused in the marriage and it is hard for me to take when someone screams at me but this behavior was not acceptable behavior for Mr. Kraft either).

June 26, 2008 I called County Police Headquarters and asked to speak with the chief about helping the police with abused woman and she said that she would transfer me to the Family Crisis office (Carol) and transferred me to Lt. Bird and we spoke. He said he would have his assistant Jennifer call me. (Lt Bird happened to be the Lt. who sent me by ambulance to Dylan after hearing my story and my sister lying about me etc.) Interesting don't you think. He remembered me and we spoke quite candidly about the issue. I could not believe that he was the person in charge of family crisis. So you see the night I complained about the officer and they told me to come back at 2:00 PM to speak to his direct supervisor, I was not speaking to his direct supervisor I was set up talking instead to the head of the family crisis division and getting affidavits from my mom and my sister to cover up a complaint about one of their officers.

I called the Chief Investigator at the Prosecuting Attorney's office and he got mad at me and said that he was not going to get involved in this and Mic said what he said that he has not prosecuted a perjury charge in the 12 years he has been there and was sorry and I said thank you and hung up.

I later called back and spoke with Officer E and he said to call back to Clay Police and talked with a Supervisor and ask if they can write a report for a theft crime about documents being taken out of a legal court file.

I called Clay Police and Chief had a voice mail saying he was out of town and to call another officer at a different number. I called and spoke with him. Captain M stated after talking with me for quite some time that he would have a detective the next day if I could wait till then and not come that day on Thursday. He stated that he would have detective Mark at the station at 8:30 AM to meet with me but that I must understand that he could only take the information and could not guarantee an investigation would be done. I said that is fine.

He then called me back and left a voice mail for me to call him back as he needed to speak to me before coming in on Friday morning as he might have to reschedule it.

I called him back right away. He said that when the call went out on the 24th and Brain showed up that the log stated that another officer was dispatched to the scene, Officer Middleton. I stated to him that only one officer showed up and talked with me and then he left and I went into the court house.

He stated that he had something other than that showing in the computer and that he needed to look into that before he had someone meet with me so he cancelled the meeting for Friday morning at 8:30 AM and said that he would call me and maybe meet later

Friday or Monday he would let me know. I said ok.

Friday morning, I went to the Library to surf the internet and my cell rang and it was Captain M. He stated that he was no longer gong to have a detective meet with me. He stated that I needed to get an attorney. I said that I have tried over and over and he said well, there is nothing we can do for you. I said ok but was really upset. Someone was getting into my home and took the subpoena that was the proof that my ex-husband had perjured himself on the witness stand by stating that he had gotten a check from his previous company for $30,000 and that is the money he started the company with and a loan from his mother. Also, the original one was taken from the file and mailed to my home by the clerk. Now the original date stamped on one and my copy of the signed served one was gone from my files at home. But most importantly was the fingerprinting I wanted it done to absolutely get the facts as to who exactly was doing this. That would never happen.

Fingerprints I would later learn is the only way to absolutely without a doubt tell who a certain person is in an investigation to prove anything to anyone. Not to mention to know the truth yourself to protect yourself.

Chapter 10

December 28, 2007, Document, Police, Company Notes, Attorneys
Discuss Alienation of My Family Members to No One—
Very Important

While I was paying Jannie to represent me, I had told her of a private investigator that I hired to look into Mr. Rule's assets and check him out, as I felt he had hidden things from me before he left. I had also asked him if he could debug my home, tell me if someone was hacking into my computer, and install a hidden camera in my home. Jannie told me not to give him any more money when I told her that I gave him $500 to do those things for me, and he came to my house and looked in all of my rooms.

I said to her, "Why would I not give him any more money or get information from him?"

She simply stated, "Don't do business with him, and don't give him any more money."

Well, I thought without a good explanation, I was going to do with my money what I wanted to do with it. She gave me no real good reason not to, just stated not to. I needed a good reason to follow that statement up.

I told him what she said, and he I said I should do what I wanted with my money if I thought it was best for me. I agreed with him and continued to talk with him.

Police had told me when I went to talk about the verbal abuse in public now to file a protection order and get my home protected, get my car checked out to see if there was a GPS tracker on it, and have someone check for bugs in my home as well. It scared me.

I had filed the protection order, was working on the case when I received an attorney who told me to drop the case because he might kill me. I was extremely scared now.

I told Mr. Raymond Kirsing, the detective, about the protection order, and he told me that he would help me the best he could. He came to my home and told me to put baby powder on the floor right inside the front door.

He said, "You will see the footprints inside the front door and know that he is in the house or not when you are gone."

I remember thinking this was a pretty primitive way of figuring out yes or no, but the simple principle was right on.

Sure enough, the first day I put the powder down, when I came home that night there were footprints in the baby powder on the white tile floor. It worked, but now I was really scared, knowing that he was in the house for sure. It would be the beginning of many sleepless nights. Some nights I was wondering if this was the last night I would be alive.

I called Mr. Kersing, and he said that I should change my locks, and he came over and looked at my condo to see how we could install a hidden camera. He spent an hour or so sitting on my balcony with me talking about how he thinks through things first to see what would be the best attack on these security issues. I think he maybe never had such a request before. Most people hire a detective to follow someone or get information. My request was very different. I needed my home debugged, my computer looked at to see if someone was hacking in, and to help me understand how someone was getting my home phone number to harass me. Someone had used my debit card online on my computer itself as it would reveal from The Geek Squad, a computer home-check company, that my computer was not hacked into. Mr. Kirsing did not know computer technology detection, but he referred me to another man he knew in his parish at church who was. Once my laptop was compromised by someone changing the password on it so I could not get into it, I knew for sure. I did not know that computers were so easy to get into; just by starting up in the safe mode, you can change the password and get in, but IT people know this and do it all the time for people. We the public think our computers are safe, but they are not unless we protect them either from someone getting their hands on them or by remote access. We can protect ourselves by just not hooking up to the Internet on a computer that we use for secure writing and put those documents on a flash drive and put them into our desktop to send wherever we need them sent. In other words, if you have things that are personal and you never want anyone to get to them, don't hook that computer to the Internet. Keep the documents on a flash drive as well, and put that drive in a safe place or safe deposit box at the bank.

Mr. Kirsing would help me for a few months meeting with me about what I could do to stop my ex-husband and to keep this from happening further. He was definitely in and out of my home; no one else would want the things from my divorce court case and evidence against him accept him. He didn't charge me anything to help me further; it was really nice of him.

I was trying to tell him that I thought he was tracking me on my cell phone. After all, he was the best at investigations in the world, why not GPS-track his wife who he had been telling people was crazy. She was nuts to ever trust him and ever believe anything that her husband told her after all he lied right when he first met her, and I believed everything hook line and sinker. He would manage to do that to me all my life. It was what made him so convincing to others all over the world in the end. He was about secrecy and would never reveal to anyone his truly twisted side, but I knew because I lived with him, and no one believed what I had to say because he covered his bad behavior by saying that I was out of control and crazy, psychotic—which, of course, I admit I had one event that was because of his treatment directed at me. He did that on purpose, you see, knowing that he could. In the investigative world, you are taught many things, but in this case, he had learned this very young and did to his first wife as well. She told me when I called her after thirty years that she did grow up with him and that he had psychological problems. No wonder why I never met her or got to speak to her ever, except for a few times when she would call to speak to Paul about their son, Joe. I wondered why would she never have told me the truth; I knew part of the reason was that now when I was not living with him any longer, I was still afraid of him and what he would do if he found out I was telling people about certain things like his behavior toward me and the yelling and screaming.

It would be very hard for me to convince people because, let's be honest, I was the very person he had been so successful in convincing me of everything that was not true because he was such a great liar, and I loved him. He did it without batting an eyelash; even if he did, he had these big, bright blue eyes with eyelashes like a woman's long and curled up like a picture you see in a magazine. You right away were drawn to his eyes and his athletic body, which was always in shape. He smiled all the time and laughed a lot about things. He made fun of things and every once in a while it would concern me as his humor was borderline way out there weird sometimes, but I just brushed it off, thinking he's being silly. We had fun together and enjoyed many things together; everyone knew this, and people saw us together and always said what a great couple and how lucky he was to have me. My aunt whom I trusted more than anyone even said to me one day, "You better hang on to that guy, he is a go-getter and had more energy than anyone I have ever met."

I told her I agreed; that was in my thirteenth year of marriage. We were now living in Springfield, and she would have us over for dinner occasionally. Little did she know that later on after she was dead, I would find out that this was all an act. Like he was an actor in a movie or something pretending for all. Nothing that came out of his mouth was to be believed by me eventually. I would come to understand that I would never understand him at all, even after someone profiled him for me as a pathological liar with obsessive-compulsive disorder and control issues. He tried to kill me, or so I think, as I have no proof and he covered up things secretively as I never knew he had a girlfriend. But when I think back about the time I moved to River Bend to be with him before we were married, he hid me in the bedroom closet when his mother and his sister arrived early at our apartment; he hid me like the dirty little secret because he did not tell his family that he had met me at all. He had left his wife, or so he told me, at the time and asked me to move in with him until the divorce was final. I realize now that he probably did not tell his mother anything, just as he had not told me anything about his new girlfriend that he had for six years while still married to me. He just tortured me and made me cry so much that soon my brain was like the salad that he kept mixing up and adding more ingredients to the bowl until it overflowed with too many bad things, and I slipped into a psychotic episode, which would be the deciding factor to most people that somehow I had a mental disease. He was lying to help his end of the puzzle; he wanted out, and he wanted it to look like it was all my fault so no one would believe anything I had to say about how he was treating me or how my life had changed so drastically because of his treatment to me. It was weird. Later, I would learn that I did not have control of life, and I was going to get it back. I did, but it would be a long struggle, and the realization that I was left with post-traumatic stress disorder from verbal and sexual/physical abuse, traumatic events that would leave me helpless to defend myself even in the simplest of situations for a while. But then I would get stronger and realized that I had a disorder now that really changed my life and how I could interact with others to a limited extent because I could not be yelled at or touched by a male without my permission. It was like I was a little girl afraid of the simplest of things like a touch. But there were good reasons, the man who was supposed to love and cherish me had torn me apart, day by day, leaving me with little respect even from my children. "How could this be true?" I used to say to myself. From love to hate he did live.

I will tell you this: it is a horrible thing to have happen to you. It strips the very core of your personality away until you feel like you are lying on the floor being beaten and no one even cares anymore. When you see the signs coming and you start to fight back, it is when they turn it on even harder for you and make your life unbearable at the time.

I remember while watching Oprah Winfrey one day on television the first year we were in our new house. He came home from work that day, and I was crying. I was standing at the ironing board ironing his shirts, and he said to me, "Why are you crying?"

I said, "I was watching Oprah today, and the topic was sodomy." I began to cry even harder.

He said to me, "Why would that make you cry?"

I said, "I was sodomized by a coworker while in training at the control tower, we dated a bit, and he invited me to his apartment one night and wanted to make love to me, I said no, so he sodomized me instead, telling me it would not hurt and it would not be breaking my vow of chastity as I had told him I was religious and was waiting till marriage to make love. He convinced me that he was not going to hurt me at all and people do this all the time instead of intercourse. I was stupid, and I told him it hurt, but he did not care. He did his deed, and I broke it off. I remember that he told me I could not go to air traffic control school any longer and I was going to marry him and live with him. I told him no, I am going to school, and no one is going to stop me from that. He came up to me in his apartment and unzipped his pants and put his penis in front of my face and said this to me, 'This is your last chance.' I got up and walked away and out the front door and never to talk to him again. He was a monster and a pervert as well. Divorced and unhappy and looking for any way to get a piece of ass any way he could. I was a nice girl and was so upset, and I had to see him at work once in a while until I left for school. I never said anything to anyone, but today on the television, Oprah made me realize that I should have." I was crying the whole time I was telling him of my past relationship, and I was not thinking rationally that this person who did this to me was now one of my husband's coworkers.

He did not hug me, and he started to ask questions. He looked angry at me and made me feel even worse like it was all my fault at the time it happened. He looked like he hated me and thought I was somehow dirty because of the story I told him.

I remember thinking that I should have never told him.

This might have been the catalyst that made him want to make me suffer and hurt me emotionally for not telling him. Maybe he thought since I slept with him, I had done this many times. I had never had intercourse with anyone except my husband. I had been sexually assaulted a few times but never raped, never penetrated by anyone except the night of sodomy when I was alone in a man's apartment that I thought cared about me and wanted to marry me. He only wanted sex any way he could get it. Many people are like this; some women like it. I was not one of those women. I would learn later on that people that I knew actually preferred this kind of sex; I found it to be barbaric, not to mention against my religion and against the law. I wished I would have prosecuted him and sent him to jail.

I was a victim. I would soon learn that a man who had loved you, had children with you, and shared your life could turn this into something that he would twist in his mind, which was twisted anyway into something that he could justify for not only leaving me but treating me like an animal he could kick around, just like our dog Henry, whom he kicked down the basement steps once for not listening to him. I remember Henry, and I became friends and stuck like glue together as this was before our children were born. I would never have sharp words with him after that event and always was on guard for his temper. This time he would use that temper to get back at me and torture me in ways that I was not ready for and most of all could not believe that he would do these kinds of things to me.

So his having a girlfriend already just gave him one more thing to hate me and make me his punching bag. After I told him that story, every time we went to a company party from work, he would watch me by staying by my side every minute. Maybe he thought that since I had slept with him and we weren't married, maybe I was lying to him about never sleeping with anyone except him. Liars oftentimes don't believe others because they lie themselves. It would reveal itself to me that other people I would meet would be the same. They sometimes did not maybe believe me because they were liars themselves, you see. Learning about liars would be my greatest success in life. It had after all destroyed my life as I knew it, so it was important for me to understand how someone could do that to me—, how I could avoid it, and most of all recognize it when I would be approached by a new man who said to me, "I will never lie to you." But it only took a few weeks for me to catch him in a lie. That would be my first lesson in searching for a new mate, as well as listening to your head and not your heart when making decisions about whom to love and whom to leave behind in the dust of life. Of course, our hearts reel us in tight, and our minds have to be strong to resist if needed.

I remember thinking at that time, "Was I never to trust anyone again?" Was I going to be alone and unloved forever? I cried many nights over this very topic. I was a very loving person. I missed someone in bed and in my life to love me and be with me but not enough to make sure that the next time it was the real thing, and that someone was not just lying to me to get an easy piece.

People would comment to me, "You're such a pretty girl, you should go out on dates and meet a new man."

I just would acknowledge the compliment and say, "Yeah, you're right." And they were, but they did not know I had such complications to get straight in my mind before I would attempt to find the right person.

First, I had to figure out why I was so gullible and believed what people said to me. I believed for a long time that people were honest and trustworthy, and then later I grew up and decided that it was not just criminals that were dishonest and not trustworthy; people in the world who had not been in prison, jail, or arrested could still be the same type of person, just never got caught or turned in by anyone.

I did not know that people would soon learn that women can be abused by a man just as a man can be abused by a woman to punish them, get relief from their anger, or just not be not interested any longer for their own selfish reasons or for reasons of jealousy. I do know that when my husband left; he said he was going to do something selfish for himself. He was out to get the company started that I told him would be a gold mine for him. He had found the woman who could make it all happen for him. I was toast and expendable. I was so sweet and nice, and I never saw it coming. I just remember that I was glad he left. I was having a party and finally free from his anger, screaming, yelling, and most of all, belittling me and controlling my life. I was finally free to think and do what I wanted.

I only know that by the time I was writing this story, I would become an advocate for anyone who was abused, lied to, and lied about in court or in life. I wanted to help victims, and I felt I had the power to help them in maybe just the simplest form of letting them know that someone believed them, that someone cared.

So when I asked Mr. Kirsing, the detective, to help me out, he would have no clue what he was getting into, neither did I at first.

We would meet occasionally as I would stop by his office to ask a question, mostly to see if he had finished the asset search on him for court. He never would do that for me, and to this day, I do not know why. He did tell me that since my attorney withdrew, he would help me by giving me an attorney's name. He told me of Mr. Porter, and I called him. Porter said he would help me, and he felt sorry for people like me. He said he would take the case from me and reformat and refile some of the things I did wrong, but he would have to read the case file and I should bring him a copy. It took me a few weeks to copy it all. So little by little, I would take three or four files to him, and he put them in a box in his office on a table.

It was Christmastime. Every year I send out Christmas cards to hundreds of people. Inside the card I include a Christmas letter from me about what has happened in the past year to me and my children and what is new and a message about the world if there is one from me at that time.

I would come to know that Mr. Rule asked me years prior why I would send a letter about him to people.

I said I did not. His own mother called me and said to me, "Paul called me and was yelling at me to send him a copy of your Christmas letter, I told him I don't know where it is, and he told me to please send him a copy of it." She was asking me to please send her a copy of the letter.

I said, "Why does he want a copy of my Christmas letter I sent out? I said nothing about him in the letter!"

She said, "Would you send me a copy?"

I was on my way into my parents' house with my children for Christmas Eve celebration. Why was she calling me on Christmas Eve to tell me that? I never said anything to my children as we were walking into my mother and father's home. But all I can think of was that I said in the letter that my son Shaun was living with his father in another state. That is all I said in reference to my son, nothing about ex-husband. I guess he did not tell his mother where he was living—because he was living with the girlfriend at her house with my son. Maybe he was lying again to his mother, just as he did when he hid me in the closet when she came to visit while he was still married to the first wife. Mothers don't like to be lied to. Mothers don't like it when their children lie about something important in their life. His mother liked me very much; we became like mother and daughter more so than most real-life mothers and daughters. People like me, people get attached to me easy; his mother was really upset, and I felt as though she had been crying. I did not know what to do, so I calmed her down and said, "I will send you a copy of the letter, don't worry." I then started walking into the house, and my son would not get out of the car.

I said to my oldest daughter, "What is going on?" as my middle daughter got back into the car with my son. She said Paul was upset about something and she would talk it through with him and we'd just go inside.

"Come on, Mom, and they will come in when they are ready."

My son came in the house with my daughter about a half an hour later.

I kept saying to my eldest, "What are they talking about?"

She said, "Don't, Mom, they will be in."

They never would tell me what they were talking about, and my son looked as though he had been crying. At the time, I did not put all these pieces together. Buy my ex-husband must have been upset that I put that in the Christmas card where my son was living and was making hell of the day that I got to spend with my children. Per the parenting plan, I got Christmas Eve and he got Christmas Day. He knew full well that my family celebrated Christmas together on Christmas Eve, which we had celebrated with them for years. He was making my day with my family and my children a wreck. It was his way.

Later, I would learn that he actually took my oldest daughter's card with the letter inside and took out the card and sent it back to me, stating that it was from his first wife with a note, telling me to stop sending her any Christmas letter as she did not care about us.

It looked as though the note inside was written by him. I kept it. Clear to me, it was his printing. "How could he manage that?" I thought to myself. I forgot about sending Alexandria a card to his house since she was living with him for a short time when she returned from New York. It was like I was Alice in Wonderland, confused and scared.

I took the card and put it in a safe place. When Mr. Roy had become a friend that I trusted, I took the card out of the closet where it had been for a few years. I gave it to him as I had asked him previously could he tell if someone's handwriting was the same. He said, "Yeah, I was trained as a handwriting expert." So I put the card in the trunk with some other evidence. I took it to his office and opened up the trunk and gave him the card inside with other examples of his writing.

He said to me very quickly, "Yes, without a doubt, this is his writing."

I said, "Great, we got him!"

He said, "Yeah, you do."

I put the card in the trunk inside the box of love letters that he had written to me years ago. I was taking them to the attorney's office. I went home and called Porter, my attorney, and told him what Mr.

Roy had said about the Christmas card and note inside sent from my ex-husband's first wife.

He said to me, "Bring it in to my office, and I will keep it for evidence."

I said, "Okay."

By the next day, I went out to the car, drove to his office, and took all the evidence I had for him inside along with the box of love letters and the Christmas card. After I got inside his office, I reached into the bag that had the box of letters and the Christmas card. The card was gone. It was only one day later, and the only people I told was Mr. Kersing and the attorney, Porter. So now someone was in the trunk of my car. Who knew it was there? Mr. Kersing and Porter. So now I was definitely suspicious of Mr. Kersing and Porter. Mr. Kersing used to work for the Corporate Investigations Organization, and I began to think he was gathering up evidence for them so that I couldn't present this in court. Because you see, it would make the Corporate Investigations Organization look bad that they had such a psycho working for them with a top-secret clearance and a very important job.

I went home and gathered up some more information. My sister called me on the telephone, and I asked her what had happened and what the private detective said to me.

She said, "Are you outside?"

This was her code to tell me to go outside since the police thought he had my condo bugged. I went outside and talked with her and told her what happened. This was proof that this psycho was more dangerous than I ever thought. Maybe it was coincidence that Mr. Kersing and Porter were talking about it; maybe he came that night and got into my trunk and took it himself. I would never know the answer to this dilemma.

But it would seem that since Mr. Kersing never gave me the asset search results for Mr. Rule, yet he gave other results for other people that I asked of him in a day. Porter, the attorney, who said he would take this case and help me out, only yanked it away from me at a very crucial point so he could stop me from pressing charges against Mr. Rule. It was all clear to me at this point. When Poter even said to me at the hearing in September that he forgot to ask the judge about my maintenance motion, I knew he was a liar. He forgot a very important thing. I thought to myself at that time, "He did nothing but jam up your hearing you had set." Later I would learn he did nothing at all. He said he read the files but sent me his accounting of what they meant, and it was all wrong. He was incompetent, and I knew it. Maybe he had just gotten too old; he didn't even use a computer.

Later, I even contacted him about my employment mess at Burger World, and he did nothing to help me. So I knew for sure. He didn't care about this case at all. His comment to me weeks after taking it was that he had a friend at the law firm of my ex-husband and would make me wonder if he did take the case and do nothing to help his friend at the law office where my ex-husband's attorney practiced. I cried about this issue for months.

I did get another cell phone that was prepaid to call people from since someone said he might be tracking me on my cell phone number. The kids had my number even though he did not. After his mother died and his sister called me to say that her mom died. It was past the funeral, and I was a bit hurt that she did not call me, but most of all, hurt by my children that they did not tell me that their grandmother had died. The girls went to the funeral; my son, I was told, did not because he had a soccer game out of town. Later, my oldest told me that her father instructed her not to tell me.

I said to her, "You would listen to him and do whatever he says, right?"

She got upset with me. I realized at that time what a hold he had on her. I was frightened by it. He told my daughter to lie to me and withhold information that was so dear to my life. I never told that to my children when my father died.

I said to them all with a phone call that their grandfather had died. None of them called me back. Alexandria and I spoke later, and she asked me what happened. I realized then they did not care about me at all. But I was not okay because I needed someone to tell me about my sister possibly killing him on purpose because she was mad at him. It was only a suspicion, but she had lied about me, and I had the proof, so in my mind, if she would treat me with such distain and lie and hurt my professional and personal reputation without blinking an eye, for sure my gut feelings about her maybe just the truest of things to be revealed.

One more thing I could never prove.

My father died.

In the middle of this mess of my personal stuff came a day that I was not prepared for but happy for my fad that he finally died. This was what happened to him.

One day I got a call that my dad had been taken to the hospital. I arrived, and some of my family were in the room.

I asked, "What happened?"

They said that Devilia, my sister, had gone to Mom and Dad's and found Dad very sick and called an ambulance. They said that Dad was ill and Mom had the flu too. Dad was admitted, and he was really looking bad and hardly able to talk either. I stayed in the room a bit and went out into the hall to chat with siblings. My father was stating that by the time visiting hours were about over, he could not ring the buzzer for the nurse if he needed her and asked if someone would stay the night with him.

I said, "Sure, Dad, I will stay with you."

My sister-in-law stated that she could as well, but I told her, "You have to work, I am unemployed right now, so go ahead to work, and I will spend the night with Dad."

She said okay.

I spent the night in the chair next to his bed, and only once did he wake me to ring the buzzer. He was really sick, and I had never seen him so ill and feeling so bad about life; he was crying from time to time. In the morning the doctor came in really early for rounds and asked me if I knew that my father was totally dehydrated and almost died.

I said, "No, no one told me that, and I'm sure it was because my mother is ill as well with the flu and probably could not get Dad what he needed either. She did not come to the hospital because she was sick."

He said, "Well, I am not going to let your father go home while this happened to him there, he could have died." He asked me questions about my mother's ability to care for him and was sort of insinuating that she neglected him and almost caused him to die.

I said, "No, my mother was ill as well. I will call my sisters and have them come here tonight to talk with the staff at the hospital to get the story correct."

I got on the phone and called my sister Cristy and told her what the doctor said.

I said, "Get everyone down here and stick up for Mom. I have to go to an attorney's office for an appointment today, but someone needs to stick up for Mom as they are accusing her of possibly letting Dad die."

She said, "Really!"

I said, "Yes."

I left and went home very tired and now upset. I took a shower and got dressed and gathered my files and notes to take to an attorney and my sister Brunhilda and my friend Cristy went along with me.

We arrived, and Brunhilda and Cristy and I were seated in a conference room. The attorney came in and pretty much said that her strategy was to just say that I was crazy and I would get a settlement much bigger if I would go with this strategy. However, since I had little income or assets, she would have to get someone else to sign the attorney client agreement that someone would be responsible for the $15,000 she was charging to finish up this case. None of my sisters would do it, and quite frankly, I did not want to go with her strategy anyway, as I was trying very hard to prove to my children that I was not crazy at all.

I went back to the hospital with my sister Brunhilda, only to find my sister-in-law and brother who asked me this: "Did you tell the nurses that mother has dementia?"

I said, "No! Who said that I said that?"

She said, "No one, the nurses are saying that someone told them that."

I said, "Well, who was here earlier was it Devilia, she's a big liar, of course."

I was insulted by that comment, and so I went out to the nurses' station and asked the nurses which one of my family members stated that my mother had dementia. They said it was not in their notes. But I knew it was Devilia. She was protecting my mother and lied to the doctors; it was her way. She had lied about me at work, telling them I was a paranoid schizophrenic when I was not. She is such a liar and just says whatever she wants. She told people I have a dual personality. She's nuts.

So since the nurses would not tell me, I just let it go. But I made it clear to my brother and my sister-in-law that I did not like them stating that I said that because I did not. Later, my sister Devilia appeared, and I asked her.

She said, "No, I did not say that to the nurses."

I said, "Well, they said that Dad has to go to rehab to learn to walk again."

Devilia piped up and said, "I will talk to them, and he can come to my house instead."

I said, "Don't you think rehab would be good for him? They would work with him to get him back on his feet."

She said, "No, he wants to go home."

I said, "Well, I know what he says, but what is best for him is what the doctor is saying, and he can't go home because Mom can't take care of him right now or in the next few weeks."

My father was a very large man who stood tall about 6'4" and weighed about 220 lbs., but he was very heavy for Mom to pick up or help get off the bed and into the chair; he was heavy even for me to pick up.

My sister said, "He will come to my house!"

I said, "Well, I guess that is up to the doctor."

She got her way. He didn't go to rehab; she took him directly to her house. I found out and went to her house that night to see how he was doing. It was myself, my mother, Devilia, and her husband, Saul, and my father all sitting in the family room. In the middle of conversation, my father spoke up and said he needed his legs adjusted in the wheelchair.

Right away Devilia said, "I will fix that for you, Dad."

She got up and went over to him and wrenched his legs around very hard, and he was yelping, "Oh my, that really hurts!"

She just kept on doing it and said he was a big baby. She had just abused my elderly father; I watched her. She looked like she enjoyed it.

He cried out to her, "Please don't do that to me again."

My mother saw the whole thing and said nothing. I was alarmed. I left her house and called my brother Jerry and told him to come and get Dad and take him home and that I saw Devilia being mean to him on purpose with malice to harm Dad.

Jerry came the next day and took Dad home.

I was so happy to know that, and I went to Mom and Dad's regularly in the next week. After that, all the children decided that we should all take a turn spending one day a week at the house, seeing if they needed anything and just being company to Dad. My day would be Saturday as I was finally working again. I loved spending the day with him.

I felt so sorry for my dad; he was in pain and asking us to pray that the Lord would take him and he would be dead.

I said to him, "Dad, I pray for many things, but not that, you may pray to the Lord to take you, but I can't do it, that would be asking for murder, you see."

I continued to go every Saturday and took him lunch either that I made as he liked homemade soups or that I would buy and bring to treat both Mom and myself and him, of course, to a nice lunch together. We would be closer now than we ever had been before as we had many hours to spend just talking about the world and watching a ballgame or two.

I was helping him use the walker to walk around the upstairs down the hall and into the two bedrooms and then back into the hall and over and over about three or four times, and we would do that about three times while I was there for the day.

One day, when I called my mother, she said that Dad was up all night and slept all day, and she could not take it any longer; she was tired, and he would not stop calling her incessantly at night while she tried to sleep.

I was going down the next day anyway since it was Friday, and I made sure to look at his pill boxes. Sure enough, she had the sleeping pills in the AM box, and they should have been in the PM box.

I said to Mom, "Mother, are you putting these pills in this container?"

She said, "No, Devilia is."

I said, "Well, Mom, they are in the wrong boxes you are giving him a sleeping pill in the morning, and that is why he is not sleeping at night."

She said, "Really!"

I said, "Yes, Mom, please tell Devilia to stop doing this. Don't let her near Dad's pills."

She said, "Okay."

I filled the container the right way and spent the rest of the day and part of the night with Dad and Mom making dinner and serving it and enjoying their company.

My sister Sophia from another state came in to visit. Dad was worse. She said he called her, and she felt like she should come. While she was there, Dad was in a horrible state, almost as if he could not take another single moment of life. He was stressed out, crying, and stated to me that Mom was not answering him and leaving him alone upstairs.

I said this to my sister and, she said, "Well, since I have been here, Dad is complaining every minute that someone is not in the room with him. He yells for Mom while she is outside hanging clothes and she can't hear him. He gets mad and takes it out on her by saying that she is not answering him. Anyway, for days he was not himself and crying and acting different. He had soiled himself in the wheelchair, and the stain was still on the carpet in the bedroom and on his stuff."

I said, "Was no one here when this happened?"

Sophia said, "Brunhilda was and didn't clean it up quick enough, and it stained."

I was upset for Dad as knowing him so well, this was a horrible event as he was the cleanest man I had ever met. Sophia cleaned it up nicely, and I took care of Dad, and we both sighed for him.

She left and went back to her home in another state, only to have to return shortly for his funeral.

On the day of his death, I got a phone call at 9:30 AM. I had gone to 7:30 AM Mass at church and had come home and was eating my breakfast. I had taken off my church clothes and was ready to sit down and enjoy the paper. The phone rang, and it was my sister Lenora.

She said, "Mom would like to talk to you."

I said, "Okay."

Mom said, "Your father is dead."

I said, "Well, Mom, I guess he got what he wanted, but what happened, how did he go?"

She said this to me: "I was getting ready for church, he fell off the bed, and I put a pillow underneath his head, he said, don't call for someone, just go to church, and we'll get me up later."

So she went to church as usual with her friend Pam, picking her up weekly, and she was a best friend of my sister Lenora. Pam was riding Mom to church every Sunday since Dad could no longer drive. She lived in the neighborhood and agreed to pick them up every Sunday. She was a very nice girl. I watched her daughter Gail for a few days when she was little as well when I lived behind my parents and babysat a few years. Pam had dropped my mom off at home, and evidently, when my mother went up the steps to get dressed and help with Dad, she found him dead.

She called my sister Lenora, who lived in the city, and she came right away.

I arrived quickly and parked my car in the street. I could see my brother and sister-in-law on the front porch.

I said, "Hi."

They said hi back to me and opened the door to let me in.

I saw my mother in the kitchen. She was just sitting all alone in the kitchen chair that Dad used to sit in. She looked stunned. I hugged her and asked her if she was all right.

She said, "Yes, I'm fine." She just took a big sigh and said, "He's gone, he got his wish, and now he's in a better place. I can't believe he's gone."

I felt so bad for her as she was with him for over sixty-five years of her life, and he was her partner and her daily living spouse to share things.

She said, "The coroner's office, the priest, and the funeral home person are all upstairs."

I said, "Well, I guess they are doing their thing." I did not want to go up to see him. I wanted to remember him alive and unique.

Just then, my sister Devilia came through the front door and ran up the steps, screaming and wailing in such a fake demeanor, "Dad! Ohhhhh, Dad, why did they have to take him?" She was wailing at the top of her lungs in a fake manner to me. It was clear to me she was putting on a show of some kind. But why? I knew something was not right. It was my gut feeling; I knew she had done something to Dad. The hateful act at her house, the pills, and now this greatest fake show on earth for the world to see, phony, and I didn't buy it.

I sat there thinking to myself that this was nothing but a big show she just put on. Why? I turned to my mother and with the thoughts of Devilia abusing my dad in my mind and then the pills being in the wrong place put there by her, I said this to my mother, "Mom, are you going to have an autopsy done? You know, it's the only way to tell why Dad died."

She simply said, "Oh, your father died of old age, he was ready to go."

I said, "Well, I know that you can't tell why someone died unless you do an autopsy. Why don't you ask for one?"

She said this to me, "Just let your father rest."

She had just lost the man whom she lived with for the last sixty-seven years of her life. Dad was ninety-one, and she was eighty-eight. She was tired, and I didn't have the nerve to insist as I loved my mother and could see that she was heartbroken and in distress, so I let it go. In retrospect, I should have asked the coroner to do one as I suspected possible murder. I was under the crazy radar at that time, so I was extremely hesitant to say anything at that point as well. Scared of my ex and my family.

I was happy that my dad had gotten his prayers answered. I was not happy that my thoughts were that my sister had something to do with it.

When I called my children, only Alexandria called back, and I asked her if she was coming. She was living in New York at the time with her sister and had told me that she did not want to come. I asked her to please come for me as a person who would care about me during this time.

She reluctantly said, "Okay."

I told her that I would pay for the ticket on my credit card, and she said, "Yeah, then I'll come."

So I paid for the ticket, and she arrived a day before the funeral, and we had fun talking, and we went to the funeral home, and there were many family members and friends and relatives that were all there to say how sorry they were that my father had passed away. My mother was sitting on a stool by the casket, and my sister was sitting with her. Everyone else was all around the room as there were ninety-one people in my immediate family when my father died. My family was very big, and we were all upset for Mom and happy for Dad.

The days prior to the funeral parlor were days of concern for me about whether to tell someone about my dad. I went for a walk with Brunhilda from work on our lunch hour, and I told her that I thought one of my siblings might have had something to do with my dad's death. I didn't know what to do. Brunhilda asked me if I had any proof.

I said, "No."

She was very nice, and we were of the same personality type as well. She was a good friend to me while I worked there.

Brunhilda and Connie, my supervisor, came to the funeral home. I was surprised and thanked them very much for coming.

It would be a very hard night as people were coming and going and asking me about my ex-husband and the court issues as well as me telling them what a big liar he was and that I thought he would be going to jail. My daughter heard me telling this to one of my best friends. She did not talk to me about it, but only said after her fiancé came to the funeral home, and they went out to eat together as no one in the family told us that there was food in the family room at the funeral home. It did not surprise me. I was not asked to participate in any of the funeral church readings, and neither was my daughter. Devilia was in charge of the getting the thing together, of course, and she did not ask me to participate at all. My nieces and nephews did readings before; his very children were even asked to do it. I thought to myself, as my sister Sophia from out of state said in the church pew, "I guess we are not good enough to do anything since Devilia is in charge."

I said, "Yeah, you're right, we divorced sinners will have to just sit and listen because we are not good enough to participate in the church ceremony since the Popess said so."

She just turned with a big smile and said, "You're right about that."

My sister Lenora had coined the phrase the *popess* to describe my sister Devilia, who was always right, always knew what was best, and planned everything for everyone every second she could. Lenora had a great tradition she started for my dad of giving him a great unordinary, sometimes homemade, one-of-a-kind birthday hat on his birthday every year. One year it was the white tall hat that the pope wears, and after his birthday, she said it was the popess's hat from now on. We all laughed and agreed with her. But I thought it was horrible that I was not asked to read or do something for my own father's funeral and church ceremony. No big deal now, huh.

My daughter, after listening to hours of the family junk at the funeral parlor, said to me, "Let's go into the back room and sit down."

I said, "All right, let's go this way."

I took her to a back empty room, and we sat chatting; my brother Tom came in and sat with us. We were all laughing and said that we had to cheer up as the room was getting weirdly sad.

My oldest brother started asking me what I was up to, and I said to him, "Well, when we talked last you said I needed to get out of the house, I spent this past summer using my credit card going to baseball games and concerts and having fun, but now are you going to pay off my credit card since you were the one who told me to get out and have fun?"

He laughingly said to me, "Heck no, man, you pay your own bills."

We all started laughing. Alexandria was glad to be out of the room, and I was sure my brother was too, as our family—or I should say Devilia—really bugged him, and he would probably like to be anywhere but where she was. All of his life they hated each other; he was so nice and kind, and she so utterly had to have it her way all the time, and she was my father's pet, as we referred to her.

My older siblings always told me what a liar she was to their faces about what happened when they were kids. I was too young to remember anything, except for the time one evening when my brother was watching TV and it was one of his favorite shows. Devilia began playing the piano in the living room upstairs. He asked Mom to have to quit playing, and Mom said no. So my brother pulled the two main fuses in the fuse box and left. We all thought it was funny, but my mother was not overjoyed. She sent us to the store to get more candles as it was getting dark. I remember laughing at how he had the balls to do that to my mom, but I'd bet he was sick of Devilia and her attitude that she ruled and she was the queen of the house. The baby grand piano that we had was quite noisy when played, and I was sure he was fed up of giving up his time to enjoy life so she could practice. The whole family thought it at times when we were all watching a TV show. She rarely gave consideration to others as my siblings would tell me. I tried to get along with her as she was so much older than me, but later in life, after I moved back home, I would begin to see that she thought she was in control of my life and my mother instead of a sister. Somehow, my two oldest sisters had become the rulers of the family other than my parents. The younger echelon, which was what we called ourselves, were sick of it. In the prior five years of my father's death, we would finally, the last five children, finally stick up for ourselves and start to buck the orders of our two oldest sisters. We were finally feeling good as the younger five to have a say about family matters. I know my sister Devilia did not like it at all. I know my sister Brunhilda started having Christmas Eve at her house for only her children and did not join the rest of the family after that time.

Alexandria and I spent the night talking and drove home. The funeral was the next day, and of course, it was very nice, and then of course, we all were invited back to Devilia's house for the luncheon. She was in charge as usual. I didn't say a thing. I do remember sitting in the living room on her new, expensive living room furniture as they had taken the pool table out of the living room.

My sister Vicki turned to me and said, "Do you realize that we have ninety-one people in our immediate family, and Dad is ninety-one when he died?"

I said, "No, Vicki, only you the mathematician would know such details."

We both started laughing. Vicki was very smart in school; even though I was smart, I was not in the National Honor Society as she was as I was an artist and my personality was very laid-back and relaxed—not into being the best, just happy. I know that I can be intelligent, but I did not know what she was about to say, and I just burst out laughing. I would remember this day very fondly because of her statement. My father, you see, was very proud of the fact that he had ten children and so many grandchildren and great-grandchildren.

In the end, when he was so sad, I said to him, "Dad, just think, you have so many children that are so good, none of us has ever been in jail or done anything wrong."

Well, I did forget that Devilia had been arrested several times for her unlawful behavior in front of abortion clinics here in Springfield. I know that some people think that sort of thing is something that you can look the other way about, but I never did. I think it's wrong to scream and yell at people and make them feel bad when they are not doing anything against the law. I think you can hand things out and ask them to talk with you, but you as an American never have the right to scream and yell at anyone who is within the law. I am a very passive person about personal being. I don't like violence. I don't like war. I especially don't like people who make others feel badly about a choice they have made in their personal life. I don't agree with abortion, but I know in this world not enough people help others in need sometimes and people make wrong decisions. I once asked a girl standing on the corner who was pregnant begging for money if she would come home with me and I would give her a place to stay for free. She said no because she did not trust me. I believed her, and it was good judgment on her part, but I still wanted to help her. She told me Birthright would only let her stay three months. I felt so compelled to do something, but money was all she would accept from me. Nothing I could do for her could stop her from sleeping in an abandoned building at night; it was summer, but I still felt that need to take her home not only to protect and help her but to let her know that someone cared about her and her baby. To this day, I wish she would have come with me.

Alexandria and I spent the night at home talking a bit, and then she said that she had to get back to New York to work. I thought she might get to stay the weekend since it was Mother's Day, but she said she had to get back. Later on, I would find out that she lied and stayed with her boyfriend in Springfield and did not take a flight back until Sunday night. I was upset and cried and told her that I did not like the fact that she lied to me. I was so hurt and didn't even get a Mother's Day card either; I spent the day alone. I guess she missed him, too, and wanted to spend alone time with him as well. I later understood but at first was so depressed about it as I wanted to talk over with her the fact that I thought Devilia might have had something to do with Grandpa's death, and I didn't know what to do about it. I thought she would be my anchor of strength, which she had in the past, and I was very grateful to her for that part of our relationship; she was a lot like me in many ways. Instead, she left, and I didn't know what to do.

So I held on and kept trying to understand the process.

I went back to work, and lo and behold, the girls had done nothing to keep up my case files, which were very crucial to the job. I was told in my absence that the supervisor and other case workers would attend to my files. It was horrible, and on top of that, the next week, I was supposed to go to a breakfast banquet about my son's high school graduation, and I had asked Lawrence, one of the hot attorneys that sat in the cube next to mine, if he would attend with me. He said he had other things that day but we could go out perhaps another time.

I said, "Sure."

I was hoping that the big, cute ex-probation officer would have come along to protect me against the devil ex-husband. But it was not to be. Later that week, I was in the bathroom at work and one of the girls who had been going to lunch with me said, after I told her that I had asked Lawrence to go, "Well, you sound like you need a psychiatrist."

I was outraged and left the bathroom and came into the office. She followed me and stated in the middle of the aisle, "You know that Frank is a big pervert."

I said to her, "I'm a big girl, and I can take care of myself, and if I were you, I would not say such insulting things about an attorney you work with, he may just sue you."

The next day I had asked the office person to have the afternoon off to go the FBI and talk about some things, and before I knew it, I was taken into an office and told that I was being let go. They gave me a letter and stated that for no reason I was being fired. I never heard of such a thing, and I left, stating to the office staff that I was let go because I said I was going to the FBI. It was horrible. My father had just died, I was trying to investigate, and now this.

I went to the FBI the next day, and they told me to put a home alarm on my condo and that they would call me to see what they could do to help. I went home and put an alarm on my condo.

My sister-in-law, my ex-husband's sister, called me to say her mother died. Three days after the funeral. The next day my ex-husband called me to say his mother died. I only said to him, "I am sorry for your loss," and I hung up. I had not talked with him for over a year. He was letting me know a message that he delivered himself because he wanted to. I then was even afraid that he might have killed his mother. I had been up to see her about six months prior, and she had nothing good to say about him and was upset that his girlfriend had sent her a check marked "PAID IN FULL" real big across the top to pay off a loan they took from her for $100,000. His mother confided in me how upset she was, and she said that she had deposited the check into the bank.

About three weeks later, his sister called me up crying stating that he was telling everyone that he, my ex-husband, had a new will that his mother made out and it said that he got everything. His mother, mind you, at the time was worth a few million dollars—the total amount I did not know, nor was it any of my business. She confided in me that he was telling everyone that she was crazy and that he had the proper will. She was crying the whole time while talking to me and making statements like, "How could he do this to me, telling everyone I'm crazy and he has a new will stating that he gets everything. He never did anything with Mom. I took care of her for years."

I said to her, "I know you did, and your mother was your life, and she adored you for looking out of her and taking care of her. You were the only person who loved her dearly until her death and saw to her everyday needs. Your mother talked about you so endearing and knew that you would do anything for her. Your brother, on the other hand, moved far away from her years ago, when I said why don't we move to Raleigh and be closer to your family and your son."

She said in a panic, "What should I do?" She was still crying.

I said to her, "Get an attorney outside of Grey Town that he would not know or another attorney in the burgh would not know. Talk to no one about what he is saying."

She said, "Okay."

I said, "Call me and let me know what happens."

She said, "I will call you back when things are figured out."

She never called me back. I did try a few times to call her. I left messages, but no one ever called me back. I have no idea to this day what happened to her.

I think either she decided to just get on with her life, or she was calling for her brother to find out what happened to me in the hospital when the police took me there. She asked me specifically what did the doctors say. She had never called me before or after the divorce. Maybe they were all crazy; maybe they killed off their mother for her money. Who knows at this point, I don't care! I do know she was lonely as she called me pretty much since I made the trip to visit her and stayed for a few days. She was lonely and had very little food in the house when I was there, she had lost a considerable amount of weight as well, and she didn't even look like herself. When I went to her house in the morning that day to visit, she was not at home. I called his sister's house, and her husband Kevin answered and said they were out shopping together. I waited at their house for them to come back. He called Alice on her cell phone, and in about two hours, they were back. Kevin and I talked about the kids, and Dominic, their son, was there and was getting ready for his ball game later that day. Cecelia, their daughter, was not home; she was at a friend's house.

Most importantly was his mother telling me about how upset she was at Paul and her son Saul as well. Alice told me that she rarely talked to either one of them and that she was left to care for her mother by herself. I thought to myself, "Is that what life is like when you are older?" I saw my parents, since they had ten kids, we were all able to take a day a week to help with other things they might need. Alice had to care for her mother by herself. It must have been hard. She cried so hard when she died as she was her best friend and had very little other friendships as she was a very quiet person who kept to herself pretty much. I liked her, but I was now wondering what in the heck this was all about because she never called me back. I don't know if she got the will that she had or if my ex her brother got the courts to approve the separate new will he had stating he got everything. I can't believe that she would have not called me if she needed me to state things about him, so I am going to suppose that she got what she wanted.

I never inquired. I didn't even ask my children. I was so angry with them over keeping things from me, like the fact that Grandma died and they didn't tell me. Not to mention that Alexandria had taken a job working for her father, my abuser, and never told me. The shock I got when I walked into his office and there she sat at the front desk next to the desk of the girlfriend—wasn't that cozy for them all. My heart cried out, and I kept my composure, but I would never forget the feeling of betrayal.

Chapter 11

I Realize I Have to Get Out of My House
You Believe Him and Not Me—Hell to the No

Why does everyone believe him and not me? Why did I lose the people I loved and friendships I had since childhood? How could he do this to me too?

It would be very calculated skills and control that would give him the upper hand in creating the destruction of my past relationships; even with my family.

This is a detailed vision in my head of how he was able to do it.

In 1997, he realized he wanted government contracts and to have his own businesses and life without me.

He put our home we renovated for eight years up for sale. I hated him for it.

He found a house we couldn't afford, but it was close to his girlfriend's house (which I didn't know at that time), so he pressured me to say yes to it. He promised me he would fix this new house up to look just like our old one—with new staircase, install wood floors, etc. I bought it all, of course, and believed him. He never did any of it, of course, because he never had any intention of doing any of it anyway. He just lied to me to be within a few miles of his girlfriend's house. The girlfriend I knew nothing about.

It would be one year in which he would ignore me, state things to me to upset me, not back me up when I asked him to on important things and decisions.

I changed jobs because a woman was not nice to me at work and someone had changed my work in the computer; he didn't even seem to care when I talked about it at home. It was clear that he did not want anything to do with me, nor did he care about how others were treating me. He was a Salieri and much more, as I would uncover later.

I resolved myself at that time to ignore him too. It worked. However, when I changed jobs and another woman would accuse me of things, he would not come to my rescue as well. I knew for sure then something was wrong.

When I went to church one night after quitting my job and resigning, he was so upset but always held back his true emotions, just did things behind my back to get even or ignore me when I needed help.

When we came home and he started the "you're crazy, you're going to the hospital," it was the first step toward building up the lies in front of my children who adored me. He had to get them to believe him and be on his side when he left me, but this was his first attempt at building up the big case that Mom was crazy so that they would not believe what I had to say at all.

That night my children heard the argument; they saw me packing a suitcase to leave him. He, of course, was not ready for that yet in the plans, so he did everything to stop it from happening. Oh, he did it right, got my sister, brother, sister-in-law to all come over and pull me by my feet out the front door of my home in front of my children to take me to a mental ward at the hospital. They stated I wanted to kill my brother's children, and they kept me. It was a lie, of course, that my evil sister Devilia told them to hurt me. She knew why, not me.

The lies began at the hospital with him and my sister telling things that were not true to get me admitted. The lies that would ruin my life as I knew it happened at that very instant and I would have no idea what was to come in the next five years and how I tried to be quiet about him as I knew I had nowhere else to go and no support from my family at all.

I knew he had convinced people of certain things, but I had no idea what until it was way too late. He and my sister had paved the way over the last five years to instill in everyone that I was crazy. I felt like I had an out of body experience that just wouldn't stop.

One by one, my neighbors, friends, and family would stop having anything to do with me.

This would be the most important lesson of my life. Someone had the ability to destroy my life and friends in my hometown on my turf in my neighborhoods and churches and schools and social events. Little by little, he weaved his web of destruction on purpose, and one by one all my friends and family took a step backward to stay away from me.

I remember the most surprising one of all was my neighbor Lizbeth, whom I had stuck up for when all the neighbors were talking about her and her children. She was close to my life, my home, my children, my holidays, and I thought to myself, "Well, if he was able to convince her, who else would believe me?" She knew me so well at that time.

Well, my sisters and brothers, children, friends, acquaintances, work relationships, one by one everyone stepped aside and had nothing to do with me. My family, I withdrew from myself after learning they were responsible as well.

He did this on purpose. Same as my sister Devilia—she, too, lied about me on purpose.

He did this with purpose. Same as my sister Devilia—she, too, did this with purpose.

The purpose was to get what he wanted. New job, new business of his own, new wife to cover his gay lifestyle with her not suspecting a thing; he was on his way to a new tunnel of life he created to get rid of the one that was so heinous to him as my family talked often about hating homosexuals. I'm sure he wanted to pull out the Uzi even though I knew he didn't own one at every one of my family functions that he had to attend.

So one by one, people stopped believing anything I had to say. All of a sudden, I was being ignored. I was not credible. I was not a viable person. I was being ignored, lied to, like I was the big family secret that no one wanted to let out.

What I didn't know until years later was that my sister was also at the same time, if you can believe it, telling everyone that I was molested by a brother when I was younger. Now, my brother did something to touch me once inappropriately as if he was exploring. It never affected me at all. He was about ten, and I was only four. I didn't even think about it until at age forty when the husband was saying I was crazy and my sister was too; she was spinning her wheels of emotional destruction as well to make me cry, upset me, and torture me.

So with both of these things happening at once, I was wondering if I was Alice in Horrorland and someone was going to wake me up any minute and tell me I was just in a sci-fi horror life-destruction movie. But I wasn't; it was my life, oh, my life indeed.

I looked in the mirror one day and said, "Is this me? Why are these people doing this to me?" I had no idea that my other sister had told everyone about the incident, including my name in her story, and everyone believed her because she said so. I hated them all. Liars and destroyers of my life.

I came home to my condo on the third floor and said, "Is this where I live?"

I said to myself after seven years of virtually no contact with my children, "Do I deserve this? Of course not! Why then is this happening to me?"

For seven years of my life, I tried to prove everything was a lie. No one listened to me, not even my children. It seemed the more I tired to set things straight, the worse they got. I gave up.

I said to myself, "I am not talking to anyone in my past. I am starting over. A new life. A new love waiting around the corner somewhere."

I started some business ideas. I networked, I worked, I went to online school full-time at a college nearby and had one class at night in the classroom.

I was on my way to a new life. I was going to put the past in the past.

But one thing I was left with as a victim of verbal abuse reared its ugly head. I had post-traumatic stress disorder from verbal abuse. I found certain situations unbearable.

Now, after several work situations I found one more that put me over the edge. I uncovered sex offenders at work. I worked with them. I sent them into the homes of my customers. I investigated, I cried, I got scared, I got fired.

Finding myself in bankruptcy from being foreclosed while I was unemployed, fired again, stressed about many things, it would break me down to the realization that I must disable myself to keep alive and paying bills. But most of all, to have a place to live.

I didn't want to. Why? I knew the past medical records that no one would listen to me about to set the story straight would get me disabled. But would they believe me this time.

I thought the golden day came. The paper said, "Yes, you are disabled and will receive benefits for PTSD and depression and stress."

Guess what—they lied on the paper. Or did they?

Later, I would learn after requesting a copy of the doctor's exam that they lied to me. They didn't reveal the doctors findings because another office decided whether you are or aren't, not the doctor.

The doctor did not state PTSD or they said that; they said I was a paranoid schizophrenic and that I needed someone to come into the office with me as they were not going to give me the records by myself.

Once again treated like a baby, lied about. No wonder people with mental diseases want to kill themselves. People treat them like dirt. Even the very people who you would think would be helping you out. But oh no, they were just the same. Secrets only to be revealed to someone else who was not crazy at all but very intelligent and wrongfully diagnosed.

I asked for a new exam. They didn't even return my calls. These people who said they would help me now ignored me like everyone else.

So I was ignored and lonely and poor. I thought to myself, "I am not giving in or giving up. I am going to prevail to my new, enriched environment. They took my house. They took my respect. They can't take my mind or my self-respect, which I have a lot of. They have tortured me with every disdain of life. They have lied about me, lied to me, and tortured me with words and lack of support. They can't take away my right to write. Write, 'I am this story for you to all learn from.' The last thing in my life I wanted to accomplish for sure before I died."

Learn from my words and life, learn from my story. Learn and keep that knowledge.

Never say never.

This, too, could happen to you.

Trust me.

Never did I ever think that anyone could do this to me. Never. Never. Never.

My beautiful spirit, my free will, my fun-loving ways, my spiritual gifts from God—how could someone want to take them from me? They did.

I fought the devils and won.

I fought life and made it mine once again.

I fought for justice, and although some may think I never got it, revealing the truth can be justice. Remember that. Revealing the ugliness of someone is in itself justice, maybe not the justice we think of, but in the long run, it is the justice of personal life.

Personal life justice: Talk loud, and let everyone hear you.

Some will believe, and others will not.

During this struggle, I realized that I needed to be a new me. Even though I was part of safety program and my mailing address was hidden for me, it would soon reveal it was not enough to keep people from finding me if they wanted to in my mind. I did secure myself; I don't think anyone horrible in my past knows where I am but also realized that if I truly wanted a new life, it had to be a new me. I never wanted to think about it ever again, "Does this person know me? Would they tell where I live or worked to anyone else?"

Change my name, change my Social.

I couldn't wait for the day.

I know it was drastic; I know it cut out my past life.

I was ready.

I was longing for the day.

Today on this Memorial Day weekend, when the pool opened, it was cloudy and the weather station stated that it may thunderstorm. For my safety, I stayed inside even though I wanted to swim so bad as it is one of my favorite things to do.

For my safety, I made the change to change myself to someone new as well.

I had gathered evidence; I had studied. I had had enough.

Once the bankruptcy, chapter 7, was over, I could change my name.

The days became days of waiting as of that day, forty-seven more days till I was completely free from old ties to my name. It would be forty-seven days of waiting for the new me, waiting patiently for the new name and new life. Those forty-seven days would be some of the most important to remember in my life.

I was finishing my story, starting on a new life and working on helping others so their lives would not be destroyed like mine.

Such intentional life destruction. Who would do this kind of thing to me? My husband. My family. My friends. My children unable to ascertain the truth from the lies. My children hurt by the very people who were supposed to love them.

I know the people who I thought were supposed to love me the most in life would ruin it, tear it to shreds, bash me, trash me, say I'm crazy. Ignore me in my hours of need, turn their backs on me.

My children who would not talk to me, my children who I thought for sure understood their mother. He had taken that from me too. I hated him the most for that.

Little by little, I gave them information so that they would know he was a liar about me and his life.

They were tired of it by that time. Tired of the strife of life when family should be and was taught to be the one thing you could count on. They learned a lesson harder than mine. Family was good for me until forty. At twenty and younger, my children's lives were ripped apart, their emotions lying on the floor, and everyone ignored them. I tried to talk to them, but they were being pulled, and I let go.

I let go—because I loved them more.

I let go—because I loved them more than myself.

I let go—because I wanted them to be happy.

I let go—because I wanted the proof I wasn't crazy before I talked with them again.

So far in 2011, on Memorial Day weekend, that had not occurred.

So seven years of bad luck, seven years of abuse, seven years of loneliness.

Now, I was in control. I might not have a lot of money, but I was working toward my new life and a new outlook. A new me now for sure to live peacefully.

My new name, I picked from a past name that someone stated in my life, and I thought it was beautiful. Like a song or a poem when spoken. I thought it would fit my new life filled with song and poems and words of love and life and happiness.

A totally new name, even in nationality, first and last; it was fun picking. I won't say what it is, because it is a true story. Or is it? I won't reveal for my safety who I am now, just hope that this helps everyone else.

I keep that to my new life. My new world. My new happiness.

Live life.

I live life.

Make life what you want it to be. When you reach a wall, climb it. If you can't seem to get over it, find another route and finish the plan.

Peace is what I offer.

I hope this story will reveal eventually how to attain peace in your life.

Strive for peace.

Live peacefully.

Demand peace.

Otherwise, you might just let people continue to treat you anyway that they want to.

Don't let them.

Live peacefully. Your way, your rules, your time, your peace. You're worth it. Trust me!

Chapter 12

A Fresh Start—Not Quite Yet!
Starting College as a Freshman at Fifty-Three, Bankruptcy, and Furniture Hut Scandal All in One Year

Who could ask for more? I'm surprised I survived.

People have been saying my life is intriguing for a few years, and I would like it to be even more common, but I guess because I am who I am, and I stand up for myself and honesty. My life is intriguing to those who don't or maybe have never had things like this happen in their lives.

I have now taken a job at Furniture Hut as a sales consultant. I interviewed for the job in my less-than-conservative clothes as I was going networking that night at a bar and needed to look like I fit in and wanted to save gas and just leave from the interview and go network.

I arrived at Furniture Hut and met with Amy, the manager. She was a tall and stout woman with blond hair in an updo and a long skirt, which made her look like the boss I thought. She said her hellos, and we sat on the showroom floor as she said to me, "Just sit down here and get comfortable, and we'll chat for bit to find out if you will be a good fit for our team here at Furniture Hut."

I thought to myself, "This is a bit unconventional an interview on the sales floor with the customers coming in and out," but it seemed like a slow day and so we began to chat. Before I knew it, we had talked for hours. She asked me about my past previous experience, and I told her I had no sales experience but that I was a natural people person. She told me I was a good listener and talked for hours about this and that and about the store and about past businesses she had with her ex-husband. We shared a bit of our divorce stories, and she, too, had been a victim of poor choice of husband and abuse involved in her life, so we connected.

We talked at great length about how we wished that there was a business that could help victims of abuse with a store and hair salon and a great place for them to stay. She went on and on about her ideas, and I shared that I had started a business to help investigate lies that people tell in court and help victims get evidence to prove that someone lied about them in court. She admired my efforts, and we talked about our love of furniture, and she was clearly a wonderful woman who had spent most of her time managing a store that sold upper-class furniture, and she was fun.

I said, "Amy, what is the most important thing to remember when selling?"

She said, "I think the fact that you are good listener, customers just want someone to listen to what they need and help them find it."

What she didn't tell me was that the company had just months prior changed their sales staff payout monthly from commission only full-time with benefits to hourly wage of only $12 an hour part-time and no benefits. Salespeople who were used to making around $65,000 a year were now making almost nothing, according to them. There was disdain and upheaval amongst them. Even worse was the new policy that they now had to dust, vacuum, and clean the bathrooms and kitchen and mop the floors and wash the windows outside of the store that were about twenty feet tall. Clearly, she told me my duties were to clean along with selling, and I told her that I had no problem with that. She, however, left out that the sales staff was not used to doing this part and they hated it; it would become a source of daily contention within the store as well.

She said, "You have to talk with Porter first, he will call you on the phone, but according to me, you have the job." She said, "He will call you later tonight."

I said, "Well, tell him that I have to go meet some people, and if I can't hear my phone ring, would he please call me on another night?"

He never called, and so the next day, I called Amy.

She said, "Oh, I guess he was busy, he may call you today."

I said, "Okay."

The call never came, so I called her at the end of the day.

She said, "Oh, what the heck, just come in and fill out the

paperwork to have your blood tested and drug test and you're hired."

I said, "Great, I'll be over to the store in just a few minutes."

The first day of work was really nice, and I got to know of the sales staff. The assistant managers were a male Chester and female Bonnie. The sales staff consisted of three men and five women other than later one other male who was hired and two males left to go to other stores.

The sales team was upset over the loss of the money they used to make and they had to clean the store. It was a usual battle to get them to do it, and I just did it, and I'd bet they hated me for being so cooperative in doing it since the company had paid someone to clean prior to that on a regular basis.

Clearly, I had stepped into a hornet's nest of angry salespeople. The assistant manager, Chester, was put in charge of me to train me and get me started seemed to really be enthusiastic at first and then did not train me any longer very well. I did not know why, and we began to drift apart from one another. I thought, "Oh, a gay man and his frustrated life," or something, but later I would learn why. It would be the noose around my neck on many occasions to make him want to get rid of me. Had I known he was keeping such a dastardly criminal secret from me, I would have not had conversations about my work in life and my studies in college of criminal justice later on some nights working there.

The job was difficult to learn, and I was doing great for getting no training as I saw others doing. The whole numbers thing for each piece of furniture would be impossible to learn, and I chose not to in order to keep my sunny disposition and stick to selling and not learning numbers, which meant nothing to customers unless they were ready to buy. So I focused on customers' needs and learned the products and custom items by myself mostly and asked questions of the sales staff on occasion.

One day I realized when I asked simple questions of Bonnie, she turned around and walked away from me. I went to Amy and told her of the moment, and Amy said to me, "You have a bad attitude, and I saw you throw that book down on the counter."

I said, "I did not throw a book on the counter."

She said, "You just wait on customers, and we'll handle this later."

She was angry and said in a tone that made me wish I had never opened my mouth.

An hour or so later, she said to me, "I want you to come into the office with me and Bonnie and discuss this issue."

I said, "Okay."

She and Bonnie proceeded to tell me that I was overreacting and that if Bonnie stepped away from me when I asked a question, she must have been with a customer.

I said just simply said, "Okay," and we walked out of her office.

Only a few weeks went by, and we all got the announcement that Amy was going to cut our hours back. I was hired at thirty hours at $11 an hour, but now there was no guarantee what hours we would get weekly. The schedule would be posted weekly.

I said to Amy, when she asked me if I would stay, "I have to find full-time work in order to support myself."

Amy said, "Don't worry, the hours will pick up again in a few weeks, just try and stick it out. Can I count on you to stay?"

I said, "Well, I'm not going to say I will stay if I can't pay my bills."

Weeks went by, and some weeks I only had sixteen hours. I was struggling but loved the job and had put in many hours of training and wanted to stay.

She told me that in July the hours would pick up, and they didn't, and in August she would give me more hours. She didn't.

She told me for sure when summer was over. She didn't and not only that, but she retired and told me one week before she left. I was aghast.

The lack of wages to me on my paycheck would be the cause of missing payments on my mortgage and asking for home modifications on my loans to stay in my home. I was living below the poverty level, and my life was a mess. Work had screwed me intentionally and didn't care.

At the same time that summer, I had started three businesses, and the ideas were good; they just needed money, which I thought would come from other sources but did not.

The first idea was to start a company for abused people but found no funding. The second idea was to renovate a mansion inside a state park and turn it into a restaurant, wedding hall, and bed-and-breakfast, but the park service failed to tell me after four months of work that the mansion was full of asbestos. The third idea was the biggest, and it was to take all schools to laptop learning with e-textbooks instead of paper books. One private school in town was already doing it for years, and I wanted to bring the technology and ideas into every school across the nation.

Now you might say, how a person with no money can think that she can start three businesses with no money. In 2009, there was stimulus money given to the states from the federal government. I went to a grant-writing seminar that a senator had, and she inspired me to think of ways to put people to work in my state during this terrible time of joblessness and foreclosures leaving people homeless and unsure of their very existence in life for the first time in America since the Great Depression. So I was a dreamer with great ideas, and I thought I could do this; I could make a difference. So I rolled up my sleeves and got to work. The idea about the park mansion was clearly the most hurried since I did not want someone else to get the privilege of the renovation project and thought it might bring home my daughter and son-in-law from New York, who were both chefs, to run the business, and of course my grandsons to live in the mansion inside the park with their parents, which was, of course, right down the street from where I lived. So Grandmama saw a way to bring her grandson from halfway across the United States to only miles from her house where she could play and run and have fun with him. The mansion was breathtaking, turn-of-the-century picturesque stately home with a main ballroom kitchen and maid quarters, five bedrooms, and of course, a view of the river that would calm any heart to want to stay forever. The beauty of the mansion in its splendor was also surrounded by 190 acres of state park and a view of the river as well. It was like a dream come true as my daughter, the pastry chef, had spent many hours of her teenage years in that park with friends and boyfriends, walking, hiking, and writing poetry under the trees to get away from the stress of life and just relax. I thought to myself, "What a treat for her to be able to live in the very park that brought such joy to her life." Now I know it's not Central Park, so when I called her to say, "Would you like to move home and live in the park in the mansion?"

She simply stated, "Mom, I don't know I'll have to think about it."

I have to admit, I was let down and a bit heartbroken, but I still pursued the idea even asking Furniture Hut if they wanted to furnish the home with furniture and be a sponsor of sorts for the project and have the name put on the front of the mansion. They never responded to my request.

But the project would soon be a massive heartbreaker for me since they were not forthcoming or just too stupid to know that the mansion had asbestos in more than the kitchen floor. It was crushing for me since I had put all my summer hours of fun instead to working on getting this project up and running quickly since it would take a year just to get the mansion in shape to open businesses. After many lies and many meetings, I scrapped the project and cried for days.

Still working on the other two projects which, of course, needed no long sentences to describe: the e-textbook idea was not welcomed by local schools who did not either like the idea or did not have the matching funds for me to get the stimulus money needed to spearhead the project. I ran out of money to even put gas in my car to further the venture and gave up the project for a while to focus on work and paying my bills.

But despite my efforts, I found myself fighting with the mortgage company's day after day one phone call every day; it seemed telling me I was behind and needed to make a payment. I was honest with them all the time, but they continued the calls and made me cry daily and weep as I had explained the situation and began to get discouraged with the process and Americans.

I had two mortgages—one original, when I bought the home, and a few years later a line of credit.

The original mortgager, I was paying regularly, as I was told that the second could not foreclose even if I owed the second one more money. So I tried very hard to pay them and keep them paid up while falling behind on the second line of credit, but I did not know that they could jack up the monthly payment for the line of credit like a credit card, and soon the payments were three times as much as they normally were. It was a nightmare, and every day I was fighting and struggling on how to pay, and I was exhausted and felt abused since I am a victim of post-traumatic stress syndrome, and when people verbally abuse me, I go limp like a noodle and digress. When that happens, my mind is incapable of functioning, and it takes days for me to recover. So day after day, the verbal abuse from collection people was taking me to a place that was not healthy for my mind. I begged and pleaded for them to stop, but they wouldn't. I begged and pleaded with the corporate office, but they wouldn't.

My mind was upset, and my body was taking a toll. My work was affected, and I was not selling like I should have been. Of course, I did not know that the furniture store I worked for had the policy that if you were not selling like they thought you should, they would cut your hours. I was caught up in a tornado of circumstances and found myself being blown around and around for days on end, never knowing when the storm would stop for me.

I had met with the staff and asked after Amy left, "Could you please give me more hours?" And my request was never granted nor acknowledged by Porter. It was as if he wanted me to leave. It was as if he hated me and thought, "I'll just ignore her request and maybe she'll get mad and leave." I was crying at home on a regular basis now, and I was tired.

I found out I could ask for a modification from my mortgagers and asked them to please grant me a modification. I asked the second line of credit mortgager first since they were the ones calling me daily, relentlessly causing me to want to kill myself as I could bear it no longer. They told me that I could not get one from them until the first gave me one.

I said okay. He said this though, which made my mind dash for an instant to that place where you know that someone was not telling you something important:

"Well, you would have to get the first mortgager to give you the modification, that is, unless we already bought your loan from them."

I said, "What do you mean by that?" I wanted to reach through the phone and grab him by the neck.

He said to me, "Just call your first mortgager and ask them to give you a modification, and then we can."

I thought to myself, "If you bought my loan, then I shouldn't be paying the first anything anymore, but I had been for a year."

His statement will be a key part of the criminal crimes that were committed as part of this story.

I called my first mortgager, and they said, "Sure, we'll start the paperwork," and faxed me the papers to sign. A few weeks later, I received the paperwork and began the three months of shorter payments so that I could catch up. I was jumping for joy.

Then the second mortgager gave me a bunch of paperwork to fill out and said, "Just fill it all out, and fax it back to us." I did it right away. I waited, and I waited, and I called and called, and all through this process the collection calls kept coming. I called the corporate office again, and they said, "The collection calls will keep coming until you are paid up."

I said, "But you agreed to a modification, and the paperwork is just not filled out yet."

They said, "Just wait for the modification, but we can't stop the collection calls." It was so hard on me.

I waited patiently with great need to get that modification paperwork and save my home. The paperwork never came. I called again; they said, "We lost your paperwork."

I said, "What? You lost my paperwork a third time? How can that be?"

I faxed it to them but first called the corporate office again. The corporate person said they would put a special person on this, and Ms. Smith faxed me more paperwork again to fill out. I filled it out and faxed it back the same day, as I was in a hurry to get the task finished.

Again, I waited and called and waited and called. Nothing. I called one day and said, "What is going on? It has been months."

They said, "The girl who was working on your modification went on family leave, and we don't have the paperwork."

By this time, I know that they are lying to me, and I stated that I had to do something. A girl I met who used to work in collections once told me that if you send a check marked "paid in full," and they cashed it, even if it was not the full amount in court, they would have to honor it as paid in full. I thought to myself, "This would surely fix these liars, and they would never be able to take my home away because they had lied to me over and over now, stating they had lost my paperwork." It was my way of sneaking in a "Here's one back at you, you dirty rotten criminals." I thought to myself, "I'll just send one to everyone except the first mortgager," and I did.

The paperwork was lost again.

I said, "That's it."

I called the corporate office again. They put a new person on the job and apologized. The new paperwork came FedExed to my home, and it was not modification paperwork. It was loan forbearance paperwork, and it was way more than I owed them for back payments, and they tacked on thousands of dollars for attorneys' fees for drawing up the paperwork, and it said it needed to be faxed back by 5:00 PM that night or else.

I was not going to sign anything in one night that did not make sense to me, and I needed to talk to them the next day.

I woke up the next morning, and at 10:00 AM, and there came a knock on my door, and it was the mailman with a certified letter. I signed for it and sat down and opened the letter.

The letter said, "You are hereby notified that we are foreclosing on your property."

I remember feeling numb after reading it and then of course had nervous breakdown, crying spell number 9, and I wept for days.

Realizing I needed to find out what I could do, I received a letter in the mail from a bankruptcy attorney, stating that I could file bankruptcy to save my home from foreclosure.

I immediately called him up and made an appointment.

We met at his office, and he said that if I thought there was some criminal aspect to the case, then if I wanted to see a criminal attorney first, I could. He was very nice.

So I began to call criminal attorneys that he had referred to me, and one by one they said no. I checked with one more, and he said yes to meet him at his office on Saturday at 1:00 PM. I drove to the office and waited outside his door; I noticed the building was empty as I made my way up the steps to the second floor.

I waited outside the office door and waited and waited. Then a man came walking by, but it was not him. He was going into the office opposite the attorneys, and he said to me, "That guy has people waiting outside this office all the time, he may not even show up."

I said, "Thanks, I think I'll wait just a bit."

I waited patiently, and soon he arrived and said, "I forgot my keys to the office, we can just go down to the lobby and talk."

I thought to myself, like, "Huh, forgot your keys."

I said, "That's no problem," and took the elevator to the first floor with him.

His assistant was with him, and she introduced herself. They both seemed very nice, and I sat down on a bench, and he looked at some of the stuff and said, "Yes, I would like to see you give me a copy of all this and meet me back here tomorrow." He didn't really want to do it tomorrow as he talked of a Memorial Day with his family in honor of his dead father the judge, and I said, "That's fine, we can do it another day." But his assistant was nagging him to just do it anyway, and he finally caved in to her and said yes. I felt sorry for him. He looked so unhappy.

I said, "Okay, I'll meet you back here again tomorrow when you call me and give me a time."

He said, "Can you make a copy of all of these files for me?"

I said, "Sure, I can go to Kinko's tomorrow and copy everything." I thought maybe he had a copy machine, but he said he didn't.

He said that he would call me. He called and said meet at noon.

I went to church and over to Kinko's to copy the file. I didn't know that they were closed on Sunday mornings and could not copy the file. I had copied everything at home except the legal papers from the mortgage companies because my copier at home did not copy legal paper, or I guess it did; I just didn't have any at home.

We were in his office now as he remembered his keys, and it was a small office, drab and military-like with hardly anything in it and very little pictures on the walls. I thought to myself going through the door, "He must not have many clients," which was fine. He told me he used to be in the attorney general's office, and I said, "Really." He showed me a picture of his father on the wall sitting with many judges in a row all lined up.

He said, "My father was a judge."

I said, "How nice, and I'm sorry that you are missing him and that family had a special day planned and you missed part of it to help me."

He said, "My father would have wanted me to do this and get this mess straightened out."

I said, "Thank you, I really appreciate it very much."

We started to go over the paperwork and get to the bottom of the criminal mess.

He looked over all the paperwork, going from pile to pile as it was in a box. He kept going. "Oh my god, and look at this." He flipped pages and made expressive comments. At one point, he said to me, after trying to put the pieces of the puzzle together, "I feel like Columbo, and we just uncovered the crime!"

I thought to myself, "Yippee!"

I said, "Well, great, tell me what you know," very anxious to hear what he had to say.

He said, "Well, last night I looked online and saw that Mortgage Hut did sell our loan to Bank 2 in 2008, all you have to do is go the Recorder of Deeds Office and get a copy of the paperwork so it can be submitted in court!"

I was elated and said, "Great, then can we file it up the street in court soon?"

He said to me, "No, I can't file anything up the street in the county courthouse, they won't let me."

I said, "What happened, did you get in trouble?"

He said, "Well, kind of."

I just let it go.

He then said, "We are going to file this in Chicago, and don't worry, we will get you up there to testify."

I said, "Why Chicago?"

He said, "Well, the racketeers are in Chicago, and James So-and-So who owns the company is a bit-time crook and racketeer."

All of a sudden, I was getting nervous.

He then said, "You file a protection order against your ex-husband and get to a shelter or safe house. I will draw up a contract tomorrow and fax it to you."

I said, "I don't have a fax machine at home, and I'll be at work. Let me call work and see if they will let me have you fax it there."

I called work, and Bonnie said, "Sure, you can fax it here."

Then he said, "I'll fax you the contract, and it will be contingent with me getting 30 percent of the awarded amount from the court."

I said, "That will be fine with me, thanks so much, I have been worried about this, and I am really happy that we are going to stop them from doing this to anyone else."

He said, "Yes, we will stop them, but you have to protect yourself right now because these people are not nice people."

I was really scared at what he said, and I said, "Okay, I will." I went home and didn't sleep well.

I got up the next day and went to work as usual, waiting anxiously for hours for the fax to come.

Bonnie came up to me and said, "You had a message to call someone, and I just am giving it to you now." The message said, "Call Glenda." I just stuck it on my desk and continued to work.

I kept looking at the fax machine, and it never came.

At 2:00 PM, on my break, I went into the break room to use my phone and call him, and he said, "You were supposed to call me at 5:00 PM."

I said, "What? You told me you would fax a contract, and if you didn't that, I need to go to a bankruptcy attorney right away that day as the bankruptcy had to be filed by Monday today."

He said, "No, I don't have a contract written up to give to you."

I said, "Well then, could you please have our assistant bring the box to me so I can go to a bankruptcy attorney's office and file."

He started to scream at me even louder. I was a nervous wreck and thought to myself, "I can't go into this difficult case with someone who is going to scream at me when he knows that I am at work." He has upset me very much so much so that I was crying.

Now, I had to wait on customers and greet them with a smile. I thought to myself, "If he is not the attorney that can work with me, and I will not work with an attorney who will not give me a written contract as I had been screwed by an employment attorney who said that for months he was on my case and then said to me, 'Did you think I was taking this case? I have given you no contract, and therefore you are not my client.' I remember how deceived I felt, and his lies had not only hurt me but also hurt the case, which would have given me compensation for lies told about me that damaged my reputation beyond repair. Those damages were never paid for as the court case was dismissed by a federal judge, who said it was frivolous. In that case, never had I been so swindled by someone who professed to take an oath to defend people as an attorney in my state, and I was betrayed. I was not about to let that happen again."

I told him I would pick up the box of evidence after I got off work at 4:00 PM.

He said, "Fine, I'll be here, and you can pick it up," and hung up on me.

I drove to the office the whole time upset and worried and feeling like I was again betrayed by someone who professed to be my hero. I remember feeling numb.

I went up to the second floor, and his office door was shut, but the office juxtaposed across the hall was open, and I could hear him talking. I was surprised that he had another office across the hall, and I thought to myself, "Who is this guy with two separate offices?" I just took the box from his assistant.

I said, "I have to check to see if it is all here."

She just handed me the box out in the hall like I was a bum.

I sat down on the floor and looked through the box. I noticed my one credit report was missing but did not know the original certified check stub from the "paid in full" to the mortgager was gone.

I called him that night and e-mailed him to say, "Please send it back."

He e-mailed me and said he did not do it intentionally and he was going to call the Bar Association to tell them so I would not make a complaint about him.

I e-mailed him back and said his father would be ashamed of him and that I just wanted back my credit report. At that time, I still did not know he kept the original copy of the certified check "paid in full." It was a nasty trick that attorneys played, and I don't know if it was intentional in this case, but he would not talk with me after that, so I let it go as I had a copy of it anyway.

Later he did mail me the original credit report. The very next day after the contract debauchery, I had to call a bankruptcy attorney.

I called the first guy I went to, and his secretary said he could not do it as his cases were full. I began to call on the phone and found someone close to the house.

I got an appointment, and he met with me, and we talked for about three hours as he wanted to hear of my other court efforts in the county courthouse against my ex-husband; he was infatuated by the story and said he would not want to read my book about it that I was writing.

He said, "That is not a book I would want to read." He said, "Come to my St. Charles office tomorrow night and bring all of your stuff, and we'll take a look."

I was happy and got everything together and check made out to him. He was really easy to talk with and a gentle spirit, it seemed, which I needed at this time in my life.

I drove to the office at the other end of town, which he had was there that night, and we met again, but this time he greeted me with the statement, "My secretary is out of town, and I can't use the software as I don't know how to, and you can't file it without using the software."

I could see he was unhappy to tell me that, and I said, "That's okay, I'll just find someone else."

He said, "Sorry, I did not know she was out of town." Clearly, he was a liar.

I called many others and found a woman who said, "Yes, come tomorrow, but first tonight you have to get online and do this online Hummingbird software credit counseling, and then bring the statement of completion to me, and we will file it."

I completed the online information and then got up and went to work. From work, I went to her office, and she seemed very nice. She entered all the information, and then we chatted a bit about the case.

I told her of the *"paid in full"* part and the other fraud information. She said since it was Thanksgiving and she was going on holiday, she would not have time to get to any of that until after the holidays were over.

I said, "Fine."

She said to me with a big smile, "You are not going to owe anyone anything. I have never had to file a motion about paid in full before but heard about this in law school, and I will have to talk with my professor and get some instruction on the proper way to do it."

I got so excited I wanted to jump for joy.

I said, "Don't worry, I'll get the evidence box over here for you to review."

I dropped the box off for her and gave it to her assistant to give to her.

Weeks went by, and soon it was December 4, the day to go to court for the meeting of the creditors.

I thought we would now get to state that the fraud was involved in the case.

We were in a room full of people. No creditors, just people all bankrupt.

I asked her what I should state, and she said, "Nothing, just state that everything filed is true."

I said, "But it is not."

She said, "Right now, we are just trying to stop the bankruptcy, so just state it."

I said, "But you have the evidence in your hand that there is criminal action to this case, and they sold my loan and kept taking money from me."

She said to me, "No, just state that everything on the paperwork is true, and we will file the other stuff later."

I said to her, "I feel like that is lying."

She said, "No, it is not, just say it."

I was never so upset and just agreed to do it her way as I had no other choice.

With only minutes till my name was called, she handed me a paper to fill out for the court that day, and I had seen other attorneys out in the outer office arriving early to have their clients fill out these papers. I thought to myself, "Where is my attorney?" Clearly, she was late and unprepared.

I brought homemade candy for her staff for her to give to them. She said, "Thank you." She never sent me a thank-you note either.

The attorneys all did nothing but just sat there. We just sat at a table with a microphone, no judge or nothing, and stated our names and took the oath and swore that everything on the paper was true. I was upset as I knew it was not, and she kept me quiet. I hated that day more than any day recent in my life. She had let me down and talked me into not speaking up when clearly it was so very important to me as always.

She then stated, "I will work on this other fraud stuff and the motion for objection to claim for the paid in full."

I said, "Okay."

She never would. She claimed that after Christmas surely, she would have time to look over this big box.

Christmas came and went, and I never heard from her.

At the same time, I was so poor I could go to college for nothing on a Pell Grant. So I seized the moment and applied and in January went to college for the first time as a student to study criminal justice and start to help others through abusive situations. I was never so happy and enthusiastic about finally at age fifty-four going to college. It was a dream I had since I was seventeen, and I was on cloud nine.

School started, and I found myself with three Internet classes online and one regular class. The online classes were simple, except for one which would pose to become a nightmare in itself. I logged onto an interactive website and paid to access and got a password. The next time, it would not let me on and it seems I did write down the log-in, but not the password, so I tried every password I could think of that I used, and none worked. I had very little time and needed the password to get online and do my homework. The professor explicitly said, "No late assignments." Well, I tried to get a new password, but there was no phone number on the website to call. I e-mailed her and said, "Could you please contact the publisher and get me a new password?"

She e-mailed back and said, "We have to have a meeting."

Ticktock, the homework clock was ticking down the homework I was not able to complete on time. I was upset.

Two weeks now without homework, and I had a meeting. I went to the wrong campus as she was not at the campus I signed up at but a south campus location of the college.

I arrived and was looking all over for this room she said to meet in, and it was nowhere. I went to admissions, and they said, "You went to the wrong campus."

I said, "Oh my, it is my mistake. I will call the professor."

I did, and she did not call me back. Until I was in the dean's office. I had the dean call her, and then she said, "Call me," which I guess upset her.

I went into admissions. They said, "Go to the criminal justice office on the second floor of the adjacent building your class on campus is in."

I went there, and the young girl greeted me and said, "How can I help you?"

By this time, I was exhausted and said, "I need a password today, and I went to the wrong location. I have been through many hoops and need help getting a password."

She said, "Let me see what I can do."

I said, "Well, the website is this, but I could not find a phone number to call anyone."

She said, "Let me see."

She tried and kept saying sorry, and I was upset, and my voice was loud, and I said to her, "I have been waiting for weeks, and my homework is not getting done, and I have to get that password tonight to do my homework."

She tried and tried and said, "Well, I'm sorry, I could not figure it out either."

I laughed and said, "Don't worry, I couldn't either."

And I left. Clearly, they were not going to help me.

I went back over to admissions, and they said, "Well, there is nothing we can do."

I said, "Well, I guess I will call my senator."

They said, "Just sit down, and we'll see if we can get ahold of your instructor." They said, "We are going to take you over to the dean's office." They walked me over there and left me at a secretary desk.

She said, "I'll call Holly and see what we have to do."

She called the number, and Holly answered, and they talked.

She hung up the phone and said, "Call Holly."

I said, "Can't I just talk to her right here in your office?"

She said, "No."

I went outside the door in the hallway and sat down on a bench. Just as I was going to call her number, my phone rang and, it was Holly, but the phone ID said, "RESTRICTED ID." I thought it was the police. I picked up the phone anyway.

She said, "Hello, this is Holly."

I said, "Hello," but could barely hear her as my reception was bad.

She was the only one talking, but the phone kept cutting in and out.

I said, "Let me go outside and call you back."

I called her back, and she said, "Did you abuse my secretary in the office?"

I said, "What? Abuse your secretary? Absolutely not. I asked for your secretary, and they said she was not in today."

Clearly, she was lying to me, and I don't talk to liars who call with a restricted ID. I was upset, betrayed, and confused, and I hung up.

I walked back into the dean's office and said to the secretary, "Did you tell Holly that I abused a secretary today?"

She got upset and then the police came walking into the office and asked me what was going on.

I said, "Nothing," and I left.

I remember thinking to myself, "They are not going to set me up with the police, that's for sure."

I left and went back to admissions to complain of what was happening, and this time I said, "Who in this building can give me a password today to get my homework done?"

They said, "You come with me."

I said, "Where?"

They said, "The dean wants to see you."

I said, "Really, then you get a police escort over here for me right now to go with me."

Two officers showed up, and we walked together to the dean's office.

I asked the officers to come into the dean's inner office with me, but they were told by the dean to stay outside. (When I came out of her office, they were gone, and they did not even stay as I instructed them to do.) Whew!

The dean said, "Scott, my assistant, can see if he can get you a password."

She took me into the adjoining office, and Scott said he would see what he could do.

I said, "Great."

He asked for all my passwords to the online website and the website for the book involved. I gave him all of them.

He called the publisher, and they said only Holly could get the password over the phone (which of course, she already knew—the jerk). He then went to the website and tried a few places, and an online chat tech told him that he would e-mail me a password in an hour.

I thanked him and left.

I never received the password, and the dean never called me the next day or later that night to see if I got one. I was crying.

I e-mailed Holly and asked for a password. I e-mailed the dean and said I wanted to have a meeting with Holly, the chief of campus police, and herself. She said she would set it up for the morning of the next few days.

I said, "That would be fine."

I then received another e-mail saying that the only time they could meet was in the afternoon.

I said, "I have an appointment in the afternoon."

She said, "Well, that was the only way we could do it." I was upset again.

I arrived for the meeting. A police officer was in the outer waiting area, and it was the same officer they called on me, not the chief.

I then talked with the police officer. He was asking me all kinds of personal questions, interrogating me, if you will. I was getting hotter under the collar by the minute. Was I divorced, any children, etc. were his questions. Way out of line.

Then I was told to come into the room. The police officer stayed in the chair and did not come with me.

So I said, "I wanted the police officer in here for the meeting."

The dean said, "That's fine if you feel it is necessary."

I said, "Yes, it is necessary."

I said, "Hello," and sat down.

Holly, the dean, and some other man but no police chief.

"Well," I said, "thank you for meeting with me."

The dean said, "We have some questions for you."

I said okay. I answered all the questions and the other man in the room, clearly Holly's boss, was implying that I knew the syllabus stated "no late assignments."

I said, "Yes, I know that is why it was imperative that I get the password quickly." I stated, "Can I ask a question?"

The dean said, "You may not ask any questions."

I said, "I asked you to schedule this meeting so I could ask questions and get a password."

She said, "No, you cannot."

I turned to the police officer, and I said, "This is why I asked for this meeting."

He said, "You have to do as they say."

I said, "What? I asked for this meeting to get answers to the questions about what has been said about me and how people have treated me." (I felt like I was in a police state and had no rights.)

The dean again said, "This meeting is over, and you may not ask any questions."

I said, "Well then."

She said, "We are taking you to my office, and we will get online and give you your password so you can get online."

I said, "Fine."

I got up mad as a hatter and walked into her office. I sat down at her desk, and she made a statement that women of my age often had trouble getting online and using computers.

I said, "Well, usually, I don't, I even have websites of my own."

She looked amazed. My hands were shaking; they had upset me so much. I don't get nervous, just abused.

It was clear they were abusing me to get even with something that they thought I did, which I did not. She was an evil woman, and I knew it for sure.

She had manipulated the situation to make me look like a bad person, and then she asked, "Would you like someone else to grade your papers for you instead of Holly? I can do that for you." It was clearly another form of a put-down and clearly not to help me.

I said, "No, that's okay, I trust Holly."

The weeks ahead were nothing but disappointment and clearly bad grades put upon me for my personal statements of displeasure with website and password issues. Nasty people treating the little guy like dirt. I remember thinking to myself, "How damaging this would even be to a much younger student in college for the first time. Horrible treatment."

They had given me to the devil, and clearly, they were the devils themselves. Long story short, in her two classes, I got two Ds. My other two classes I received an A and a B. It would prove later to show that they had screwed me over so bad that I could not transfer to another school that I wanted to and would need to find another. Very sad for me.

Chapter 13

Valentine's Day
A Decade of Valentines Alone

Valentine's Day, my day for romance even if it is all by myself. I have been alone for a decade of them now, and this one for sure special even in my loneliness as I had to appear in court for a hearing on contempt of three banks on four counts of contempt for $3.5 million each. A decade of Valentine's alone, I would write a poem to show myself that being alone was part of live sometimes. Maybe that would ease my pain and sting inside.

But I was hoping that the night before, or maybe even the week before, or maybe any time that my friend who asked me out on a date the weeks prior would say to me, "How about the two of us do something together on Valentine's Day?" but he didn't. I just said, "Well, it is not meant to be between the two of us even as friends." He hadn't even called me since he asked me out two weeks ago. I guess I made an impression on him that he could forget, but I must admit, I was weary of his stories about his wife and since she tried to kill him whilst his daughter still lived in the same house with her and his children. It was upsetting to me that he did not see that she could surely kill them, too, or hurt him.

I tried telling him that, and maybe he did not like my personal comments. As private investigators, I said, "Well, I think it is something you should think about." Only because I know my ex-husband had done things to hurt my children to punish me. But it was his life and his children, so I didn't say anything else. I just kept quiet. But I know from others that I had helped, that when I give them the truth of possibilities, they tend sometimes to take it out on me. I don't care; I just think to myself, "Well, if what I said and what I brought to their attention would in some way help someday, maybe they might think about me at that moment and smile and say, 'She cared about me.'"

Anyway, I went to bankruptcy court that day and arrived early as usual. I was sitting in the back of the courtroom, and several attorneys were in the benches in front of me. They said that a friend of theirs was in New York and were talking about how expensive things were but that they were staying with friends in order to go to the dog show that weekend. They were talking about making reservations and how expensive rooms were, and I told them that I used to work for doctors and do their travel and one time I went to New York and found on Expedia a package deal for flight and hotel at the Waldorf Astoria. When I called my daughter in New York to tell her where I was staying, she said, "Mother, you are not!"

I said, "Yes, I am, the room was cheap, I guess as it was not the busy season, it is August, and my grandson was born, so I guess that would be the cheap time to go to NYC and get a good rate on a room, flight, and I also booked a New York Broadway show, too, at one low price. I know that sounds too good to be true, but that is where I am staying."

She said to me, "Mother, that is one of the most expensive hotels in New York."

I said, "Well, is there only one Waldorf Astoria?"

She said, "Yes."

I said to her, "Well then, it's where I'm staying, and I have the receipt to prove it."

It was funny to me to hear her reaction. Sometimes my children forget that Mom had skills she had learned doing menial work for others that could pay off in her personal life as well.

The attorneys said, "Yeah, that sounds like a great deal."

I told them as well, "The door to my room even had a doorbell."

We all laughed a bit. I needed a laugh. One of the attorneys said that he heard that the IRS was not going to approve any longer any company giving out the rapid refund loans any longer.

I said to him, "Yeah, I heard that from someone from the IRS, I took a tape recorder into the Miracle Tax Preparer Office and caught the guy lying to me on tape. The company, of course, makes him say what they want him to say." And I told them that the woman at the IRS said there won't be any more of these loans being made since I made my complaint to them.

Now it was time to begin, and the clerk said, "All rise." The judge came out of her chambers and into her seat on the bench up at the beautiful desk she had in this gorgeous courtroom of the new building that was the federal courthouse in Springfield. I was so eloquent and direct as the judge called my name and the names of the three banks and attorneys 1, 2, 3 spoke out their names.

Judge heard from them and then asked me, "Was there anything else I wanted to say?"

I said, "Well, just one thing. Bank 3 had one of their presidents call me from North Carolina after I made a complaint to the OCC, and she called me directly and said that she wanted a copy of the checks and asked me if I could fax her a copy of them. I said, 'I don't have a fax machine at home, so ask your legal office they can supply the copies as I gave them many copies of all the checks when they received the subpoena.' She said, 'Well, all right.' I said, 'Why don't you give me the fax number so that if you don't get a copy, I can fax them to you!' She gave me a fax number that was a telephone number of someone named George. I called the OCC and said to them, 'Please don't give out my personal number to these people if you are not going to do an investigation.' A few days later, he would send me a letter stating that I should seek legal advice, and it was on Bank 3 letterhead."

The judge then said, "Well, Bank 3 submitted a response on Friday to this motion."

I said, "Well, I did not receive a copy of that since it takes me five days to get my mail."

The attorney for Bank 3 then said, "I will give her a copy of what I submitted on Friday," and he handed it to me at the podium. I tried to read it over while everyone was talking, but I could not concentrate.

The judge, knowing I have post-traumatic stress disorder, said to me, "Ms. Rule, would you like a few minutes to review that response to make your statement?"

I said, "Yes, Your Honor." Thank God!

I left the courtroom and went out into the hall outside the bankruptcy court. I read over the statements, and clearly they had submitted more lies to the judge. I read over each response; there were about eight of them. One even said that they had submitted a spreadsheet of all the checks and account numbers, etc. I had to laugh out loud but could not. I chuckled to myself now that they wrote more lies about things they never did as well; this was clear-cut fabrication of documents that they told the judge they gave to her. They had not submitted a spreadsheet nor had they complied with the full request of the subpoenas.

I had spent many hours on this case. Clearly, the judge now had all the information to prove in court that I was right, and they were all in contempt.

She said, "Well, I will take these all under submission and rule by the end of this week."

I was overjoyed and left the courtroom feeling wonderful. I had a great day in court and was finally winning this game of motion after motion to refute the lies and innuendoes of me being confused, not knowing I was in the wrong place and most of all that someone was unaware that they had received a subpoena at all. I thought to myself later, "If this was school, the teacher would say, 'Very creative things to say that you don't have your homework done and for that you get an F.' Well, I wanted the judge to give them all an F, which would make me a very rich woman for sure, but would also send a message from that judge that in her court, you better submit the clear-cut truth and the information requested so as not to make her courtroom a joke or something that was clearly not in the interest of justice."

I waited a week, and on Friday, called the office back to see what the ruling was, anxiously awaiting to hear that I was a millionaire. But she had not ruled as of yet what was the answer to be yes or no, granted or denied. So my grand day of celebration must be put off yet another weekend or so, and my anxiety growing daily as I wanted this to be over, and I could move on gloriously with my life and never have to look back at this place I called home for fifty-five years of my life, but I could move to wherever I felt it safe to live and be happy and most of all find peace.

So on Valentine's Day, after I left the courthouse a bit disappointed, I stopped at the store, bought a steak, and made myself a great dinner and bought flowers the day before in the Dollar Store, pink peonies four stems, and put them in a vase on my coffee table. They looked beautiful while I ate dinner and watched a movie, and it was indeed a lonely Valentine's Day dinner. But the food, flowers, movie, and the courtroom day made it one of the most memorable ones I would ever have up to this point in my life. I was going to win without a doubt. The proof was all there for the judge to rule in my favor. No doubts.

For you see, if there is one thing I have learned up to now, I can make myself happy. I don't need another person to do that for me.

It would be, oh, so grand if I did have a Valentine of my own, but for now, a decade of Valentines I would write a poem about this day and a decade alone on the lover's day to appreciate each of the ten Valentines Days. It is my own fun in writing when I am most inspired about my own life as well as others, to keep a memory written on paper about how I felt this day.

The poem reads:

> I spent the past Decade Alone on Valentine's
> After all a romantic wants someone to say you're mine
> At first lonely and forlorn
> Since you have made it an extra special day since you were born
> Realizing that I am special myself on any day
> I began to treat myself in a special way
> On Valentine's, flowers, new dress, dinner out
> Was my way of saying I can do without
> By the third or fourth year wanting a pair
> I found one who didn't dare
> He actually didn't ask me out
> A Valentine who made me pout
> Thinking to myself after that affair fizzles out
> I can go out all alone and have fun without a doubt
> But I must admit beware of the stares
> Especially when your ring finger is bare
> People gave me looks—what a dork

I just sat and ate my marinated pork
A drink I might have had
But dessert was never too bad
My advice to everyone who is single
When that day makes you want to mingle
Go out—even by yourself if you please
Just look like a summer breeze
Put on your best dress or pants
Look confident; even get up and dance
Go someplace you love
Maybe you just might find your turtle dove
A decade may seem long
But just stay strong
Romantic remain
Always the same

I was also inspired as I watched my favorite movie since I was a little girl, *The Diary of Anne Frank.* I remembered as a young girl how this movie made me feel and how it made a clear cut difference in my life. I was surely not going to ever forget what it taught me and when I went out to the Jewish center and viewed the building dedicated to teaching people about the Holocaust, I remembered what it was that made me think—that I would be any different in the world. We might not have Hitler any longer, but we have a world where like the Jews in the workplace, we are told, "You are out of work for no reason," when they are clearly hiring other people, and they don't care if we lose everything or can't eat or buy what we need. It is about control; Hitler was about control. I know this may be a long stretch for some people to understand my thinking, but in the workplace now, you are fired because of what you think, what religion you are, what you believe or don't believe politically. This is true. Hitler was no different; only he actually took part in the killing of these dear people's bodies as well. He did bury them to his shame.

In my state, if you die and have no money, they will bury you or give your body to science. It is a good thing they do for people that are poor.

My state has supplied me with food, money for unemployment from the employer when I'm out of work (not enough to pay your bills though), and my local county agency has paid my fuel bill so I would stay warm and have hot water and a place to lay my head on a pillow that would make me secure. I remember a time when I had no hot water and it was winter. I put my head under the faucet in the kitchen sink to wash my hair. The water was so cold it gave me a severe headache, and I thought to myself while crying, "Well, the Frank family had it much worse than me, I can bear this for a while." But it did make me cry. I thought to myself, "No one cares about me." It was true; I felt it in the harshest way ever, straight to the core of my cold, shattering brain.

The rest of the night was quiet, and I went to bed dreaming of helping others, and most of all knowing that I loved myself greatly and deeply more than ever before. I now know that I can be alone and it's all right until Mr. Right comes along. I have plenty of love to give, and I also have plenty of stories to tell. Maybe a man could love me the way I am and the way I fight for rights; if not, they are missing out on a very special person, one who knows especially how to love unconditionally.

It was now a week after Valentine's, and no one had called.

Friday, I received a call in the afternoon from the office where I had gone asking for a free counselor to help figure out and talk through what has happened to me at Furniture Hut and at Fundgate. Since May, I had called and asked over a dozen places, and even though this one had said they would help me for sure with a counselor, instead they gave me this call.

She said to me, "Hi, this is Karen from Safe Place, I am calling you to say that since we talked once and you brought in your medical records the team and I have decided that you should think about seeing one of our doctors on staff before you see a counselor."

I said very calmly, "Well, Karen, I specifically asked you if I could see a counselor for free, no doctor, just someone needed to listen to me, and you said, 'Oh, for sure we will give you a counselor, no problem at all with that,' do you remember saying that to me?"

She said, "Well, that was before I saw your medical records, and when you were in my office, you said hurtful things to me."

Clearly, this bitch was no different than any of the other incompetent people who lied to me, saying, "Yes, we will help you, we won't do an intake and then give you no one to talk to." Clearly, they were no different at all. Making up bad things about me to coincide with the medical records that were incorrect; I was once again Alice in Wonderland going down the hole without a rope.

I said nothing hurtful to her at all except I wanted to call her a liar, but felt it not appropriate to call her on the telephone. She had done just the very same thing that others had done and the very thing that she made a direct promise to me that she would not do. I felt like she was a snake rearing up her ugly head to once again put me in my place of saying you need a pill lady your crazy. She did it to me just like everyone else had done before. The phrase "Same shit different day" might be one of my favorite sayings at this point on this agenda.

I told her that I did not appreciate this call and hung up.

I immediately called the office and asked to speak with the manager. They put me in her voice-mail. She never even bothered to call me back. These offices get money from our tax dollars and from people who think they were helping people. They did what they wanted just like employers. They didn't care. They made decisions that were good for them, not the very people that needed help.

I then sent an e-mail to the counselor on the business card that she gave to me. I stated that she could not treat me this way. I had called another place and would see a counselor next week. I wanted to tell her how much that hurt me further but what would have been the point. She did not care about me—same shit, different day.

I told them that I was not a client any longer. I attached to the e-mail my proposal that I wrote to gain funding to help people. I e-mailed to them that this was what people needed. "I needed only a counselor from your office. You said you would give me one, but then went back on your word." In other words, she lied to me. "A snake such as yourselves and your team do nothing but hurt the abused even further. Think about it, and your life will haunt you until you stop treating people this way. Just because we are in need does not give people the right to treat us with contempt and disdain and lie to us to manipulate what they want and not what we need."

They want money and people to say they have a client and get paid because they log you in as a client, then they kick out the door and get paid for it.

If I asked for a counselor; I should get one. Period. I had just found someplace else. I thought. It had been a long road of people and counselors, and I grew tired of it. Truly tired.

I looked forward to the counselor at YWCA, a place where they know how important it was to be honest and tell people up front the truth, and oh yeah, the most important thing—schedule an appointment to see a counselor. It was that easy, one phone call. Sure wish I had known that years ago, and it was free to victims of sexual abuse.

Later, however, after about six sessions, she told me that I would not be served best by them. She gave me a list of other places to get counseling, and I said, "But I want to come here."

She said, "I think you would be best to pick a place that fits you and where you're comfortable." She told me I needed a counselor for trauma as this was the worst thing in my life, and I needed help with it. I remember taking the list and looking at her and thinking, "Same shit different day" all over again. I remember thinking, "This would be the last place. No more chances anyplace else."

I stood my ground and called no one on the list. About three weeks later after I had moved and gone through quite a hard time, even giving up my home and dropping the keys off at an attorney's office, she would never tell me again anything at all. She called me and stated that she had time to look at all the things I gave to her and that I had truly been through quite a bit of trauma in my life and if I wanted to, I could still come to see her, and she would get the copy of the report of the exam the Social Security Disability Office did on me that they wouldn't give to me. At first I thought, "No way!" Then I slept on it and decided to call her.

I told her that I would come in for a visit but that I start a new job next week and I was not sure of the hours and so I couldn't make an appointment at this time. I told her she could get the copy of the report from the SSA office, which I signed a release for weeks ago. She told me she would definitely give me a copy of it.

I said, "Great, you get the report, and I will get the schedule for work and call and make an appointment." I think others were telling her I needed help from other offices and not her—who knows at this point; I don't even care who decided this or that. I just wanted help and didn't care at this point who it was from.

I went to bed that night and decided to write a poem titled, "Simmered Away—A Recipe for Liars" so that one would know what to include if one wanted to become a liar or if one just wanted to know what to look for to stay away from liars. Either way, I had fun with this poem, and I am including it in this story of my life to show others that when someone has taken you down to the very core of your goodness to destroy your happiness, especially when it is someone who you have taken into your confidence who says they will help you, just remember this recipe, and you won't feel that you are the only one who has been betrayed in your life or in your quest for help from abuse and the feelings it leaves you with for the rest of your life.

The poem makes me laugh not only at myself but knowing that others will read my poem and belly-laugh if it relates at all to their lives, knowing we all need laughter to make us happy and keep us healthy.

Read and laugh out loud, no matter where you are, when you read this part. It is my wish.

Simmered Away—A Recipe for Liars
Recipe for Getting Rid of Liars—Simmered Away—
Smell That Smoke

Ingredients:

1 pinch of stenchy foul mouth

1 cup of slithering pointed snake tongue dash of back stabbing

1/2 heaping teaspoon of I thought you told me this (when they know all along you didn't)

1 cup of sweet voice thick like syrup (remembering syrup cooks to black when boiled)

1 large great big smile—phony, of course pint of statements all untrue about you

1 tablespoon of—I never said that dash of—my

retirement is all gone

1 statement—honey, even though we got divorced, my accountant says we can file jointly

Cooking Instructions:

Stir up all the ingredients into the pot and let them simmer, making sure you are sipping on your favorite drink of choice and have your fun tunes playing in the background to get you into a good mood and dance if you feel the beat, all the while knowing you have just dumped all the parts of the biggest liar in a pot and cooked it till it's all gone. Not reducing it, not bringing it to a boil, just simmering it nice and slow and taking in all the satisfaction that this liar is no longer in your life anymore.

This is my surefire way to get rid of a liar.

Ciao, baby! And most of all, bon appétit!

I could have given you a recipe for Arsenic Wassail Bowl, but that's someone else's style.

Maybe just maybe, some years of the decade, it was good to be *alone*. No one to lie to me or make me cry, no one to hurt my feelings telling me that I was not living my life the way he thought I should. No jerks to ruin my day.

Then, alone and feeling blue, your heart reminds you of why you would like a nice person to love you and hold you and kiss you good night and say good morning. Hoping every day I would meet my prince, my dream come true again, yet spending many lonely days and nights alone.

Someday I hope to meet that special person, and until that day, I remind myself that God, the mystery man in my life is good for today, and maybe just maybe I'll meet the man of my dreams tomorrow. I haven't stopped dreaming, just stopped wondering why it's taking so long.

Chapter 14

Final Chapter
My Shimmering Inspiration—The Sky and All That Lies Within
New Name—New Me
Private Investigator—Begin Living Life and Helping Victims
A New Life—A New Style
An Ending of Abuse
Not What I Dreamed Of, but in My Dreams, I'm an Author

I reached a day in court whereby the words from an attorney threatening me, saying, "It's time we sanction Ms. Rule," would be true, oh, so true, as I learned before the attorneys in court play games and make statements that they know they can attain by playing out the cards that they have and hurt you because you told the truth and called them a liar.

Amazing at a time in court when I was waiting for the contempt charges to be handed down and I would walk with $20 million. Instead they played out the hand, and I received nothing except the words to their attorneys: "You can lift the stay and take her home since she has proved nothing and servicing does not mean that Mortgage Hut sold her house." The judge said along the lines of those words—yes, she did. I stood there, my emotions paralyzed. I listened and went home to call my daughter as I could not believe that they were taking my home after I proved that they deceitfully took money and promised modification and gave loan forbearance instead with a monthly amount added to increase the payment again for thirty years to the tune of an additional $141. Talk about added fees and racketeering.

Yes, indeed, I was in an emotional volcano in which I was thrown after fighting the good fight with all my might. I called and left a message on my daughter's phone to please call me. I was not crying yet, but I thought for sure she could hear in my voice at that very day at that very moment in time I needed to talk to someone who cared about me.

She never called.

About three days later, I sent her an e-mail. It was not very nice, and it said that I would not be taking the train for a visit, and I did not say why. I told her that I would send the presents by mail unless she hated me and wanted me to give them to the poor. I had very little money and spent the money to cheer her and her husband and the kids up by buying them some things they needed and was going to mail to them so they would get there when I arrived by train to get hugs and kisses I desperately needed. I knew she was off work because she was in the hospital with an emergency appendectomy and was not paid for being off, and they were stressed about that as well. I felt bad, but I still had learned that I didn't let people disregard me, especially my children.

Well, she responded to my e-mail by calling me and yelling and screaming at me telling me that I called on a day that she spent with her husband the only day off she had and the only time they had to spend with each other. She was screaming so bad that I remember stating these words: "I have post-traumatic stress disorder, Bella, and I can't listen to you screaming, and I am hanging up." I remember crying when I hung up. Crying because at that very instant I was reminded that no one cared about me at all—no one. It was the most awful feeling and especially reminded me that my own children whom I gave birth to, whom I supported through thick and thin, whom I gave up many things for to raise and encourage would once again remind me how they cared nothing about me at all.

It's been two years, and she had never called me back. She didn't even send me a Mother's Day card or an e-mail. It was then six months, and still she hadn't called to say sorry or find out how I was at all; I knew she cared nothing about me. This shows how my life changed in ways I could not stop.

I gave up with her. I remember that on a given day, even when someone took away my home, no one cared about me at all. No one. Not even my daughter whom I gave birth to and took care of her whole life and gave all the things she needed and spent my money on her instead of myself most of her life growing up. *I gave up.*

I decided that I was never letting anyone treat me that way ever again. I wouldn't.

I would rather spend every day alone than with someone yelling at me; I have learned that for sure. I cut them loose and live in peace. That is my mantra for life—*peace.*

I did call my one older sister who years before told me that I could come and live with her and her husband. I was so distressed I thought maybe I could live with them for a few months to gather my composure for life. I went for a visit, and her husband who had just had surgery said, "No way, no one is living in our house, we just buried my mother, and she lived with us for the last year, and one day she had poop on her hands and put her hands in the ice cube tray to get ice and got poop on everything."

I remember thinking to myself, "I'm only fifty-five and in excellent health, I don't have poop on my hands ever."

I was highly insulted. I understood he was upset, but I didn't have to sit there and take it. He left the room and went to lie down. I spent the rest of the afternoon with my sister, and we had fun talking.

They also told me of their suspicions of their son-in-law who lied and did not put Social Security money into the account of his brother-in-law who worked for him and his wife. My sister was afraid that if he lied about that, what else he might have lied about. She knew what I went through, and it was not fun. I knew that I would help them but told them it did not mean that he had done other things as well.

I called her the next day to say thank you for lunch she gave to me. I invited her over to my condo for lunch, and she said, "So you have a place yet?" I said, "I will find one."

The next day I spent all day searching websites for things that might connect criminal activity and found some people of same name from the state that their son-in-law came from, but never having seen his father, I just printed out the information and sent it to her in the mail. I told her with instructions to not tell Kay until school let out as if it was something that applied to her and it would make her upset; that I did learn from my own experiences of finding things out about my ex-husband while at work and crying really hard about it, which was not seen as a great thing at work. I was fired once because when I found out about his girlfriend for six years while married to me, I felt like dying of embarrassment at that very moment and could not stop crying.

Now, I didn't think there was anything to the fact that my niece's husband did anything else, as I felt he was just upset over losing his business and was depressed, but I didn't say anything to anyone except myself as one never knew until one checked it out. That is what I say to people, "Just relax until you find something that is tangible, otherwise you will be upsetting yourself over nothing. The things you do find out are bad enough, no need to conjure up something that is not true."

So then I searched for apartments, and I did find one quickly on the Internet. It was downtown and with a view of the river in downtown Springfield. One large picture window with a scenic view of the city of Springfield would sell me. I thought, *Let's see what the rent is.* The studio apartment was just in line with my budget, and I was excited. I called up and went to see the apartments. They were nice, and the view from the picture window of the river was a surefire way to inspire me to do and finish all the things I needed to do and would also give me a place to set my easel and paint to inspire me to do anything I wanted to do.

My new home would be called my royal safe house.

I called my sister back and told her I found a place with a billion-dollar view. I couldn't tell her where because I was part of the safe home program, and she was a bit upset at me as she thought I moved away from Springfield two years ago when I joined the program, but I did not. I could not tell her, and she was mad. My family does not communicate; they decide what is and what isn't without discussion I hated that about them as I was so different. If I thought she could keep the secret, I would have told her, but she still was friends with my sister Devilia, who put me in the mental hospital, lying about me to the police and to other family members. Of course, that incident destroyed me in the workplace professionally for a while until I got away from all the connections, friends and family who would continue to gossip all the lies that ruined my life.

In other words, I did not trust her and her family, I guess. It is hard for me to trust people after they treat me a certain way. I don't let abusive people in any longer; I don't and won't ever let cruel people in my life no matter who they are.

She came for lunch at my old place which I called home for seven years. At that time, I made a very nice lunch of quiche, salad, and dessert. It was a very nice St. Patrick's Day–themed lunch with green snake bread that I bought at the store as well. We ate and talked and had fun. Later when we were talking, she told me that my other sister had told everyone years ago that I was molested by a sibling, and I had no idea that she had said that. She did it to hurt me further as she had, along with my sisters, decided to destroy me. They continued to think something that was untrue and, I guess, decided to punish me for being quiet about something that in their minds was created to destroy my brother, and I was not going to let them. They hated him his whole life; his genius and my father's love for him different from the love for the daughters, and they were jealous and that I knew for sure most of my life, watching them in disgust.

I now knew the reason why my brother yelled at me on the phone years ago and said, "FUCK YOU!" and hung up on me, which was never the way he talked to me in my whole life. I had no idea that my sister had told others about my life experience when I was young. Who gave her the right to do that? What my brother did when he was ten had no effect on me whatsoever and was not perverted in any way. Why then would they make a big deal out of it? It was funny to me that the real things that were abusive in my life, my sisters knew nothing about because they couldn't handle anything that might have seemed like criminal action nor would they probably believe me anyway. I was told even by my own daughter that I must have done something to get attention from another man while I was married when he kissed me out of the blue at a church dance when he was drunk. At that very moment, I realized how people were cruel to each other. My own daughter on my birthday in a restaurant telling me I must have done something. Well, that spoke billions to me. I would never expect anyone to ever have pity on my feelings. Never. I didn't care anymore.

My sister, even though I knew she meant well, had found a way to upset me again in a way that was very damaging to my mental well-being at a time when I had lost my home and had to move to a one room apartment and had to move by myself since no one could know where I was moving. I hated her for that. How could she? She had no concern of others' lives and their feelings of what was the best time to tell anyone. It was what my family did, and they had been doing it to me for years; I just used to ignore it. It was why I stopped talking to them at all. I will never call any of them ever again except maybe to inquire about my sister, Sophia, who is ill, I may call her daughter, but her daughter didn't even call me to say that she was ill and in the hospital. I guess she thinks I don't care about her because we haven't talked directly in an ongoing basis and I don't want to upset her either. I quit calling her when the family junk got ugly. I thought it best to not talk to her since she tells my other siblings things about me. In other words, if I could cut them off completely, then they would know nothing about me at all. Later, we talked, and she said, "I promise to you, I won't tell them anything about you." She was a true sister that I knew I could trust, but I cut her off for a few years to give her relief from my mess, which I knew upset her because she knew how much it devastated my life.

She was nice and brought me food because she thought I needed it. She also brought me toilet paper and soap and shampoo, and I told her that I got food stamps. She just looked at me, and I never asked her for food. My family does what they want they don't ask. They don't inquire; they just do.

It's why I don't talk to any of them at all. It has been five years since I spoke to most of them. Now at least I know why almost all of them stopped sending me Christmas cards. Except for a few family members that still send me a card, about six or seven maybe when it used to be three hundred. Big changes in my life, but numbers always show the truth to us even on days when we don't want to admit it.

It had been a month, and my sister had not called me back, not even to say thank you for the information that I took the time to search for about her son-in-law. I guess she thought what she thought about me. I guess she thought since I wouldn't tell her where I lived, that I didn't trust her. I guess I didn't in that respect because my family had a way of getting things out of people when they least expected it. I didn't want to put her in that position where she would have to say "I can't tell," or telling when she had a weak moment. I guess it's up to her to call me if she wants to. She has my new number. It is part of the agreement that I not tell anyone where I live. Her daughter did call me one night to chat, and I told her we should do lunch and chat about her teaching school and maybe the possibility of taking on the business idea that I had about e-text on laptops for all schools across the nation and maybe eventually the world. I knew with me being bankrupt, I would never get a loan for the start-up, and the schools had no money. Maybe at this time they might, I don't know. But for right now, I have to think about me paying bills and living while I'm finishing my book. I thought that she and her husband might get back on track and have their own business again and be a happy couple and family once again. That is important to me to help others to be happy and save relationships I think are worth saving. She and her husband are clearly two people I feel are meant to be together in every way. She never called me back months later and almost August.

I know that people felt that way about me and my husband's relationship, but I feel that one ever knows who a person truly is sometimes. It does not make me negative about men or other people's relationships.

I know that she meant well; she just does not know emotional intelligence. It is something my parents didn't teach us; some of us learned, and some of us didn't.

It took me a few years to get emotionally intelligent and most of all to protect myself emotionally so that no one could hurt me anymore.

I felt good about moving into royal safe house. It had 24-7 security cameras and swipe cards to get in and private parking underground. It would be a smart decision even though I had to switch into living in one room. I knew the view of the river my shimmering inspiration would give me the creative juices to not only finish my book but keep me on track to happiness and peacefulness within my living area which is very important in my life. My royal home is everything to me, and I spend a lot of time there even though I am an extravert who goes out usually quite a bit and have fun in life no matter what I am doing.

I paid the rent for the apartment at royal safe house three weeks prior to moving day, which gave me time to paint and get my space ready for moving in and getting things ready to be perfect so I would not be upset at all about anything. Well, that was great. I picked out a pretty, sensuous pink and a light apple-green paint. I put pink on the top of the walls and green on the bottom. I then created a border from black grow grain ribbon, which I ran along the wall around the room, and ran a second strand about eight inches from the first and painted a really cute, whimsy pattern, which was how I signed my cards under my name my whole life, and that would please me every time I looked at it.

I began to bring my paintings in and hang them. The room was filling with my flowers, and I made curtains that turned out really cute and hung them on a black rod with clear transparent rod ends that were really cute. The kitchen I painted green with pink trim on the top of the ceiling wall that came down about ten inches, and it was really adorable. I placed everything just right, and my flowers in vases and pots turned the room into an indoor garden for sure. Some of the pots by the picture window to view my greatest garden part at the view of the river while the flowers were my reminder that flowers existed, too, without a backyard of my own. My enriched environment had turned out exactly as I wanted it to.

I met a guy in the lobby one day when I was getting my mail. His name was Terry, and we introduced ourselves, and he said, "Let's go up and sit down in the party room and chat." He could see I was stressed out from moving as we talked about getting in shape, and I said I needed yoga and meditation. He said that he taught meditation to friends. Turned out he was not of American descent, and his mother taught him holistic ways of calming and relaxing. We talked about everything, and it turned out he was interested in my legal mess as he went to law school. It was fun, and he was encouraging and was a business accountant and financial adviser. We talked, and he could see my stress; he was nice and massaged my neck and feet, and we chatted and talked.

Finally, I said, "Let's go get a drink and something to eat."

He said, "Okay."

He walked me to a restaurant with the name that I gone to many years in my youth—Coco's, just a few blocks away. The night was very nice, and the air was calm and crisp. We ate pizza and drank a drink together and talked about everything. He was very engaging and kept letting me know he was attracted to me. I was not sure about anything. I was so tired and stressed. He walked me home around 2:00 AM, which was late for me, but it was about six years since I had been on a date, and I was happy that he thought of me that way. He walked me to my apartment, and I asked if he wanted to see the paint job in my apartment that I did, and he said yes. We sat again, and we talked all night until 4:30 AM on the floor of my new apartment. We kissed, and he went down the elevator, and I went home to sleep. He asked me to go out the next night, but I was too tired. I called him and told him that I was tired and could not go out dancing.

I said we could do it another night.

He was very nice. I was not sure if I wanted a serious relationship as I had asked him to be friends first and he kissed me anyway. I guess men don't want to be friends as I have found that out in some cases, but later, he would be one to me once in a while with a call to say, "Happy Fourth of July."

So I began to pack up all of my stuff—well, not all; I had to get rid of two bedrooms full and a kitchen set as well. Turned out my neighbors took it since they were out of work and needed the money by selling the items and using the money to pay their rent. These would be the two people who moved in last January, both cars with different out-of-state license plates. I was suspicious of them both. After the fire last June in our complex, I was suspicious of him for sure. But it was a neighbor down several streets that lit the fire.

Anyway, I packed everything I needed. The movers were hired. I changed everything I needed to and was ready.

Moving day came, and they arrived in the afternoon and began to load the truck. It was sad to see my home emptied out one box at a time, and then the couch and chair and lamps that would never light that space. I was glad actually because that condo was a place I never wanted to go, didn't like living there as it was like a retirement area, and it was on the third floor. So watching everything go was sort of a good thing for me. No longer would the person who was in and out of my home for years be able to get into my things ever again and mess with my mind and my happiness.

The apartment I was moving to had security cameras everywhere just about, or so I thought. You had to swipe a card to get into every outside door. The underground parking had cameras as well. I found a secure place for me and my work and my personal things.

But before Cinderella would be secure, as she unpacked her boxes, her portable hard drive was missing. It was a copy of every file I had created since 2005. I was really upset. As I tried to backtrack and figure out who could have taken it, I exhausted myself and found out there were no cameras in the parking area where they unload the truck, so when we were up and down the elevator with my stuff, the truck was open and unguarded. As when they moved the boxes out, they were taking them down three flights and leaving them at the bottom and then transferring them to the truck, so they sat there for a bit with no one watching them. I was tired of trying to figure out who took it and when. I was exhausted.

There were other items missing too. My personal Social Security papers, my receipts for the last three years for things I had bought. I was upset.

Later I would learn that most of the things turned up; I was so used to being suspicious that I still to this day get a little mini panic attack if anything is missing, and I take a deep breath and keep looking. Nothing has been missing since I moved in months ago. Life is good.

That Sunday was Easter, and I told myself that I would not upset myself anymore. I asked Nicole, my friend, to come for dinner, and she said yes. I asked her if I could invite Terry, my new friend, and she said yes.

Easter came and, they were to arrive at 2:00 PM. I went to church at 10:30 AM and was ready at noon. Around 12:30 PM, my friend Nicole called to say she was not feeling good and would not be coming. I was upset and thought she was lying, later found out she was lying to me; she did not want to come to dinner because of Terry. Why would she not tell me in the first place? It made me cry on Easter. She hurt the very thing that every man had done as well—lied to me.

Then Terry called at 2:00 PM to say he would be coming later around five-ish. I thought to myself, "I can't believe in my new place the first time I invited people, no one showed." I cried myself to sleep and woke up around 8:00 PM when Terry called and the phone woke me up.

Terry had come earlier, and he said and no one answered the door. Maybe I did that on purpose while I was napping. I was upset. It took me hours to prepare the meal, and I was tired from moving. No one cared about disappointing me. I would rather be alone.

Well, turned out Terry and I ate and had fun. He took the

conversation a little too quick for me in the relationship, and he stayed until 2:00 PM, talking again before he left and taking himself to a place of sexual offering that I was not interested in that night. It was clear he liked me a lot, or was it just that he wanted sex? I felt bad because I was not sure how I felt at all. I did not want the pushing sex he was turning on. I was trying to tell him, but he was not listening.

Over the next few weeks, I was able to calm down over my missing things. My friend Nicole and I had gone and done a few things together, and I had helped her fix things at her home and helped her shop for groceries since she was disabled and used a motorized cart when she shops. I was beginning though to feel that she was using me to do the things she needed as I was pushed to do this and that when I was stating that I was tired from moving. She didn't seem to care about me at all. It hurt.

I was trying to cheer her up, but in fact, I was making myself miserable. I knew I was letting someone push me around once again. I asked her what she would like to do for Mother's Day. She said, "Let's go to lunch at Amy's Tea Room."

I said that would be fine and I would make reservations. She said, "I will pick you up at 1:00 PM, but make the reservation for 2:45 PM, and we will have time to shop a bit before we eat."

I said, "Fine."

Mother's Day came, and she picked me up at 1:00 PM, and we drove there and arrived at 1:30 PM, and she looked at things she wanted to purchase and had me put them at the front counter.

She then said, "You should tell them we are here."

I said, "Well, our reservation isn't until 2:45 PM," and she insisted that I tell them we were there.

I said, "Fine."

Sure enough, they called my name in the next ten minutes, and I didn't get to shop, but I thought that was fine; I would shop after we ate. We sat at a table, and Nicole was unhappy with the fact that she was hot because of the door behind her as they were going in and out.

I said, "Why don't you switch seats with me?"

We switched. She was there for a few minutes and looked hot; I noticed the air-conditioning register was under my chair, and it was cool.

I said to her, "Do you want to switch chairs again as the air is coming out under my seat?"

She said, "Fine."

Then she was happy. She kept admiring the floral arrangement hung behind me and said, "I'm going to buy that when we are done with lunch."

I said, "Fine."

We ate a wonderful lunch and dessert, and then she said, "I'm going to pay for that item and the ones you left at the front desk."

I said, "Fine."

She paid and then said, "Let's go."

I was upset but said nothing as the last time we were there, I did not get to look around as well, and she said that the next time we went there, she would let me look. Here it was Mother's Day, and she didn't care about me at all.

I said nothing as she drove away. She drove to the place she wanted to go to look on the Great Road in Lisa along the river. She stopped and bought more things at one shop; she then had me go into the fudge shop to get her fudge as she waited in the car, and then she said, "Well, let's go to the fish restaurant and get fish as I have to go to the bathroom."

I said, "Fine," but I could not believe that we just ate two hours earlier, and I was stuffed. I just did what she wanted. I could not believe that she had to climb about fifteen steps up to the restaurant, and she did it. The woman who couldn't walk anywhere and go up steps was doing just that. Was she lying to me about that as well? When we got to the top, I said, "How about sitting down while we wait for a table?"

She said, "No, I don't have to."

I then knew she was lying.

We ate fish dinner and left.

She said, "No, I don't want to go straight home, I want to go to the grocery store."

I said, "Whatever!" as I had told her earlier when we were driving there and she mentioned that she needed to go to the grocery store. I told her, "No I don't want to shop for groceries on Mother's Day."

Clearly, she had no regard for me or my happiness at all.

I said, "Fine," as she was driving.

She said, "I have to stop at home first to let my dog Pansy out."

I said, "Fine."

On the way home going through her neighborhood, she was bashing the people who did drugs.

I said, "Well, a few weeks ago, you admitted to me that you buy pot, and that is illegal as well."

She got really upset.

I said, "Well, anything that is against the law is a crime."

She didn't like that statement. When we got to her house, she got out of the car and started to yell at me and stated that this was her house and she could do what she wanted. I just said fine again and wanted to leave but could not. She pulled something she bought out of the trunk and said, "Unwrap this for me." Really mean. I just stood there and did nothing. She unwrapped it fine by herself. She was a lying bitch and was going to hurt me now since I told her that she was committing a crime as well as the crack buyers. She was a person who would get back at others that did not agree with her. I was not going to let her do this to me anymore. I didn't care about her life anymore at that very point. She scared me.

She drove to the grocery store and once again got her mobile cart and started to drive, and she said to me, "Where is the pharmacy?"

I said, "Nicole, I don't shop here, but you do. Where is it?"

She knew, and I was upset.

Then she said, "Let's get some kitty litter."

So I walked to the aisle, and she went somewhere else. I turned around, and she was not behind me. That did it; she was someplace else, getting something else she needed.

I said, "You could have told me."

She said, "Oh, I knew you wouldn't care."

I went off on her in the store and said, "Yes, I do, and I'm not letting you treat me this way on Mother's Day, and I told you directly that I did not want to go to the grocery store on Mother's Day, but you did want you wanted because it's what you do."

She said, "Don't yell at me."

I said, "Well, you yelled at me at your house, now how does it fell on Mother's Day to get yelled at?"

She said, "We are leaving."

I said, "Good."

She drove me home and pretended to be lost as she got off on the wrong exit for downtown—as *if.* She was horrible, and when the car stopped, she told me again how awful I was and that was why my family had nothing to do with me; she said this would be the last time she saw me as she hurt people.

I said, "You're right my family are criminals like you, and they are not allowed in my home either," and I shut the door. I was so happy that she made the comment that she did not ever want to see me again. I did the right thing at the right time to get rid of her, and it was her idea. She would never contact me again. I was happy.

Abuse comes in many forms. Verbal abuse is one thing that I don't put up with from anyone anymore. So her comments about smoking pot since she was fifteen and the fact that she sold porn with her husband to other couples made me sick. I know did not trust anything about her and her life. What else had she lied about, who else had been criminalized in her life? Clearly, she was a liar.

Terry had called me in the morning to say, "Happy Mother's Day." It was sweet of him, and I liked him as a friend. However, his lie that he was a practicing religious person and the fact that he would not tell me his age and when I asked for a paper to prove he had no venereal disease, he said he knew that no woman he had ever been with had disease. I thought to myself, "Well, I guess you underestimate me for sure." When I say something and someone does not give the correct answer or says they don't care what I want, it is a clear sign they don't listen and care about what the other partner wants. Crystal clear. So all the other things being very forward, not showing up for Easter, and coming on to me constantly sexually after I asked to be friends first were clear signs that I could be friends with him, but that's it.

When people don't listen to what you want, they disregard you as a person. Terry and Nicole had both in their own ways showed to me that they did not care about me at all other than to call and talk and go where they want to go.

Terry was nice, but I had too many gut nos to take the relationship any further.

So my new life was just that, new. New place to live, new ideas, but most of all that I was not going to let anyone ever hurt me again in anyway. I may cry for a while, but that is all the hurt I will feel as I have not given my heart to anyone. For if someone did hurt me again, for sure they don't have me even as a friend; I had decided that for my life. That would be my reward for being hurt; I just walk. I am my own hero, my own protector, because I have studied and learned and have no one else to help me with that at this moment.

I had learned to love myself finally. Being alone does hurt and is lonely, but being with someone who hurts you is worse than being alone. I learned that the hard way. I was finally in control of my emotional life. For once I was in control and proud of myself. I was now in a different place, but I was the same and in control of myself.

People who are victims of abuse learn the hard way to never let anyone hurt them. No one would hurt me, not even a friend. I had finally learned the lesson that would save me emotionally for the rest of my life.

I would rather spend every holiday alone than with someone who would hurt me. Yes, indeed, that lesson is hard and true. I hope that everyone who is abused and turns their life around learns that lesson quickly.

I now walk and go wherever and whenever I want to. It is a good feeling. Maybe living alone again taught me to be tough again when I had lost that from being married.

I told Terry when I met him that I told my children when they meet someone, they need to ask two questions: (1) How do you feel when you are with them? (2) How does that person treat you? If the answers are negative, then the story is told, and you need to end the relationship. I use that for friends as well. It works for me.

Mother's Day would be remembered by Nicole abusing me verbally and reminding me that if I have to spend a holiday alone, it is fine with me.

I know that I am in control of my life now.

Further paperwork arrived in the mail about my chapter 7, "Bankruptcy." It said that it was a motion to foreclose and that I intended to surrender my property. I did surrender the property on April 27, 2011, to the attorney for the creditors; she represented both Bank 2 and Mortgage Hut Financial Company. Why then was I getting this from the original foreclosure company for Bank 2?

I made some calls, and the man whose name was on the motion didn't write it. Instead of him returning my call, a woman returned my call and knew nothing about this case and did not know that I gave the house keys and surrendered the property to the attorney weeks prior.

The most interesting part of the motion was the statement that they had superior rights to the property.

I had to laugh out loud and stated to myself, "Isn't the judge going to love this?" In other words, in the chapter 13 case, I was trying to prove that Bank 2 had the superior rights because the courts gave them the right to foreclose on the property in the first place in 2009, but in court, the judge let Mortgage Hut Financial present information and sided with their case. They still owned the first loan and gave them the rights to lift the stay with no workout plan approved and take my property.

The property was then surrendered after I requested a modification and a refinance from Mortgage Hut Financial because all were denied. I had no other choice.

I called and asked Mortgage Hut Financial how to turn the property over to them, and they stated that I could give the keys to Ms. Tammy Jon, their lawyer.

I said, "Okay, I can do that shortly after I find an apartment to move into."

I found one quickly and set the wheels in motion to move.

I moved in a few weeks—three to be exact. I took the keys to Ms. Jon's office one rainy morning. As I walked into the building, which was fully owned by the law firm, I inquired about her, and as they were calling for her, she walked through the front door with her lunch, and I gave the keys, talked a bit about the property, I had her sign the paper stating that I gave her keys on that day.

I said, "Would you like to copy this paper?"

She said, "No." I in turn copied it when I got home and mailed her a copy.

So when I got his motion stating that I intended to surrender the property, I was upset again.

Then after writing the response to their motion, I got my mail, and in the mail was yet another motion from Ms. Jon to appear the next week in court for a hearing as well with her on the same issue, and it stated as well that I intended to surrender this property.

Well, I was so upset I wanted to scream out loud, but I didn't as I had to drive to a meeting for my new job. There was a staff meeting at someone's house for a meeting and eating. I had map quested the directions but did not take into consideration that it was a new website, and it had two sets of mileages on the outer page. Well, without my reading glasses on when I drive, upset about reading this shit again, I drove past the turnoff as I thought it was miles further looking at the paper in my car with the directions.

I was so pissed off, and when I called my boss on his cell, as we were talking, I got disconnected. I began to drive again and could not find it. I realized it was almost 7:40 PM and the meeting was over at 8:00 PM. So I made an executive decision to turn back and go home for the night. I did call the main number and leave a message for my boss that I got lost.

I was clearly upset again over this court shit even after they took my home.

I was angry. Yes, I'll say that again. I was angry. I didn't even have to pay anyone to state that myself. I was angry.

So in the next few days, I wrote the response to that motion as well and took them both to court to file and filed a subpoena to be served on Ms. Jon to appear at the first hearing that the other foreclosure company called in court. I thought to myself, "Let's get this over with right away." She could tell the judge herself that I gave her the keys and surrendered the property.

I was sick of this shit. I wanted this over. I gave them my house and even left the refrigerator, stove, and washer and dryer. I even painted over the holes and dark spots in the living area. Now, this nice person had reached her limit.

Yes, I had reached the nice limit. No more nice stuff from me. Now, in court I would go for the hearings so the judge could know firsthand that I surrendered my property to Ms. Jon.

There was nothing else to do. I owed nothing to anyone. Chapter 7—the end. They took my home and my peace of mind for the future of my financial life, but they didn't take my peace of life. I live peacefully and honestly, and I won't ever let anyone take that from me.

I will let no one ever do that again to me. Ever.

So now that I am in my space, even though it is my place, it belongs to a company, and I rent. I don't have to put up with anyone's anything anymore. I just pay rent.

My space is small, but when I think about when I started out in my first apartment, it was a studio and a park was across the street. It was small, but it was mine, and I got to do what I wanted.

Now thirty-five years later, I have my space, which is a small studio and across the street, is a park, and it is small but it is mine, and I get to do what I want. I guess I have come full circle right back to where I started on my own in the world. Doing what I do best, pleasing people and living honestly—this time with a view into the human souls of people who reveal to me the liar or the truth-sayer. This is true!

I have peace. Yes, I have peace. I get to decide who comes in my world and who does not in order to keep the peace of my life.

When in this world we wonder what is important. Peace, of course, from the Almighty God above as well. Love one another as you would like to be loved.

Love and peace.

Now I do have to call a few people after this case is dismissed, and I owe nothing to anyone. Hopefully they can determine what is what and if anything else is needed to be done to stop criminals from doing what they do.

After that, it is my turn to change the wheels of time and start completely over.

Love and peace.

I will change my name and Social and become someone new. I have waited years to get this finished and over so I can move on with my life in safety and live life even more fully and have fun.

However, I will always be the same good person my parents brought into this world; no one could ever change that, nor did I want them to. They did try, but I'm glad to report they failed.

I started a new job at a place that I won't state. I found liars, people who didn't care, and gray areas to the policies actually written by the corporation no different than any other place I had worked. I ignored it all. Even the parts about me challenging people and asking too many questions. I just became quiet. I don't help people who call me names and see me as a problem. I just ignore them. I do my job then and go home. My genius is just that I had finally become smart and knowledgeable about the why of what people do and how they do it.

I made friendly talk as well with one of the cleaning people. Her son had been kidnapped, and I told her that I help people who are victims. We started to share information, and I stopped communicating to her when she made me feel that a member of the place was a friend of hers who could be trusted.

He came up to me at the front desk one day when I was really busy and started to ask me questions about myself and did I have a husband, boyfriend, etc.

I said, "No," and he continued with personal questions and then asked for my phone number. I gave it to him for being persistent.

He called me a few days later, and we talked. We talked about two hours, and he asked many personal questions. I remember thinking, "Is he interrogating me?"

He said in finality, "How about coffee tomorrow morning, we'll meet."

I said, "Okay, what time?"

He said, "I'll call you tomorrow."

He called me back the next day about 10:00 AM and said, "How about lunch instead?"

I said, "Fine."

He said, "Can I pick you up?"

I said, "No, I'll meet you there as I am part of the safe at home program, and I can't tell people where I live."

He said back, "You're being awfully secretive!"

I said, "I am not, I told you, I can't tell you, okay?"

He said, "All right, I'm not pressing." He then went on to add, "Where would you like to eat?"

Since he was Italian and lived in the area which was the Italian section of Springfield, I picked a place near his house.

I said to him, "I'm a cheap date, you can take me to Amies"—the best sandwich place in town.

He said, "No way, that place is for everyone who is not Italian!"

I was shocked by his statement as it was my favorite lunch spot for an authentic Italian sandwich. He was full of it.

I then said, "How about Mia's? I love that place!"

Again, he said, "No, we're not going there."

With that second no, I knew I was talking to a controlling man who wanted everything his way.

I said, "Well, you pick where you want to go."

He said, "Okay, where would you like to meet?"

Then he told me to meet at the grocery store parking lot after stating, "Let's meet at work."

I stated, "No, I'm not going to work on my day off."

It was really getting weird, and I almost didn't want to go any longer.

I said, "Okay, I'll meet in the parking lot at the grocery store by work at 11:30 AM."

He said, "Okay, see you then."

I arrived at 11:30 AM and found him in his black Corvette sitting in the parking lot. I parked my car and got out.

He walked over to me and said, "Hello."

I said, "Hi, Mr. Casual," as he told me to dress casual.

I got into his car, and the gentlemen held the car door open and closed it after I got in—but was he truly a gentleman? We talked a bit, and he gave me a business card that was gold, and it talked about loaning money. He then told me he was a loan shark.

I said, "You're kidding." I almost choked. I said, "Really?" as I put the business card into my purse.

We drove around the area up and down the streets passing by many restaurants. He then pulled into a very small place with only three tables and pulled into a parking spot next to the building. It was a pizza sandwich shop. He asked me what I wanted to get, and I said, "Well, you talked about pizza, why don't we share one."

He said, "Okay, pick one out."

I did, and we ordered salads as well. Then we talked. He asked me more personal questions about my past marriage, children, and my life. He was not social-minded, and I told him that I helped victims of abuse. I knew he would not like that since he had previously told me that he had perpetrated domestic violence upon his ex-wife. He said people changed on the phone. I know they did, but the personality did not.

We can change small things about ourselves to someone; but when you are seventy-one years old, to change who you grew up to be is not possible. I know I don't want to change either. I grew up a certain way, and I don't want to change, nor could I change the very core of my honest upbringing. He could not change the dishonesty at his core any more than I could change myself, nor did I want to.

He was telling me all the reasons why I was living my life the wrong way. We finished lunch, and he said, "Let's go for a ride."

The more I talked, the more he told me how I was not living my life correctly. We passed by my old neighborhood on the highway, and I said, "If you want to see the home I grew up in, get off the next exit."

He said, "Okay," and he got off and drove by my mom's house, all the while telling me that I should be talking to my mother.

I was not getting into the family junk and gossip with a strange man I met for an hour, and I guess he didn't like that either. Too bad! This guy was prying into my life far more than I wanted to, and I guess I took it one step further.

Since he stated that I was being secretive, I thought to myself I should take him past where I just moved from.

I said, "Get off the 25 exit, and I'll show you where I moved from last." He drove down the street and into the condo area.

He said, "This is really nice."

I said, "Yes, it is why lived here for seven years."

He then drove back down the main road, still telling me how I should live my life. I then pointed to my old subdivision where I lived with my ex-husband and I said, "I used to have a real big house down there, why don't you drive down that street, and my church I used to go to is back there as well."

He said, "No."

I said, "Well, I guess that's enough about my secretive life."

He said, pointing his finger at me, that I need to change how I live etc..

I said, "Well, for someone who is a loan shark I guess you have the right to tell people how to live their lives huh." I said, "Well, I help victims and some of the people help me as well."

We talked a bit more, and the conversation got ugly.

I said on the highway, "You take me back to my car right now." That was after I said, "I help victims and have talked with the county executive's office."

Since he made connotations to Nigger's earlier, I thought I would tell him that I had friends and acquaintances that were Black. My great niece was, but I did not tell him that as he was a clear bigot in the twenty-first century who needed soap in his mouth.

Clearly not a person I would even want to spend any time with at all.

I said, "Take me back to my car right now."

He said, "Okay."

When we pulled in the parking lot, he said, "I'll let you out of the car," and got out on his side. I looked down and found the secret button to let me out.

He said, "Oh, you found it?"

Getting out, I said, "Yes, I did, I told you I was smart!" My way of telling him that loan sharks were criminals. I couldn't wait to drive home. In a couple of hours, I knew this guy was a jerk—the quickest I had ever gotten over being with anyone. I hated him.

I got into my car and drove away fast. I went home and got on my bathing suit and jumped into the pool and said to the girls, "I had a date with a loan shark today, believe it or not!"

I even told one of the guys whom I had become friends with me, and he looked surprised as well. I actually was very attracted to him, but my friend at the pool said her daughter was interested in him, so I backed off at that point on, wondering if he would be someone for me as I didn't want to get involved in a mess if her daughter and he were in a relationship. Which I didn't know, but I guess I think the guy should say something if he was interested. That I know for sure.

When I returned to work, I told one of the supervisors about him being a loan shark and approaching me at the front desk for a date.

She said, "What you do in your personal life is up to you, and it is your business."

I said, "Okay," and was surprised.

I thought the other girls at the front desk should know in case he was hitting on others as well.

I asked one of the girls who had been there a long time, and she said, "Oh yeah, he hits on a lot of the girls, and one of them, he brought lots of jewelry who used to work up here."

I said, "Really, I wonder why no one told me that. But they don't even tell the front desk people about calling the police on two members who broke into a fight."

It was clear to me that they were not sharing information about the security of people.

The next few days, I told every woman whom I thought needed to know. That Sunday, an employee called in after vacation and asked what was new there.

I said, "This and that," and she said, "Did they ever find the music equipment missing from the studio?"

I said, "I didn't even know it was taken."

She said, "Yeah."

I said, "Well, if they found it, I wouldn't know that either."

The place was a security mess, and I felt like I was being put in the middle of the junk again. This time I was not being used for $9.50 cents an hour to protect anyone.

I had learned that lesson working at Naldo Burger World. I would never do that again. I do what I am told; other than that, unless they ask me for assistance on security issues, I will not say anything ever again. I have been upset enough.

Sammy came in the next day on my first day back, and I saw him quick enough that I could go to the back and would not have to talk to him.

The next day on my shift, at the beginning, he walked in again as I was counting money way down at the other end of the counter not where you scanned in, and he put his face down in mine while I was counting money and said, "Hi, Julia!" I don't go by Biggie. But I ignored his comments and kept counting. He was showing me that he was going to bug me even though the date did not work out.

The next day as well he came up to me on his way out and stuck out his hand again and said to me, "No hard feelings, right?"

I said, "Right." I wanted to say, "Please stop bugging me at work."

The next day Sammy, the cleaning woman, his friend came up to me with a diamond ring and said, "She found it."

She said, "Do you think it's real?" Karl took a look at it, and I looked as well.

I said, "Take it to a jeweler."

She said, "Maybe I should have Sammy look at it. Maybe I'll give it to him."

It was her way of sticking it to me about him. I would never talk to her about anything any longer. I had already thought that she was keeping stuff downstairs so she could have it herself or sell it. The dialogue had already been had over a woman who lost her son's swimsuit and left it behind the night before and called in and it was not in the lost and found. They didn't bring stuff up from downstairs, stating that they were too tired to bring it up. I knew the person stopped her membership because of it. She was angry.

I told the boss, and he had dialogue. After that, it was the same as usual. I told myself I didn't care any longer at all about the office problems related to theft. They clearly didn't care about the property of others.

I stayed in the house a lot lately due to the abusive words from the guy I went out with. It reminded me why I am writing this book.

My chapter 7 bankruptcy was over but still today in the mail, I received yet another letter from Bank 2 about my loan and my home, which I surrendered to their attorney's months ago.

Just for the hell of it, I called the number on the letter that stated we could work something out. I called, and the girl Jan said, "There is no such loan number."

I laughed and said, "That is why I called, you need training, you already took my home in court, yet you harass me further," and I hung up.

It felt good to me in my own nice way telling them to *get lost*. I had to wait for six weeks while looking for a job for my unemployment.

I had to talk with someone and fax a letter stating that I could work full-time. Because I was disabled, they said, I needed a doctor's statement stating that I could work full-time.

I said, "I don't have health insurance, what would you like me to do?"

This is America; there is no insurance for the poor. Not even someone who is federally disabled; they make you wait two years before you get free Medicaid and Medicare to help with what is wrong with you. I was disabled federally, and no insurance. Americans need to rise up and speak out about what is wrong. We are killing ourselves. We don't have to wait for terrorists.

My friends I see in tents inside the city plaza in Springfield standing up for what's wrong in America called Occupy Springfield are doing what I might have been forced to do if I was not able to disable myself with PTSD. Otherwise, when I was foreclosed on, I would have been put out on the street. No money and no place to live.

One of my family members said years ago when I thought they were not happy about me writing this book that I could write my book from my car because I would probably be living in it. My own family cared nothing about me in the end except for one sibling, and the rest probably were angry about me writing this book. For once in my life, I don't care what they think. My new life with a new name will help me to get past the hurt and live with the hope of happiness again in my life. I have achieved it, and I won't let anyone take it away ever again for any reason.

So I did give an on-camera interview with a local TV station while

Occupy Springfield was protesting in front of Bank 3 while President Obama was in town and hoping to get his attention to fix the things that were so wrong. I hope one day that he will see it and start action against the bank and mortgage problems that are intentional.

While I'm not in a tent, I am hiding out in one room, and I am very careful about where I go and usually go by myself other than one friend I made where I live. She had understood somewhat but finds my lifestyle a bit different. I am grateful for her friendship as it has been a long time since anyone cared at all. She has been my constant rock of support through a lonely time.

She celebrated with me when I called to say I was going forward after seven years of writing this book to have a drink out. It was fun and exciting to share my great accomplishments.

I hope that my readers know that this book is about helping people and changing the world. I hope this book helps many people and changes some laws. Domestic violence is just that violence that we can get rid of by getting away and never talking about it ever again, unless of course you want to. I wanted the readers to know they are not alone and it happens to the best of us.

I encourage men and women alike to report anything the moment they feel someone was abusive. Make yourself a *hero* and report.

Find the inner peace that lies within yourself, and, Americans, please be honest and strive for justice.

That is my prayer and wish for America.

Get up, get out, and change something. YES, YOU CAN! Remember to be anonymous!

This past week, I attended a meeting that the attorney general set up for the public, and they said that the Department of Justice and the attorney generals from all the states in America struck a deal with the major bad banks, one of them being the one in my case, and decided for all the people that instead of prosecuting them for it and getting back our houses, they fined them one fee of $155 million to be divided between all the states, and if there was enough money, we could each get a possible maximum of $2,000 until the money ran out. If the bank failed to pay us, then the attorney general's office gets $1 million per each account that the bank didn't pay out. Now, I lose my house to criminals, and the attorney generals and the DOJ make a deal with the crooks to give them money. Does this seem like something that should happen in America? Of course not! White-collar crime being slapped on the wrist and not put in jail by prosecuting each case. The feds are good at that. They are worried about terrorists—well, you are feeding into the worst ones I know of in America. I guess that's my opinion, now, isn't it? Rightly so, can't wait for my $2,000. Maybe I'll go on vacation and look for a house in another country.

I wanted the book to end stating that I finally met a good man, you know, finally my prince had come which believe it or not he may have come—that is to be determined by him and me. One thing was sure trying lately, that I gave more concessions than I ever thought I would, and we are ongoing to understand each other and know that it may not be a lifelong relationship yet or ever for that matter, but I hope it will. Life's surprises pop up sometimes when we least expect them or need them to. I told him he was a surprise as we met unexpectedly. We are now more than friends, maybe in our minds only. He is here for a short time, and I don't know if my world and beliefs can mesh with his idea of life. We're going to try and see. Love is a possibility, and he is a prince for real—yes, for real in his country. True. Coming in America.

I wanted the book to end stating that I have a piece of paper stating I'm not crazy after trying to get one for seven years to prove I'm not and what I stated to people was the truth over the last seven years. My new counselor that said she could do that for me last week, and the next week she said that she said that in haste and it may take six months to get it. Hum! Well, well. We'll see if I can change that! Find a good friend, and skip the counselors; they just want to do homework and take everything that comes out of your mouth as an answer exactly to what they propose it means and not what you intended at all. Find a good friend and have a cup of coffee or a drink, and get on with the happy part of your life; this is my best advice.

If you haven't figured out the book yet—I hate liars and make them disappear as quickly as I can. I highly recommend it in life. Then peace will be yours. Read the "Recipe for Liars" poem I have written within my book on occasions when you need to get rid of one. It works!

The end.

For you and for me.

The beginning.
A new me.
And new life too!
Sophia.
Love always.
Ciao, baby.

Chapter 15

My American Terrorists Continued
"The" Real End One Year Later
"Truly Now"
The Beginning Again
A New Me
And New Life Too!
Sophia
Love Always

Finally, a year later, here is the chapter we were dreaming of, Sophia!

Well, well, just when I thought I was finished with this story, it absolutely made an unconventional turn for the better, and as I watched it unfold for a year, it tore me apart and made me cry and then elated me when I received a phone call. I cried tears of joy! You must remember when reading that while I was working on my case, I somehow got involved in a case that was so unbelievable that I wondered why I ever started to help victims. I hope you enjoy the thrill of an unjust case and the threats and verbal abuse that came again my way by way of ugly, black, charred souls unleashed. This chapter is more of a diary of statements made by me. I'm tired of saying what people said, and now I'm talking about me and what I think and what I observe. It's more interesting, trust me.

So while I thought my life was new and peaceful once again, things started to happen that made me continue further to protect myself from years of harassment, and my persistence became even more fervent, and I was called resilient, and the following words will convince you that, indeed, I am.

The ending chapter in this book will remind you that one can achieve what one sets out to achieve; it may just take years longer than it should. I now have my paper saying I'm not crazy. Here is the story continuing for one more year of important information that will help victims and inform others how people can and will manipulate your mind to make you even think that you are crazy!

When I changed my name in court to get my new Social Security and it was denied, I was devastated, of course, and thought, "What do I do now?" I was bound and determined to get what I needed, but I was tired and running out of ways to convince people. I had gone to everyone I could think of to help me, and now I was financially in trouble again, and it was stressing me out. I decided after numerous conversations with the Social Security people that I needed to see a counselor for my stress. I knew myself better than anyone else, and I could not lose it at this point psychologically because I needed to stay strong to complete my trek and get what I needed: a new me with a new number.

So I tried and tried talking and resubmitting several times the evidence I needed, and when it didn't work, I sought a counselor to help get through this tough period. I went to a low-cost health center in Springfield and was able to get reduced payments because I was living in poverty at the time. Poverty levels are set by the government and people on disability are usually living in the income of poverty because they say we can work and add to the income we receive. But in 2012, finding work during the recession was not easy. So in May 21, I found help at the health center and signed up for counseling. He made me feel good about myself and made me laugh as well.

He said, "Well, if you were able to change your name, then no one would have the past medical mental health information on you, so don't worry about what was said in the past!" He made me laugh so hard. He was being so honest about it, and from a man's point of view, he was just so nonchalant about just getting on with life and forgetting about what people had said. We talked about coping skills, and I said that I had some now and that I had been working on them for years. Writing, painting, music, watching movies, meditating, walking, and just lying still and doing nothing. Those skills would help me to get rid of the moments of stress and help me to live life more fully in peace.

I had connected once again with a victim help service to see if they could intervene and help me with the Social Security Department.

They took my evidence and a week later said no, there was nothing they could do for me.

I was once again let down.

I wrote in my diary,

No one loves me… No one calls no hugs or kisses!

Wow, what powerful statements from me in writing. How sad my beautiful heart was so broken and ill.

I called the YWCA the next day to see if there was anything they could do, and for legal reasons they could not, and I understood.

> I'm scared now to even roam through my building since someone put on Facebook what the view is from my window which of course is him telling me I know where you live. It is amazing what the mind will think when our buttons are pushed. It is alarming to me and I know I will get over it in time. Time the only healer of the mind and heart. Time is ours and how we use it.
>
> I have Peace true Peace in my apartment. I let no one in and have resigned myself to the fact that I can live this way for a while and keep my mind peaceful. That is the important thing for me.

May 27, a month later, I wrote:

> I am feeling better. On the TV the Dali Lama says America is more peaceful than it used to be on the Piers Morgan show—it is nice for him to say that in my skeptical outlook on American people he sure did make me feel better about someone from the outside looking in at us sees us as more peaceful. If I could talk to God, I would ask his opinion as well, but that hasn't happened in my life so I just talk to my priest at church.

I write,

Alone today—used to it—hate it!

May 28, I wrote,

Memorial Day—and I'm thinking about my father who died a few years ago. My one sister abused him in front of me and messed with his meds, which is why I think he died. Upsetting now as ever that she may have been the one who actually killed him and that he didn't die from a heart attack. We'll never know because an autopsy was never done.

The man who had come into my life and back out had texted me that day as well and said, "Am I doing OK without him? Am I alone?" I said, "Yes I am alone and you can call me." He did not.

That night I sat down and wrote some children's stories to be published later that would be cute for children. Part of my coping skills in action since his call upset me once again. Why does he keep calling me—I don't know. Maybe it's torture from him to me for breaking up with him.

I'm still job searching and it is getting so hard to find anything. Every day searching and searching.

Today I got an email stating that they shut down my PayPal account since someone was using my account that was not me. I was really upset. I did my nails and made dinner and tried to not think about it.

The next day I tried to get someone from a Women's legal advocacy office to help but the answer was no once again. I tried one more place—no.

I talked with my sister and she said don't worry about liars and business people because in a perfect life people would care more about the truth. I made dinner and went to sleep.

Today after fighting with a publisher I got my money back and can publish any way I wish now. I was so happy as I did not trust them any longer with my book. I got a full refund of my money. That was only because I pitched to them the aspect of lying to me initially stating that they would protect my writing legally with a lawyer and that was not true. They never had a lawyer look the book over. So, they agreed with me that I deserved a full refund. They had me get the copyright when they do that it means when someone wants to sue you that the holder of the copyright gets sued first not the publisher because I was the author and so I would not be protected by their legal office. What a rip off and how smart of them. It was someone in my writers' group that advised me of that very important piece of information. So, hanging with writers for years made me more knowledgeable than I ever thought I would be. It was alarming the amount of information to just publish something. At times it made my head spin and stopped me from writing because I would get stressed out about it.

The man in my life who left today in June was texting me again. "Hi Babe, How are you?" he would text me. Asked me if I could wire him $100.00 so he could come visit next weekend. At first, I said yes to see what he would say. The money man who had lots of money was now asking me for money to drive to see me. What was up with that! I didn't know what to think. I called my sister and she said don't you dare send him money. If he has money why is he asking you for it. I guess he gets it wherever he can I suppose. I cried that night since I had almost thought of sending it to him and bought a new dress to go out with him. I had to sit awhile and think and talk before I realized that he was using me. Loneliness is a very dangerous mind game.

I feel so much better now.

A few days later he texted me again saying are you going to sleep with me when I come home! I texted back NO. I cried that night and fell asleep. What is wrong with some men. What?

The next day I got my food stamps on my card so I can go get some food! YEAH! I also got my money back from my book. YEAH!

I went to the local garden area to rest and relax and think about life. It helps me too. I walk and write poems and had a wonderful lunch in the café. There is a hidden secret spot I like to go to where there are tables and chairs behind a building that not many people know about and I sit and dream and write. There was a concert in the garden that night so I stayed and it was fun to listen and watch all the people having fun. Alone was I but fun was the night.

I called the Attorney General's office about the foreclosure mess and they still stated that I did not meet the criteria for any refund from their office. I said you have got to be kidding me. I just laughed about the world once again. Our own officials are keeping money that was given to help all of those who were illegally foreclosed on and our local state office was keeping the money for themselves. Wasn't that interesting?

Today I had an SSA person hang up on me. She was the person who was supposed to be helping me gather evidence and submit it. I was appalled and called back to talk with a supervisor. She said she would send on my information to Security and Integrity.

Tonight, I went to the outdoor gardens for a festival and stayed all night taking pictures and enjoying the crowd and artists work.

It's Sunday and I attend church and relax the rest of the day watching TV and talking with my sister.

Today I saw my counselor and he gave me other places to call that might help me. I did receive my results from tests of no sexual diseases and my dental appointment said I had no cavities as well. I was in great shape other than being overweight and stressed out sometimes due to my life and continuing efforts to get my life in order and start over anew.

I drove to the small town about an hour away and went to the courthouse to look at the file for the person I had been helping. I was told that the file is now confidential and I can't look at it. The trial is coming up soon. I was surprised that I could not look at the file.

I'm still job searching and stressed out. I've been watching the Trayvon Martin case on TV and loved it when CNN gave some very important facts that showed in my opinion that Mr. Zimmerman was not being truthful to the Judge about money. It was so interesting to me and I'm sure the world.

Today I called Catholic Charities to see if they offered any help. They said they have psychiatrists for $95.00 a visit and that the first initial visit would be $180.00. Well, well, that is out of the question. Being poor is just that being poor.

June 23, I wrote:

> The man is texting me again stating that he wants to see me. I said when you left town you slept with a woman you met at a party that night instead of spending your last night with me. He said, "No I didn't." I said, "Yes you did you are lying to me." He said no I'm not I only went to the party. I was so upset I thought I was going to blow a gasket. How do people lie to each other. Clearly the 10 Commandments are there but many ignore them. I don't. Just think if everyone believed them and lived their life accordingly no one would be hurt. Why or why don't they.

> Tonight, I watched a movie about a man who drove a woman crazy to get her money. It was an old movie and I thought to myself—why did they believe her and not me. It was so parallel to my life. I wanted to make a movie myself. Maybe one day I will.

> June 26th and it's the first day of the trial of the man I agreed to help on trial for murdering his girlfriend he lived with. True story of an innocent man who was set up by evidence to be guilty of a murder when in fact it was a man who came home one night and a jealous woman pulled a gun and threatened him because he was with another woman that night in a bar where they had met. He tried to get the gun from her to protect her and himself and the gun goes off and shoots her in the face and kills her.

> The woman who said she would be the go between and backed out. I would learn later in the story why and it would be unbelievable once again in life how people

treat me and why. She never even called me to say the trial was starting that day. I drove to the courthouse by myself and I think she was surprised to see me there. She was late the first day and I was on time and the jury selection had begun. She had dinner with me at a burger joint during the recess at 5PM and we talked a bit. She told me to be quiet in the burger joint as I was talking too loud about the case. I looked around and no one was in the place where they could hear me talking to her and I was not talking loud.

I wondered what she was up to. When we returned to the courthouse, she said to the security guards that we were family. I was not, I wanted to say it, but kept quiet. The guards told us we could not enter the building any longer as it was closed. I said, "Well the Judge stopped the court proceeding for a break for dinner so we left to eat dinner." He said I don't care you can't get back in the building. So, I did not get to witness first hand the actual selection of the jurors. I later knew why and that she was instrumental in keeping me out long enough so that I would not be there. It was amazing in my opinion.

The next day I drove again by myself to the courthouse and sat and took notes all day during testimony of several witnesses. It was very sad to listen to. My car overheated and I stopped twice to let it cool down. My radiator is leaking and I don't have the $700.00 to get it fixed. I keep pumping anti-freeze into the engine. I got home at midnight.

Next day up at 6AM and left at seven; drove to courthouse. Court began at 8AM and more testimony by people and then from the man I was helping. I believe him no doubt in my mind. I took notes all week and my hand was hurting to say the least from writing. I ate lunch with one of the potential jurors who was not picked again and she was interested in the case. I drove home and my car overheated again and I had to pull over on the road to fix it. I sat crying and got off the next exit and saw a movie while my car cooled down. I drove home. So tired and it was 11:00 PM.

Next day up at 6AM left at seven again. Court began at 8AM with more testimony by the man I was helping and others. Closing arguments and I had lunch again with a woman who was a potential juror not picked. She was anxious to see what the jury would say. So, from noon until one we ate and talked. We walked back to the courthouse, and until 4:30 the jury deliberated and then returned to the courtroom for the delivery of the decision. Guilty the jury would say again only this time 10 years for murder and 10 for Armed Criminal Action not life. It was good but not great. It was a bone thrown out for a bit of life but not freedom that he so longed to hear. I looked over at his face and he was crying. He looked over at me and said, "Why!" It made me want to find out for him. His whole family burst into tears and cried. The most interesting part of waiting was the other family of the girl who laughed for 20 minutes after the jury gave its guilty verdict. I thought to myself and wrote in my notes how unusually cruel it seemed to me that for 20 solid minutes they laughed out loud over and over for 20 minutes it continued. I wanted to walk over to them and ask what is so funny. But later I realized that they are grieving and I knew I better just hold my tongue so that I would not get thrown out of the courtroom. I found it so horrible though and noted it several times so I would not forget that moment.

I drove home and stopped to see a movie The Lucky One. It made me feel good and feel better about the day. I cried in the movie about the man who was innocent returning to prison for a murder he did not commit. I drove the rest of the way home and slept 10 hours. I was up and cried. I called my sister and cried. I ate that night and cried some more. I was upset about the injustice of the justice system. I was upset that an innocent man was again sent to prison for maybe 20 more years of his life. I was upset about everything. I sent an email to a writer at the local paper and she responded stating that she, too, thought he was guilty therefore was not going to do an article about anything about the trial as she thought justice was completed.

It's Sunday and I'm home from church and eating my breakfast I cried some more and later that night I did make dinner and watch TV.

It's Monday and I called his lawyer. He said he was calling him to tell him what we talked about. He said he thought he had won. He could not believe he did not win. I made some calls to the local area about the prosecuting attorney but no one cared at all about what I had to say about what I witnessed in court. The lies and fabrication of evidence to me was unacceptable. I job searched, talked to my sister, and went to bed.

July 3rd I called and made an appointment at the jail to see the man I was helping so I could see him in person and talk on Saturday. I did laundry and ate and job searched some more.

I called the police department from where she worked to talk about allegations that she (the girlfriend) had been having an affair with her boss the police chief. I got no reply only left a message that was not returned.

I was so tired and weary at 2:00 PM I went out that night and ate ribs for dinner. It was so good and I treated myself for job well done for a week at the trial of course I get paid nothing for helping people because I do it for free so they know I am doing this from my heart not from my wallet.

Today is the 4th of July and the little town I live in had a fair with music and fireworks and food and fun. It was a fun day for all the families that live here.

The next day or so in the news was a story about a girl who was walking along the highway and a police car picked her up. She stated that she was on her way to the hospital to get checkout or mental problems and in the car the gun goes off, and she's dead. How does that happen? She had walked 10 miles and only minutes from the hospital the police pick her up and she's dead. They said she was shot by herself with the police weapon that she took from his belt in the front seat. Later it was revealed that she was shot in the back of the head. I guess someone lied huh! When do the lies end? When do people get punished for lying in this country? We have got to find a way to make it happen that is what I was thinking at the time. You know a law for liars if you lie you go to jail no matter who you are.

It's Saturday and I'm feeling better I watched TV and ate and then drove to watch a few movies at the local theatre. I drove later to the jail to visit with the man I was helping. They told me at the jail that I was not signed up for a visit. That I would have to come back at another time. I was upset and said I did call in and I will just wait to see if no one else shows up. A girl in the lobby told me that it has happened to her several times she shows up and they say you're not on the list come back another time. I said that is unacceptable I drove almost an hour to get here. So, I waited and they let me go up and talk with him.

He was so happy to see me and he said that his friend the woman who asked me to help him was no longer returning his calls. I told him to be careful of her as she was saying things about him during the trial that we're not exactly great for him and that she was angry with me and isn't really talking to me either. I did not tell him that she was stating that people change in prison and he is a womanizer who knows that he learned his lessons in life and needs to learn and move on to a better life. I felt so sorry for him that she had once again given up on helping him. She did that after the first trial and somehow thought he would win this time and they would be together forever. He said he was not interested in her that way. He said no way I am not going to be with her in life. I said well that is what she was telling me. He said that his lawyers never gave him a copy of my notes from the trial that I sent to them a year ago. So, I said OK I'll send you a copy.

Sunday and I'm resting after church and feel happier. I did nothing absolutely nothing.

Monday, I called SSA again to try to get someone to help me. Once again that was not happening. I had applied in May and it was now July and nothing. I was very upset that night and called a hotline to talk to someone who would understand my stress.

Today I was on fire (you know that song "This Girl Is On Fire!" by Alisha Keys) and I was determined to get somewhere in this SSA mess. So...I called the White House and got 6 other numbers to call and complain about SSA. Then I got headquarters SSA and she and I had words then she said she would look into my case and she would call me back on Friday. She never called.

I was shaking and upset by the time I had finished

with that days calls. My PTSD was in motion and I had to find a way to calm down. I called a hotline again today and a nice guy talked with me. I laid on the couch watching TV and eating pizza. I called the lawyer of the man I was helping and he said he would call me back at 6:30 PM.

Today I called and talked with the Chief Medical Examiner and he said yes someone can shoot someone from across the room at a 40 degree angle in the face. I said how can that happen. He said this is not my case so I can't talk about the case in particular. I could tell he was upset at me.

The director of the Y said that she could not help me further because of legal reasons. I was shaking unrelenting and slept for four hours. I am emotionally raw at this point I got a no from the person who could help the most. I hate the world sometimes I wrote in my diary that night. I wonder why!

Today on the news is a story at the owner of a National Bank in the USA he got sanctioned 5.8 Billion dollars for being a bad boy. I guess that made me feel better in some ways since it was his bank that illegally foreclosed on my property and put me out on the street to find anything, I could afford which was one room. I guess the Lord works in small ways and sometimes in large ways for others. I was happy about it I can tell you that.

Still job searching and no phone call from SSA.

On July 15, I wrote:

> I decided to take the bull by the horns and go straight to the top. So I typed up a letter and faxed it to the White House to the President himself talking about how SSA had treated me and how they lied about the 2 year time frame of evidence submission when it is stated no where in the policies or online anywhere but they are stating it to me now and saying it is why I am being denied my request. How bold was I but when I heard President Barrack Obama speak on television and he said that he was doing the right thing; I believe him. He was a man who would do the right thing no matter what it took to help others. How bold was I—I didn't care anymore. I was going to the top and complaining and asking for help.

> I'm now eligible for Medicare part B and Medicaid because it has been two years since I am disabled. It takes a two-year waiting time frame for the disabled to get insurance—does that make sense. When we talk about the people who have mental disease and we disable them but then state that they have to wait two years to get medical medicine! We wonder why the people in our American borders are falling to the wayside and not getting the attention they need to help them lead a normal life free of stress and with medical attention if they so need it. Not true. I said to myself they disabled me with the worse mental disease in the books (a lie) yet state that I have to wait 2 years for medicine. How does that make any sense? So, when we want to wonder why people with mental disease go off the chart and start shooting people it's because they are not getting the medical attention the need. We have to wake up and start to see what is happening in this country. We have to stop ignoring the needs of the poor and unemployed when financial disease strikes people get depressed

and they have no healthcare. Then when they do lash out; we say let's kill them since they are insane let's put them to death since they killed others. They take no responsibility in that they did not see to it they got the help they needed in either case. They were let alone—to strive on their own and their minds get twisted and start to make bad decisions. We the people have the ability to help and we turn away and are afraid to talk about mental anything. I hope these cases make us learn more and become educated. I know I became educated only when it began to affect my life. I know that others had no clue so they speculated what was wrong with me and lied about me. It was horrible what they did to my life. I am a special person and I was able to hold it together but fell apart many times having to call hotlines to find someone who would understand. Searching daily for the truth about what was wrong with me and it was PTSD from verbal abuse that over the years had fallen in my life without me knowing it. I had no idea you get PTSD from verbal abuse and stress. I had no idea until I began to search myself. No clinician helped me with it. I was shoved from one place to another. I was told everything but the truth. No one was listening to me. No one was listening to me. Listening to me. Listening to me. No one was listening to me. That would be the key—how do I get someone to listen to me. Here is the truth from me. I would focus on that issue for a time.

I was trying to get the local Vocational Rehabilitation office to get me a job where I could work without worry of stress or verbal outbursts that would upset me. They said no, I did not meet the criteria. Meaning I was not taking medication so no. The doctor for SSA said I had a severe mental disease and when I requested another opinion, they said no. The EN that works with Vocational Rehab stated that they find us a job with the intent that we get off disability and work a full-time job.

Their office is about getting people off disability not helping them get back on their feet—just finding them a job to get them off disability. I still had many things to accomplish and get trauma counseling which I have not had yet. Oh well, later we'll see.

Car trouble and I'm tired. An older car is wonderful since you have no car payment. My car has been very, very good to me. But on this day, it's trying my patience a bit with an overheating engine even after I pull out of the car dealer after an oil change and check.

I had thought that the local University would help me with the testing for mental disease. They said they had to check with my counselor but they never did. They said they couldn't reach his office. He was on vacation. I guess they didn't know to call back next week. I find people's lack of follow-up for others to be quite something that I don't understand because I'm an A type who used to be an administrative assistant who followed up on things. I hope we get better at it. I have four more months until I am eligible for Medicare and Medicaid so I will wait a few months more. Wait and wait is what I have to do—I'm tired of it.

Today in the news the Colorado shooting of people in a movie theatre proves my point. This young man was a University student seeing a psychiatrist—yet he does this! I guess we did something wrong huh! I hope we figure it out and get it right for individuals such as this and the victims of such events that rock our world and lead people to say kill this man, he's insane. Makes no sense to me.

Today I realize I'm so tired of people referring to me as crazy myself. I wish someone would acknowledge my trauma and quit calling me crazy. I'm upset and crying and called my sister who cares. What if I had no one who cared! No one who cares. I think some of these people have no one who really cares and they reach a very dark place and act out. People don't like to admit anyone related to them has mental problems or depression. We see it as a weakness and we hate week people. I don't know why. The week need help, the week usually have big hearts that get so hurt we get depressed. Let's help the good hearts to get back to living life peacefully and in a goodness that makes them feel wonderful about themselves.

The next day I lay around all day distressing. Being disabled I was afforded the time to do such things to make me feel better. Thank God for that. Thank God for the Federal Government Benefit that helps people and cares. Thank God we have figured that part out. Thank God that someone cares—my government. When people have such awful things to say—I can say not true. Maybe it takes awhile to get there but they do care. The food that fed me was from the USDA my government who cares. My neighbors, my church, my friends did not care. Most upsetting most of my family did not care. Big family only one person who cared enough about me. Only one out of 100. Not good odds is it. I'm not a betting person but those odds tell a tale of how hard it is for some people who have no person that really cares. But our government does. You can take that to the bank.

My sister tells me to learn the lesson to not tell family what my social life is about and who I see and what I do. My family is very judgmental. I chose to just leave them out of my life thus far since many of them lied about me as well. I don't trust them with anything so why have anything to do with any of them. That is a lesson I learned with my family. When everything is going great—oh yeah you're the greatest. When things are going bad they forget about you. Move on I say and learn the lessons of life. My one sister and I agree on most things so she showed me that no matter what she was there for me. I thank God for her. My counselor says I'm lucky to have her. So many people don't have that one person to help them no matter what. So, she is a gift from God and my parents and I thank God for her everyday.

I told her that my children used to make me happy and I missed them and it hurt that they didn't anymore. It hurt that they didn't care enough to listen to me but believed others instead. It hurt but I knew I had to let them go if I was to continue with a happy life for myself. It is what I had to do.

I was surprised that my church's society to help others refused me as I would not tell them my address where I lived. I told them I was in a safety program and for my safety I do not tell people where I live. They said we have rules and if you don't tell us we won't help you. I thought to myself was that very Christian in thinking. I even approached the Archbishop on a night after mass when the society was all in church having a celebration of years of service to others and I told him that I did not receive help and he said talk to them not me and walked away from me. I guess I understood at that point that they did not care about me at all. Not at all. My church I had belonged to for years of my life did not care. Well, I said you go on and understand they are just people—not the kind God would approve of for sure and move on with your life.

The next day I fought again with people in the food stamp office that talked so terrible to me and hung up on me four times. They treat people they believe have a mental disease in such a way. I realized that even though I had no mental disease they were treating me as if I did and they were treating me horrible. I thought to myself these people are so ugly hearted and I hope God punishes them. I called and reported her to the higher office and they said they would look into it. They never really told me what they did and I was upset for sure. Sick of people treating people who were poor like trash. Shame on those individuals who do such things. I was shaking she had upset me so much. Yes, I said I was shaking; someone did that to me in a food stamp office. Why, I guess they have the power trip and want to hurt others they feeling superior over me. It was a sad day.

I called again the next day to inquire as to whether this treatment was because I got a food stamp case worker fired years past and they said they would look into it. They never called me back to verify yes or no. I do know if she was guilty, they would never tell me. How sad for me.

The Olympics started and I have the time to write a bit about each event and write poems too. It was so fun and I love the Olympics. It's swimming season now and I'm in the pool every day I can get there swimming laps and getting a tan and resting whilst talking to people at the pool which is fun.

Fab 5 wins Gold and so does Men's Swimming Relay team that night and Michael Phelps won his 19th medal the most Olympic medals won by one person in the Gold section. Olympic History in action whether team or individual it was an exciting Olympics in London.

I get a call stating I can't see my counselor any longer at the reduced-price Health Center because I have Medicaid. I said I do not. I have the ability but I can't afford it so I don't have it. I was horrified again. I remember crying.

I was still searching for a job. While calling for a job helping victims, I found a place that gave free counseling to victims of crime and I said can I come for counseling and he said sure. He did tell me of another place that was hiring and I applied but was not hired. I did however start counseling there and for 8 months saw a counselor every week for an hour for free. Unbelievable. For years I had searched and called every place and phone number given to me to find free counseling and there was none I was told. They had lied to me. This place did and so did the YWCA Assault Center but no one had ever told me. Why not—I guess they will have to answer for that.

My car needed a radiator so I decided to bite the bullet and get it fixed to the tune of $700.00 and I have no credit card at the time because of me staying on the outs with someone connecting me to an address so I had do really dig deep and pay my rent a week late with an added fee in order to get my car fixed. I remember it was stressful for me.

My new job I accepted part time at a card shop would need a car to get me there so I had made the decision to get the car fixed so I could get to work. Then the work did not equate to the number of hours they promised me. It was hard to take. But then one night she said that I have something in the back office in my purse and I knew she meant a gun. They were not allowed in the mall and she was hiding the fact. She scared me as she had a temper. When someone stole something from the store; she yelled at me as if I had anything to do with it. The store had a policy where we were not to approach anyone even if we knew they stole something. So why was she getting so mad at me. She scared me so I quit the job stating she lied to me. Which she did but I left out the part that she had a gun in her purse in the break room. What an experience once again.

Today I get a text while I'm at the pool—Leroy how are you. It's from the guy I broke up with. Leroy he's calling me Leroy. I picked up the phone and called him and said why are you calling me Leroy. In my mind he was playing games with me. I said I was up at the pool if he is in town come up and sit with me. He said he was still not there yet but coming back to school in a couple weeks. I wished he would go away. He wanted some of the things he asked me to keep for him in my apartment. He didn't want to talk to me he called just to get his stuff back. He said he had been at the Olympics and in London, Paris, and other places over the summer. I said wonderful and hung up.

It's mid August and I had a dream about Ice and I don't dream so I don't know what that was all about.

Today I met with my counselor and I realize that I need to let go of the people at the SSA office and switch offices. I called another local office and found someone who said they would love to help me apply under the victim's harassment rules and she would be happy to help me. I was overjoyed and found someone who cares. Thank God for her. So SSA has a great employee and I found her.

Someone in the building where I lived came to me and told me that she thought that someone put something in her drink at the bar and it was two women who live in the building. I told her without proof she should be careful of what she says even though she believes it happened. She got upset with my comment but I tried to help her. We were friends again for a few weeks until she started to talk bad to me and I let her go. She said she didn't want people in the building to know we were friends because of the gossip. So, the next time she called me for a ride I said no I don't want people in the building to gossip so I better not. She hung up and I never heard from her again which was fine with me. People tend to use me and then abuse me when they are upset—they forget I have stress related PTSD from verbal abuse so when they talk bad to me it affects me horribly. Not to mention how rude it is towards me.

Today the Empire State Building had a shooting and 10 people died. Why I don't know.

I drove to the town of the courthouse where I was helping my friend. I got the permission by writing a letter to Judge that I wanted to see the file. He gave me permission and I sat and looked at what was added. I requested to see the evidence in the case and they said the prosecuting attorney has the evidence downstairs go ask them. I went to the office and asked to see the evidence and they said I had to wait I said I have to see my friend in jail in a few minutes so I will wait 15 minutes and then I have to go. They said nothing and I left. I had a visit with him at the jail and it was nice to talk to him. He was such an inspiration to me as an innocent man stuck in prison again for something, he did not do not to mention the stress of another trial listening to everyone lying in the case. It was hard for me to listen to.

A few days later I drove back down to the court house and inquired some more of the file and pages I needed from the transcripts which I can't copy in the court house I can only get a copy from the court clerks. Why, I don't know they say the court reporters own the pages. I think if they get paid by the tax payers the pages belong to the tax payers and I should be allowed to copy them. They want to charge $1300.00 for the transcript of just one trial who has that kind of money to throw around. It is unbelievable and outrageous but they did let me copy just a few pages which was nice of them to get to the evidence of perjury of one of the witnesses. I was happy.

It's September 3rd Monday Labor Day. I worked and this would be my last day. Yes, a holiday and I had to go in for 4 hours and after 2 ½ she said you can go home. I said you bet I am. The next day I called in and quit and called unemployment.

The very next day the out of town break up man texted me again he's in town now and wants to know if he can come over and get a hug. Get a hug. Oh yeah, come get a hug. I met him in the lobby where I live and he got a hug and I talked with him in the office area. He never said let's go out for a drink and talk nothing. He wanted his stuff from my apartment that he asked me to hold onto for him. Believe that one. I said not tonight my knee is hurting you said you only wanted a hug today. So, I made him wait for a couple days. Then I dragged his clothes and mess downstairs to the lobby and he took it and put in his car. I said your table and chairs which I have you will have to help me so come up and get them. So, I let him up to my apartment to get those things and we put them on the elevator and went down to his car and put them in his car. He drove away. Never came back. Never took me out. He said he's living in another area than me. That's all he said. I said wonderful. He left and I was glad.

Depressed the next day I picked up my last check at work and got rid of the bum who was dragging me around all last year using me for this and that when he needed something. I knew and wanted to see just how far he would take a woman and dump her. Oh, it was interesting to say the least. Right down to the last day of school which I'll save for later in the chapter. Oh, My what a not a nice guy!

I'm still trying to see the evidence from the court file case on my friend and exchanging calls which got me nowhere but statements that I could view them soon.

That day I also got an email from both my daughters stating they wanted to contact me on Facebook as friends. Since I had once asked them and they did not reply I thought I would approach it in a different way. I also received an email from one of them and so I responded to the email and called them both. The first one my middle daughter picked up the phone and said Hi Mom I've moved back home and would love to see you. I was so excited and said come on over right now later today and see me. She said fine and that her husband and the two boys my grandsons would come along as well. I was overjoyed and ran around cleaning and preparing food. I also called my other daughter and left a message for her. She never called back.

Later that day in the late afternoon they arrived out front and drove up the driveway as I came out the door. Lisa was driving and I told them to pull into a parking spot. They all got out and they all looked great. We hugged and kissed and the boys were running around the fountain out front while we talked. We then came in the building and went up to my apartment. They were surprised I was living in an apartment but nonetheless it was what it was. A small studio apartment that I had fixed up really nice to look great. I had a decorating flair that most people liked when they viewed it. My son-in-law even commented how nice it was and did I do this myself. My grandsons were so inquisitive and went around the room looking at everything. It had been so long since I had children in my living area, I found it so fun. We read from books I had for the children and myself and we talked a bit. I put out a tray of appetizers and we chatted. The boys were running around and the older one fell against the coffee table and hit his head and put a big gash in it that was bleeding pretty badly. They both rushed towards him as I was sitting across the room and said call 911. I ran to get a rag to stop the bleeding and said just apply pressure and take him to an ER as an ambulance will cost an outrageous amount. She did not look happy and ran out the front door with her husband holding him and the smaller one in tow running behind for the elevator. As they got on the elevator, I said call me and tell me where you go. They never called. I called and called that night several times with no call back.

I called the following morning around 10AM and she told me he got stitches and he's fine they were sleeping as they were in the hospital till midnight waiting for him to get stitched up. I never thought that would be the last time I would see my grandsons but it was for a long time.

After months went by and other things happened, I never did see my grandsons and its one year later and I miss them and their parents are monsters for not letting me see them again.

The next day was a Saturday and I watched the movie <u>Charade</u> which I watched yesterday as well right before I started to write this; it is one of my favorites for sure. Starring Audrey Hepburn and Cary Grant and the movie is a thriller and love story all rolled into one which is my favorite plots in a movie. Love and Intrigue the two things I love which I will write about later in my life for my first fictional novel. How fun is that for me.

That day I found out that one of the jurors in the case of my friend was related to the Prosecuting Attorney whose office tried the case. Later I will tell you what another prosecuting attorney said to me about that kind of selection. Out of one hundred people with only 12 to pick and 2 alternates they picked her as one of the jurors. Why! Well, well I guess we all know the answer to that one.

That next day the man I broke up with called me again late one night and said you know I love you. I said I know you do and I hung up. He knew he didn't he just liked saying it to me. He thought that would get what he wanted; me to pay attention to him while he was in town again this year. But I didn't fall for his lies this time.

I called some of the jurors that night to see if they would talk with me about the case and how they felt about the decision of guilty and why and how they came about deciding that over innocent in the case. Two of them were willing to talk and said quite a few things which I wrote down so that my friend could know the why of the guilty verdict which he asked me about. I said the only way I would know why is to talk with the jurors. Some would say it took guts to call them up but I guess I have the guts to ask anyone nicely anything. If you want to know you have to ask. Being an investigator,

I had no problem completing that task at all. I'm nice and the ones who did not want to talk I said no problem I'll never call you back again and I didn't.

The next day more calls to the police to see the evidence but no reply only voicemail. I was getting so tired of this treatment and I was getting emotionally upset about it. My children had upset me as well. Why contact me and then nothing. Were they trying to hurt me again? Were they trying to upset me once again in my life? Yes, would be the answer as they never called me again and its one year later.

Today I had to call my sister and ask if I could borrow $200.00 to pay my bills this month. She said no problem and sent the money. I remember crying that I was tired of living in poverty as the fight to stay afloat and alive had me in overload. Emotional overload once again and now I had to control why and get rid of what was upsetting me. I did do that for sure this time around.

I had two free tickets to a museum and asked a friend to go with me as she was an artist as well and wouldn't you know on that day I went to the court house to submit the paperwork to change my name and it was unreal how I was treated like shit. The Judge in the case said how do I know your poor and can't pay the fee since I filed In-Pauperus which means free; no fee is applied because you are too poor. He grilled me over that paperwork and said I get hundreds of these why should I believe you. I felt so insulted for sure. Then the paperwork back and forth while we tried to get it right. I was so upset and he would not schedule a hearing quickly for me to get the name change and I was so upset and in the elevator called him a bastard and the clerk in court when we got off the elevator on the first floor told the security guard at the front desk while she yelled it out at the top of her lungs to see to it I got out of the building. I was so embarrassed and arrived at the museum late for my friend.

We saw the exhibit and I told her what happened. She looked upset and said she was so sorry that happened; she was so consoling and we looked at the exhibits and then it was time to leave so we never had time for lunch together which was a shame. I never went to work that night I was so upset and talking to people on the phone is not done correctly if you are upset. So, I called in and stayed home and felt sorry for myself. I wondered no more why it was hard for me to find friends and I could not wait until this part of my life was over and I could live a normal life.

I remember writing how I was waiting for someone to take me dancing. I wrote a few poems and rested.

The day came for my friends sentencing hearing. The first time I would attend a sentencing hearing. I was worried about him and sat outside the courtroom early looking over my notes. First his parents showed up and sat across the bench from me. I gave them a copy of the notes from the jurors and the notes about the trial that I had for him. They took them and didn't seem too impressed. They were nice but you could tell they were so upset about their son. His lawyer showed up and I approached him to talk about the one juror and he got upset with me and called me crazy out loud and said the Judge was going to sanction me. Knowing how nasty lawyers get—I just backed up and sat down in my bench and said nothing to him. The lawyer looked over at his parents and said who is she and they said we don't know. He called me crazy that bastard and his parents stated they don't know who I am—why the heck am I even doing this on my own dime. Then when his Aunt came in the hall waiting area the lawyer talked with her but she never came over to talk with me.

The Bailiff opened the doors to the court room and everyone went in. I stopped and waited and sat way against the wall by myself and took notes. Then it was my friends turn and the Judge had him stand up and said that he got 10 and 10 and he was running them consecutively which meant 20 years not 10 and that he had to serve 11.5. He had served 5 already which meant he had another 6.5 years to serve before he could get out. It was 2012 and so that would mean he would serve 6.5 and in 2018 he would get a hearing. Oh, my not what we wanted to hear but nonetheless it was what it was. I could see he was upset but I could not talk with him at that moment. You can't approach the prisoner while he's sitting in cuffs in court. I had to wait until he called me the next day. He was upset and said well maybe they'll let me out sooner since I'm so good. I said I don't know what they will do. He said that Probation and Parole do what they want. But what he didn't know is that they told me later that the Judge said 11.5 so they pretty much have to follow that. So, I was upset and thought we'll wait and see.

After I left the court room that day his Aunt said can I talk to you about the lawyer incident and I said sure outside. I walked outside and they were all behind me. The woman who had asked me to get involved in the case but then ignored me came along outside as well. When we got outside his Aunt said I need to wait for the lawyer and talk to him. I said really. Then the woman friend of his said to me that the lawyer said there were crazy people in the court house and he had to come outside instead to talk. I said really. I could see I was being set up and I quickly said you know what I have to go home you can call me after you talk with the lawyer. She piped up and said I was there when the lawyer said those things to you and I said you were not.

She said yes, I was and I said no you weren't. I said I'm going home. I had had enough of liars in my life and she was the biggest I had ever met.

I drove home and relaxed thinking about my friend who did not get concurrent sentence which meant he might have been out in a few years now he has consecutive 10 and 10 which is 10 and Judge said must serve 11.5 of the 20 at the least. I was upset. I went to sleep. His Aunt never called me that night either.

It is now September 18, 2013 I am really upset about how people are treating me again in my life and seem to be slipping into a small depression again. I was upset when I thought my pajamas were missing and barely slept. The next day I realized I left them in one of the washers in the laundry room and realize that when that starts to happen, I am really stressed out and my brain can't even function properly. I now later would watch myself when I get stressed to actually see what is stressing me out and how my brain reacts to it.

So, I sleep, eat, and cook when I'm feeling like people are hateful towards me after I've been nice. Now I realize that I don't like people that aren't nice to me and I have to stick to my gut and say I don't want to be friends any longer with people that treat me in such a way.

One other person I didn't like where I lived a few days later ask to talk with me. I feel sorry for her and brought lunch up on the roof to eat with her. I let her talk and I listened. She gossips about people which upsets me but I realized her life is just talking about other people since she has no one on a regular basis that talks with her. I feel sorry for her but know that she is not good for me as a friend.

I was still job searching as I was unemployed for over a year and I needed a job desperately. Meanwhile I was still trying to get someone at the criminal court house to investigate my ex-husband and of course that went no where fast as usual. I try and try and get no where. I think I did learn something about how people see victims of domestic violence—they don't think we are important at the court house or the police department. It was a very sad conclusion to come to even though I was now in a different area with different people.

I did go to the food pantry to get food as I was living in poverty. I was tired of being poor and feeling like a beggar.

After a peaceful weekend I got back on the trial case and started to make calls again. I went to counseling and made a pie for the girl's group there. It was fun to share and get to know some of the people.

I tried expert after expert to act on behalf of the victim I was helping in court and I couldn't find one. It was exhausting and upsetting for me. His Aunt said she would get a copy of the file for me but in reality, she never did one year later even. People amaze me at how much they lie and don't care about me or my time I give for free. I tried calling some lawyers and found no one that was even remotely interested in helping this case out.

I was so tired of this case and stressed out I didn't write any notes the whole next month. I was fed up and tired of liars again. I was talking to him from prison, and it was almost December and Christmastime. I found out I got a job and would start in a few weeks. I was elated.

Today I watched It's a Wonderful Life and wrapped some Christmas presents while watching a soccer game which LA Galaxy won the MLS Championship.

I called my sister to tell her of the good news about me getting a job offer and she was so excited for me. I had started the search for the correct doctor to get the paper saying I was not crazy and the trek became somewhat interesting. The first Primary Care Physician treated me rotten and I left. I had to get another appointment and then an appointment with a PH.D. who could administer the test for Post-Traumatic Stress Disorder (PTSD) and I found one. The insurance company had to approve the visits and I was off to a great start to finally having the paper I needed to prove that people had lied to me. I was feeling wonderful to say the least. It took seven years and many people treated me rotten during that time and stopped being friends with me and I didn't care any longer I was on the way to my new life.

I was still trying with the Social Security office to change my number and she said she would send my application. I was overjoyed.

I had a counseling visit at the crime victims place and took my friend that lived in my building as well to show her where the office was. She was so cruel to me on the way stating that I was raped and this and that. I wanted to open the door and shove her out but I didn't. I had told the counseling place to not schedule her with me but they forgot and I had to take her. I wanted to rip her lips off and remembered that from that point on I was going to be selective about who I helped and who I made friends with. While she was in a session, I went down the street to see a friend.

My friend worked in an art studio that taught people as well. She was working on a project of fiber art that she was inspired by one of my poems called Balloon Glow about hot air balloon races but the night before the race there is a glow party and all the balloons are on the ground lit up like a birthday cake. I was so honored that she was using one of my poems to create a work of art about life in general. My friend had honored me on a day when I sure needed to hear that someone thought something nice of me and my talents.

My friend was done with her session and so I met her in a diner and she actually got angry again at me. I had enough and I was not taking abuse from anyone any longer that I tried to help. It was a pattern of blaming me since I was around and I can't take it any longer. She then asked me to take her to another store to pay a bill and she asked me if I knew a computer hacker as she needed one. I could not believe what she said to me. I said no I don't and that is illegal.

The next few days I worked on some ethics courses for work at home and found it was refreshingly so great to see a company that taught ethics.

The other friend I had in the building where I lived saw me in the elevator stating that she missed me. I told her that all she had to do was say she was sorry for screaming at me in my apartment. She said nothing and got out! Almost 6 months later she died never having apologized to me. I felt bad that I didn't even know when she passed away. Such is life. I guess I was missing her but really proud of myself for finally caring about me and not allowing abusive actions or words around me.

I went to the Christmas party in the building and it ended in someone from the office yelling at a woman sitting near me. I could not believe what I was hearing and it was the same girl who had previously yelled at me in the office about the printer. What is happening to people in the world and how are they learning to treat people so abusively. I am so sick of it.

Then the Newtown shooting happened in America and I would watch the television reporting the story for days and months and years. It was so sad and we will never forget it. People need guns to do what. Kill each other that is what for and who needs that! That is how I feel about that story. It is so sad all those children dead and for what nothing!

I stopped in the Probation and Parole office in my area and the woman there informed me that as long as my friend was a good boy in prison and had a job to go to; he should be out in the least time.

I started work on a training shift of four hours a day and was enjoying the work and training. Later a week or two the one trainer got upset at me for asking a question. I could not believe her tone and aggressive nature towards me. I would not ask another question of her at all. She let me know at the end of training that she did not appreciate my questioning her. I just ignored it and stuck to the work. She never bothered me again. So, I got over it and she never had to train me again so everything was fine. I did receive one night of yelling at work that upset me but I held my tongue and said nothing just shook on Valentine's Day after I left work and went to see a movie. It had really affected me greatly. My PTSD was showing for sure. How sad for me on a day of love when I knew the man who said he would marry me and take me out didn't even call either. I guess I learned about many things this year.

It was Christmas Eve and I had not heard from my daughter or son-in-law and had presents for them and my two grandsons. They would sit for months until I put them into the Goodwill bin still all wrapped up in March right after my birthday which they did not honor as well. I had enough of them as well. It was clear they were being hateful to me.

So, who loves me I said to myself! My sister and one niece who called me on New Years Eve and my friend in prison who called to wish me well and say I love you. I shared with him about my children and he was an inspiration to me for being so upbeat and happy and cheered me up.

I wrote the word *HURTFUL* in my diary really large about my children or one child who did not contact me. It is and will always be a very hard hurtful subject for me. I have just blocked it out now for good as far as I am concerned.

I am communicating by mail with my friend in prison as he was transferred to another state and that state will not let me talk by phone unless I give them my address. I said I won't so we have to write to one another instead of talking. It is really upsetting for him and for me his advocate. The world; just when I think people can't treat me any worse for being a victim— and oh yes, they could.

New Year's Eve big flakes were falling as I stare out my window to the world. My friend from prison called me to say Happy New Year and we had fun talking about music and I know how he feels alone and sad at the holidays just like me. My heart sighs for him and for me lonely and we had one phone call to console each of our lonely hearts on New Year's Eve. Then I went to sleep.

Oh yeah, my ex-boyfriend did text me... I miss u.... I texted back I'm on my way to church and he said he's in D.C. I remember thinking miss u... like cleaning...cooking...what? I lay around the next day and cried a bit.

A few days later I met my friend the artist and gave her my quilt my mom made for me as I knew she would enjoy it so much. I was never going to appreciate the quilt at all for many reasons such as why she made it for me and my ex and that she lied to the police about me which she could never take back since she has dementia so I'm told now. So, so hurtful for me to say the least but I have learned a lot about things in life and what I needed to do to move on and never look back. It helps me greatly.

I scheduled a visit to give her the quilt and earlier that day I had called the social security office to see if they approved my new number. As I walked out of her office my phone rang and it was a message from my contact at Social Security and it said YES YOU HAVE BEEN APPROVED FOR A NEW NUMBER! I listened to it over and over and while I walked down the grand avenue with my phone right past my counselor's office, I remember thinking that I should have a star in the side walk of shame for all the victims to see. A walk of shame showing that offenders make us victims stars. Get it! Walk of shame on them and a star for victims. I immediately began to sob and tears of joy ran fiercely down my face. I was able to dial my sister and told her the great fantastic news. Pinch me for sure I'm Alive. I'll shout tears of joy to the world. My sister told me not to sue my ex and to move on with my life. I was crying and saying I'm not sure what I will do at this point but I would love it now that he can't hurt me any longer.

The next few days were happy and working on the case for my friend in prison. We chatted a bit about his book but he doesn't want to write it or contribute so I'm putting it on hold until he gets out. I may write a few chapters off my notes but I wanted it to be from his outlook and words and he's not really interested in that part now. I think he wants to stay positive and it's too hard for him right now to think about. I totally understand his heart for sure. I'll wait as long as he wants or not at all if he never wants to ever.

At work I had to drive to social security and pick up a letter stating I had the changes approved and that was on January 4, 2013. I ran into work early with the letter so they could make the important change which was faxed to the main office so my paychecks would reflect the new number.

I talked with my sister and said I was stupid about jobs and people and I'm fine but was crying really hard and it was not her fault as I was tired of being alone. I had such wonderful personal news but yet my personal life where I lived, I had no one to share my great news and I was tired of that feeling. I took down my Christmas Decorations earlier than usual.

I had to go to court and change my name. The Judge was so nasty and would not schedule a hearing right away but made it for 6 weeks later. He was so rude to me and insulted me and then on the way down the elevator I called him a bastard and one of the clerks yelled as I got off that they should make sure I got out of the building to the security guards. What a bitch!!!! And by the way the Judge was a bastard no doubt about it! This victim had been through so much and now this jerk Judge telling me there was no rush on my name change. I hated him. What a royal jerk!!!!!!!

I went to see the movie Zero Dark Thirty about getting Osama Bin Laden and I remember I had written the poem about the President after watching Brian Williams interview him after they had achieved the end.

But then I thought it poetic to send a thank you letter for him helping me get my new number and start a new life so I wrote the letter and attached the poem and faxed it to the White House and I know he appreciated my thanks and my poem even though I never heard back from him at all. I didn't need to.

On January 14, 2013 I received a call from my friend in prison's daughter who threatened me by saying that she would call my ex-husband and tell him where I lived. I said where did you get this information? The only person in the case who knew where I lived was his friend who got mad and quit talking to me. I had so much to handle and now this. She insulted me, threatened me and never met me. What a bitch. I was so upset that I told her I was going to call the police. I told her that I would call the Judge. I told her that I would call the police where she lived and knew where she worked during the trial. She sounded upset then and hung up.

The next time I wrote to my friend I told him that I called his Aunt and sure enough his friend had called her that morning and said that she had been talking to his daughter. Those women were cruel after I had helped him and now, they wanted to hurt me. Not anymore.

I wrote to him and said I want her address. He said he would find out and get it to me. Six months later and I never got the address from him. [Skip to months later.] Then he called on the 4th of July and said that he put an address down for me so he could call me. I didn't ask what address he put down and was of course upset that he lied to be able to call me. Nonetheless he did not tell me her address on the phone either. I was very upset to say the least that this guy after over a year of me helping him would do such a thing and not answer my question. I guess we find out about things in ways that make us sad. I know he must have been desperate to talk with me and that's why he did it. Desperate to talk to someone who cared about him just even for a day. Little did he know I did care but was upset that he lied about my address and I know he was lonely?

I hate liars.

I received a text from the last boyfriend he wanted to see me again. I said let's meet somewhere he said no you come over. I said no. Let's meet somewhere he said you can come over next week. I said sure. Again, not willing to meet me anywhere but then he said this to me: I want to marry you and live in town here and get a job at a non-profit agency. I was shocked and of course I knew he was lying. To get what? To hurt me? What? What? So of course, I met him that night at 9:00 PM after he got home. All he wanted to tell me was that he was going to study at another prominent University in New York. And of course sleep with me which I was not going to do. I left and stated you want to take me out on Valentine's Day to dinner and go dancing and he said yes. He never called. So, I called days later and I told him off. Never heard from him again. Thank God. I learned so much about liars from him and manipulators who will say anything to get in bed with anyone.

I am beginning to write a fictional novel about some great story I made up and for the first time I am having so much fun writing. This time writing about something that makes me energized and excited and figuring out what will happen next because I said so in words. It was fun. Finally writing for fun was fun. Not this stuff.

I'm back to work at my job. Busy with hours of work and I'm finally making money again. It has been very hard being so poor for so long.

Finally, the best day in years has arrived. I had a visit with a PhD who gave the tests for non-craziness. It is called a "Comprehensive Psychiatric Evaluation" which involves written tests like an SAT where you read a question and fill in the circle for the right answer. It took 4 hours and then I returned for the results a week later. It was done in a Psychiatric office but by a Psychologist PhD. The test only costs $250. I waited years with no insurance because no one would see me and this test cost less than the tires on my car. What a sad day to figure that out.

One week later I returned to this fabulous doctor's office to get the good news that I am clinically not a Paranoid Schizophrenic but indeed I do have Post-Traumatic Stress Disorder from years of verbal abuse and trauma from my ex-husband. I was elated and now could move forward with my life.

I met a man at work who befriended me stating he has been through similar stuff and months of listening to this man day after day and over a coffee how messed up his life was, he began to turn on me and attack me emotionally here and there. It was such an education to watch and learn why people do what they do and the reasons behind it. This man knew nothing of love nor showing it to anyone. Clearly his past of no love from anyone had permeated his life with the inability to feel anything for anyone except himself. Once again; another jerk in my life who later I ditched by avoidance.

My friend in prison called me to say that he was moved to a different state. I felt bad for him.

His aunt called me and we had words. I never

called her again. Bravo for me.

It is now April and it's my birthday for sure. I woke up and ate quiche drove to the bank got some money and went to my favorite restaurant and shops to have a fun day. While shopping I received a call from his probation officer who informed me that they would get him a copy of his release date and hearing date (even on my birthday I had to deal with someone else's problems). I was so happy all alone. I even saw a movie that night and was elated to see Jack the Giant Slayer.

Clearly my Birthday in life had come. I had a new name new number and could now go on without harassment in life. I was overjoyed.

Many months have passed and things needed to be changed at work in my file for the newness of me. It took a very long-time months and months and it made me sad.

But finally, the change came and I was free to live.

Live Free Finally in Peace.

So even though I don't have a man in my life to call my prince of peace or even prince or even boyfriend. I have found peace. Maybe I'll find Mr. Perfect along the way the Lord knows I pray.

So, my readers and my friends in victims past, this victim and now survivor hopes that you have learned everything you needed to in order to complete your new lives.

Simple Steps to Life Change

1. Visit SSA then gather up evidence from police of abuse/harassment. (Make sure SSA will change the number first then continue.)
2. Erase every financial thing attached to your Social (it may take

years to do but do it).

3. Close all accounts banking/credit cards.
4. Visit Social Security to request change in number due to abuse.
5. Change name only after they agree to change the Social Security number. Make sure you make them both change on January 1 of a certain year.
6. Know that your driver's license has to change numbers and get that figured first as well. (Know that your new name will be searchable by plates by police if you have a car.)
7. Get your new birth certificate, and voilà! Live anew!

The best scenario is that you are not working at this time. The change happens and then go apply for a new job or reapply where you used to work if you trust them. Just know that you can't use past experience knowing they will contact people. Try to have references of the past from people you trust. Never give out information to anyone, even relatives. Try very hard to keep it all to yourself. You can also contact a victims unit in your area, and maybe they will have a lawyer that will help you as well. This can be very overwhelming to do by yourself. Trust me, I know.

Don't ever forget to realize that you can become someone else to save your life and start over. The starting over is not fun at first, and getting used to a totally new name is quite weird at first, but then it's fine. Trust me on this one. Even though I had to get a car loan at 26 percent because I didn't have any credit history, it was fine. I could at least get a car because I knew the person who owned the dealership, and what a friend he was indeed. Be careful to put all past paperwork in a safe deposit box or someplace where people can't read it. The hard part is running into people who know me in the old name. I try very hard to not let that happen. Seclusion in some ways works, and be careful how you let it get back to normal. Best to keep this change to yourself if you are a talker, and later you can be vague and not say anything at all if you wish. Moving to a different state or country when completed is best, but for me, it was a matter of this victim not letting her abuser win on that issue at all. After all I was born here in this great state in this wonderful city…my city…and I wasn't leaving!

I may move if the right man asked me to for the right reasons…

who knows?

So, my readers, I hope that this book has filled your minds with day-to-day stories of a person who had a life and then started a totally new one. Life is worth living. It's the living that one must focus on. Don't ever give up, and on your worst day, know that God loves you.

Love always, America.

The End
The real end for sure, or...

I have started to help others, in which I find great satisfaction to stamp out abuse and resolve myself to at least say I tried to rid America of abusive relationships and help others get out and get support since I did not have but very little help at all. I would say that this was the very saddest part of the story aside of the direct abuse to me. The very people that I thought would stick by me through thick and thin abandoned me one by one, even lying about me along the way, making my life even more difficult for me emotionally until it was unbearable. I am a very sweet lady who maybe does see life through rose-colored glasses because, after all, it is more fun that way!

Now, I live in peace, and peace I try to bring to the world. I live life. Finally.

However, things have not changed, and you need to know that. The very week of editing this book before I wrote the last chapter, I was asked by a government agency to have something investigated by the police. They said, "Was anything taken?" And I said no. They said even though someone had violated my personal information by using it to mess with my mind that they could and would not do an investigation. Interesting, isn't it? I cried a bit and then persisted anyway to get what I wanted. That is the most important thing to remember for the reader. Persist to get what you want, and if you have a bad day, let it go for a few days and cry if you want. Then get back up and empower yourself to get it done as your emotions come into play and make us so tired.

I am making new friends very carefully and very happily. Finally.

I wish I could tell you want I want to write about next, but it will be under a different name; maybe you'll be able to figure it out if you are a good investigator. I hope you are, after reading my book!

Acknowledgments

Writers, professors, police officers, office staff, and counselors who encouraged me to keep myself empowered, but most of all, to my high school girl friends who said one night at my house, "You have got to write a book about this, it's so hard to believe," and later they didn't believe the ending either. So it in itself tells a bizarre story about people and the way life can drastically change in a second.

This book is about people, like you and me.

And to Professor Benjamin at a university who on my lowest day told me I should not change and I should just be myself, which meant it was okay to always tell the truth about myself and my life whether at work or in my personal life. *Cool.*

Coldplay, one of my favorite music groups, sings a song this year called "Paradise." Listen often.

"In God We Trust." Where oh where did we ever lose that trust in the one so easy to trust? Like children who don't want to follow rules, we took his out of schools. What have we done? What have they become? Let people pray and give them leave to do all the things our forefathers came here to do.

About the Author

I am dedicated to helping others escape abusive relationships and find support for a mission born from my own experiences of limited help and abandonment. Despite the emotional toll of these betrayals, I remain optimistic and strive to bring peace to the world.

I do believe in persistence and self-empowerment.

I carefully build new friendships.

I look forward to writing more under a different name.

Perhaps you'll uncover my identity if you're a keen investigator.

Peace and be lovely always.

www.ingramcontent.com/pod-product-compliance
Lightning Source LLC
Chambersburg PA
CBHW020916140626
46545CB00015B/68